NATIONAL GEOGRAPHIC

BIRDER'S JOURNAL

NATIONAL GEOGRAPHIC

BIRDER'S JOURNAL

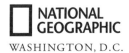

NATIONAL GEOGRAPHIC
WASHINGTON, D.C.

Contents

Checklist

The following checklist is a taxonomic listing of all bird species illustrated in this book and the *National Geographic Field Guide to the Birds of North America*. The nomenclature and taxonomy of this checklist are based on *The Check-list of North American Birds* (1998) published by the American Ornithologists' Union (AOU), and this checklist incorporates subsequent revisions through 2006. To be of most use to birders, we include in this volume some species that are not found on the AOU checklist. Most of these are exotic species that are regularly seen but not officially accepted as established in North America.

Checklists are, by their nature, always evolving. Species are split or lumped, higher-level taxonomy is adjusted, scientific and English names are revised, new species are recorded, introduced populations die out, or native species may become extinct. The most current list is available at *www.aou.org/checklist.* Many birders use the American Birding Association's (ABA) checklist; the 6th edition was published in 2002 and an updated version is available at *www.americanbirding.org/checklist.* See page 480 of this book for an explanation of the differences between the AOU checklist and the checklist prepared by the ABA.

(Adapted with permission from *The Check-list of North American Birds,* 7th Edition, AOU, 1998.)

Key: **BOLDFACE** indicates order.
CAPITALS indicate family.
Check boxes indicate individual species.

ANSERIFORMES

Ducks, Geese, and Swans: ANATIDAE

☐ Black-bellied Whistling-Duck *Dendrocygna autumnalis*
☐ Fulvous Whistling-Duck *Dendrocygna bicolor*
☐ Swan Goose *Anser cygnoides*
☐ Bean Goose *Anser fabalis*
☐ Pink-footed Goose *Anser brachyrhynchus*
☐ Graylag Goose *Anser anser*
☐ Greater White-fronted Goose *Anser albifrons*
☐ Lesser White-fronted Goose *Anser erythropus*
☐ Bar-headed Goose *Anser indicus*
☐ Emperor Goose *Chen canagica*
☐ Snow Goose *Chen caerulescens*
☐ Ross's Goose *Chen rossii*
☐ Brant *Branta bernicla*
☐ Barnacle Goose *Branta leucopsis*
☐ Cackling Goose *Branta hutchinsii*
☐ Canada Goose *Branta canadensis*
☐ Mute Swan *Cygnus olor*
☐ Trumpeter Swan *Cygnus buccinator*
☐ Tundra Swan *Cygnus columbianus*
☐ Whooper Swan *Cygnus cygnus*
☐ Egyptian Goose *Alopochen aegyptiacus*
☐ Common Shelduck *Tadorna tadorna*
☐ Ruddy Shelduck *Tadorna ferruginea*
☐ Muscovy Duck *Cairina moschata*
☐ Wood Duck *Aix sponsa*
☐ Mandarin Duck *Aix galericulata*
☐ Gadwall *Anas strepera*
☐ Falcated Duck *Anas falcata*
☐ Eurasian Wigeon *Anas penelope*
☐ American Wigeon *Anas americana*
☐ American Black Duck *Anas rubripes*
☐ Mallard *Anas platyrhynchos*
☐ Mottled Duck *Anas fulvigula*
☐ Spot-billed Duck *Anas poecilorhyncha*
☐ Blue-winged Teal *Anas discors*
☐ Cinnamon Teal *Anas cyanoptera*
☐ Northern Shoveler *Anas clypeata*
☐ White-cheeked Pintail *Anas bahamensis*
☐ Northern Pintail *Anas acuta*
☐ Garganey *Anas querquedula*
☐ Baikal Teal *Anas formosa*
☐ Green-winged Teal *Anas crecca*
☐ Canvasback *Aythya valisineria*
☐ Redhead *Aythya americana*
☐ Common Pochard *Aythya ferina*
☐ Ring-necked Duck *Aythya collaris*
☐ Tufted Duck *Aythya fuligula*
☐ Greater Scaup *Aythya marila*
☐ Lesser Scaup *Aythya affinis*
☐ Steller's Eider *Polysticta stelleri*
☐ Spectacled Eider *Somateria fischeri*
☐ King Eider *Somateria spectabilis*
☐ Common Eider *Somateria mollissima*
☐ Harlequin Duck *Histrionicus histrionicus*

☐ Labrador Duck *Camptorhynchus labradorius*
☐ Surf Scoter *Melanitta perspicillata*
☐ White-winged Scoter *Melanitta fusca*
☐ Black Scoter *Melanitta nigra*
☐ Long-tailed Duck *Clangula hyemalis*
☐ Bufflehead *Bucephala albeola*
☐ Common Goldeneye *Bucephala clangula*
☐ Barrow's Goldeneye *Bucephala islandica*
☐ Smew *Mergellus albellus*
☐ Hooded Merganser *Lophodytes cucullatus*
☐ Common Merganser *Mergus merganser*
☐ Red-breasted Merganser *Mergus serrator*
☐ Masked Duck *Nomonyx dominicus*
☐ Ruddy Duck *Oxyura jamaicensis*

GALLIFORMES

Curassows and Guans: CRACIDAE

☐ Plain Chachalaca *Ortalis vetula*

Partridges, Grouse, Turkeys, and Old World Quail: PHASIANIDAE

☐ Chukar *Alectoris chukar*
☐ Himalayan Snowcock *Tetraogallus himalayensis*
☐ Gray Partridge *Perdix perdix*
☐ Ring-necked Pheasant *Phasianus colchicus*
☐ Ruffed Grouse *Bonasa umbellus*
☐ Greater Sage-Grouse *Centrocercus urophasianus*
☐ Gunnison Sage-Grouse *Centrocercus minimus*
☐ Spruce Grouse *Falcipennis canadensis*
☐ Willow Ptarmigan *Lagopus lagopus*
☐ Rock Ptarmigan *Lagopus muta*
☐ White-tailed Ptarmigan *Lagopus leucura*
☐ Dusky Grouse *Dendragapus obscurus*
☐ Sooty Grouse *Dendragapus fuliginosus*
☐ Sharp-tailed Grouse *Tympanuchus phasianellus*
☐ Greater Prairie-Chicken *Tympanuchus cupido*
☐ Lesser Prairie-Chicken *Tympanuchus pallidicinctus*
☐ Wild Turkey *Meleagris gallopavo*

New World Quail: ODONTOPHORIDAE

☐ Mountain Quail *Oreortyx pictus*
☐ Scaled Quail *Callipepla squamata*
☐ California Quail *Callipepla californica*
☐ Gambel's Quail *Callipepla gambelii*
☐ Northern Bobwhite *Colinus virginianus*
☐ Montezuma Quail *Cyrtonyx montezumae*

GAVIIFORMES

Loons: GAVIIDAE

☐ Red-throated Loon *Gavia stellata*
☐ Arctic Loon *Gavia arctica*
☐ Pacific Loon *Gavia pacifica*
☐ Common Loon *Gavia immer*
☐ Yellow-billed Loon *Gavia adamsii*

PODICIPEDIFORMES

Grebes: PODICIPEDIDAE

☐ Least Grebe *Tachybaptus dominicus*
☐ Pied-billed Grebe *Podilymbus podiceps*
☐ Horned Grebe *Podiceps auritus*
☐ Red-necked Grebe *Podiceps grisegena*
☐ Eared Grebe *Podiceps nigricollis*
☐ Western Grebe *Aechmophorus occidentalis*
☐ Clark's Grebe *Aechmophorus clarkii*

PROCELLARIIFORMES

Albatrosses: DIOMEDEIDAE

☐ Yellow-nosed Albatross *Thalassarche chlororhynchos*
☐ Shy Albatross *Thalassarche cauta*
☐ Black-browed Albatross *Thalassarche melanophris*
☐ Light-mantled Albatross *Phoebetria palpebrata*
☐ Wandering Albatross *Diomedea exulans*
☐ Laysan Albatross *Phoebastria immutabilis*
☐ Black-footed Albatross *Phoebastria nigripes*
☐ Short-tailed Albatross *Phoebastria albatrus*

Shearwaters and Petrels: PROCELLARIIDAE

☐ Northern Fulmar *Fulmarus glacialis*
☐ Great-winged Petrel *Pterodroma macroptera*
☐ Herald Petrel *Pterodroma arminjoniana*
☐ Murphy's Petrel *Pterodroma ultima*
☐ Mottled Petrel *Pterodroma inexpectata*
☐ Fea's Petrel *Pterodroma feae*
☐ Bermuda Petrel *Pterodroma cahow*
☐ Black-capped Petrel *Pterodroma hasitata*
☐ Hawaiian Petrel *Pterodroma sandwichensis*
☐ Cook's Petrel *Pterodroma cookii*

☐ Stejneger's Petrel *Pterodroma longirostris*
☐ Bulwer's Petrel *Bulweria bulwerii*
☐ Parkinson's Petrel *Procellaria parkinsoni*
☐ Streaked Shearwater *Calonectris leucomelas*
☐ Cory's Shearwater *Calonectris diomedea*
☐ Cape Verde Shearwater *Calonectris edwardsii*
☐ Pink-footed Shearwater *Puffinus creatopus*
☐ Flesh-footed Shearwater *Puffinus carneipes*
☐ Greater Shearwater *Puffinus gravis*
☐ Wedge-tailed Shearwater *Puffinus pacificus*
☐ Buller's Shearwater *Puffinus bulleri*
☐ Sooty Shearwater *Puffinus griseus*
☐ Short-tailed Shearwater *Puffinus tenuirostris*
☐ Manx Shearwater *Puffinus puffinus*
☐ Black-vented Shearwater *Puffinus opisthomelas*
☐ Audubon's Shearwater *Puffinus lherminieri*
☐ Little Shearwater *Puffinus assimilis*

Storm-Petrels: HYDROBATIDAE

☐ Wilson's Storm-Petrel *Oceanites oceanicus*
☐ White-faced Storm-Petrel *Pelagodroma marina*
☐ European Storm-Petrel *Hydrobates pelagicus*
☐ Black-bellied Storm-Petrel *Fregetta tropica*
☐ Ringed Storm-Petrel *Oceanodroma hornbyi*
☐ Fork-tailed Storm-Petrel *Oceanodroma furcata*
☐ Leach's Storm-Petrel *Oceanodroma leucorhoa*
☐ Ashy Storm-Petrel *Oceanodroma homochroa*
☐ Band-rumped Storm-Petrel *Oceanodroma castro*
☐ Wedge-rumped Storm-Petrel *Oceanodroma tethys*
☐ Black Storm-Petrel *Oceanodroma melania*
☐ Least Storm-Petrel *Oceanodroma microsoma*

PELECANIFORMES

Tropicbirds: PHAETHONTIDAE

☐ White-tailed Tropicbird *Phaethon lepturus*
☐ Red-billed Tropicbird *Phaethon aethereus*
☐ Red-tailed Tropicbird *Phaethon rubricauda*

Boobies and Gannets: SULIDAE

☐ Masked Booby *Sula dactylatra*
☐ Nazca Booby *Sula granti*
☐ Blue-footed Booby *Sula nebouxii*
☐ Brown Booby *Sula leucogaster*
☐ Red-footed Booby *Sula sula*
☐ Northern Gannet *Morus bassanus*

Pelicans: PELECANIDAE

☐ American White Pelican *Pelecanus erythrorhynchos*
☐ Brown Pelican *Pelecanus occidentalis*

Cormorants: PHALACROCORACIDAE

☐ Brandt's Cormorant *Phalacrocorax penicillatus*
☐ Neotropic Cormorant *Phalacrocorax brasilianus*
☐ Double-crested Cormorant *Phalacrocorax auritus*
☐ Great Cormorant *Phalacrocorax carbo*
☐ Red-faced Cormorant *Phalacrocorax urile*
☐ Pelagic Cormorant *Phalacrocorax pelagicus*

Darters: ANHINGIDAE

☐ Anhinga *Anhinga anhinga*

Frigatebirds: FREGATIDAE

☐ Magnificent Frigatebird *Fregata magnificens*
☐ Great Frigatebird *Fregata minor*
☐ Lesser Frigatebird *Fregata ariel*

CICONIIFORMES

Bitterns, Herons, and Allies: ARDEIDAE

☐ American Bittern *Botaurus lentiginosus*
☐ Yellow Bittern *Ixobrychus sinensis*
☐ Least Bittern *Ixobrychus exilis*
☐ Great Blue Heron *Ardea herodias*
☐ Gray Heron *Ardea cinerea*
☐ Great Egret *Ardea alba*
☐ Chinese Egret *Egretta eulophotes*
☐ Little Egret *Egretta garzetta*
☐ Western Reef-Heron *Egretta gularis*
☐ Snowy Egret *Egretta thula*
☐ Little Blue Heron *Egretta caerulea*
☐ Tricolored Heron *Egretta tricolor*

☐ Reddish Egret *Egretta rufescens*
☐ Cattle Egret *Bubulcus ibis*
☐ Chinese Pond-Heron *Ardeola bacchus*
☐ Green Heron *Butorides virescens*
☐ Black-crowned Night-Heron *Nycticorax nycticorax*
☐ Yellow-crowned Night-Heron *Nyctanassa violacea*

Ibises and Spoonbills: THRESKIORNITHIDAE

☐ White Ibis *Eudocimus albus*
☐ Scarlet Ibis *Eudocimus ruber*
☐ Glossy Ibis *Plegadis falcinellus*
☐ White-faced Ibis *Plegadis chihi*
☐ Roseate Spoonbill *Platalea ajaja*

Storks: CICONIIDAE

☐ Jabiru *Jabiru mycteria*
☐ Wood Stork *Mycteria americana*

New World Vultures: CATHARTIDAE

☐ Black Vulture *Coragyps atratus*
☐ Turkey Vulture *Cathartes aura*
☐ California Condor *Gymnogyps californianus*

PHOENICOPTERIFORMES

Flamingos: PHOENICOPTERIDAE

☐ Greater Flamingo *Phoenicopterus ruber*

FALCONIFORMES

Hawks, Kites, Eagles, and Allies: ACCIPITRIDAE

☐ Osprey *Pandion haliaetus*
☐ Hook-billed Kite *Chondrohierax uncinatus*
☐ Swallow-tailed Kite *Elanoides forficatus*
☐ White-tailed Kite *Elanus leucurus*
☐ Snail Kite *Rostrhamus sociabilis*
☐ Mississippi Kite *Ictinia mississippiensis*
☐ Bald Eagle *Haliaeetus leucocephalus*
☐ White-tailed Eagle *Haliaeetus albicilla*
☐ Steller's Sea-Eagle *Haliaeetus pelagicus*
☐ Northern Harrier *Circus cyaneus*
☐ Sharp-shinned Hawk *Accipiter striatus*
☐ Cooper's Hawk *Accipiter cooperii*
☐ Northern Goshawk *Accipiter gentilis*
☐ Crane Hawk *Geranospiza caerulescens*
☐ Common Black-Hawk *Buteogallus anthracinus*
☐ Harris's Hawk *Parabuteo unicinctus*
☐ Roadside Hawk *Buteo magnirostris*
☐ Red-shouldered Hawk *Buteo lineatus*
☐ Broad-winged Hawk *Buteo platypterus*
☐ Gray Hawk *Buteo nitidus*
☐ Short-tailed Hawk *Buteo brachyurus*
☐ Swainson's Hawk *Buteo swainsoni*
☐ White-tailed Hawk *Buteo albicaudatus*
☐ Zone-tailed Hawk *Buteo albonotatus*
☐ Red-tailed Hawk *Buteo jamaicensis*
☐ Ferruginous Hawk *Buteo regalis*
☐ Rough-legged Hawk *Buteo lagopus*
☐ Golden Eagle *Aquila chrysaetos*

Caracaras and Falcons: FALCONIDAE

☐ Collared Forest-Falcon *Micrastur semitorquatus*
☐ Crested Caracara *Caracara cheriway*
☐ Eurasian Kestrel *Falco tinnunculus*
☐ American Kestrel *Falco sparverius*
☐ Merlin *Falco columbarius*
☐ Eurasian Hobby *Falco subbuteo*
☐ Red-footed Falcon *Falco vespertinus*
☐ Aplomado Falcon *Falco femoralis*
☐ Gyrfalcon *Falco rusticolus*
☐ Peregrine Falcon *Falco peregrinus*
☐ Prairie Falcon *Falco mexicanus*

GRUIFORMES

Rails, Gallinules and Coots: RALLIDAE

☐ Yellow Rail *Coturnicops noveboracensis*
☐ Black Rail *Laterallus jamaicensis*
☐ Corn Crake *Crex crex*
☐ Clapper Rail *Rallus longirostris*
☐ King Rail *Rallus elegans*
☐ Virginia Rail *Rallus limicola*
☐ Sora *Porzana carolina*
☐ Paint-billed Crake *Neocrex erythrops*
☐ Spotted Rail *Pardirallus maculatus*
☐ Purple Swamphen *Porphyrio porphyrio*
☐ Purple Gallinule *Porphyrio martinica*
☐ Common Moorhen *Gallinula chloropus*
☐ Eurasian Coot *Fulica atra*
☐ American Coot *Fulica americana*

Limpkins: ARAMIDAE

☐ Limpkin *Aramus guarauna*

Cranes: GRUIDAE

☐ Sandhill Crane *Grus canadensis*

☐ Common Crane *Grus grus*
☐ Whooping Crane *Grus americana*

CHARADRIIFORMES

Thick-kees: BURHINIDAE

☐ Double-striped Thick-knee *Burhinus bistriatus*

Lapwings and Plovers: CHARADRIIDAE

☐ Northern Lapwing *Vanellus vanellus*
☐ Black-bellied Plover *Pluvialis squatarola*
☐ European Golden-Plover *Pluvialis apricaria*
☐ American Golden-Plover *Pluvialis dominica*
☐ Pacific Golden-Plover *Pluvialis fulva*
☐ Lesser Sand-Plover *Charadrius mongolus*
☐ Greater Sand-Plover *Charadrius leschenaultii*
☐ Collared Plover *Charadrius collaris*
☐ Snowy Plover *Charadrius alexandrinus*
☐ Wilson's Plover *Charadrius wilsonia*
☐ Common Ringed Plover *Charadrius hiaticula*
☐ Semipalmated Plover *Charadrius semipalmatus*
☐ Piping Plover *Charadrius melodus*
☐ Little Ringed Plover *Charadrius dubius*
☐ Killdeer *Charadrius vociferus*
☐ Mountain Plover *Charadrius montanus*
☐ Eurasian Dotterel *Charadrius morinellus*

Oystercatchers: HAEMATOPODIDAE

☐ Eurasian Oystercatcher *Haematopus ostralegus*
☐ American Oystercatcher *Haematopus palliatus*
☐ Black Oystercatcher *Haematopus bachmani*

Stilts and Avocets: RECURVIROSTRIDAE

☐ Black-winged Stilt *Himantopus himantopus*
☐ Black-necked Stilt *Himantopus mexicanus*
☐ American Avocet *Recurvirostra americana*

Jacanas: JACANIDAE

☐ Northern Jacana *Jacana spinosa*

Sandpipers, Phalaropes, and Allies: SCOLOPACIDAE

☐ Terek Sandpiper *Xenus cinereus*
☐ Common Sandpiper *Actitis hypoleucos*
☐ Spotted Sandpiper *Actitis macularius*
☐ Green Sandpiper *Tringa ochropus*
☐ Solitary Sandpiper *Tringa solitaria*
☐ Gray-tailed Tattler *Tringa brevipes*
☐ Wandering Tattler *Tringa incana*
☐ Spotted Redshank *Tringa erythropus*
☐ Greater Yellowlegs *Tringa melanoleuca*
☐ Common Greenshank *Tringa nebularia*
☐ Willet *Tringa semipalmata*
☐ Lesser Yellowlegs *Tringa flavipes*
☐ Marsh Sandpiper *Tringa stagnatilis*
☐ Wood Sandpiper *Tringa glareola*
☐ Common Redshank *Tringa totanus*
☐ Upland Sandpiper *Bartramia longicauda*
☐ Little Curlew *Numenius minutus*
☐ Eskimo Curlew *Numenius borealis*
☐ Whimbrel *Numenius phaeopus*
☐ Bristle-thighed Curlew *Numenius tahitiensis*
☐ Far Eastern Curlew *Numenius madagascariensis*
☐ Slender-billed Curlew *Numenius tenuirostris*
☐ Eurasian Curlew *Numenius arquata*
☐ Long-billed Curlew *Numenius americanus*
☐ Black-tailed Godwit *Limosa limosa*
☐ Hudsonian Godwit *Limosa haemastica*
☐ Bar-tailed Godwit *Limosa lapponica*
☐ Marbled Godwit *Limosa fedoa*
☐ Ruddy Turnstone *Arenaria interpres*
☐ Black Turnstone *Arenaria melanocephala*
☐ Surfbird *Aphriza virgata*
☐ Great Knot *Calidris tenuirostris*
☐ Red Knot *Calidris canutus*
☐ Sanderling *Calidris alba*
☐ Semipalmated Sandpiper *Calidris pusilla*
☐ Western Sandpiper *Calidris mauri*
☐ Red-necked Stint *Calidris ruficollis*
☐ Little Stint *Calidris minuta*
☐ Temminck's Stint *Calidris temminckii*
☐ Long-toed Stint *Calidris subminuta*
☐ Least Sandpiper *Calidris minutilla*
☐ White-rumped Sandpiper *Calidris fuscicollis*
☐ Baird's Sandpiper *Calidris bairdii*
☐ Pectoral Sandpiper *Calidris melanotos*
☐ Sharp-tailed Sandpiper *Calidris acuminata*
☐ Purple Sandpiper *Calidris maritima*

☐ Rock Sandpiper *Calidris ptilocnemis*
☐ Dunlin *Calidris alpina*
☐ Curlew Sandpiper *Calidris ferruginea*
☐ Stilt Sandpiper *Calidris himantopus*
☐ Spoon-billed Sandpiper *Eurynorhynchus pygmeus*
☐ Broad-billed Sandpiper *Limicola falcinellus*
☐ Buff-breasted Sandpiper *Tryngites subruficollis*
☐ Ruff *Philomachus pugnax*
☐ Short-billed Dowitcher *Limnodromus griseus*
☐ Long-billed Dowitcher *Limnodromus scolopaceus*
☐ Jack Snipe *Lymnocryptes minimus*
☐ Wilson's Snipe *Gallinago delicata*
☐ Common Snipe *Gallinago gallinago*
☐ Pin-tailed Snipe *Gallinago stenura*
☐ Eurasian Woodcock *Scolopax rusticola*
☐ American Woodcock *Scolopax minor*
☐ Wilson's Phalarope *Phalaropus tricolor*
☐ Red-necked Phalarope *Phalaropus lobatus*
☐ Red Phalarope *Phalaropus fulicarius*

Coursers and Pratincoles: GLAREOLIDAE

☐ Oriental Pratincole *Glareola maldivarum*

Gulls, Terns, and Skimmers: LARIDAE

☐ Laughing Gull *Larus atricilla*
☐ Franklin's Gull *Larus pipixcan*
☐ Little Gull *Larus minutus*
☐ Black-headed Gull *Larus ridibundus*
☐ Bonaparte's Gull *Larus philadelphia*
☐ Heermann's Gull *Larus heermanni*
☐ Gray-hooded Gull *Larus cirrocephalus*
☐ Belcher's Gull *Larus belcheri*
☐ Black-tailed Gull *Larus crassirostris*
☐ Mew Gull *Larus canus*
☐ Ring-billed Gull *Larus delawarensis*
☐ California Gull *Larus californicus*
☐ Herring Gull *Larus argentatus*
☐ Yellow-legged Gull *Larus cachinnans*
☐ Thayer's Gull *Larus thayeri*
☐ Iceland Gull *Larus glaucoides*
☐ Lesser Black-backed Gull *Larus fuscus*
☐ Slaty-backed Gull *Larus schistisagus*
☐ Yellow-footed Gull *Larus livens*
☐ Western Gull *Larus occidentalis*
☐ Glaucous-winged Gull *Larus glaucescens*
☐ Glaucous Gull *Larus hyperboreus*
☐ Great Black-backed Gull *Larus marinus*
☐ Kelp Gull *Larus dominicanus*
☐ Sabine's Gull *Xema sabini*
☐ Black-legged Kittiwake *Rissa tridactyla*
☐ Red-legged Kittiwake *Rissa brevirostris*
☐ Ross's Gull *Rhodostethia rosea*
☐ Ivory Gull *Pagophila eburnea*
☐ Brown Noddy *Anous stolidus*
☐ Black Noddy *Anous minutus*
☐ Sooty Tern *Onychoprion fuscatus*
☐ Bridled Tern *Onychoprion anaethetus*
☐ Aleutian Tern *Onychoprion aleuticus*
☐ Least Tern *Sternula antillarum*
☐ Large-billed Tern *Phaetusa simplex*
☐ Gull-billed Tern *Gelochelidon nilotica*
☐ Caspian Tern *Hydroprogne caspia*
☐ Black Tern *Chlidonias niger*
☐ White-winged Tern *Chlidonias leucopterus*
☐ Whiskered Tern *Chlidonias hybrida*
☐ Roseate Tern *Sterna dougallii*
☐ Common Tern *Sterna hirundo*
☐ Arctic Tern *Sterna paradisaea*
☐ Forster's Tern *Sterna forsteri*
☐ Royal Tern *Thalasseus maximus*
☐ Sandwich Tern *Thalasseus sandvicensis*
☐ Elegant Tern *Thalasseus elegans*
☐ Black Skimmer *Rynchops niger*

Skuas and Jaegers: STERCORARIIDAE

☐ Great Skua *Stercorarius skua*
☐ South Polar Skua *Stercorarius maccormicki*
☐ Pomarine Jaeger *Stercorarius pomarinus*
☐ Parasitic Jaeger *Stercorarius parasiticus*
☐ Long-tailed Jaeger *Stercorarius longicaudus*

Auks, Murres, and Puffins: ALCIDAE

☐ Dovekie *Alle alle*
☐ Common Murre *Uria aalge*
☐ Thick-billed Murre *Uria lomvia*
☐ Razorbill *Alca torda*
☐ Great Auk *Pinguinus impennis*
☐ Black Guillemot *Cepphus grylle*
☐ Pigeon Guillemot *Cepphus columba*
☐ Long-billed Murrelet *Brachyramphus perdix*
☐ Marbled Murrelet *Brachyramphus marmoratus*
☐ Kittlitz's Murrelet *Brachyramphus brevirostris*

☐ Xantus's Murrelet *Synthliboramphus hypoleucus*
☐ Craveri's Murrelet *Synthliboramphus craveri*
☐ Ancient Murrelet *Synthliboramphus antiquus*
☐ Cassin's Auklet *Ptychoramphus aleuticus*
☐ Parakeet Auklet *Aethia psittacula*
☐ Least Auklet *Aethia pusilla*
☐ Whiskered Auklet *Aethia pygmaea*
☐ Crested Auklet *Aethia cristatella*
☐ Rhinoceros Auklet *Cerorhinca monocerata*
☐ Atlantic Puffin *Fratercula arctica*
☐ Horned Puffin *Fratercula corniculata*
☐ Tufted Puffin *Fratercula cirrhata*

COLUMBIFORMES

Pigeons and Doves: COLUMBIDAE

☐ Rock Pigeon *Columba livia*
☐ Scaly-naped Pigeon *Patagioenas squamosa*
☐ White-crowned Pigeon *Patagioenas leucocephala*
☐ Red-billed Pigeon *Patagioenas flavirostris*
☐ Band-tailed Pigeon *Patagioenas fasciata*
☐ Oriental Turtle-Dove *Streptopelia orientalis*
☐ African Collared-Dove *Streptopelia roseogrisea*
☐ Eurasian Collared-Dove *Streptopelia decaocto*
☐ Spotted Dove *Streptopelia chinensis*
☐ White-winged Dove *Zenaida asiatica*
☐ Zenaida Dove *Zenaida aurita*
☐ Mourning Dove *Zenaida macroura*
☐ Passenger Pigeon *Ectopistes migratorius*
☐ Inca Dove *Columbina inca*
☐ Common Ground-Dove *Columbina passerina*
☐ Ruddy Ground-Dove *Columbina talpacoti*
☐ White-tipped Dove *Leptotila verreauxi*
☐ Key West Quail-Dove *Geotrygon chrysia*
☐ Ruddy Quail-Dove *Geotrygon montana*

PSITTACIFORMES

Lories, Parakeets, Macaws, and Parrots: PSITTACIDAE

☐ Budgerigar *Melopsittacus undulatus*
☐ Rose-ringed Parakeet *Psittacula krameri*
☐ Monk Parakeet *Myiopsitta monachus*
☐ Carolina Parakeet *Conuropsis carolinensis*
☐ Blue-crowned Parakeet *Aratinga acuticaudata*
☐ Green Parakeet *Aratinga holochlora*
☐ Mitred Parakeet *Aratinga mitrata*
☐ Red-masked Parakeet *Aratinga erythrogenys*
☐ Dusky-headed Parakeet *Aratinga weddellii*
☐ Black-hooded Parakeet *Nandayus nenday*
☐ Thick-billed Parrot *Rhynchopsitta pachyrhyncha*
☐ White-winged Parakeet *Brotogeris versicolurus*
☐ Yellow-chevroned Parakeet *Brotogeris chiriri*
☐ Red-crowned Parrot *Amazona viridigenalis*
☐ Lilac-crowned Parrot *Amazona finschi*
☐ Yellow-headed Parrot *Amazona oratrix*
☐ Orange-winged Parrot *Amazona amazonica*

CUCULIFORMES

Cuckoos, Roadrunners, and Anis: CUCULIDAE

☐ Common Cuckoo *Cuculus canorus*
☐ Oriental Cuckoo *Cuculus optatus*
☐ Yellow-billed Cuckoo *Coccyzus americanus*
☐ Mangrove Cuckoo *Coccyzus minor*
☐ Black-billed Cuckoo *Coccyzus erythropthalmus*
☐ Greater Roadrunner *Geococcyx californianus*
☐ Smooth-billed Ani *Crotophaga ani*
☐ Groove-billed Ani *Crotophaga sulcirostris*

STRIGIFORMES

Barn Owls: TYTONIDAE

☐ Barn Owl *Tyto alba*

Typical Owls: STRIGIDAE

☐ Flammulated Owl *Otus flammeolus*
☐ Oriental Scops-Owl *Otus sunia*
☐ Western Screech-Owl *Megascops kennicottii*
☐ Eastern Screech-Owl *Megascops asio*
☐ Whiskered Screech-Owl *Megascops trichopsis*
☐ Great Horned Owl *Bubo virginianus*

- ☐ Snowy Owl *Bubo scandiacus*
- ☐ Northern Hawk Owl *Surnia ulula*
- ☐ Northern Pygmy-Owl *Glaucidium gnoma*
- ☐ Ferruginous Pygmy-Owl *Glaucidium brasilianum*
- ☐ Elf Owl *Micrathene whitneyi*
- ☐ Burrowing Owl *Athene cunicularia*
- ☐ Mottled Owl *Ciccaba virgata*
- ☐ Spotted Owl *Strix occidentalis*
- ☐ Barred Owl *Strix varia*
- ☐ Great Gray Owl *Strix nebulosa*
- ☐ Long-eared Owl *Asio otus*
- ☐ Stygian Owl *Asio stygius*
- ☐ Short-eared Owl *Asio flammeus*
- ☐ Boreal Owl *Aegolius funereus*
- ☐ Northern Saw-whet Owl *Aegolius acadicus*

CAPRIMULGIFORMES

Goatsuckers: CAPRIMULGIDAE

- ☐ Lesser Nighthawk *Chordeiles acutipennis*
- ☐ Common Nighthawk *Chordeiles minor*
- ☐ Antillean Nighthawk *Chordeiles gundlachii*
- ☐ Common Pauraque *Nyctidromus albicollis*
- ☐ Common Poorwill *Phalaenoptilus nuttallii*
- ☐ Chuck-will's-widow *Caprimulgus carolinensis*
- ☐ Buff-collared Nightjar *Caprimulgus ridgwayi*
- ☐ Whip-poor-will *Caprimulgus vociferus*
- ☐ Gray Nightjar *Caprimulgus indicus*

APODIFORMES

Swifts: APODIDAE

- ☐ Black Swift *Cypseloides niger*
- ☐ White-collared Swift *Streptoprocne zonaris*
- ☐ Chimney Swift *Chaetura pelagica*
- ☐ Vaux's Swift *Chaetura vauxi*
- ☐ White-throated Needletail *Hirundapus caudacutus*
- ☐ Common Swift *Apus apus*
- ☐ Fork-tailed Swift *Apus pacificus*
- ☐ White-throated Swift *Aeronautes saxatalis*
- ☐ Antillean Palm-Swift *Tachornis phoenicobia*

Hummingbirds: TROCHILIDAE

- ☐ Green Violet-ear *Colibri thalassinus*
- ☐ Green-breasted Mango *Anthracothorax prevostii*
- ☐ Broad-billed Hummingbird *Cynanthus latirostris*
- ☐ White-eared Hummingbird *Hylocharis leucotis*
- ☐ Xantus's Hummingbird *Hylocharis xantusii*
- ☐ Berylline Hummingbird *Amazilia beryllina*
- ☐ Buff-bellied Hummingbird *Amazilia yucatanensis*
- ☐ Cinnamon Hummingbird *Amazilia rutila*
- ☐ Violet-crowned Hummingbird *Amazilia violiceps*
- ☐ Blue-throated Hummingbird *Lampornis clemenciae*
- ☐ Magnificent Hummingbird *Eugenes fulgens*
- ☐ Plain-capped Starthroat *Heliomaster constantii*
- ☐ Bahama Woodstar *Calliphlox evelynae*
- ☐ Lucifer Hummingbird *Calothorax lucifer*
- ☐ Ruby-throated Hummingbird *Archilochus colubris*
- ☐ Black-chinned Hummingbird *Archilochus alexandri*
- ☐ Anna's Hummingbird *Calypte anna*
- ☐ Costa's Hummingbird *Calypte costae*
- ☐ Calliope Hummingbird *Stellula calliope*
- ☐ Bumblebee Hummingbird *Atthis heloisa*
- ☐ Broad-tailed Hummingbird *Selasphorus platycercus*
- ☐ Rufous Hummingbird *Selasphorus rufus*
- ☐ Allen's Hummingbird *Selasphorus sasin*

TROGONIFORMES

Trogons: TROGONIDAE

- ☐ Elegant Trogon *Trogon elegans*
- ☐ Eared Quetzal *Euptilotis neoxenus*

UPUPIFORMES

Hoopoes: UPUPIDAE

- ☐ Eurasian Hoopoe *Upupa epops*

CORACIIFORMES

Kingfishers: ALCEDINIDAE

- ☐ Ringed Kingfisher *Ceryle torquatus*
- ☐ Belted Kingfisher *Ceryle alcyon*
- ☐ Green Kingfisher *Chloroceryle americana*

PICIFORMES

Woodpeckers and Allies: PICIDAE

☐ Eurasian Wryneck *Jynx torquilla*
☐ Lewis's Woodpecker *Melanerpes lewis*
☐ Red-headed Woodpecker *Melanerpes erythrocephalus*
☐ Acorn Woodpecker *Melanerpes formicivorus*
☐ Gila Woodpecker *Melanerpes uropygialis*
☐ Golden-fronted Woodpecker *Melanerpes aurifrons*
☐ Red-bellied Woodpecker *Melanerpes carolinus*
☐ Williamson's Sapsucker *Sphyrapicus thyroideus*
☐ Yellow-bellied Sapsucker *Sphyrapicus varius*
☐ Red-naped Sapsucker *Sphyrapicus nuchalis*
☐ Red-breasted Sapsucker *Sphyrapicus ruber*
☐ Great Spotted Woodpecker *Dendrocopos major*
☐ Ladder-backed Woodpecker *Picoides scalaris*
☐ Nuttall's Woodpecker *Picoides nuttallii*
☐ Downy Woodpecker *Picoides pubescens*
☐ Hairy Woodpecker *Picoides villosus*
☐ Arizona Woodpecker *Picoides arizonae*
☐ Red-cockaded Woodpecker *Picoides borealis*
☐ White-headed Woodpecker *Picoides albolarvatus*
☐ American Three-toed Woodpecker *Picoides dorsalis*
☐ Black-backed Woodpecker *Picoides arcticus*
☐ Northern Flicker *Colaptes auratus*
☐ Gilded Flicker *Colaptes chrysoides*
☐ Pileated Woodpecker *Dryocopus pileatus*
☐ Ivory-billed Woodpecker *Campephilus principalis*

PASSERIFORMES

Tyrant Flycatchers: TYRANNIDAE

☐ Northern Beardless-Tyrannulet *Camptostoma imberbe*
☐ Greenish Elaenia *Myiopagis viridicata*
☐ Caribbean Elaenia *Elaenia martinica*
☐ Tufted Flycatcher *Mitrephanes phaeocercus*
☐ Olive-sided Flycatcher *Contopus cooperi*
☐ Greater Pewee *Contopus pertinax*
☐ Western Wood-Pewee *Contopus sordidulus*
☐ Eastern Wood-Pewee *Contopus virens*
☐ Cuban Pewee *Contopus caribaeus*
☐ Yellow-bellied Flycatcher *Empidonax flaviventris*
☐ Acadian Flycatcher *Empidonax virescens*
☐ Alder Flycatcher *Empidonax alnorum*
☐ Willow Flycatcher *Empidonax traillii*
☐ Least Flycatcher *Empidonax minimus*
☐ Hammond's Flycatcher *Empidonax hammondii*
☐ Gray Flycatcher *Empidonax wrightii*
☐ Dusky Flycatcher *Empidonax oberholseri*
☐ Pacific-slope Flycatcher *Empidonax difficilis*
☐ Cordilleran Flycatcher *Empidonax occidentalis*
☐ Buff-breasted Flycatcher *Empidonax fulvifrons*
☐ Black Phoebe *Sayornis nigricans*
☐ Eastern Phoebe *Sayornis phoebe*
☐ Say's Phoebe *Sayornis saya*
☐ Vermilion Flycatcher *Pyrocephalus rubinus*
☐ Dusky-capped Flycatcher *Myiarchus tuberculifer*
☐ Ash-throated Flycatcher *Myiarchus cinerascens*
☐ Nutting's Flycatcher *Myiarchus nuttingi*
☐ Great Crested Flycatcher *Myiarchus crinitus*
☐ Brown-crested Flycatcher *Myiarchus tyrannulus*
☐ La Sagra's Flycatcher *Myiarchus sagrae*
☐ Great Kiskadee *Pitangus sulphuratus*
☐ Social Flycatcher *Myiozetetes similis*
☐ Sulphur-bellied Flycatcher *Myiodynastes luteiventris*
☐ Piratic Flycatcher *Legatus leucophaius*
☐ Variegated Flycatcher *Empidonomus varius*
☐ Tropical Kingbird *Tyrannus melancholicus*
☐ Couch's Kingbird *Tyrannus couchii*
☐ Cassin's Kingbird *Tyrannus vociferans*
☐ Thick-billed Kingbird *Tyrannus crassirostris*
☐ Western Kingbird *Tyrannus verticalis*
☐ Eastern Kingbird *Tyrannus tyrannus*
☐ Gray Kingbird *Tyrannus dominicensis*

☐ Scissor-tailed Flycatcher *Tyrannus forficatus*
☐ Fork-tailed Flycatcher *Tyrannus savana*

Incertae Sedis

☐ Rose-throated Becard *Pachyramphus aglaiae*
☐ Masked Tityra *Tityra semifasciata*

Shrikes: LANIIDAE

☐ Brown Shrike *Lanius cristatus*
☐ Loggerhead Shrike *Lanius ludovicianus*
☐ Northern Shrike *Lanius excubitor*

Vireos: VIREONIDAE

☐ White-eyed Vireo *Vireo griseus*
☐ Thick-billed Vireo *Vireo crassirostris*
☐ Bell's Vireo *Vireo bellii*
☐ Black-capped Vireo *Vireo atricapilla*
☐ Gray Vireo *Vireo vicinior*
☐ Yellow-throated Vireo *Vireo flavifrons*
☐ Plumbeous Vireo *Vireo plumbeus*
☐ Cassin's Vireo *Vireo cassinii*
☐ Blue-headed Vireo *Vireo solitarius*
☐ Hutton's Vireo *Vireo huttoni*
☐ Warbling Vireo *Vireo gilvus*
☐ Philadelphia Vireo *Vireo philadelphicus*
☐ Red-eyed Vireo *Vireo olivaceus*
☐ Yellow-green Vireo *Vireo flavoviridis*
☐ Black-whiskered Vireo *Vireo altiloquus*
☐ Yucatan Vireo *Vireo magister*

Crows and Jays: CORVIDAE

☐ Gray Jay *Perisoreus canadensis*
☐ Steller's Jay *Cyanocitta stelleri*
☐ Blue Jay *Cyanocitta cristata*
☐ Green Jay *Cyanocorax yncas*
☐ Brown Jay *Cyanocorax morio*
☐ Florida Scrub-Jay *Aphelocoma coerulescens*
☐ Island Scrub-Jay *Aphelocoma insularis*
☐ Western Scrub-Jay *Aphelocoma californica*
☐ Mexican Jay *Aphelocoma ultramarina*
☐ Pinyon Jay *Gymnorhinus cyanocephalus*
☐ Clark's Nutcracker *Nucifraga columbiana*
☐ Black-billed Magpie *Pica hudsonia*
☐ Yellow-billed Magpie *Pica nuttalli*
☐ Eurasian Jackdaw *Corvus monedula*
☐ American Crow *Corvus brachyrhynchos*
☐ Northwestern Crow *Corvus caurinus*
☐ Tamaulipas Crow *Corvus imparatus*
☐ Fish Crow *Corvus ossifragus*
☐ Chihuahuan Raven *Corvus cryptoleucus*
☐ Common Raven *Corvus corax*

Larks: ALAUDIDAE

☐ Sky Lark *Alauda arvensis*
☐ Horned Lark *Eremophila alpestris*

Swallows: HIRUNDINIDAE

☐ Purple Martin *Progne subis*
☐ Cuban Martin *Progne cryptoleuca*
☐ Gray-breasted Martin *Progne chalybea*
☐ Southern Martin *Progne elegans*
☐ Brown-chested Martin *Progne tapera*
☐ Tree Swallow *Tachycineta bicolor*
☐ Mangrove Swallow *Tachycineta albilinea*
☐ Violet-green Swallow *Tachycineta thalassina*
☐ Bahama Swallow *Tachycineta cyaneoviridis*
☐ Northern Rough-winged Swallow *Stelgidopteryx serripennis*
☐ Bank Swallow *Riparia riparia*
☐ Cliff Swallow *Petrochelidon pyrrhonota*
☐ Cave Swallow *Petrochelidon fulva*
☐ Barn Swallow *Hirundo rustica*
☐ Common House-Martin *Delichon urbicum*

Chickadees and Titmice: PARIDAE

☐ Carolina Chickadee *Poecile carolinensis*
☐ Black-capped Chickadee *Poecile atricapillus*
☐ Mountain Chickadee *Poecile gambeli*
☐ Mexican Chickadee *Poecile sclateri*
☐ Chestnut-backed Chickadee *Poecile rufescens*
☐ Boreal Chickadee *Poecile hudsonica*
☐ Gray-headed Chickadee *Poecile cincta*
☐ Bridled Titmouse *Baeolophus wollweberi*
☐ Oak Titmouse *Baeolophus inornatus*
☐ Juniper Titmouse *Baeolophus ridgwayi*
☐ Tufted Titmouse *Baeolophus bicolor*
☐ Black-crested Titmouse *Baeolophus atricristatus*

Penduline Tits and Verdins: REMIZIDAE

☐ Verdin *Auriparus flaviceps*

Long-tailed Tits and Bushtits: AEGITHALIDAE

☐ Bushtit *Psaltriparus minimus*

Nuthatches: SITTIDAE

☐ Red-breasted Nuthatch *Sitta canadensis*
☐ White-breasted Nuthatch *Sitta carolinensis*
☐ Pygmy Nuthatch *Sitta pygmaea*
☐ Brown-headed Nuthatch *Sitta pusilla*

Creepers: CERTHIIDAE

☐ Brown Creeper *Certhia americana*

Wrens: TROGLODYTIDAE

☐ Cactus Wren *Campylorhynchus brunneicapillus*
☐ Rock Wren *Salpinctes obsoletus*
☐ Canyon Wren *Catherpes mexicanus*
☐ Carolina Wren *Thryothorus ludovicianus*
☐ Bewick's Wren *Thryomanes bewickii*
☐ House Wren *Troglodytes aedon*
☐ Winter Wren *Troglodytes troglodytes*
☐ Sedge Wren *Cistothorus platensis*
☐ Marsh Wren *Cistothorus palustris*

Dippers: CINCLIDAE

☐ American Dipper *Cinclus mexicanus*

Bulbuls: PYCNONOTIDAE

☐ Red-whiskered Bulbul *Pycnonotus jocosus*

Kinglets: REGULIDAE

☐ Golden-crowned Kinglet *Regulus satrapa*
☐ Ruby-crowned Kinglet *Regulus calendula*

Old World Warblers and Gnatcatchers: SYLVIIDAE

☐ Middendorff's Grasshopper-Warbler *Locustella ochotensis*
☐ Lanceolated Warbler *Locustella lanceolata*
☐ Willow Warbler *Phylloscopus trochilus*
☐ Wood Warbler *Phylloscopus sibilatrix*
☐ Dusky Warbler *Phylloscopus fuscatus*
☐ Yellow-browed Warbler *Phylloscopus inornatus*
☐ Arctic Warbler *Phylloscopus borealis*
☐ Lesser Whitethroat *Sylvia curruca*
☐ Blue-gray Gnatcatcher *Polioptila caerulea*
☐ California Gnatcatcher *Polioptila californica*
☐ Black-tailed Gnatcatcher *Polioptila melanura*
☐ Black-capped Gnatcatcher *Polioptila nigriceps*

Old World Flycatchers: MUSCICAPIDAE

☐ Narcissus Flycatcher *Ficedula narcissina*
☐ Mugimaki Flycatcher *Ficedula mugimaki*
☐ Taiga Flycatcher *Ficedula albicilla*
☐ Dark-sided Flycatcher *Muscicapa sibirica*
☐ Gray-streaked Flycatcher *Muscicapa griseisticta*
☐ Asian Brown Flycatcher *Muscicapa dauurica*
☐ Spotted Flycatcher *Muscicapa striata*

Thrushes: TURDIDAE

☐ Siberian Rubythroat *Luscinia calliope*
☐ Bluethroat *Luscinia svecica*
☐ Siberian Blue Robin *Luscinia cyane*
☐ Red-flanked Bluetail *Tarsiger cyanurus*
☐ Northern Wheatear *Oenanthe oenanthe*
☐ Stonechat *Saxicola torquatus*
☐ Eastern Bluebird *Sialia sialis*
☐ Western Bluebird *Sialia mexicana*
☐ Mountain Bluebird *Sialia currucoides*
☐ Townsend's Solitaire *Myadestes townsendi*
☐ Orange-billed Nightingale-Thrush *Catharus aurantiirostris*
☐ Black-headed Nightingale-Thrush *Catharus mexicanus*
☐ Veery *Catharus fuscescens*
☐ Gray-cheeked Thrush *Catharus minimus*
☐ Bicknell's Thrush *Catharus bicknelli*
☐ Swainson's Thrush *Catharus ustulatus*
☐ Hermit Thrush *Catharus guttatus*
☐ Wood Thrush *Hylocichla mustelina*
☐ Eurasian Blackbird *Turdus merula*
☐ Eyebrowed Thrush *Turdus obscurus*
☐ Dusky Thrush *Turdus naumanni*
☐ Fieldfare *Turdus pilaris*
☐ Redwing *Turdus iliacus*
☐ Clay-colored Robin *Turdus grayi*
☐ White-throated Robin *Turdus assimilis*
☐ Rufous-backed Robin *Turdus rufopalliatus*
☐ American Robin *Turdus migratorius*
☐ Varied Thrush *Ixoreus naevius*
☐ Aztec Thrush *Ridgwayia pinicola*

Babblers: TIMALIIDAE

☐ Wrentit *Chamaea fasciata*

Mockingbirds and Thrashers: MIMIDAE

☐ Gray Catbird *Dumetella carolinensis*
☐ Northern Mockingbird *Mimus polyglottos*

☐ Bahama Mockingbird *Mimus gundlachii*
☐ Sage Thrasher *Oreoscoptes montanus*
☐ Brown Thrasher *Toxostoma rufum*
☐ Long-billed Thrasher *Toxostoma longirostre*
☐ Bendire's Thrasher *Toxostoma bendirei*
☐ Curve-billed Thrasher *Toxostoma curvirostre*
☐ California Thrasher *Toxostoma redivivum*
☐ Crissal Thrasher *Toxostoma crissale*
☐ Le Conte's Thrasher *Toxostoma lecontei*
☐ Blue Mockingbird *Melanotis caerulescens*

Starlings: STURNIDAE

☐ European Starling *Sturnus vulgaris*
☐ Common Myna *Acridotheres tristis*
☐ Crested Myna *Acridotheres cristatellus*
☐ Hill Myna *Gracula religiosa*

Accentors: PRUNELLIDAE

☐ Siberian Accentor *Prunella montanella*

Wagtails and Pipits: MOTACILLIDAE

☐ Eastern Yellow Wagtail *Motacilla tschutschensis*
☐ Citrine Wagtail *Motacilla citreola*
☐ Gray Wagtail *Motacilla cinerea*
☐ White Wagtail *Motacilla alba*
☐ Tree Pipit *Anthus trivialis*
☐ Olive-backed Pipit *Anthus hodgsoni*
☐ Pechora Pipit *Anthus gustavi*
☐ Red-throated Pipit *Anthus cervinus*
☐ American Pipit *Anthus rubescens*
☐ Sprague's Pipit *Anthus spragueii*

Waxwings: BOMBYCILLIDAE

☐ Bohemian Waxwing *Bombycilla garrulus*
☐ Cedar Waxwing *Bombycilla cedrorum*

Silky-flycatchers: PTILOGONATIDAE

☐ Gray Silky-flycatcher *Ptilogonys cinereus*
☐ Phainopepla *Phainopepla nitens*

Olive Warbler: PEUCEDRAMIDAE

☐ Olive Warbler *Peucedramus taeniatus*

Wood-Warblers: PARULIDAE

☐ Bachman's Warbler *Vermivora bachmanii*
☐ Blue-winged Warbler *Vermivora pinus*
☐ Golden-winged Warbler *Vermivora chrysoptera*
☐ Tennessee Warbler *Vermivora peregrina*
☐ Orange-crowned Warbler *Vermivora celata*
☐ Nashville Warbler *Vermivora ruficapilla*
☐ Virginia's Warbler *Vermivora virginiae*
☐ Colima Warbler *Vermivora crissalis*
☐ Lucy's Warbler *Vermivora luciae*
☐ Crescent-chested Warbler *Parula superciliosa*
☐ Northern Parula *Parula americana*
☐ Tropical Parula *Parula pitiayumi*
☐ Yellow Warbler *Dendroica petechia*
☐ Chestnut-sided Warbler *Dendroica pensylvanica*
☐ Magnolia Warbler *Dendroica magnolia*
☐ Cape May Warbler *Dendroica tigrina*
☐ Black-throated Blue Warbler *Dendroica caerulescens*
☐ Yellow-rumped Warbler *Dendroica coronata*
☐ Black-throated Gray Warbler *Dendroica nigrescens*
☐ Golden-cheeked Warbler *Dendroica chrysoparia*
☐ Black-throated Green Warbler *Dendroica virens*
☐ Townsend's Warbler *Dendroica townsendi*
☐ Hermit Warbler *Dendroica occidentalis*
☐ Blackburnian Warbler *Dendroica fusca*
☐ Yellow-throated Warbler *Dendroica dominica*
☐ Grace's Warbler *Dendroica graciae*
☐ Pine Warbler *Dendroica pinus*
☐ Kirtland's Warbler *Dendroica kirtlandii*
☐ Prairie Warbler *Dendroica discolor*
☐ Palm Warbler *Dendroica palmarum*
☐ Bay-breasted Warbler *Dendroica castanea*
☐ Blackpoll Warbler *Dendroica striata*
☐ Cerulean Warbler *Dendroica cerulea*
☐ Black-and-white Warbler *Mniotilta varia*
☐ American Redstart *Setophaga ruticilla*
☐ Prothonotary Warbler *Protonotaria citrea*
☐ Worm-eating Warbler *Helmitheros vermivorum*
☐ Swainson's Warbler *Limnothlypis swainsonii*
☐ Ovenbird *Seiurus aurocapilla*
☐ Northern Waterthrush *Seiurus noveboracensis*
☐ Louisiana Waterthrush *Seiurus motacilla*
☐ Kentucky Warbler *Oporornis formosus*
☐ Connecticut Warbler *Oporornis agilis*

☐ Mourning Warbler *Oporornis philadelphia*
☐ MacGillivray's Warbler *Oporornis tolmiei*
☐ Common Yellowthroat *Geothlypis trichas*
☐ Gray-crowned Yellowthroat *Geothlypis poliocephala*
☐ Hooded Warbler *Wilsonia citrina*
☐ Wilson's Warbler *Wilsonia pusilla*
☐ Canada Warbler *Wilsonia canadensis*
☐ Red-faced Warbler *Cardellina rubrifrons*
☐ Painted Redstart *Myioborus pictus*
☐ Slate-throated Redstart *Myioborus miniatus*
☐ Fan-tailed Warbler *Euthlypis lachrymosa*
☐ Golden-crowned Warbler *Basileuterus culicivorus*
☐ Rufous-capped Warbler *Basileuterus rufifrons*
☐ Yellow-breasted Chat *Icteria virens*

Incertae Sedis

☐ Bananaquit *Coereba flaveola*

Tanagers: THRAUPIDAE

☐ Hepatic Tanager *Piranga flava*
☐ Summer Tanager *Piranga rubra*
☐ Scarlet Tanager *Piranga olivacea*
☐ Western Tanager *Piranga ludoviciana*
☐ Flame-colored Tanager *Piranga bidentata*
☐ Western Spindalis *Spindalis zena*

Emberizids: EMBERIZIDAE

☐ White-collared Seedeater *Sporophila torqueola*
☐ Yellow-faced Grassquit *Tiaris olivaceus*
☐ Black-faced Grassquit *Tiaris bicolor*
☐ Olive Sparrow *Arremonops rufivirgatus*
☐ Green-tailed Towhee *Pipilo chlorurus*
☐ Spotted Towhee *Pipilo maculatus*
☐ Eastern Towhee *Pipilo erythrophthalmus*
☐ Canyon Towhee *Pipilo fuscus*
☐ California Towhee *Pipilo crissalis*
☐ Abert's Towhee *Pipilo aberti*
☐ Rufous-winged Sparrow *Aimophila carpalis*
☐ Cassin's Sparrow *Aimophila cassinii*
☐ Bachman's Sparrow *Aimophila aestivalis*
☐ Botteri's Sparrow *Aimophila botterii*
☐ Rufous-crowned Sparrow *Aimophila ruficeps*
☐ Five-striped Sparrow *Aimophila quinquestriata*
☐ American Tree Sparrow *Spizella arborea*
☐ Chipping Sparrow *Spizella passerina*
☐ Clay-colored Sparrow *Spizella pallida*
☐ Brewer's Sparrow *Spizella breweri*
☐ Field Sparrow *Spizella pusilla*
☐ Worthen's Sparrow *Spizella wortheni*
☐ Black-chinned Sparrow *Spizella atrogularis*
☐ Vesper Sparrow *Pooecetes gramineus*
☐ Lark Sparrow *Chondestes grammacus*
☐ Black-throated Sparrow *Amphispiza bilineata*
☐ Sage Sparrow *Amphispiza belli*
☐ Lark Bunting *Calamospiza melanocorys*
☐ Savannah Sparrow *Passerculus sandwichensis*
☐ Grasshopper Sparrow *Ammodramus savannarum*
☐ Baird's Sparrow *Ammodramus bairdii*
☐ Henslow's Sparrow *Ammodramus henslowii*
☐ Le Conte's Sparrow *Ammodramus leconteii*
☐ Nelson's Sharp-tailed Sparrow *Ammodramus nelsoni*
☐ Saltmarsh Sharp-tailed Sparrow *Ammodramus caudacutus*
☐ Seaside Sparrow *Ammodramus maritimus*
☐ Fox Sparrow *Passerella iliaca*
☐ Song Sparrow *Melospiza melodia*
☐ Lincoln's Sparrow *Melospiza lincolnii*
☐ Swamp Sparrow *Melospiza georgiana*
☐ White-throated Sparrow *Zonotrichia albicollis*
☐ Harris's Sparrow *Zonotrichia querula*
☐ White-crowned Sparrow *Zonotrichia leucophrys*
☐ Golden-crowned Sparrow *Zonotrichia atricapilla*
☐ Dark-eyed Junco *Junco hyemalis*
☐ Yellow-eyed Junco *Junco phaeonotus*
☐ McCown's Longspur *Calcarius mccownii*
☐ Lapland Longspur *Calcarius lapponicus*
☐ Smith's Longspur *Calcarius pictus*
☐ Chestnut-collared Longspur *Calcarius ornatus*
☐ Pine Bunting *Emberiza leucocephalos*
☐ Little Bunting *Emberiza pusilla*
☐ Rustic Bunting *Emberiza rustica*
☐ Yellow-throated Bunting *Emberiza elegans*

- ☐ Yellow-breasted Bunting *Emberiza aureola*
- ☐ Gray Bunting *Emberiza variabilis*
- ☐ Pallas's Bunting *Emberiza pallasi*
- ☐ Reed Bunting *Emberiza schoeniclus*
- ☐ Snow Bunting *Plectrophenax nivalis*
- ☐ McKay's Bunting *Plectrophenax hyperboreus*

Cardinals, Saltators, and Allies: CARDINALIDAE

- ☐ Crimson-collared Grosbeak *Rhodothraupis celaeno*
- ☐ Northern Cardinal *Cardinalis cardinalis*
- ☐ Pyrrhuloxia *Cardinalis sinuatus*
- ☐ Yellow Grosbeak *Pheucticus chrysopeplus*
- ☐ Rose-breasted Grosbeak *Pheucticus ludovicianus*
- ☐ Black-headed Grosbeak *Pheucticus melanocephalus*
- ☐ Blue Bunting *Cyanocompsa parellina*
- ☐ Blue Grosbeak *Passerina caerulea*
- ☐ Lazuli Bunting *Passerina amoena*
- ☐ Indigo Bunting *Passerina cyanea*
- ☐ Varied Bunting *Passerina versicolor*
- ☐ Painted Bunting *Passerina ciris*
- ☐ Dickcissel *Spiza americana*

Blackbirds: ICTERIDAE

- ☐ Bobolink *Dolichonyx oryzivorus*
- ☐ Red-winged Blackbird *Agelaius phoeniceus*
- ☐ Tricolored Blackbird *Agelaius tricolor*
- ☐ Tawny-shouldered Blackbird *Agelaius humeralis*
- ☐ Eastern Meadowlark *Sturnella magna*
- ☐ Western Meadowlark *Sturnella neglecta*
- ☐ Yellow-headed Blackbird *Xanthocephalus xanthocephalus*
- ☐ Rusty Blackbird *Euphagus carolinus*
- ☐ Brewer's Blackbird *Euphagus cyanocephalus*
- ☐ Common Grackle *Quiscalus quiscula*
- ☐ Boat-tailed Grackle *Quiscalus major*
- ☐ Great-tailed Grackle *Quiscalus mexicanus*
- ☐ Shiny Cowbird *Molothrus bonariensis*
- ☐ Bronzed Cowbird *Molothrus aeneus*
- ☐ Brown-headed Cowbird *Molothrus ater*
- ☐ Black-vented Oriole *Icterus wagleri*
- ☐ Orchard Oriole *Icterus spurius*
- ☐ Hooded Oriole *Icterus cucullatus*
- ☐ Streak-backed Oriole *Icterus pustulatus*
- ☐ Bullock's Oriole *Icterus bullockii*
- ☐ Spot-breasted Oriole *Icterus pectoralis*
- ☐ Altamira Oriole *Icterus gularis*
- ☐ Audubon's Oriole *Icterus graduacauda*
- ☐ Baltimore Oriole *Icterus galbula*
- ☐ Scott's Oriole *Icterus parisorum*

Fringilline and Cardueline Finches and Allies: FRINGILLIDAE

- ☐ Common Chaffinch *Fringilla coelebs*
- ☐ Brambling *Fringilla montifringilla*
- ☐ Gray-crowned Rosy-Finch *Leucosticte tephrocotis*
- ☐ Black Rosy-Finch *Leucosticte atrata*
- ☐ Brown-capped Rosy-Finch *Leucosticte australis*
- ☐ Pine Grosbeak *Pinicola enucleator*
- ☐ Common Rosefinch *Carpodacus erythrinus*
- ☐ Purple Finch *Carpodacus purpureus*
- ☐ Cassin's Finch *Carpodacus cassinii*
- ☐ House Finch *Carpodacus mexicanus*
- ☐ Red Crossbill *Loxia curvirostra*
- ☐ White-winged Crossbill *Loxia leucoptera*
- ☐ Common Redpoll *Carduelis flammea*
- ☐ Hoary Redpoll *Carduelis hornemanni*
- ☐ Eurasian Siskin *Carduelis spinus*
- ☐ Pine Siskin *Carduelis pinus*
- ☐ Lesser Goldfinch *Carduelis psaltria*
- ☐ Lawrence's Goldfinch *Carduelis lawrencei*
- ☐ American Goldfinch *Carduelis tristis*
- ☐ Oriental Greenfinch *Carduelis sinica*
- ☐ Eurasian Bullfinch *Pyrrhula pyrrhula*
- ☐ Evening Grosbeak *Coccothraustes vespertinus*
- ☐ Hawfinch *Coccothraustes coccothraustes*

Old World Sparrows: PASSERIDAE

- ☐ House Sparrow *Passer domesticus*
- ☐ Eurasian Tree Sparrow *Passer montanus*

Weavers: PLOCEIDAE

- ☐ Orange Bishop *Euplectes franciscanus*

Estrildid Finches: ESTRILDIDAE

- ☐ Nutmeg Mannikin *Lonchura punctulata*

Ducks, Geese, Swans (Family Anatidae)

Greater White-fronted Goose *Anser albifrons*

DATE LOCATION

Bean Goose *Anser fabalis*

DATE LOCATION

Pink-footed Goose *Anser brachyrhynchus*

DATE LOCATION

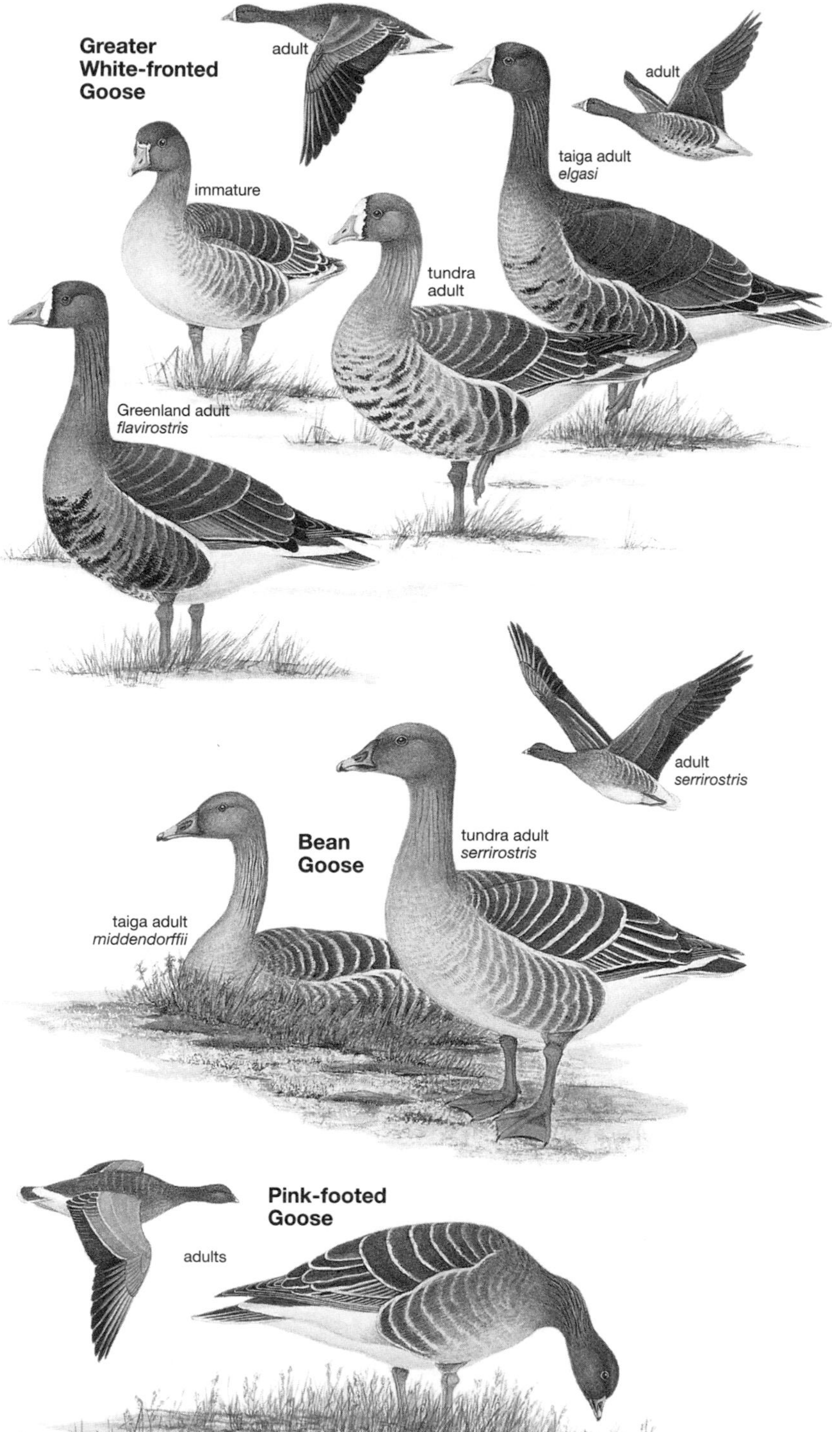
Greater White-fronted Goose
adult
adult
taiga adult
elgasi
immature
tundra adult
Greenland adult
flavirostris
adult
serrirostris
Bean Goose
tundra adult
serrirostris
taiga adult
middendorffii
Pink-footed Goose
adults

Snow Goose *Chen caerulescens*

DATE LOCATION

Ross's Goose *Chen rossii*

DATE LOCATION

Emperor Goose *Chen canagica*

DATE LOCATION

Barnacle Goose *Branta leucopsis*

DATE LOCATION

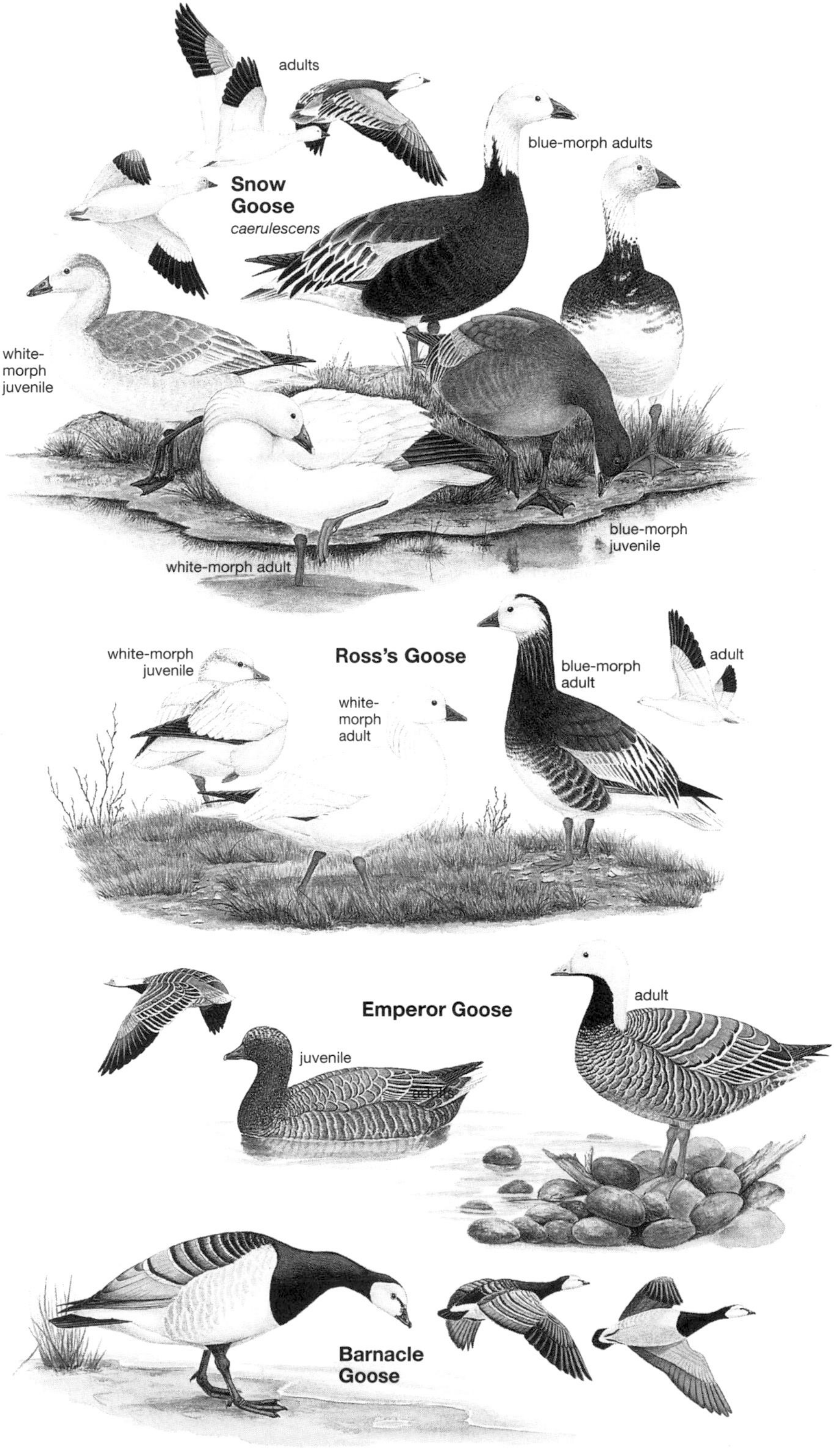
adults
Snow Goose
caerulescens
blue-morph adults
white-morph juvenile
blue-morph juvenile
white-morph adult
Ross's Goose
white-morph juvenile
white-morph adult
blue-morph adult
adult
Emperor Goose
adult
juvenile
adults
Barnacle Goose

Swans

Tundra Swan *Cygnus columbianus*

DATE LOCATION

Whooper Swan *Cygnus cygnus*

DATE LOCATION

Trumpeter Swan *Cygnus buccinator*

DATE LOCATION

Mute Swan *Cygnus olor*

DATE LOCATION

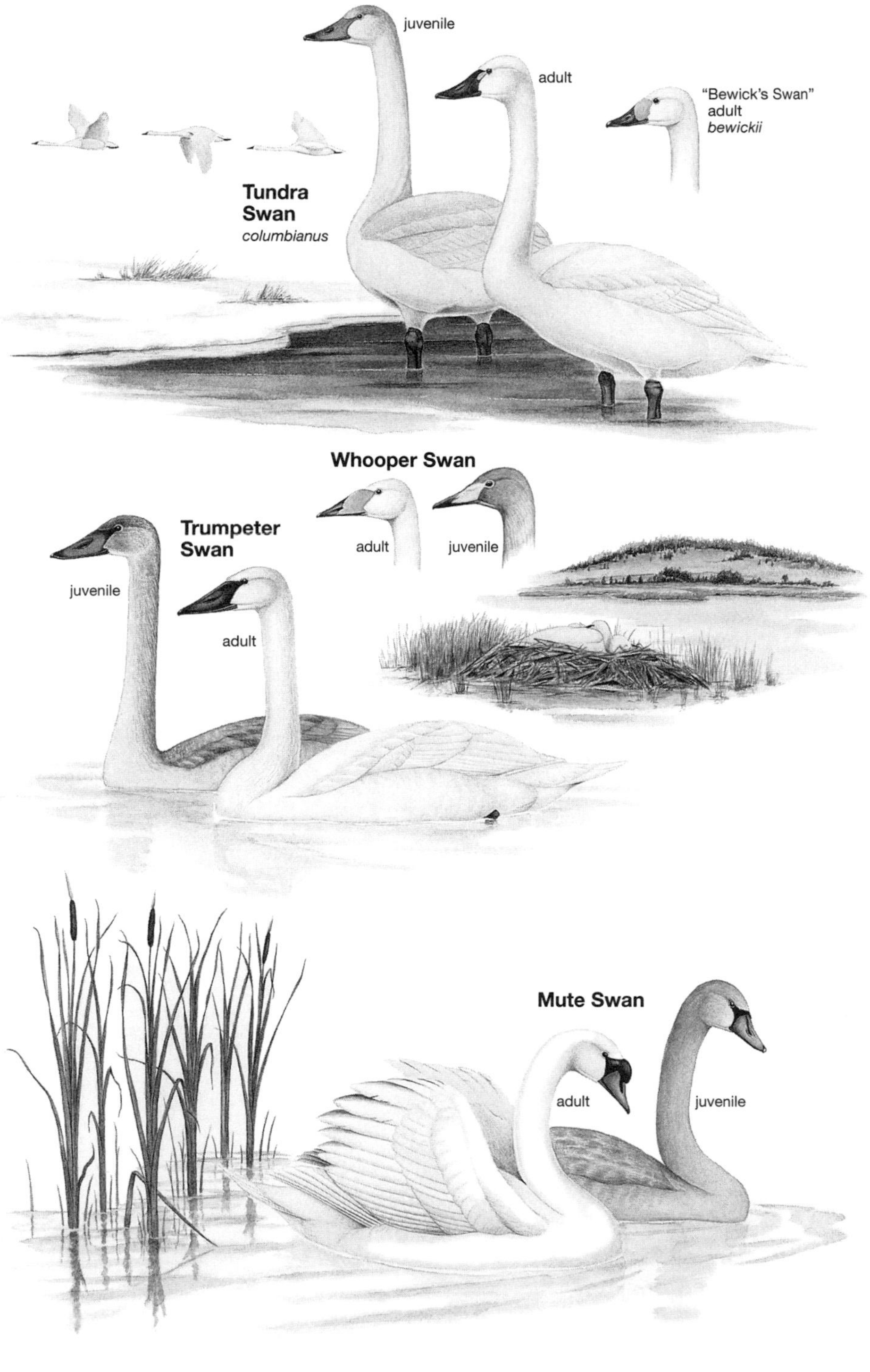
juvenile
adult
"Bewick's Swan"
adult
bewickii
Tundra
Swan
columbianus
Whooper Swan
Trumpeter
Swan
adult
juvenile
juvenile
adult
Mute Swan
adult
juvenile

Whistling-Ducks

Fulvous Whistling-Duck *Dendrocygna bicolor*

DATE LOCATION

Black-bellied Whistling-Duck *Dendrocygna autumnalis*

DATE LOCATION

Perching Ducks

Wood Duck *Aix sponsa*

DATE LOCATION

Muscovy Duck *Cairina moschata*

DATE LOCATION

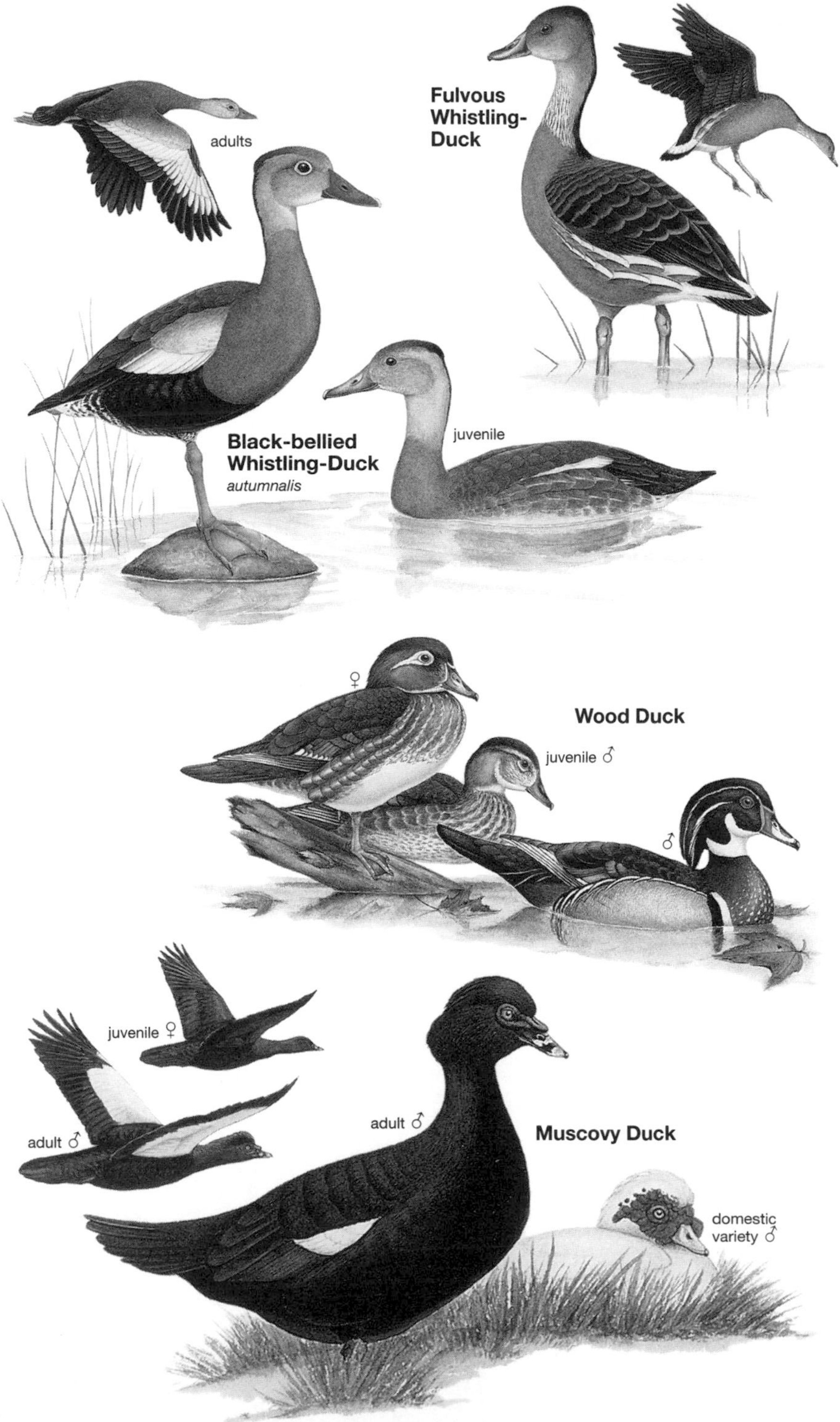
adults
Fulvous Whistling-Duck
Black-bellied Whistling-Duck
autumnalis
juvenile
♀
Wood Duck
juvenile ♂
♂
juvenile ♀
adult ♂
adult ♂
Muscovy Duck
domestic variety ♂

Dabbling Ducks

Mallard *Anas platyrhynchos*

DATE LOCATION

Mottled Duck *Anas fulvigula*

DATE LOCATION

American Black Duck *Anas rubripes*

DATE LOCATION

Spot-billed Duck *Anas poecilorhyncha*

DATE LOCATION

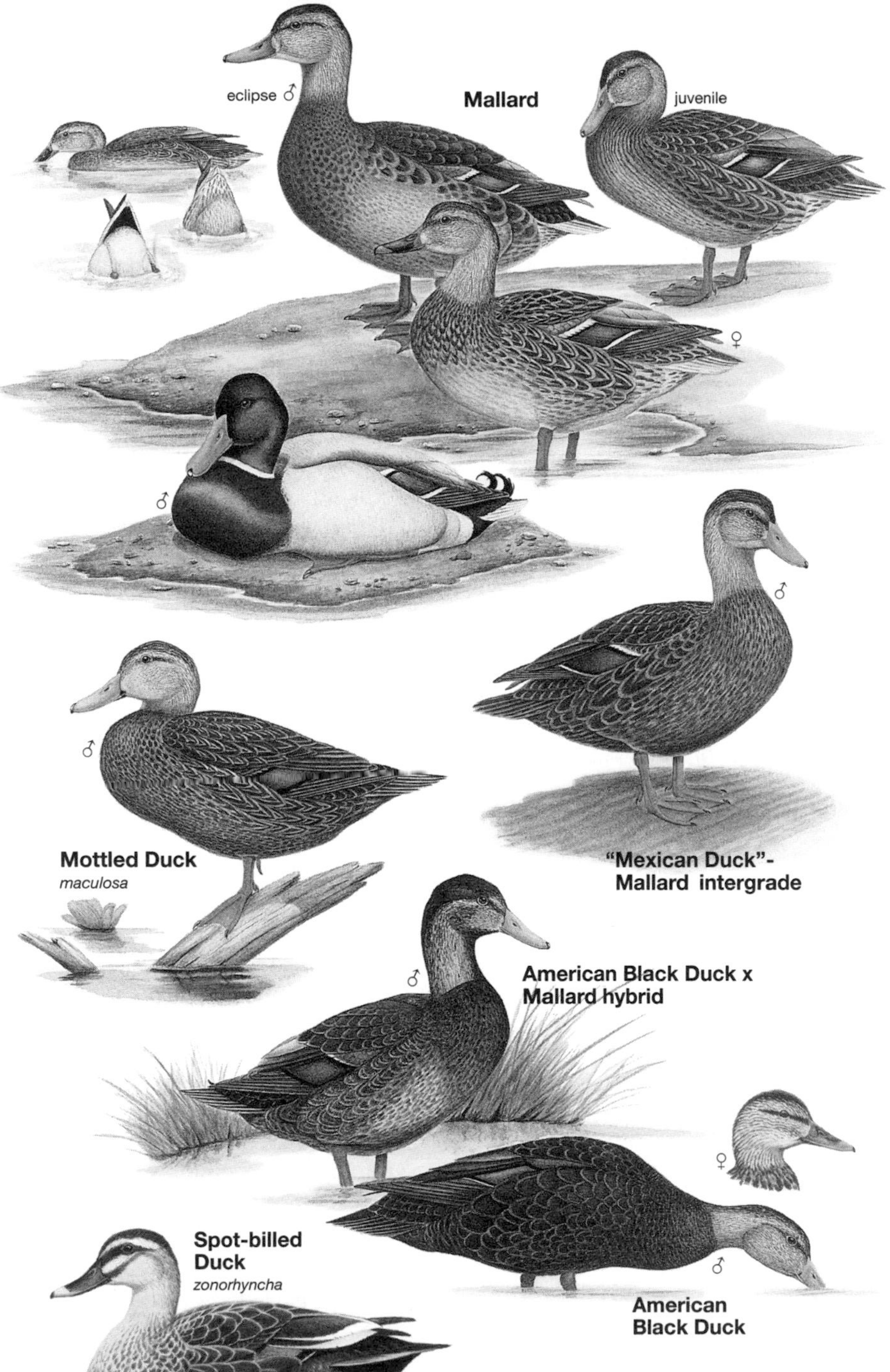
eclipse ♂
Mallard
juvenile
♀
♂
♂
Mottled Duck
maculosa
♂
"Mexican Duck"-
Mallard intergrade
♂
American Black Duck x
Mallard hybrid
♀
Spot-billed
Duck
zonorhyncha
♂
American
Black Duck

Gadwall *Anas strepera*

DATE LOCATION

Falcated Duck *Anas falcata*

DATE LOCATION

Green-winged Teal *Anas crecca*

DATE LOCATION

Baikal Teal *Anas formosa*

DATE LOCATION

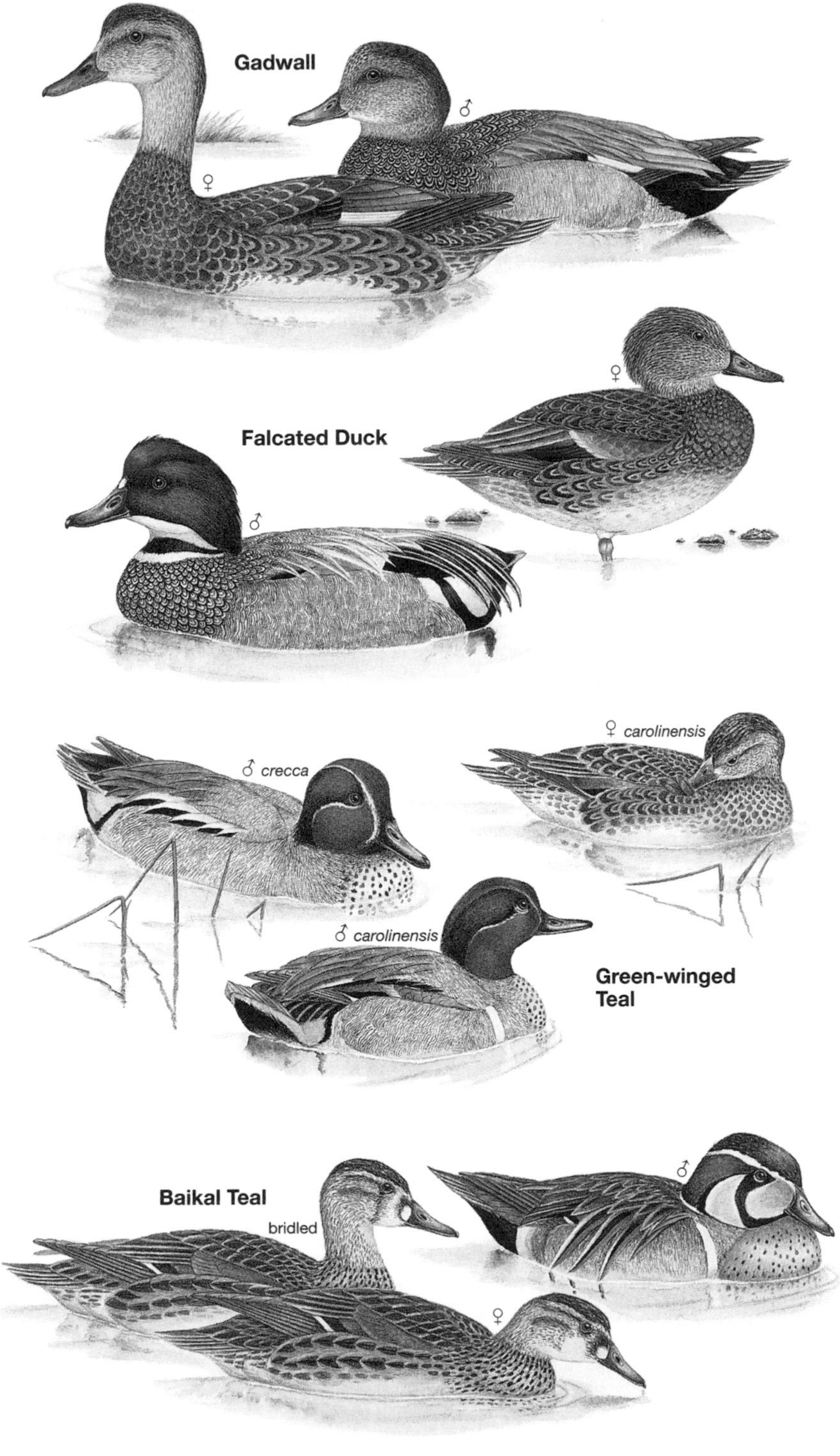
Gadwall
♀
♂
Falcated Duck
♀
♂
♂ crecca
♀ carolinensis
♂ carolinensis
Green-winged Teal
Baikal Teal
bridled
♂
♀

American Wigeon *Anas americana*

DATE LOCATION

Eurasian Wigeon *Anas penelope*

DATE LOCATION

Northern Pintail *Anas acuta*

DATE LOCATION

White-cheeked Pintail *Anas bahamensis*

DATE LOCATION

American Wigeon
adult ♂
eclipse adult ♂
♀
rufous-morph ♀
gray-morph ♀
adult ♂
Eurasian Wigeon
immature ♂
♀
♂
Northern Pintail
♂
White-cheeked Pintail
bahamensis

Northern Shoveler *Anas clypeata*

DATE LOCATION

Blue-winged Teal *Anas discors*

DATE LOCATION

Cinnamon Teal *Anas cyanoptera*

DATE LOCATION

Garganey *Anas querquedula*

DATE LOCATION

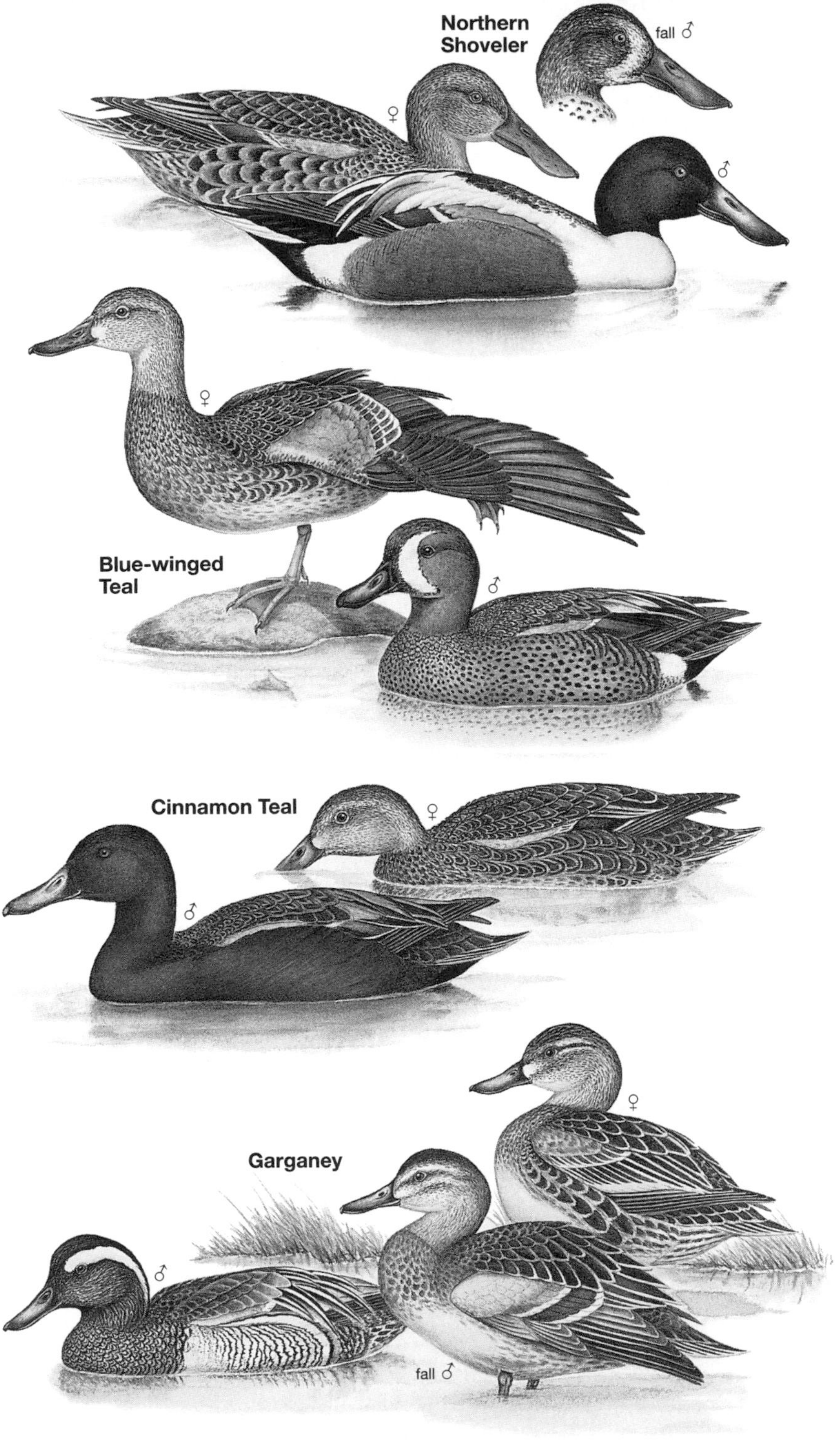

Northern Shoveler
fall ♂
♀
♂
♀
Blue-winged Teal
♂
Cinnamon Teal
♀
♂
♀
Garganey
♂
fall ♂

Pochards

Canvasback *Aythya valisineria*

DATE LOCATION

Common Pochard *Aythya ferina*

DATE LOCATION

Redhead *Aythya americana*

DATE LOCATION

Canvasback

Common Pochard

Redhead

Ring-necked Duck *Aythya collaris*

DATE LOCATION

Tufted Duck *Aythya fuligula*

DATE LOCATION

Greater Scaup *Aythya marila*

DATE LOCATION

Lesser Scaup *Aythya affinis*

DATE LOCATION

Ring-necked Duck
adult ♂
♀
Tufted Duck
♀
♀
1st winter ♂
adult ♂
Greater Scaup
nearctica
♀
1st winter ♂
♀
adult ♂
Lesser
Scaup
♀
adult ♂

Eiders

Common Eider *Somateria mollissima*

DATE LOCATION

King Eider *Somateria spectabilis*

DATE LOCATION

Spectacled Eider *Somateria fischeri*

DATE LOCATION

Steller's Eider *Polysticta stelleri*

DATE LOCATION

Common Eider
eclipse adult ♂ v-nigrum
♀ v-nigrum
♀ dresseri
1st winter ♂ dresseri
adult ♂ dresseri
adult ♂ v-nigrum
1st winter ♂
adult ♂
King Eider
♀
adult ♂
Spectacled Eider
♀
Common Eiders in flight
1st winter ♂
adult ♂
Steller's Eider
♀

Sea Ducks

Black Scoter *Melanitta nigra*

DATE LOCATION

White-winged Scoter *Melanitta fusca*

DATE LOCATION

Surf Scoter *Melanitta perspicillata*

DATE LOCATION

Harlequin Duck *Histrionicus histrionicus*

DATE LOCATION

Black Scoter
americana
1st winter ♂
adult ♂
adult ♀
White-winged Scoter
deglandi
1st winter ♀
1st winter ♂
adult ♂
adult ♀
adult ♂
stejnegeri
Surf Scoter
adult ♀
1st winter ♀
adult ♂
1st winter ♂
Harlequin
Duck
♀
1st winter ♂
adult ♂

Long-tailed Duck *Clangula hyemalis*

DATE LOCATION

Barrow's Goldeneye *Bucephala islandica*

DATE LOCATION

Common Goldeneye *Bucephala clangula*

DATE LOCATION

Bufflehead *Bucephala albeola*

DATE LOCATION

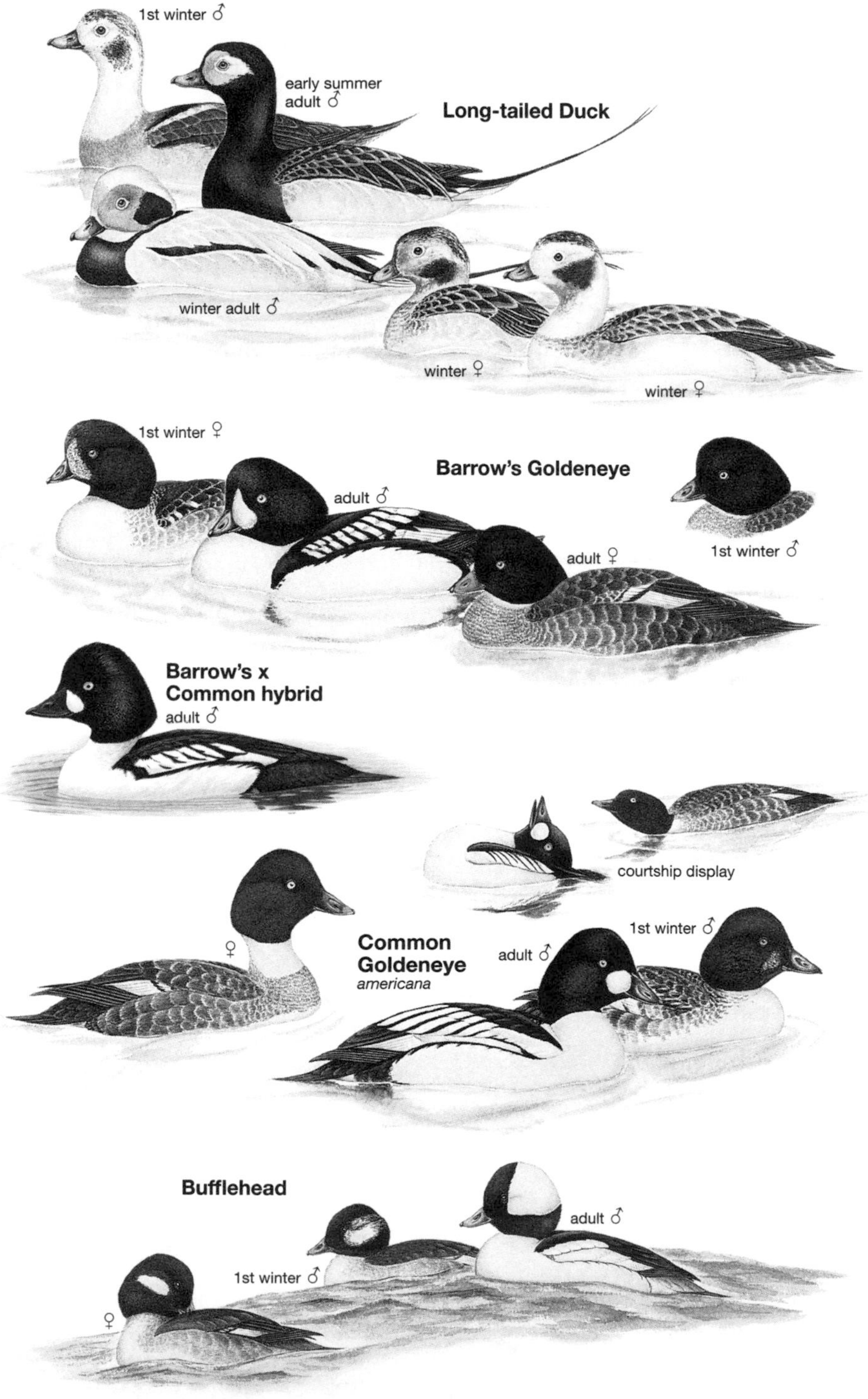
Long-tailed Duck
1st winter ♂
early summer adult ♂
winter adult ♂
winter ♀
winter ♀
Barrow's Goldeneye
1st winter ♀
adult ♂
adult ♀
1st winter ♂
Barrow's x Common hybrid
adult ♂
courtship display
Common Goldeneye
americana
♀
adult ♂
1st winter ♂
Bufflehead
adult ♂
1st winter ♂
♀

Mergansers

Common Merganser *Mergus merganser*

DATE LOCATION

Red-breasted Merganser *Mergus serrator*

DATE LOCATION

Hooded Merganser *Lophodytes cucullatus*

DATE LOCATION

Smew *Mergellus albellus*

DATE LOCATION

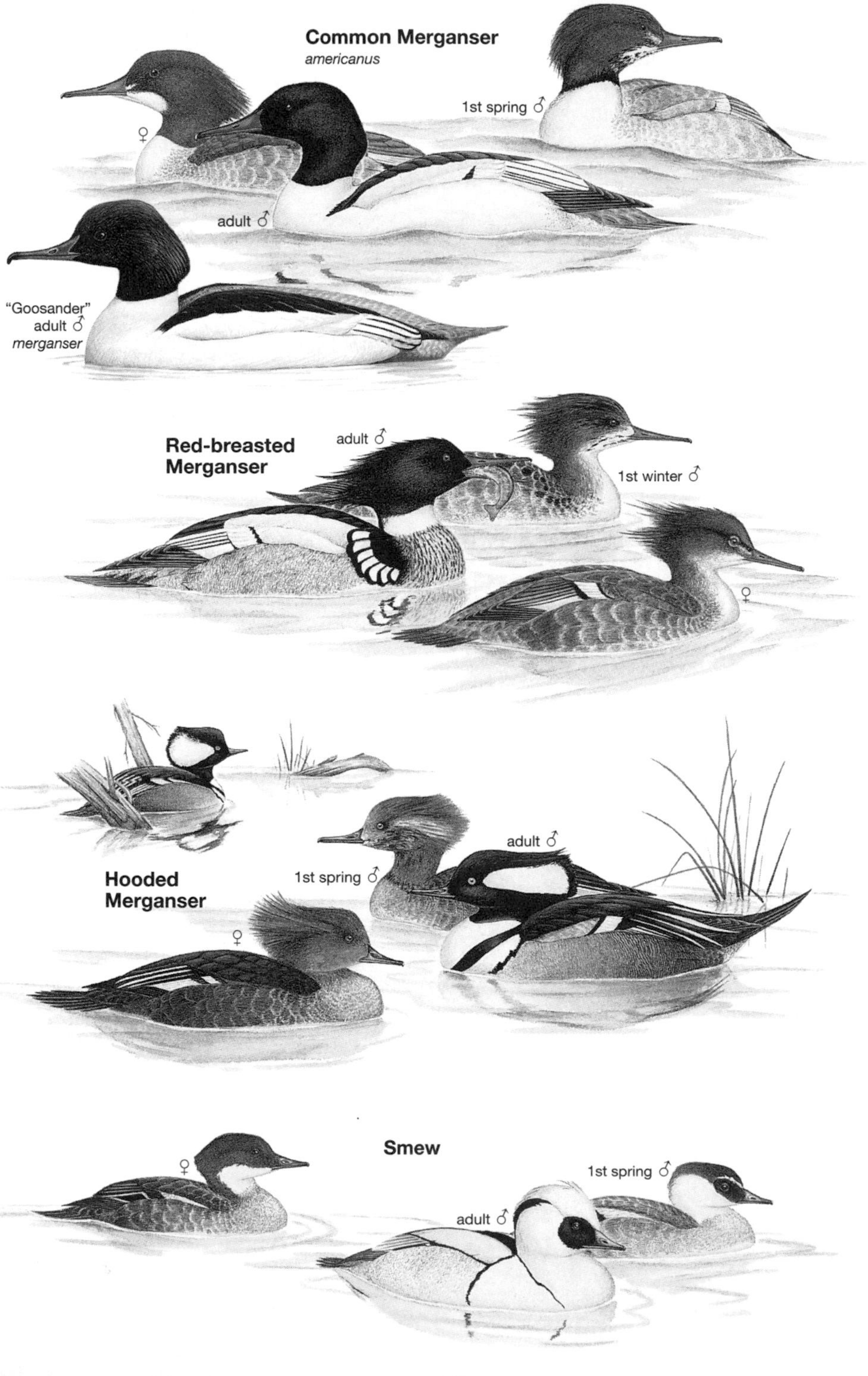

Common Merganser
americanus
♀
adult ♂
1st spring ♂
"Goosander"
adult ♂
merganser
Red-breasted
Merganser
adult ♂
1st winter ♂
♀
Hooded
Merganser
1st spring ♂
adult ♂
♀
Smew
♀
1st spring ♂
adult ♂

Stiff-tailed Ducks

Ruddy Duck *Oxyura jamaicensis*

DATE LOCATION

Masked Duck *Nomonyx dominicus*

DATE LOCATION

Exotic Waterfowl

Ruddy Shelduck *Tadorna ferruginea*

DATE LOCATION

Common Shelduck *Tadorna tadorna*

DATE LOCATION

Egyptian Goose *Alopochen aegyptiacus*

DATE LOCATION

Swan Goose *Anser cygnoides*

DATE LOCATION

Mandarin Duck *Aix galericulata*

DATE LOCATION

Bar-headed Goose *Anser indicus*

DATE LOCATION

Graylag Goose *Anser anser*

DATE LOCATION

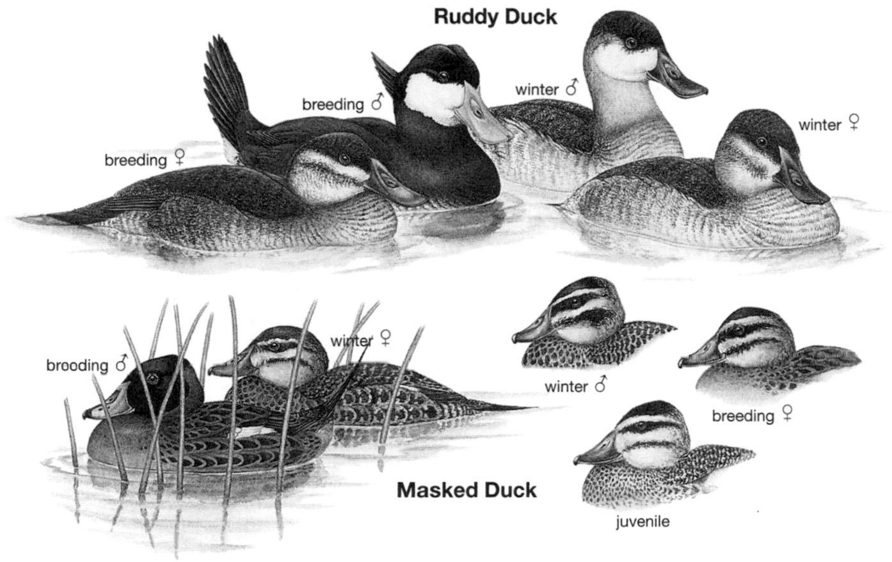
Ruddy Duck
breeding ♂
winter ♂
winter ♀
breeding ♀
brooding ♂
winter ♀
winter ♂
breeding ♀
juvenile
Masked Duck

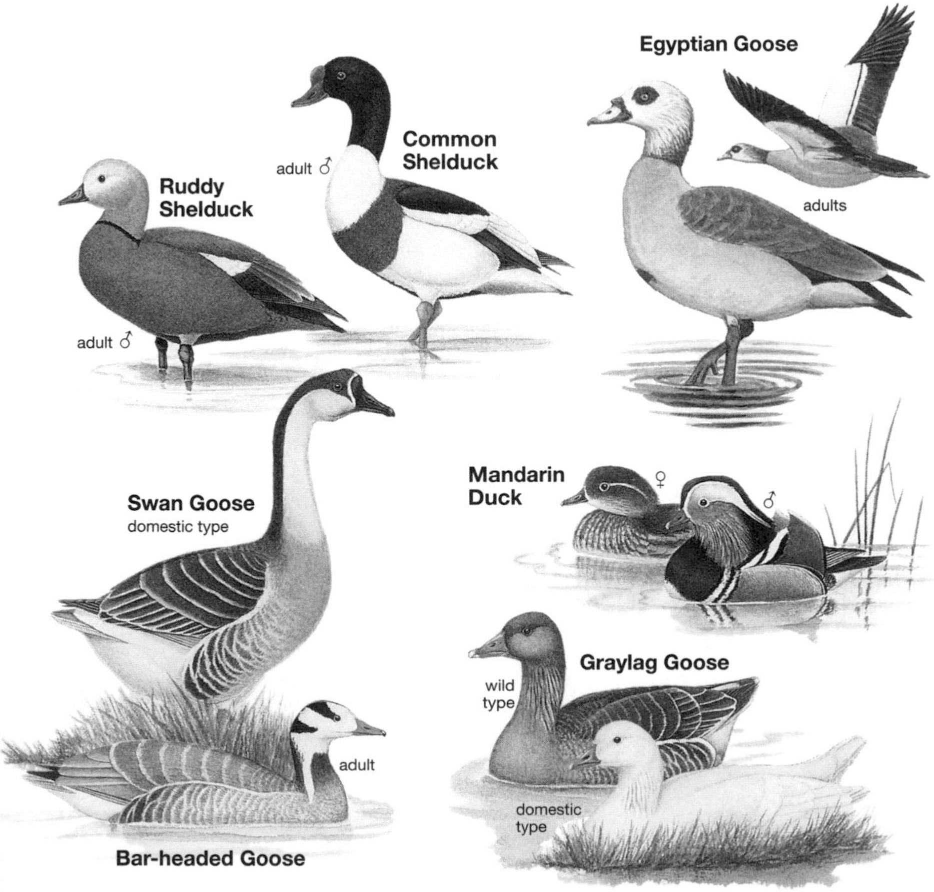
Egyptian Goose
adults
Common Shelduck
adult ♂
Ruddy Shelduck
adult ♂
Swan Goose
domestic type
Mandarin Duck
♀
♂
Graylag Goose
wild type
domestic type
adult
Bar-headed Goose

Ducks in Flight

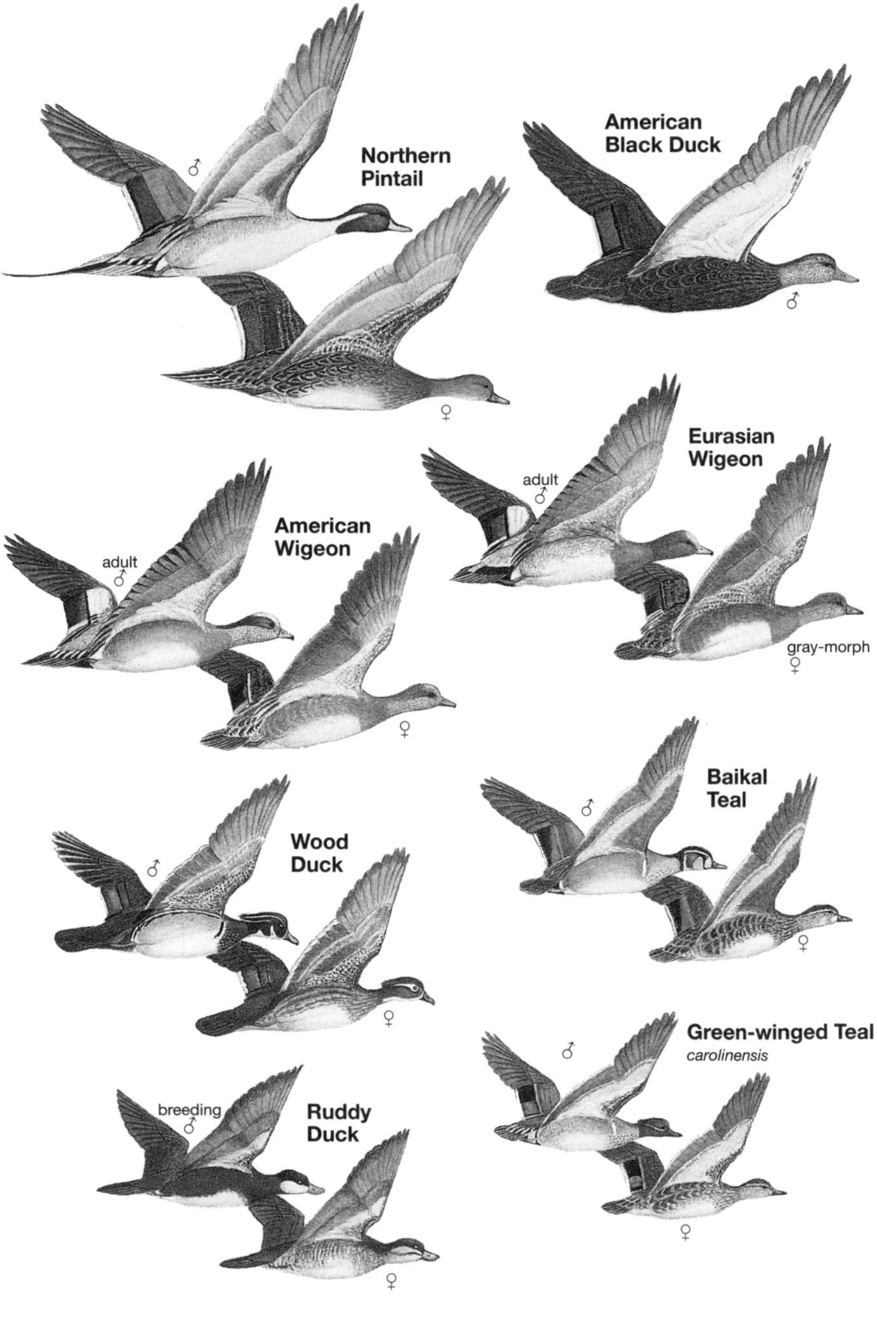
Northern Pintail
♂
♀
American Black Duck
♂
Eurasian Wigeon
adult ♂
gray-morph ♀
American Wigeon
adult ♂
♀
Baikal Teal
♂
♀
Wood Duck
♂
♀
Green-winged Teal
carolinensis
♂
♀
Ruddy Duck
breeding ♂
♀

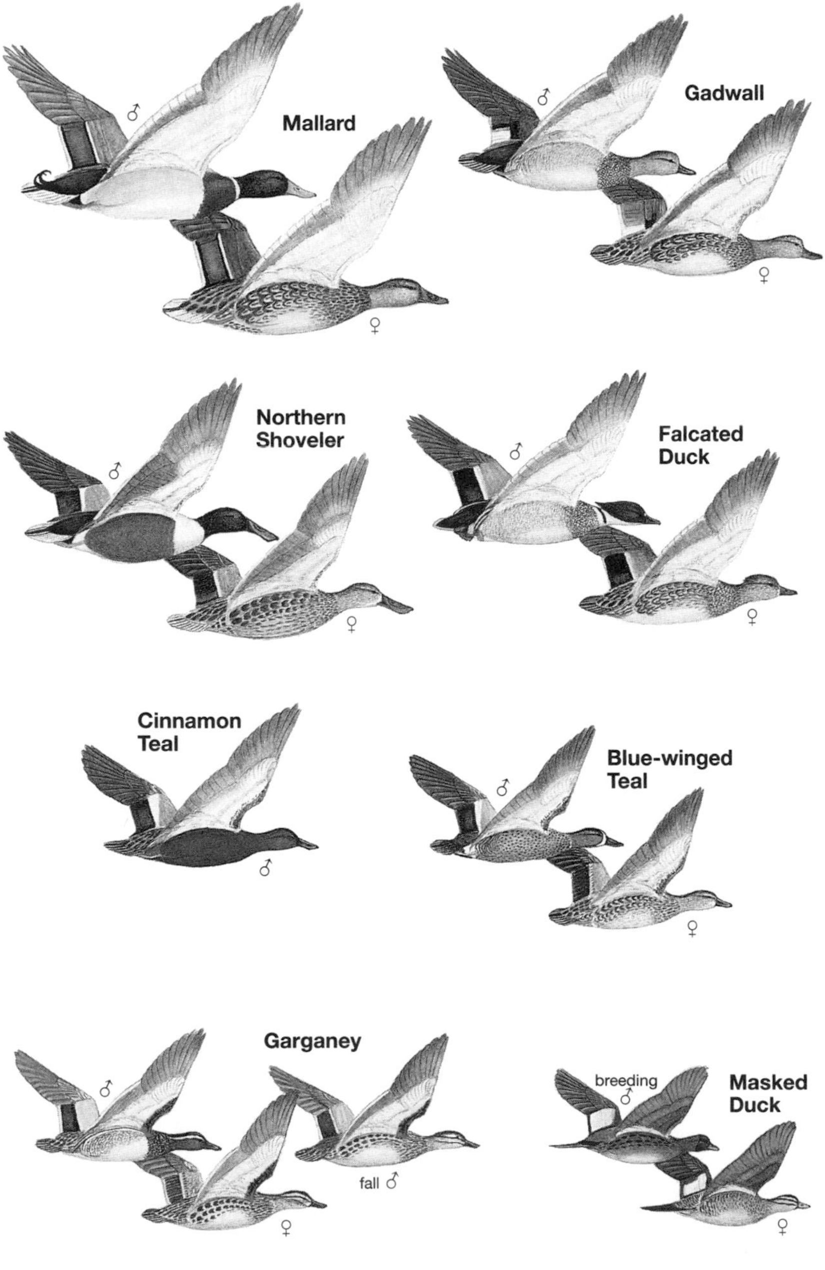
Mallard
♂
♀
Gadwall
♂
♀
Northern Shoveler
♂
♀
Falcated Duck
♂
♀
Cinnamon Teal
♂
Blue-winged Teal
♂
♀
Garganey
♂
fall ♂
♀
Masked Duck
breeding ♂
♀

Ducks in Flight

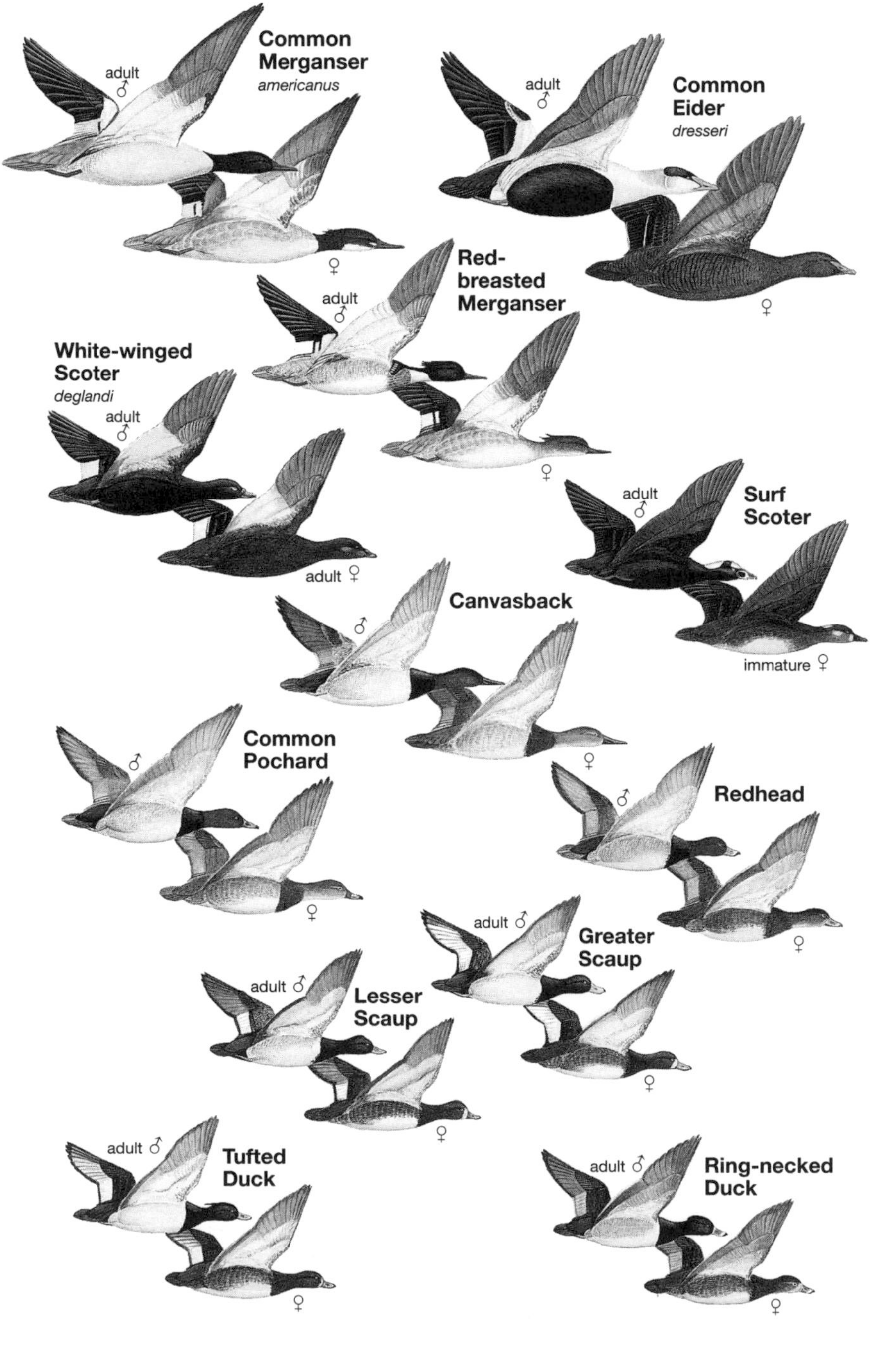

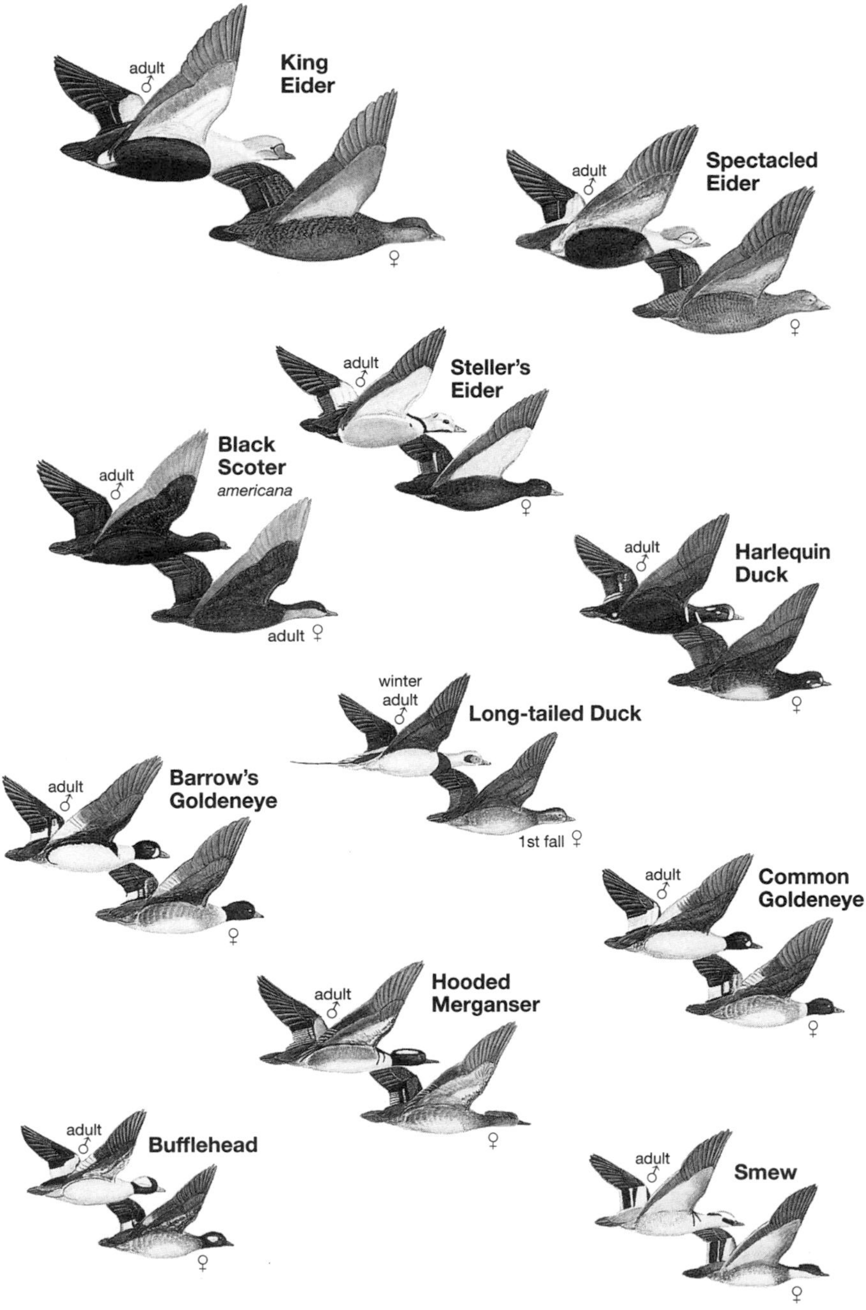
King Eider
adult ♂
♀
Spectacled Eider
adult ♂
♀
Steller's Eider
adult ♂
♀
Black Scoter
americana
adult ♂
adult ♀
Harlequin Duck
adult ♂
♀
Long-tailed Duck
winter adult ♂
1st fall ♀
Barrow's Goldeneye
adult ♂
♀
Common Goldeneye
adult ♂
♀
Hooded Merganser
adult ♂
♀
Bufflehead
adult ♂
♀
Smew
adult ♂
♀

Curassows, Guans (Family Cracidae)

Plain Chachalaca *Ortalis vetula*

DATE LOCATION

Partridges, Grouse, Turkeys, Old World Quail
(Family Phasianidae)

Chukar *Alectoris chukar*

DATE LOCATION

Gray Partridge *Perdix perdix*

DATE LOCATION

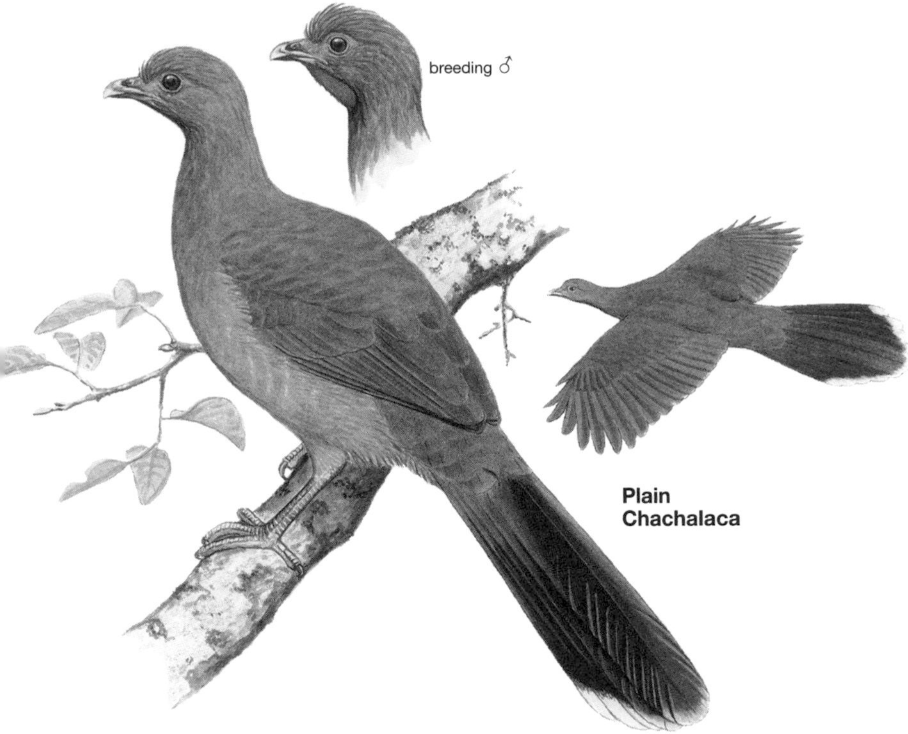
breeding ♂
Plain
Chachalaca

Chukar
adults
juvenile

Gray
Partridge
♀
♂

Ring-necked Pheasant *Phasianus colchicus*

DATE LOCATION

Wild Turkey *Meleagris gallopavo*

DATE LOCATION

Himalayan Snowcock *Tetraogallus himalayensis*

DATE LOCATION

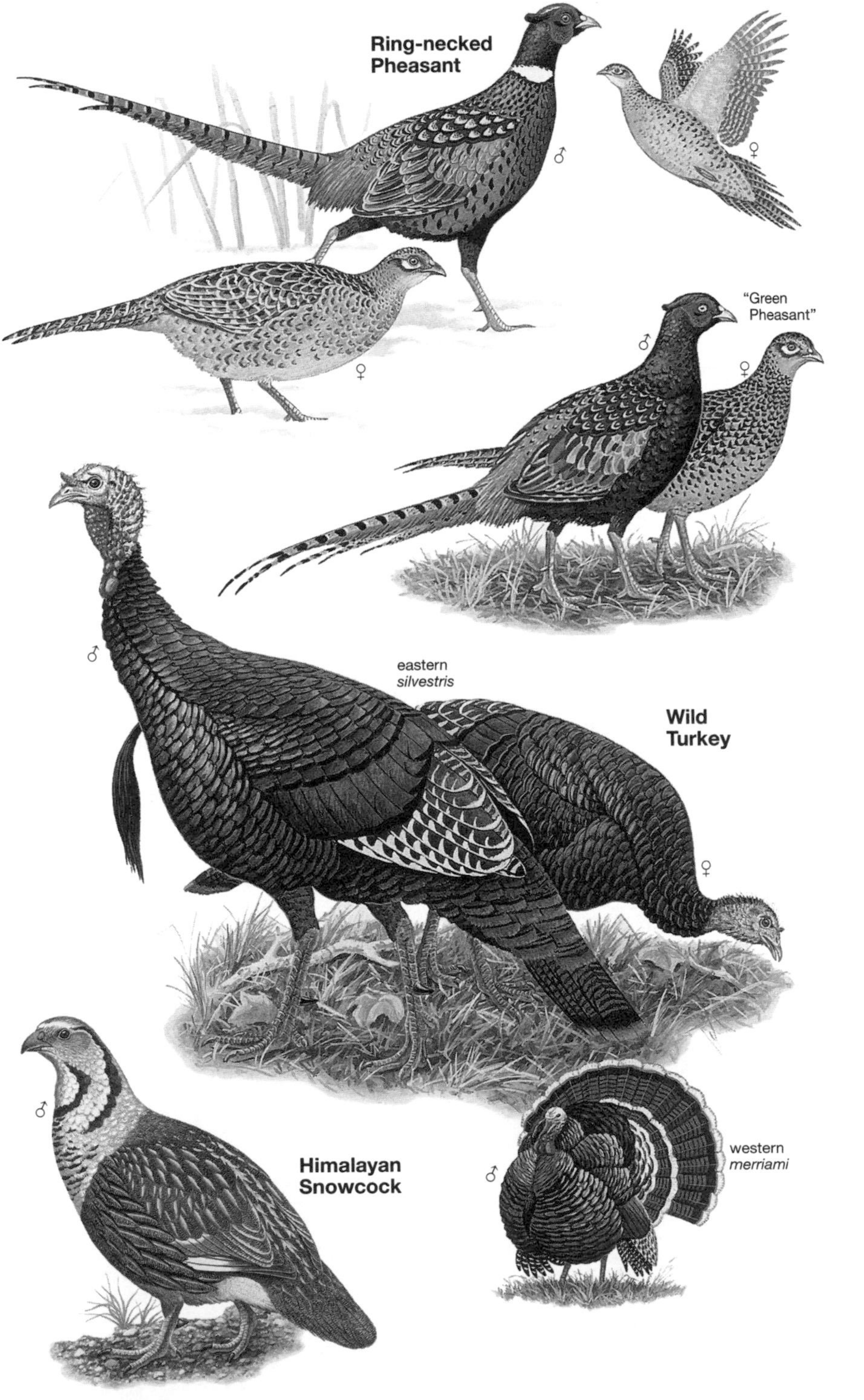

Ring-necked Pheasant
♂
♀
♀
"Green Pheasant"
♂
♀
eastern
silvestris
♂
Wild Turkey
♀
♂
Himalayan Snowcock
♂
western
merriami

Ruffed Grouse *Bonasa umbellus*

DATE LOCATION

Spruce Grouse *Falcipennis canadensis*

DATE LOCATION

Sooty Grouse *Dendragapus fuliginosus*

DATE LOCATION

Dusky Grouse *Dendragapus obscurus*

DATE LOCATION

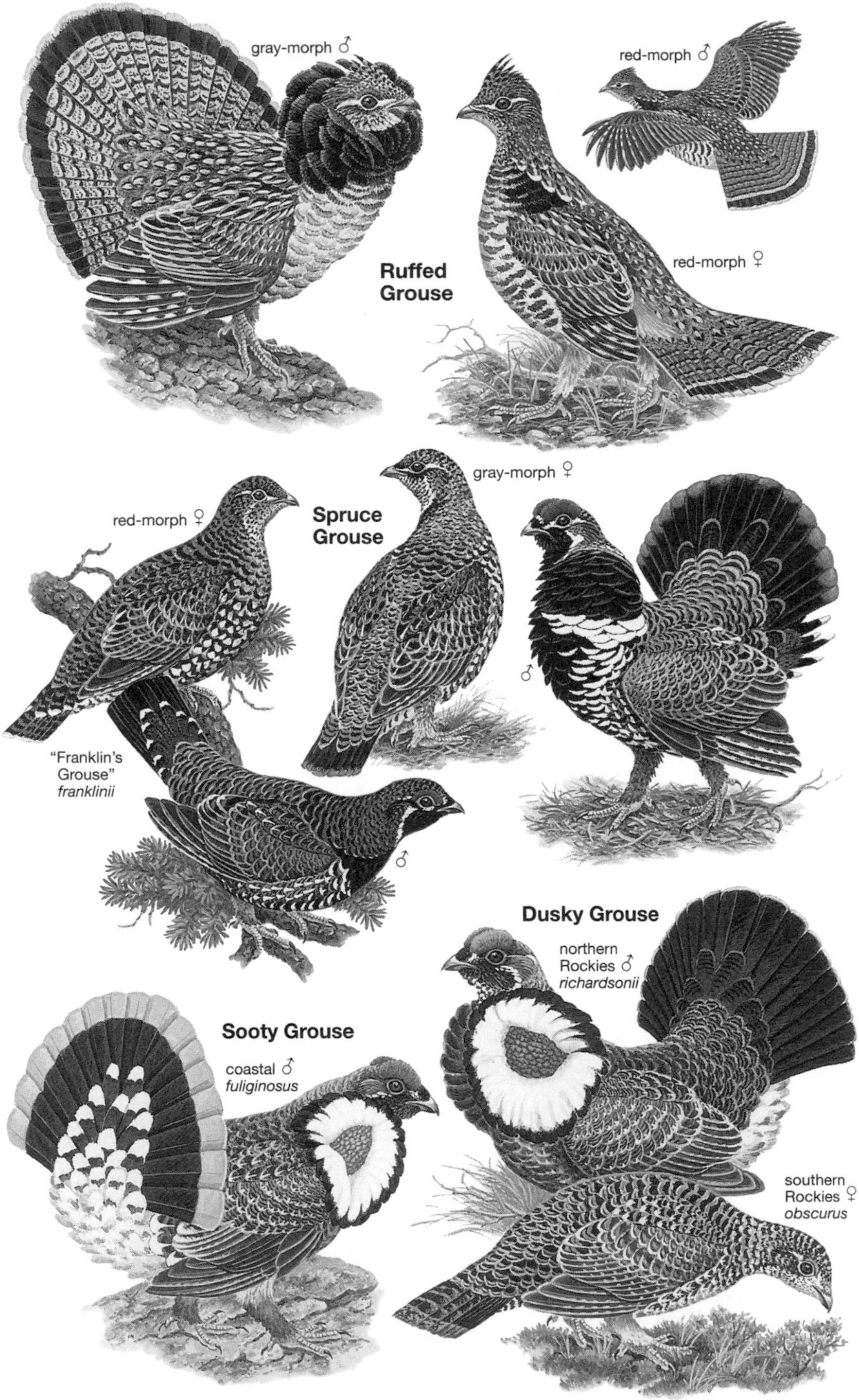
gray-morph ♂
red-morph ♂
Ruffed Grouse
red-morph ♀
gray-morph ♀
red-morph ♀
Spruce Grouse
♂
"Franklin's Grouse"
franklinii
♂
Dusky Grouse
northern Rockies ♂
richardsonii
Sooty Grouse
coastal ♂
fuliginosus
southern Rockies ♀
obscurus

White-tailed Ptarmigan *Lagopus leucura*

DATE LOCATION

Rock Ptarmigan *Lagopus muta*

DATE LOCATION

Willow Ptarmigan *Lagopus lagopus*

DATE LOCATION

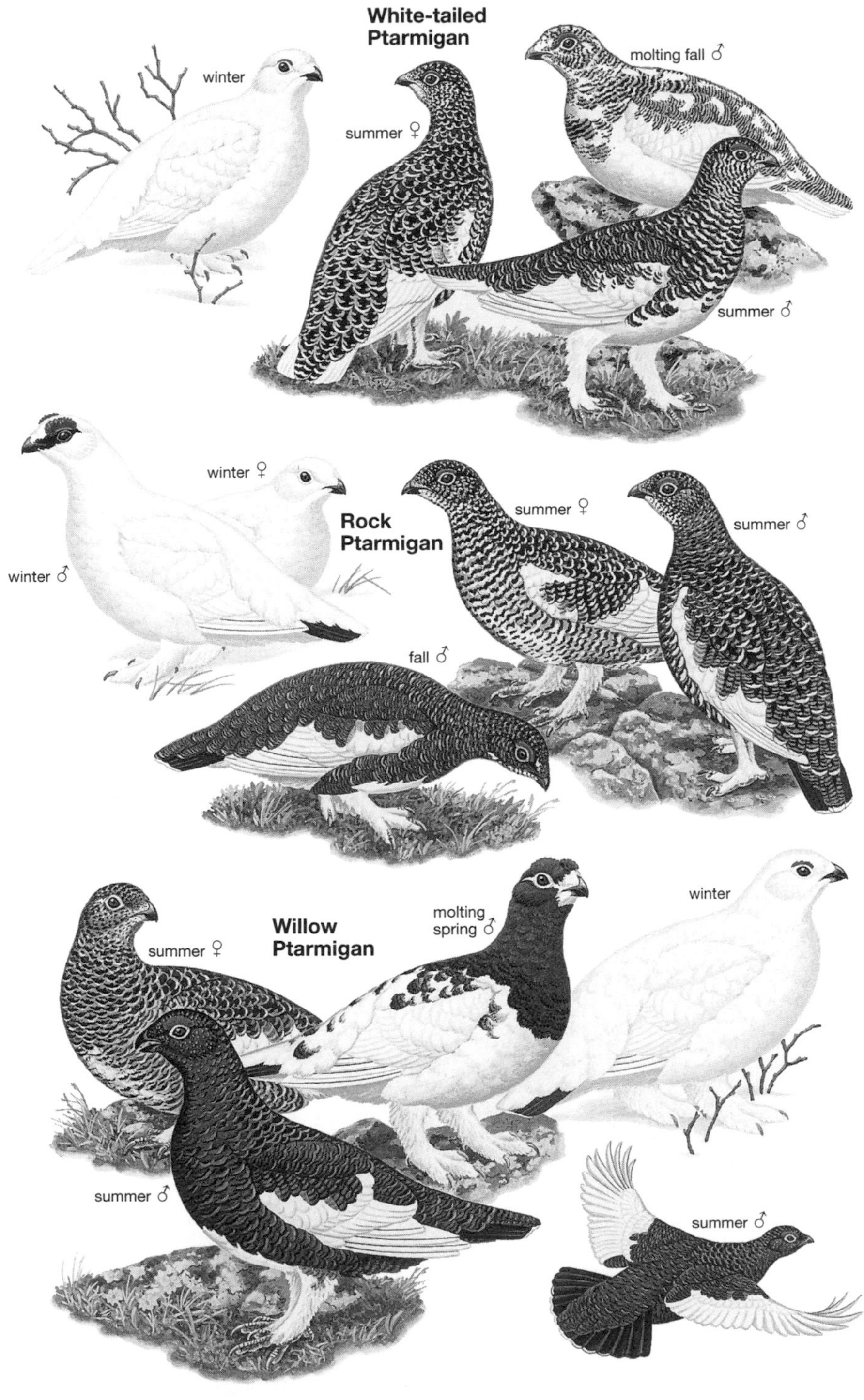
White-tailed Ptarmigan
winter
summer ♀
molting fall ♂
summer ♂
Rock Ptarmigan
winter ♀
winter ♂
summer ♀
summer ♂
fall ♂
Willow Ptarmigan
summer ♀
molting spring ♂
winter
summer ♂
summer ♂

Greater Prairie-Chicken *Tympanuchus cupido*

DATE LOCATION

Lesser Prairie-Chicken *Tympanuchus pallidicinctus*

DATE LOCATION

Sharp-tailed Grouse *Tympanuchus phasianellus*

DATE LOCATION

Gunnison Sage-Grouse *Centrocercus minimus*

DATE LOCATION

Greater Sage-Grouse *Centrocercus urophasianus*

DATE LOCATION

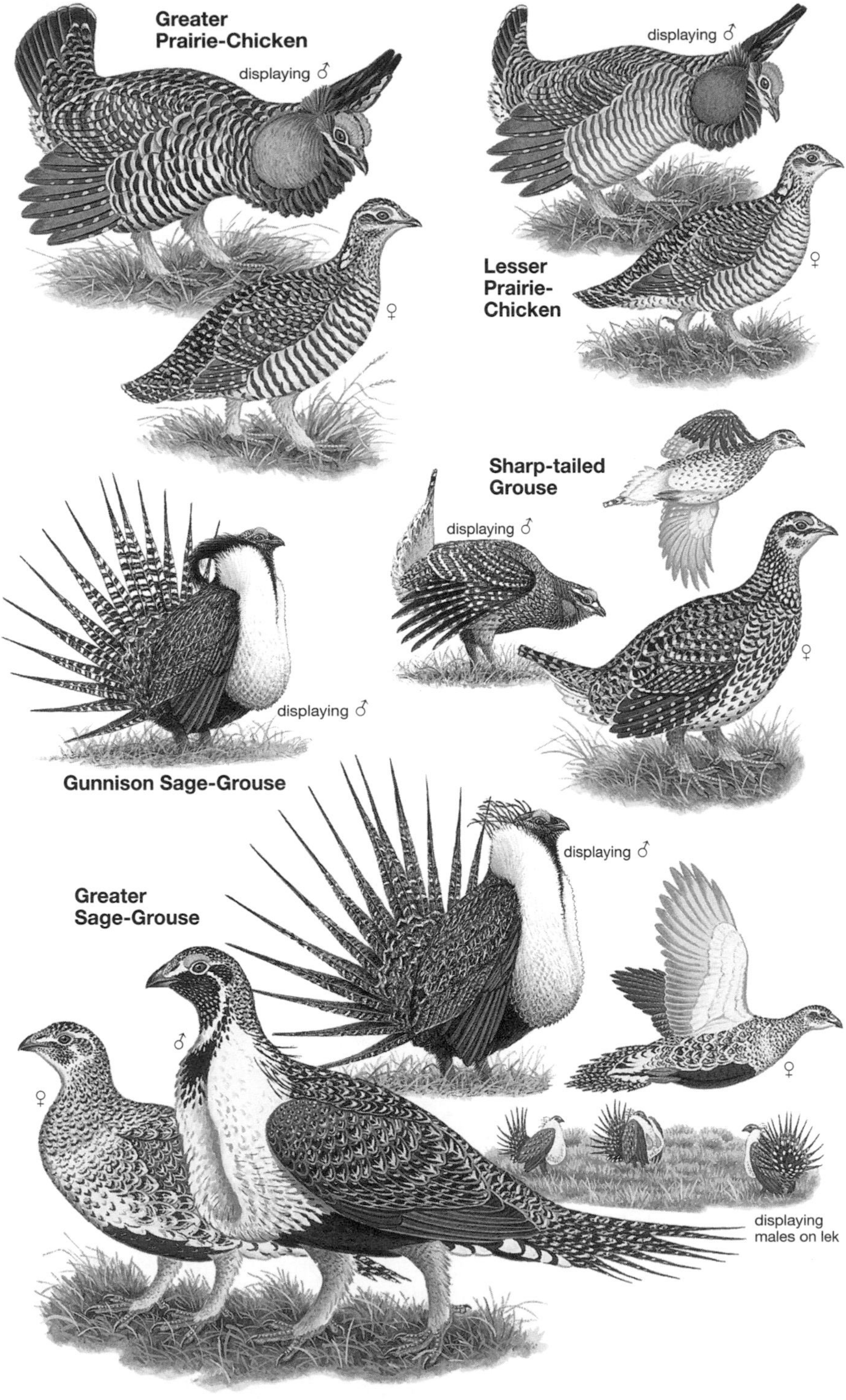
Greater Prairie-Chicken
displaying ♂
♀
displaying ♂
Lesser Prairie-Chicken
♀
Sharp-tailed Grouse
displaying ♂
♀
displaying ♂
Gunnison Sage-Grouse
displaying ♂
Greater Sage-Grouse
♂
♀
♀
displaying males on lek

New World Quail (Family Odontophoridae)

Gambel's Quail *Callipepla gambelii*

DATE LOCATION

California Quail *Callipepla californica*

DATE LOCATION

Mountain Quail *Oreortyx pictus*

DATE LOCATION

♂
♀
juvenile
Gambel's Quail
Scaled x Gambel's hybrid
♂
♀ californica
coastal ♀ brunescens
California Quail
coastal juvenile brunescens
♂ californica
coastal ♂ palmeri
interior ♀
Mountain Quail
juvenile

Northern Bobwhite *Colinus virginianus*

DATE LOCATION

Montezuma Quail *Cyrtonyx montezumae*

DATE LOCATION

Scaled Quail *Callipepla squamata*

DATE LOCATION

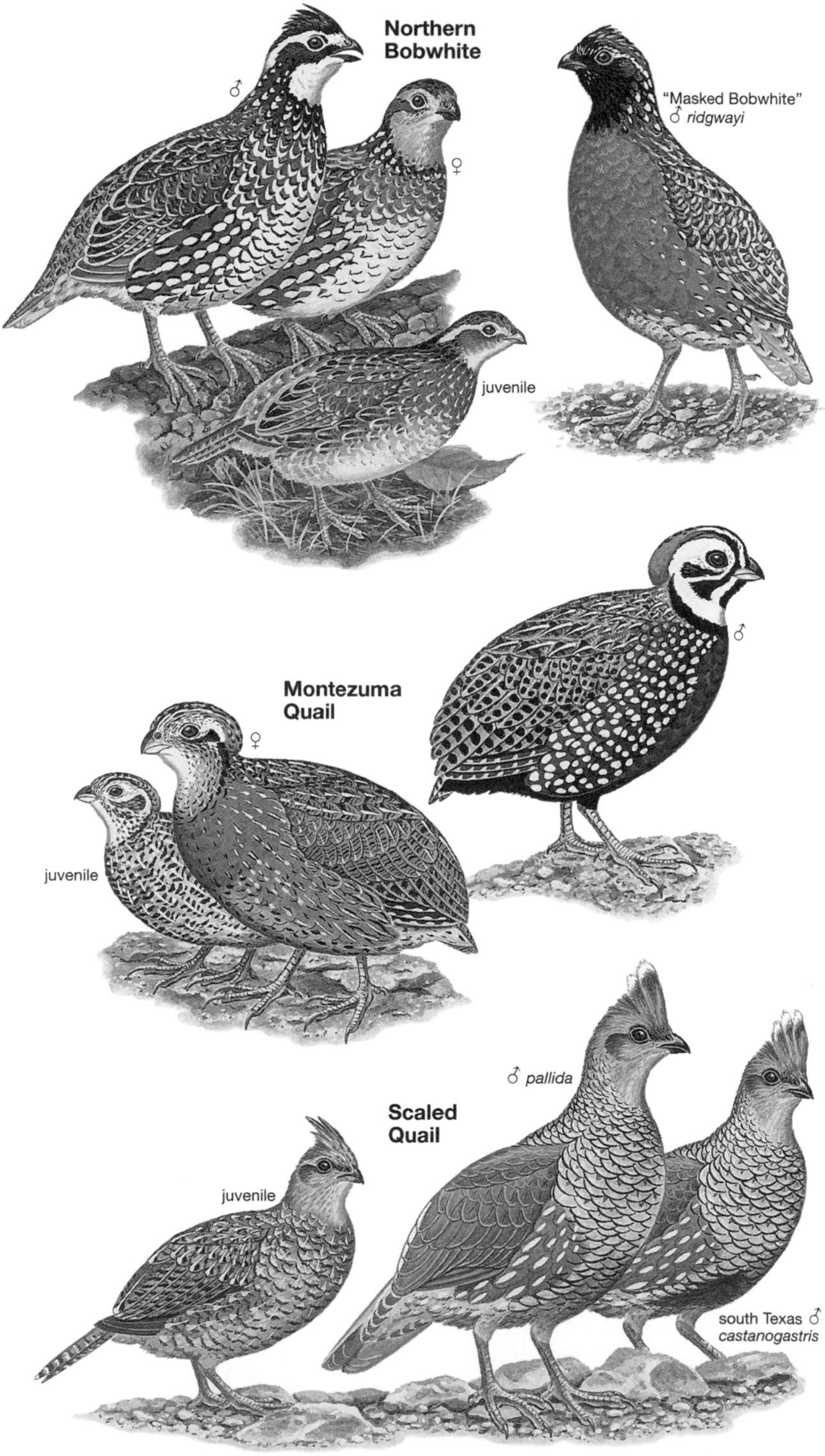
Northern Bobwhite
♂
♀
juvenile
"Masked Bobwhite"
♂ *ridgwayi*
Montezuma Quail
♂
♀
juvenile
Scaled Quail
♂ *pallida*
juvenile
south Texas ♂
castanogastris

Loons (Family Gaviidae)

Red-throated Loon *Gavia stellata*

DATE LOCATION

Pacific Loon *Gavia pacifica*

DATE LOCATION

Arctic Loon *Gavia arctica*

DATE LOCATION

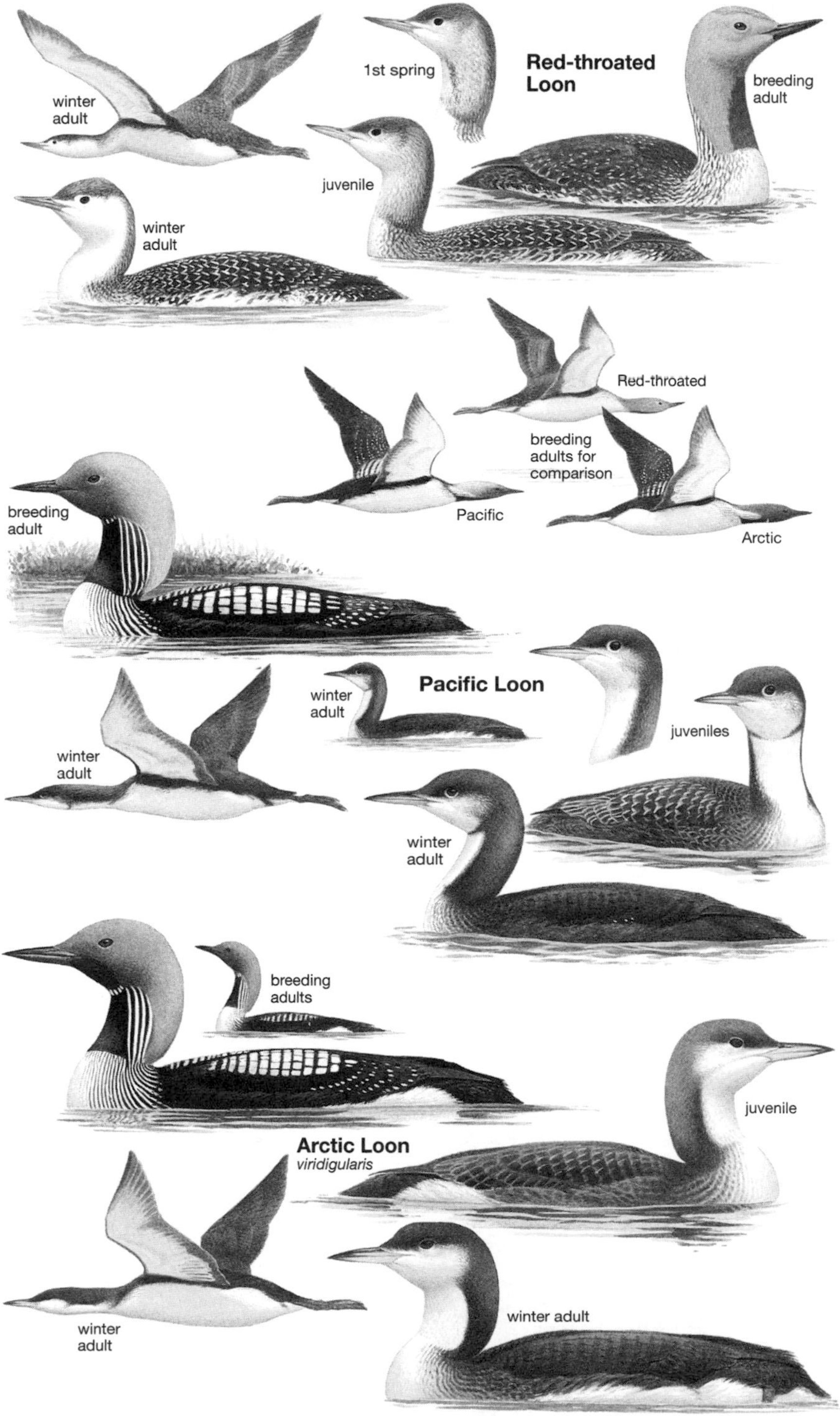

Red-throated Loon
winter adult
1st spring
breeding adult
juvenile
winter adult
Red-throated
breeding adults for comparison
Pacific
Arctic
breeding adult
Pacific Loon
winter adult
winter adult
juveniles
winter adult
breeding adults
juvenile
Arctic Loon
viridigularis
winter adult
winter adult

Common Loon *Gavia immer*

DATE LOCATION

Yellow-billed Loon *Gavia adamsii*

DATE LOCATION

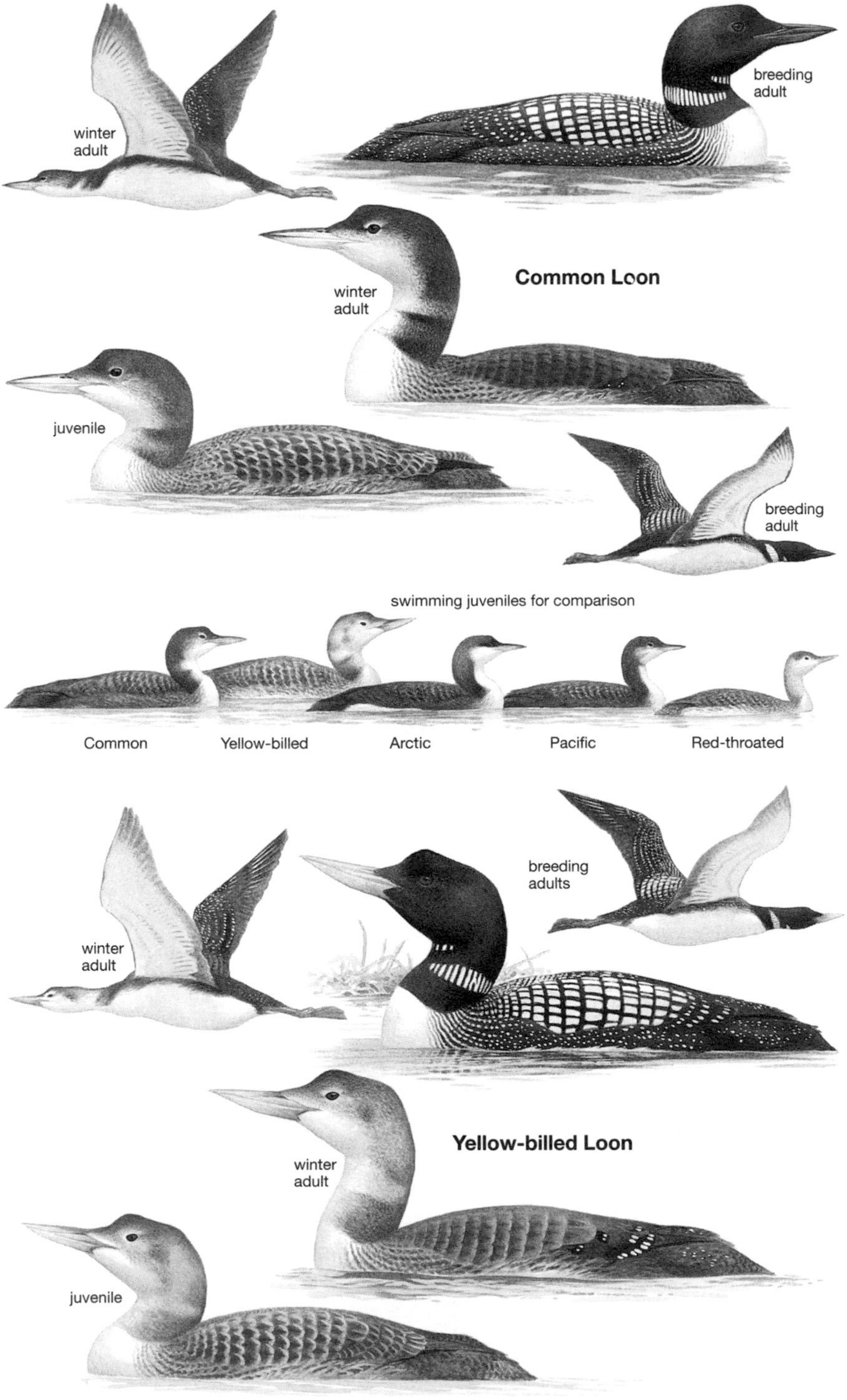
winter
adult
breeding
adult
Common Loon
winter
adult
juvenile
breeding
adult
swimming juveniles for comparison
Common
Yellow-billed
Arctic
Pacific
Red-throated
breeding
adults
winter
adult
Yellow-billed Loon
winter
adult
juvenile

Grebes (Family Podicipedidae)

Least Grebe *Tachybaptus dominicus*

DATE LOCATION

Pied-billed Grebe *Podilymbus podiceps*

DATE LOCATION

Horned Grebe *Podiceps auritus*

DATE LOCATION

Eared Grebe *Podiceps nigricollis*

DATE LOCATION

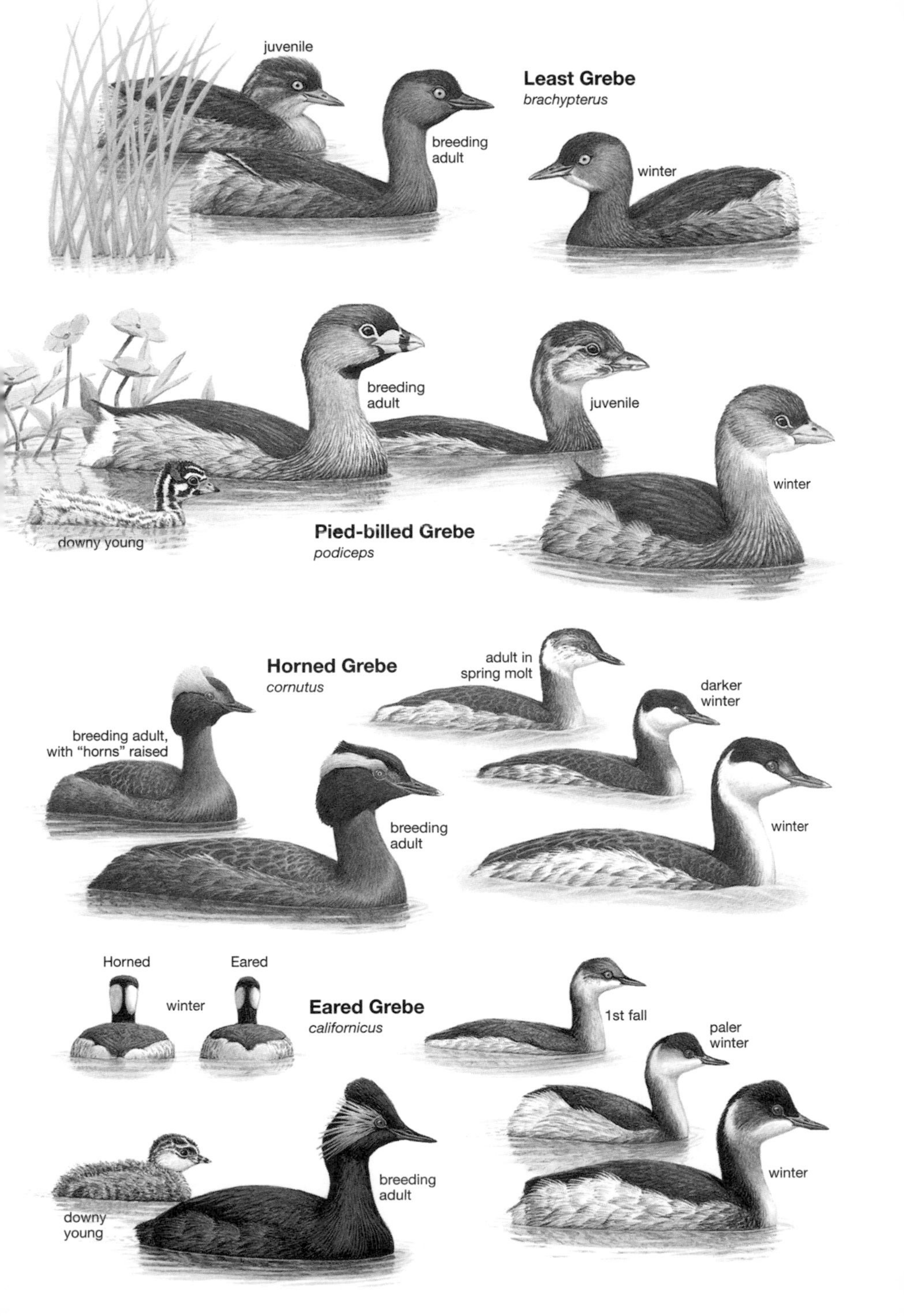

Least Grebe
brachypterus
juvenile
breeding adult
winter
Pied-billed Grebe
podiceps
breeding adult
juvenile
winter
downy young
Horned Grebe
cornutus
adult in spring molt
darker winter
breeding adult, with "horns" raised
breeding adult
winter
Horned
Eared
winter
Eared Grebe
californicus
1st fall
paler winter
breeding adult
downy young
winter

Red-necked Grebe *Podiceps grisegena*

DATE LOCATION

Clark's Grebe *Aechmophorus clarkii*

DATE LOCATION

Western Grebe *Aechmophorus occidentalis*

DATE LOCATION

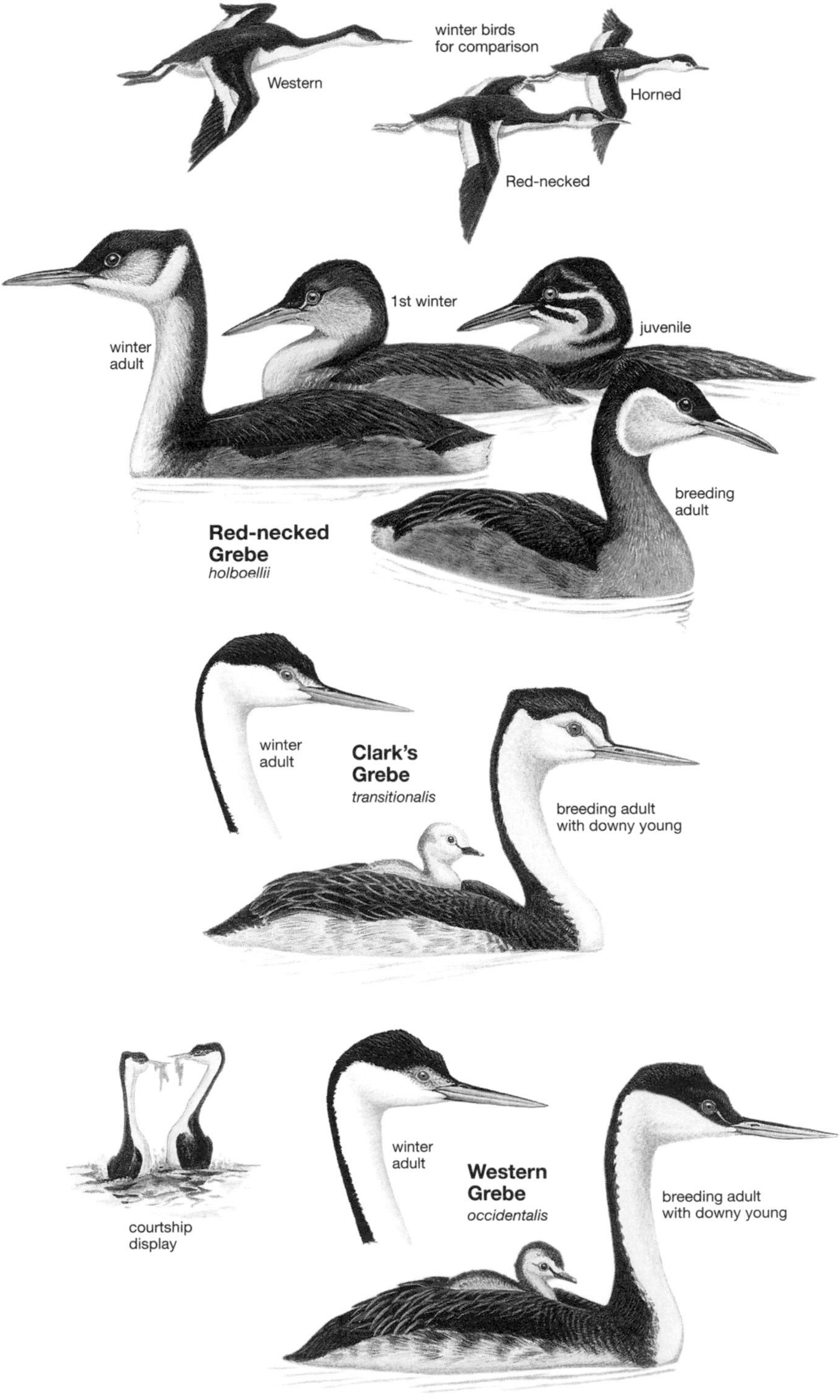

winter birds
for comparison
Western
Horned
Red-necked
winter
adult
1st winter
juvenile
breeding
adult
Red-necked
Grebe
holboellii
winter
adult
Clark's
Grebe
transitionalis
breeding adult
with downy young
courtship
display
winter
adult
Western
Grebe
occidentalis
breeding adult
with downy young

Albatrosses (Family Diomedeidae)

Short-tailed Albatross *Phoebastria albatrus*

DATE LOCATION

Laysan Albatross *Phoebastria immutabilis*

DATE LOCATION

Black-footed Albatross *Phoebastria nigripes*

DATE LOCATION

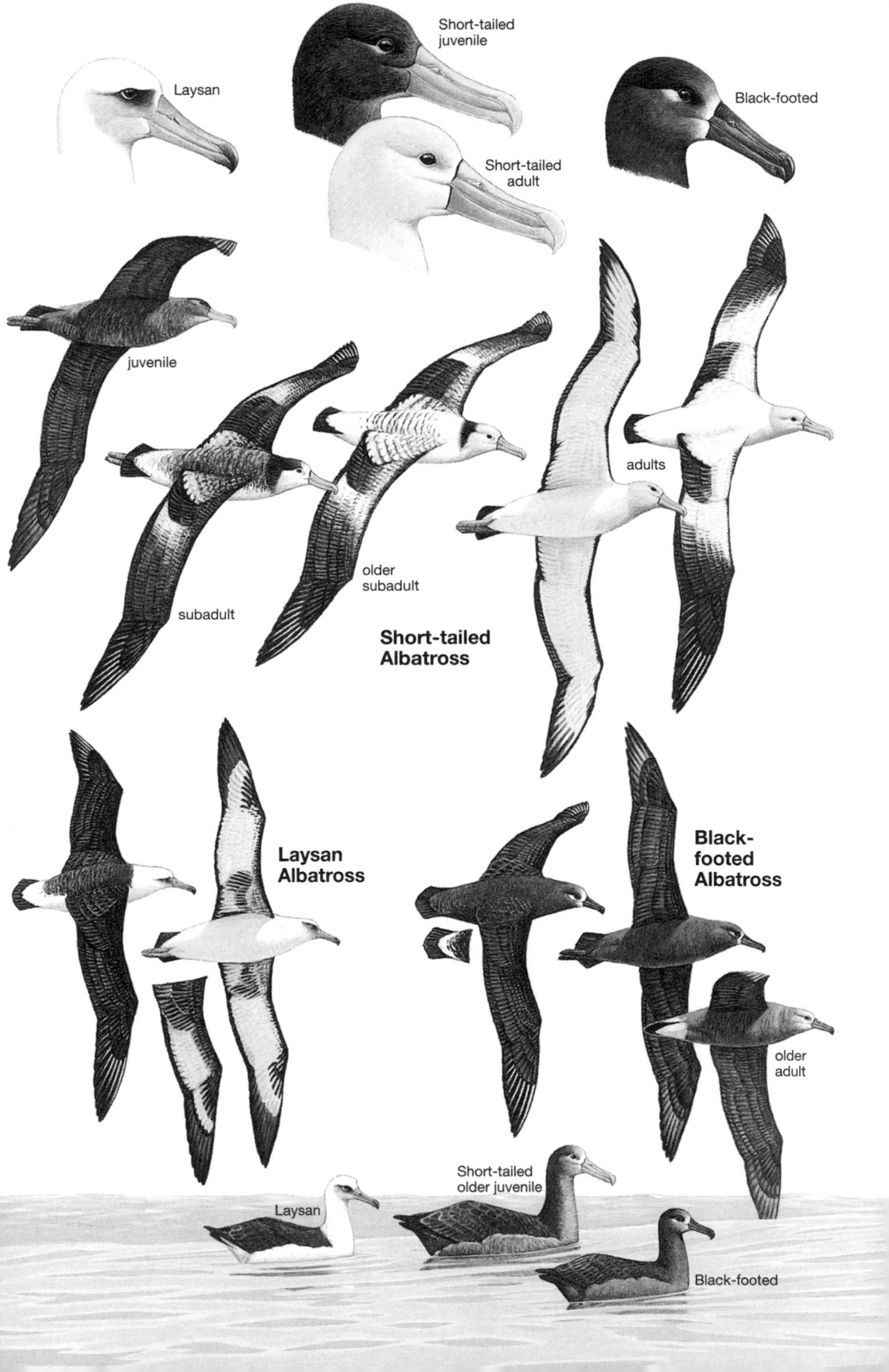

Short-tailed juvenile
Laysan
Black-footed
Short-tailed adult
juvenile
adults
older subadult
subadult
Short-tailed Albatross
Laysan Albatross
Black-footed Albatross
older adult
Short-tailed older juvenile
Laysan
Black-footed

Shy Albatross *Thalassarche cauta*

DATE LOCATION

Yellow-nosed Albatross *Thalassarche chlororhynchos*

DATE LOCATION

Black-browed Albatross *Thalassarche melanophris*

DATE LOCATION

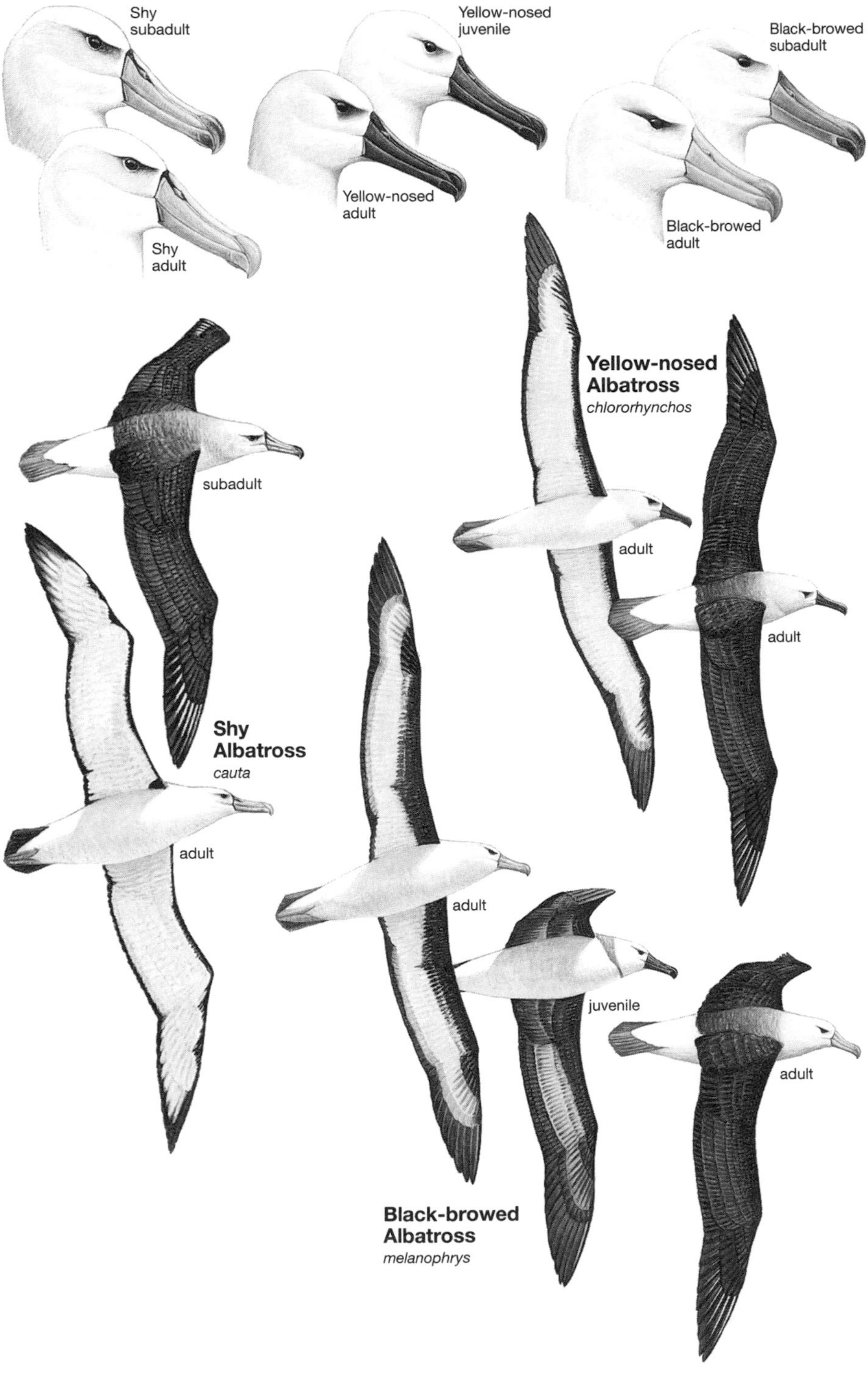
Shy
subadult
Shy
adult
Yellow-nosed
juvenile
Yellow-nosed
adult
Black-browed
subadult
Black-browed
adult
Yellow-nosed
Albatross
chlororhynchos
adult
adult
subadult
Shy
Albatross
cauta
adult
adult
juvenile
adult
Black-browed
Albatross
melanophrys

Shearwaters, Petrels (Family Procellariidae)

Northern Fulmar *Fulmarus glacialis*

DATE LOCATION

Parkinson's Petrel *Procellaria parkinsoni*

DATE LOCATION

Gadfly Petrels

Great-winged Petrel *Pterodroma macroptera*

DATE LOCATION

Murphy's Petrel *Pterodroma ultima*

DATE LOCATION

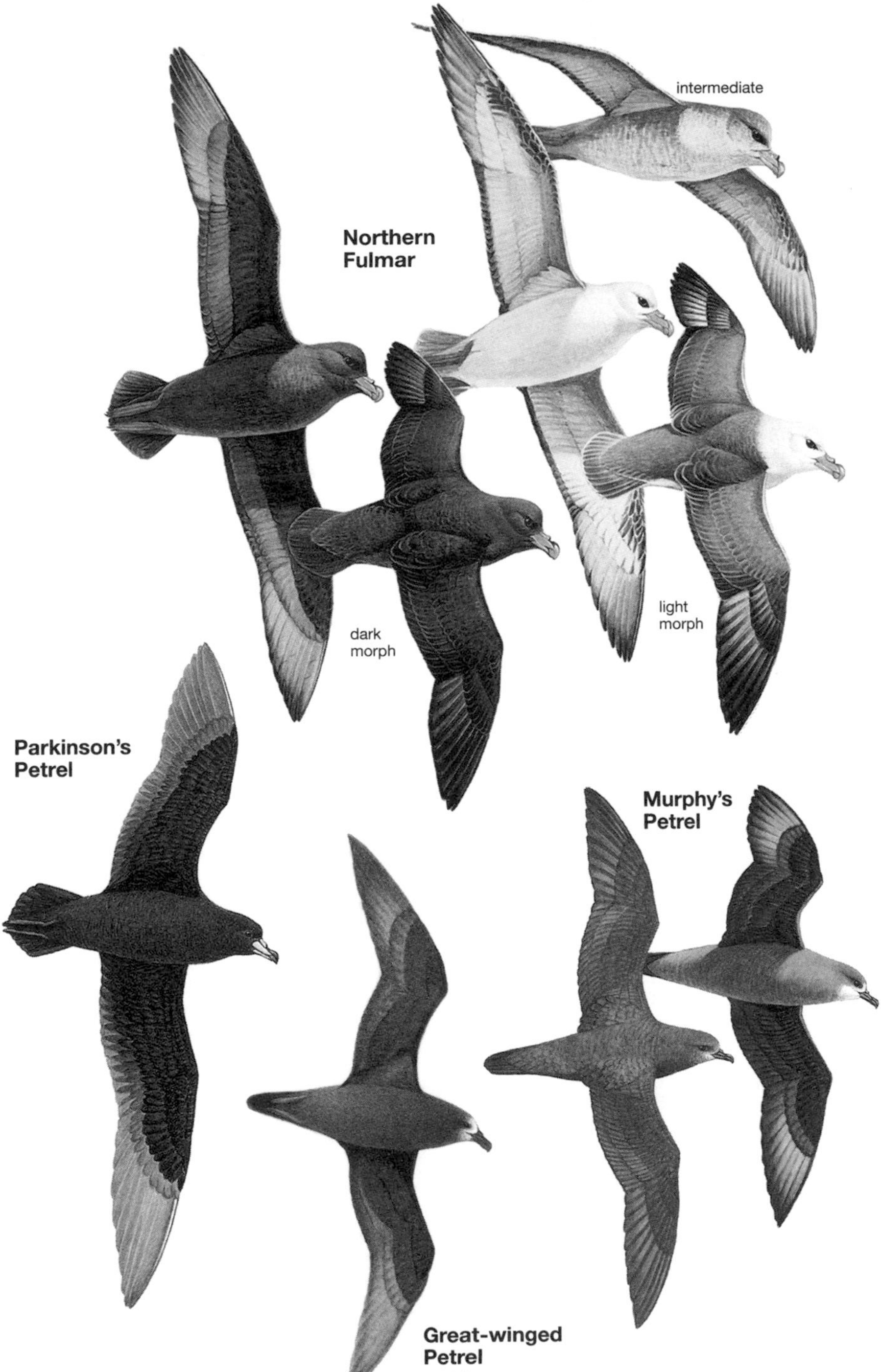
intermediate
Northern Fulmar
dark morph
light morph
Parkinson's Petrel
Murphy's Petrel
Great-winged Petrel
gouldi

Hawaiian Petrel *Pterodroma sandwichensis*

DATE LOCATION

Mottled Petrel *Pterodroma inexpectata*

DATE LOCATION

Cook's Petrel *Pterodroma cookii*

Stejneger's Petrel *Pterodroma longirostris*

DATE LOCATION

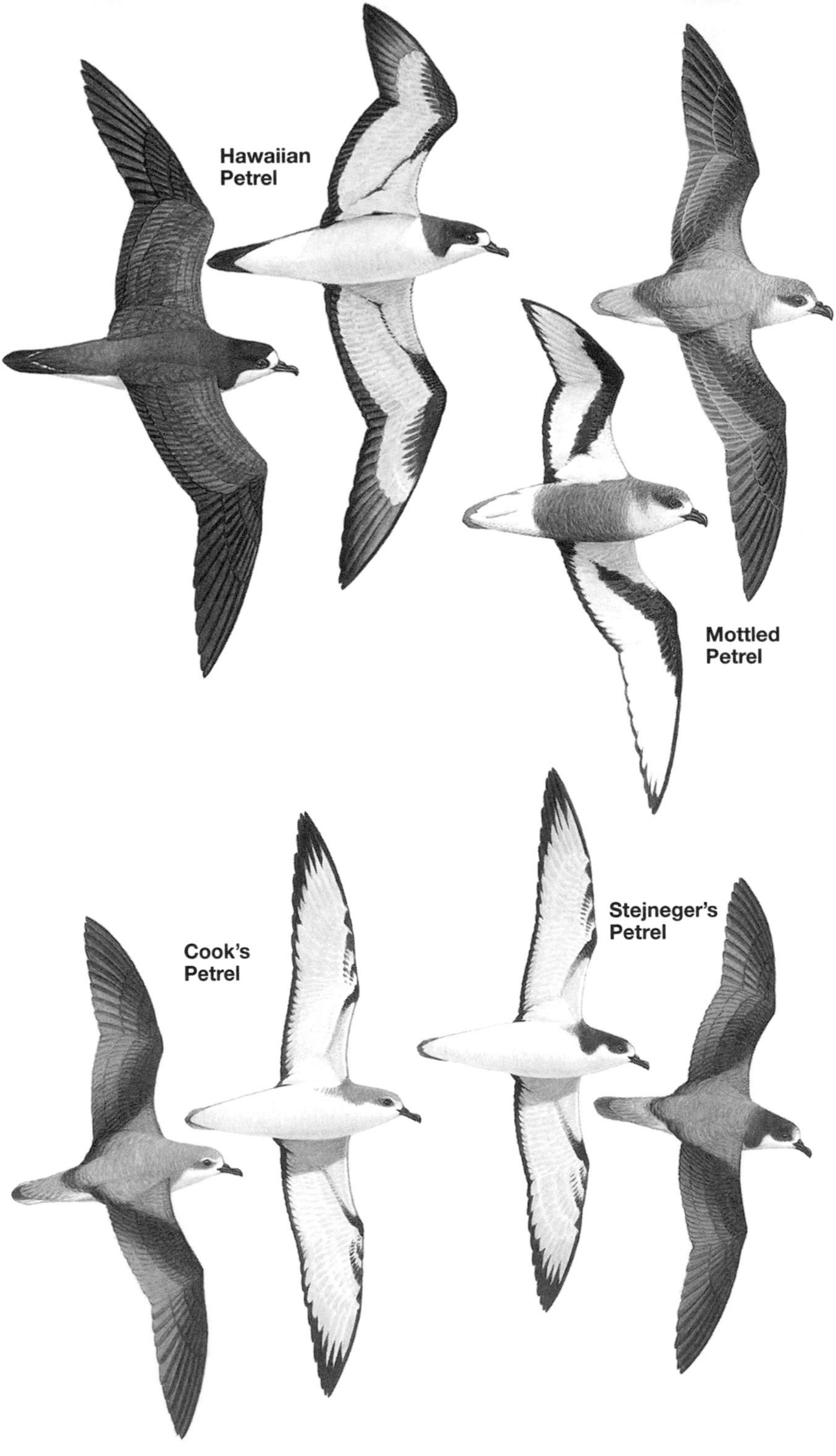
Hawaiian
Petrel
Mottled
Petrel
Cook's
Petrel
Stejneger's
Petrel

Black-capped Petrel *Pterodroma hasitata*

DATE LOCATION

Fea's Petrel *Pterodroma feae*

DATE LOCATION

Bermuda Petrel *Pterodroma cahow*

DATE LOCATION

Herald Petrel *Pterodroma arminjoniana*

DATE LOCATION

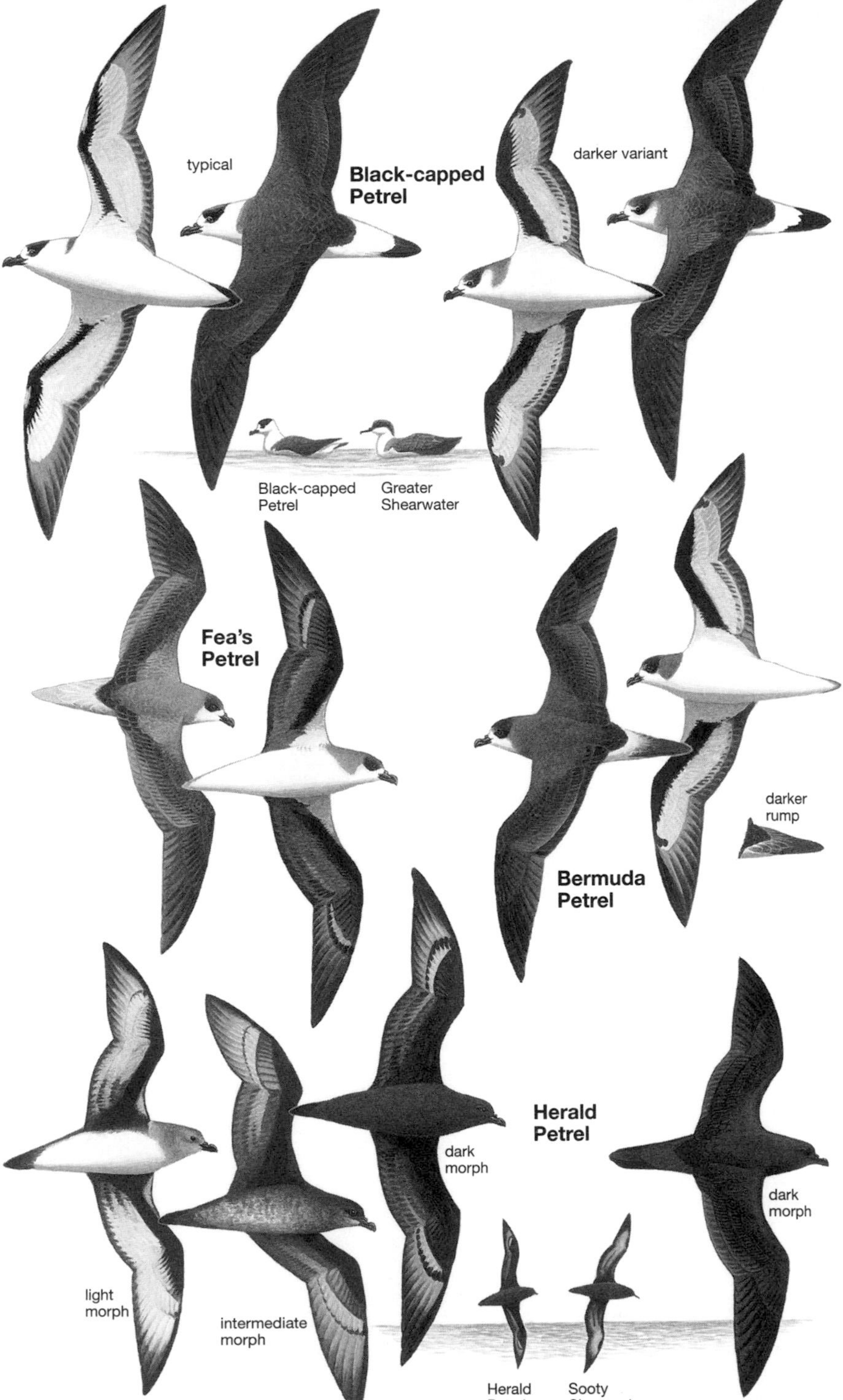
typical
Black-capped Petrel
darker variant
Black-capped Petrel
Greater Shearwater
Fea's Petrel
darker rump
Bermuda Petrel
Herald Petrel
dark morph
dark morph
light morph
intermediate morph
Herald Petrel
Sooty Shearwater

Cory's Shearwater *Calonectris diomedea*

DATE LOCATION

Cape Verde Shearwater *Calonectris edwardsii*

DATE LOCATION

Greater Shearwater *Puffinus gravis*

DATE LOCATION

Manx Shearwater *Puffinus puffinus*

DATE LOCATION

Audubon's Shearwater *Puffinus lherminieri*

DATE LOCATION

Little Shearwater *Puffinus assimilis*

DATE LOCATION

Cory's
Shearwater
borealis
diomedea
Cory's
Greater
Cape Verde
Shearwater
Black-
capped
Petrel
Greater
Shearwater
Manx
Shearwater
Audubon's
Shearwater
lherminieri
Little
Shearwater
baroli

Wedge-tailed Shearwater *Puffinus pacificus*

DATE LOCATION

Flesh-footed Shearwater *Puffinus carneipes*

DATE LOCATION

Bulwer's Petrel *Bulweria bulwerii*

DATE LOCATION

Short-tailed Shearwater *Puffinus tenuirostris*

DATE LOCATION

Sooty Shearwater *Puffinus griseus*

dark morph
dark morph
Flesh-footed Shearwater
Wedge-tailed Shearwater
light morph
Bulwer's Petrel
Short-tailed Shearwater
Short-tailed
Sooty
Sooty Shearwater

Buller's Shearwater *Puffinus bulleri*

DATE LOCATION

Streaked Shearwater *Calonectris leucomelas*

DATE LOCATION

Pink-footed Shearwater *Puffinus creatopus*

DATE LOCATION

Black-vented Shearwater *Puffinus opisthomelas*

DATE LOCATION

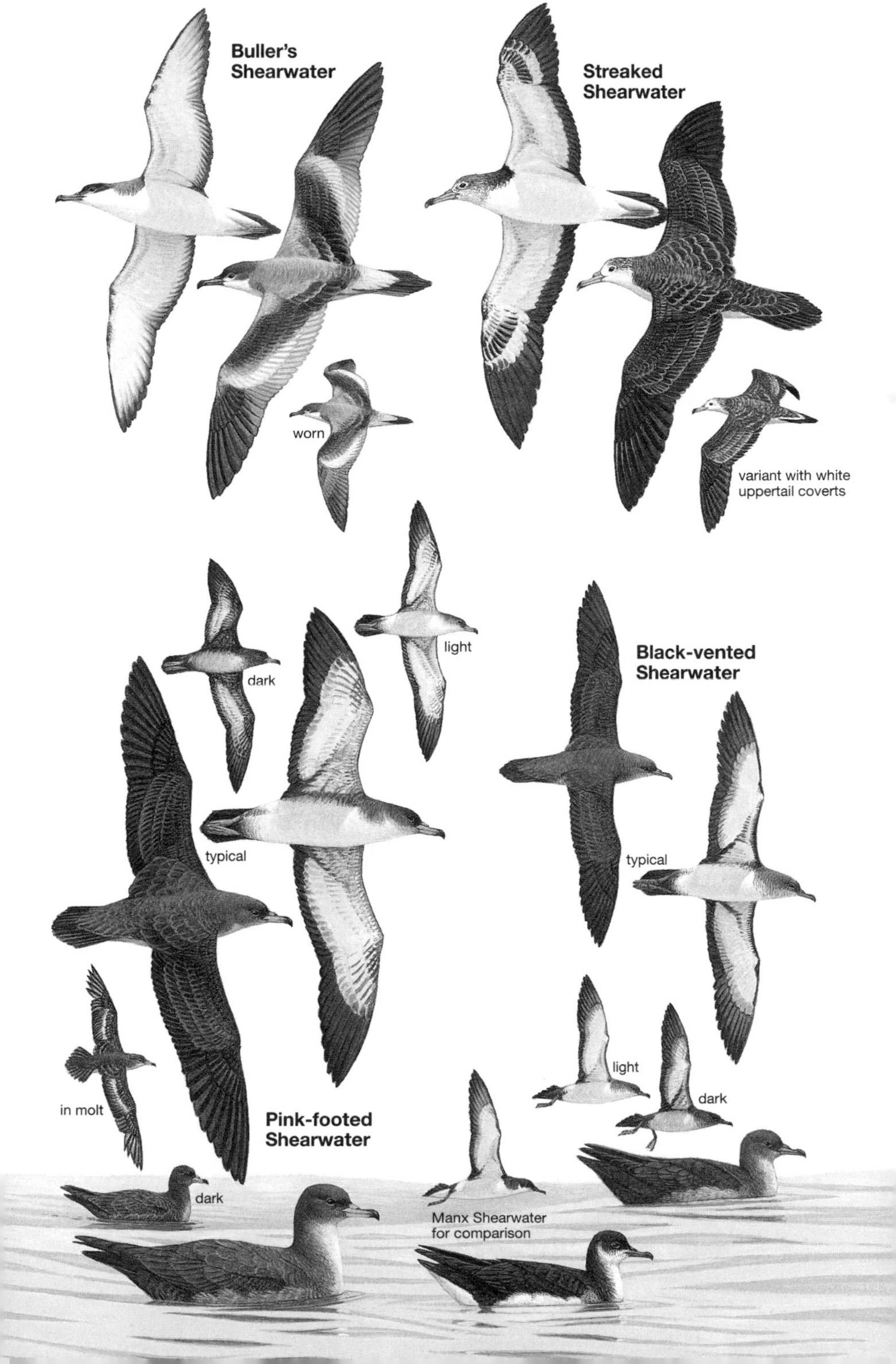
Buller's Shearwater
worn
Streaked Shearwater
variant with white uppertail coverts
dark
light
Black-vented Shearwater
typical
typical
in molt
light
dark
Pink-footed Shearwater
dark
Manx Shearwater for comparison

Storm-Petrels (Family Hydrobatidae)

European Storm-Petrel *Hydrobates pelagicus*

DATE LOCATION

Wilson's Storm-Petrel *Oceanites oceanicus*

DATE LOCATION

Band-rumped Storm-Petrel *Oceanodroma castro*

DATE LOCATION

Leach's Storm-Petrel *Oceanodroma leucorhoa*

DATE LOCATION

White-faced Storm-Petrel *Pelagodroma marina*

DATE LOCATION

European
Storm-Petrel
Wilson's
Storm-Petrel
Band-rumped
Storm-Petrel
Leach's
Storm-Petrel
leucorhoa
White-faced
Storm-Petrel
Wilson's
Band-rumped
Leach's
West Coast
northern
intermediate
southern
Wedge-rumped
kelsalli

Black Storm-Petrel *Oceanodroma melania*

DATE LOCATION

Ashy Storm-Petrel *Oceanodroma homochroa*

DATE LOCATION

Least Storm-Petrel *Oceanodroma microsoma*

DATE LOCATION

Fork-tailed Storm-Petrel *Oceanodroma furcata*

DATE LOCATION

Wedge-rumped Storm-Petrel *Oceanodroma tethys*

DATE LOCATION

Ashy
Storm-Petrel
Black
Storm-Petrel
Fork-tailed
Storm-Petrel
Least Storm-Petrel
Wedge-rumped
Storm-Petrel
kelsalli

Frigatebirds (Family Fregatidae)

Magnificent Frigatebird *Fregata magnificens*

DATE LOCATION

Tropicbirds (Family Phaethontidae)

White-tailed Tropicbird *Phaethon lepturus*

DATE LOCATION

Red-billed Tropicbird *Phaethon aethereus*

DATE LOCATION

Red-tailed Tropicbird *Phaethon rubricauda*

DATE LOCATION

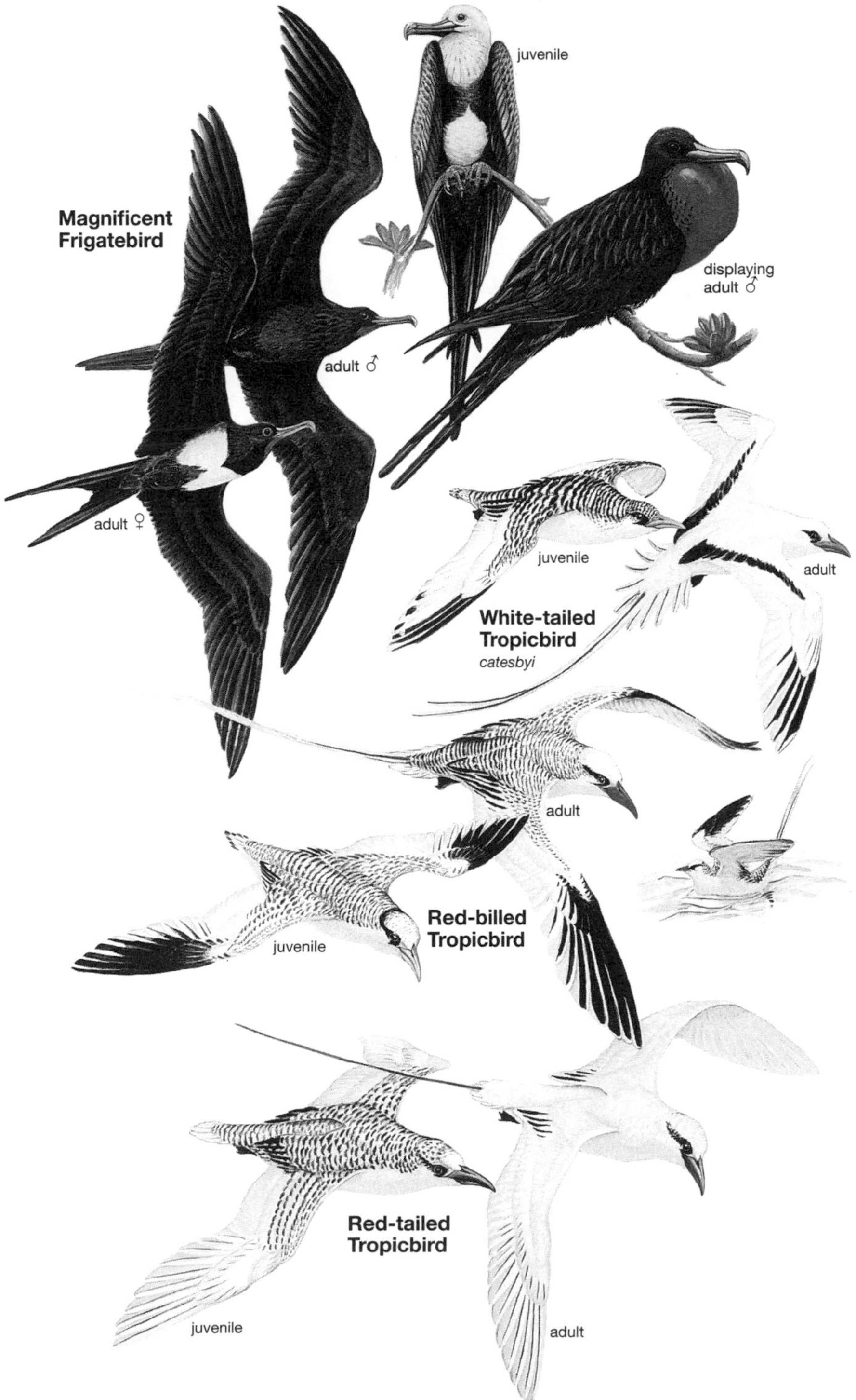

Magnificent Frigatebird
juvenile
displaying adult ♂
adult ♂
adult ♀
juvenile
adult
White-tailed Tropicbird
catesbyi
adult
Red-billed Tropicbird
juvenile
Red-tailed Tropicbird
juvenile
adult

Boobies, Gannets (Family Sulidae)

Red-footed Booby *Sula sula*

DATE LOCATION

Brown Booby *Sula leucogaster*

DATE LOCATION

Blue-footed Booby *Sula nebouxii*

DATE LOCATION

Masked Booby *Sula dactylatra*

DATE LOCATION

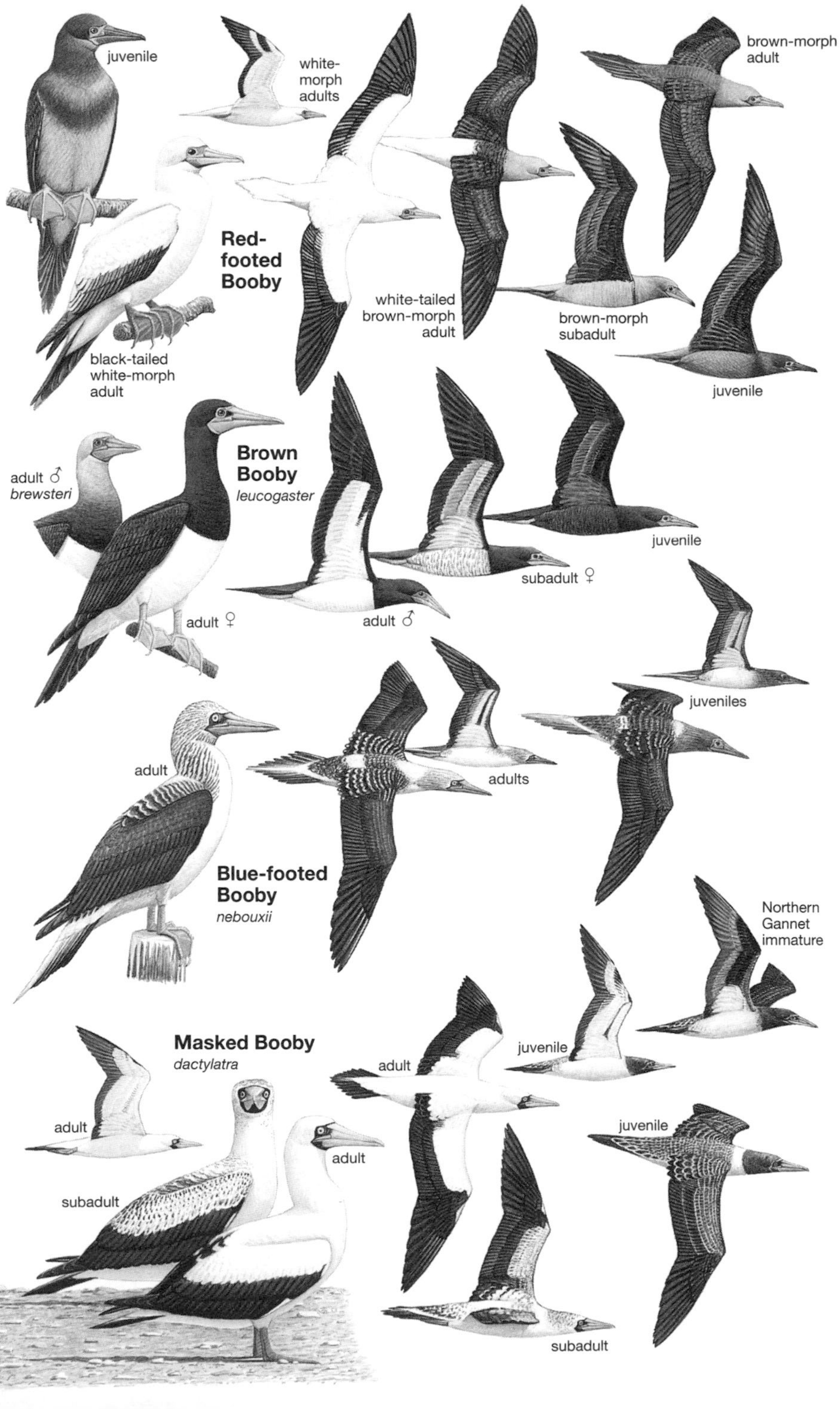
juvenile
white-morph adults
brown-morph adult
Red-footed Booby
white-tailed brown-morph adult
brown-morph subadult
black-tailed white-morph adult
juvenile
Brown Booby
leucogaster
adult ♂
brewsteri
juvenile
subadult ♀
adult ♀
adult ♂
juveniles
adult
adults
Blue-footed Booby
nebouxii
Northern Gannet immature
Masked Booby
dactylatra
juvenile
adult
adult
adult
juvenile
subadult
subadult

Northern Gannet *Morus bassanus*

DATE LOCATION

Pelicans (Family Pelecanidae)

American White Pelican *Pelecanus erythrorhynchos*

DATE LOCATION

Brown Pelican *Pelecanus occidentalis*

DATE LOCATION

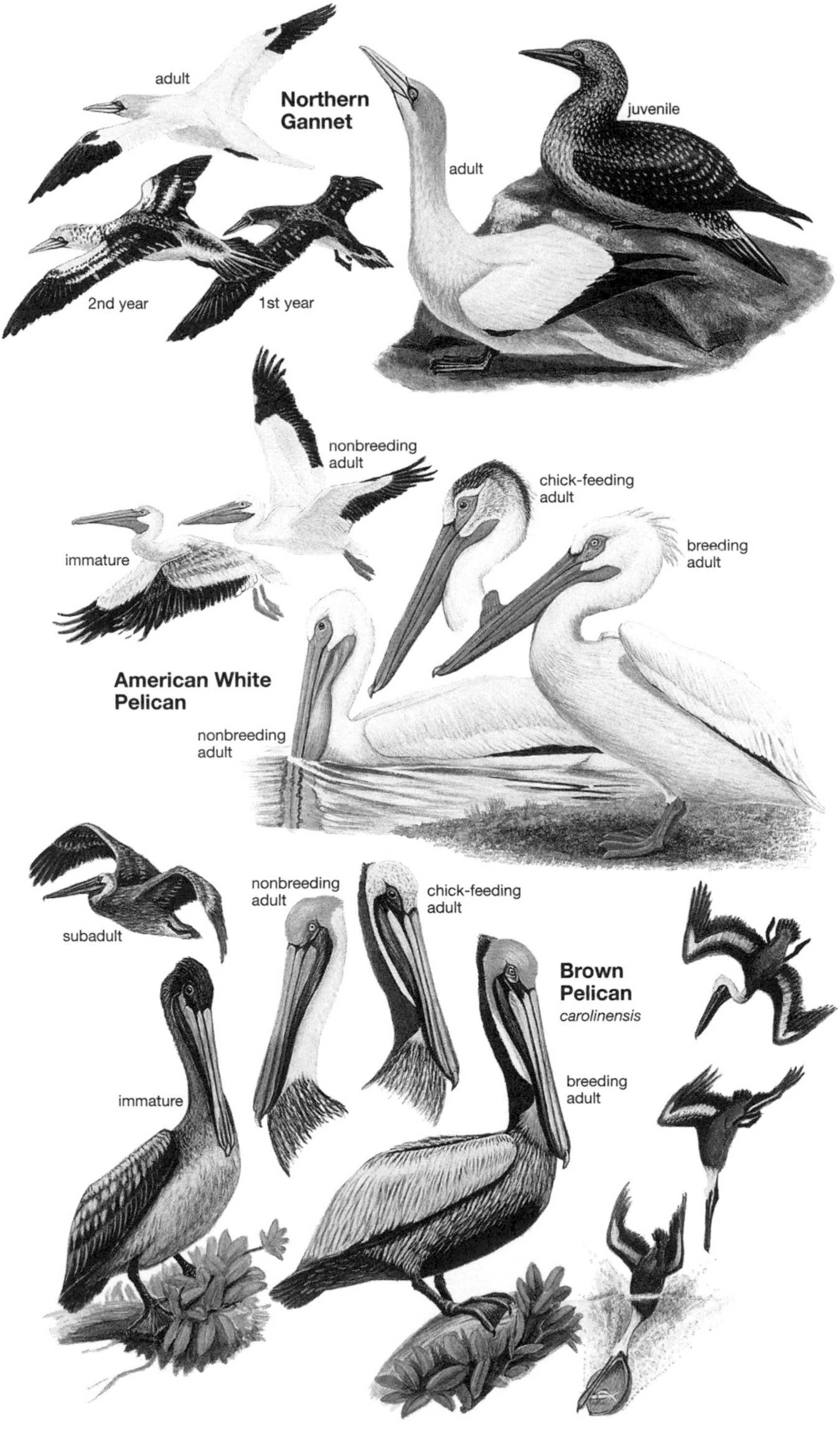
adult
Northern Gannet
juvenile
adult
2nd year
1st year
nonbreeding adult
chick-feeding adult
breeding adult
immature
American White Pelican
nonbreeding adult
subadult
nonbreeding adult
chick-feeding adult
Brown Pelican
carolinensis
breeding adult
immature

Darters (Family Anhingidae)

Anhinga *Anhinga anhinga*

DATE LOCATION

Cormorants (Family Phalacrocoracidae)

Neotropic Cormorant *Phalacrocorax brasilianus*

DATE LOCATION

Great Cormorant *Phalacrocorax carbo*

DATE LOCATION

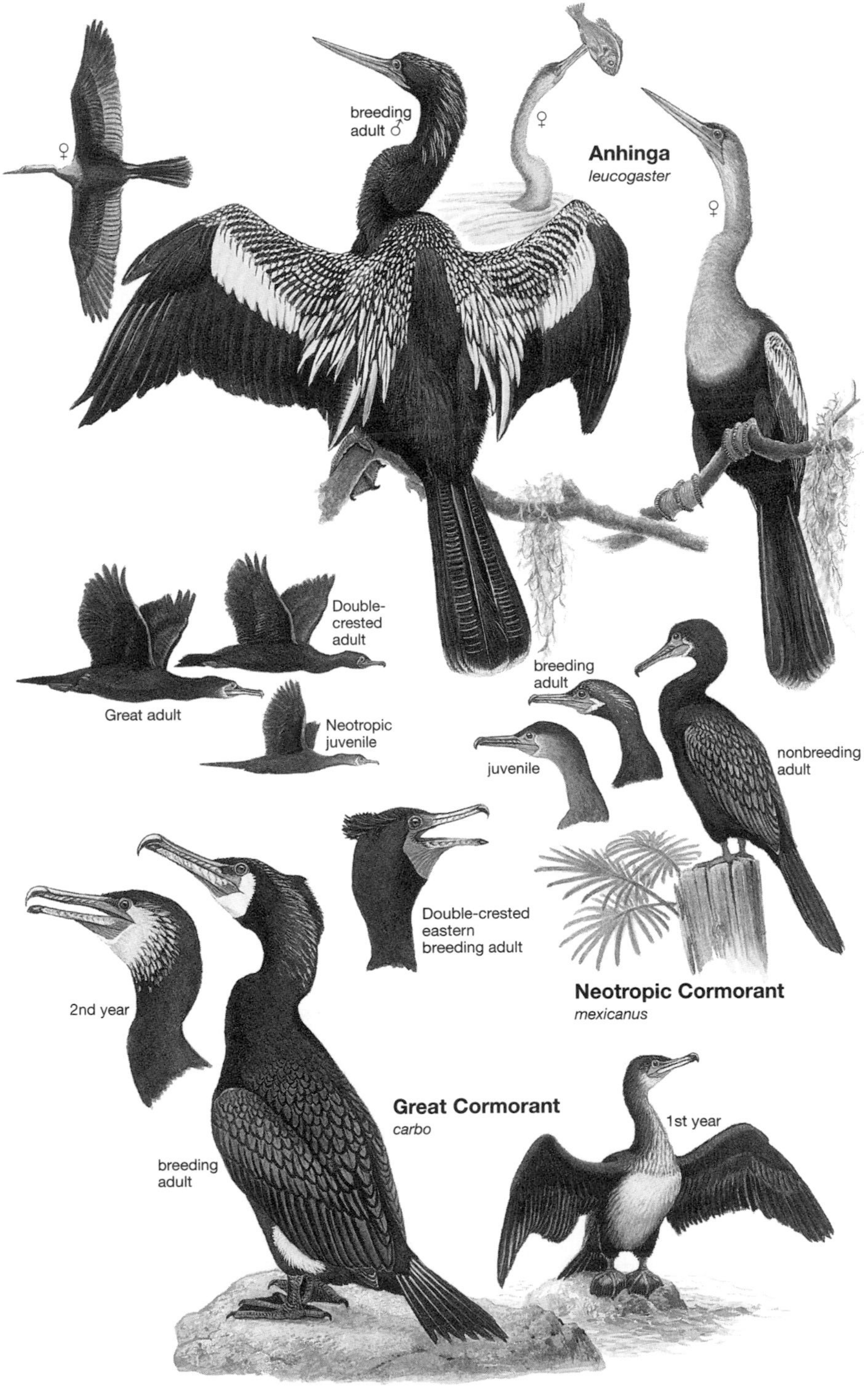

♀
breeding
adult ♂
♀
Anhinga
leucogaster
♀
Double-
crested
adult
Great adult
Neotropic
juvenile
breeding
adult
juvenile
nonbreeding
adult
Double-crested
eastern
breeding adult
2nd year
Neotropic Cormorant
mexicanus
Great Cormorant
carbo
1st year
breeding
adult

Pelagic Cormorant *Phalacrocorax pelagicus*

DATE LOCATION

Red-faced Cormorant *Phalacrocorax urile*

DATE LOCATION

Brandt's Cormorant *Phalacrocorax penicillatus*

DATE LOCATION

Double-crested Cormorant *Phalacrocorax auritus*

DATE LOCATION

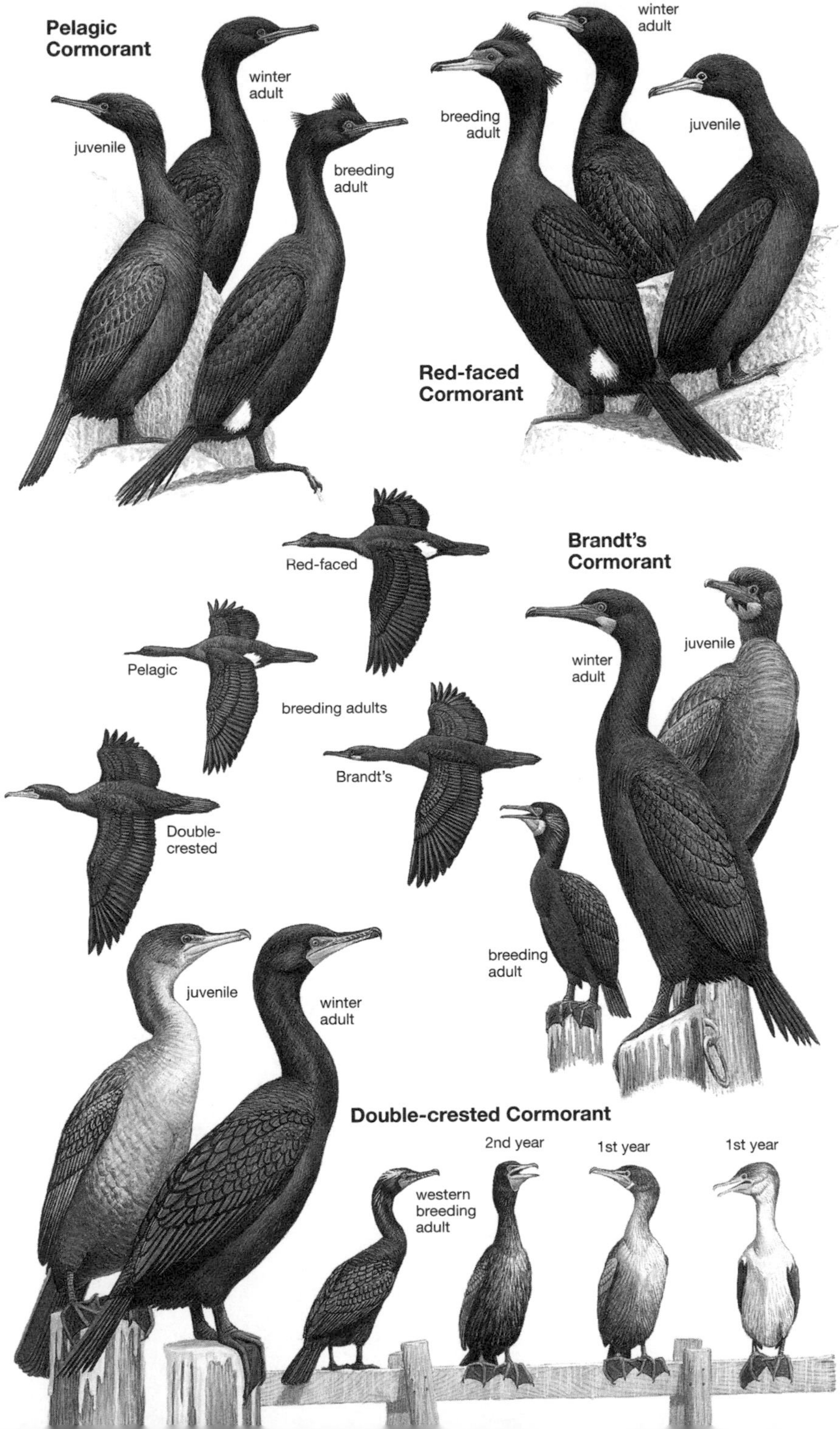
Pelagic Cormorant
juvenile
winter adult
breeding adult
breeding adult
winter adult
juvenile
Red-faced Cormorant
Red-faced
Pelagic
breeding adults
Brandt's
Double-crested
Brandt's Cormorant
winter adult
juvenile
breeding adult
juvenile
winter adult
Double-crested Cormorant
western breeding adult
2nd year
1st year
1st year

Herons, Bitterns, Allies (Family Ardeidae)

American Bittern *Botaurus lentiginosus*

DATE LOCATION

Least Bittern *Ixobrychus exilis*

DATE LOCATION

Yellow-crowned Night-Heron *Nyctanassa violacea*

DATE LOCATION

Black-crowned Night-Heron *Nycticorax nycticorax*

DATE LOCATION

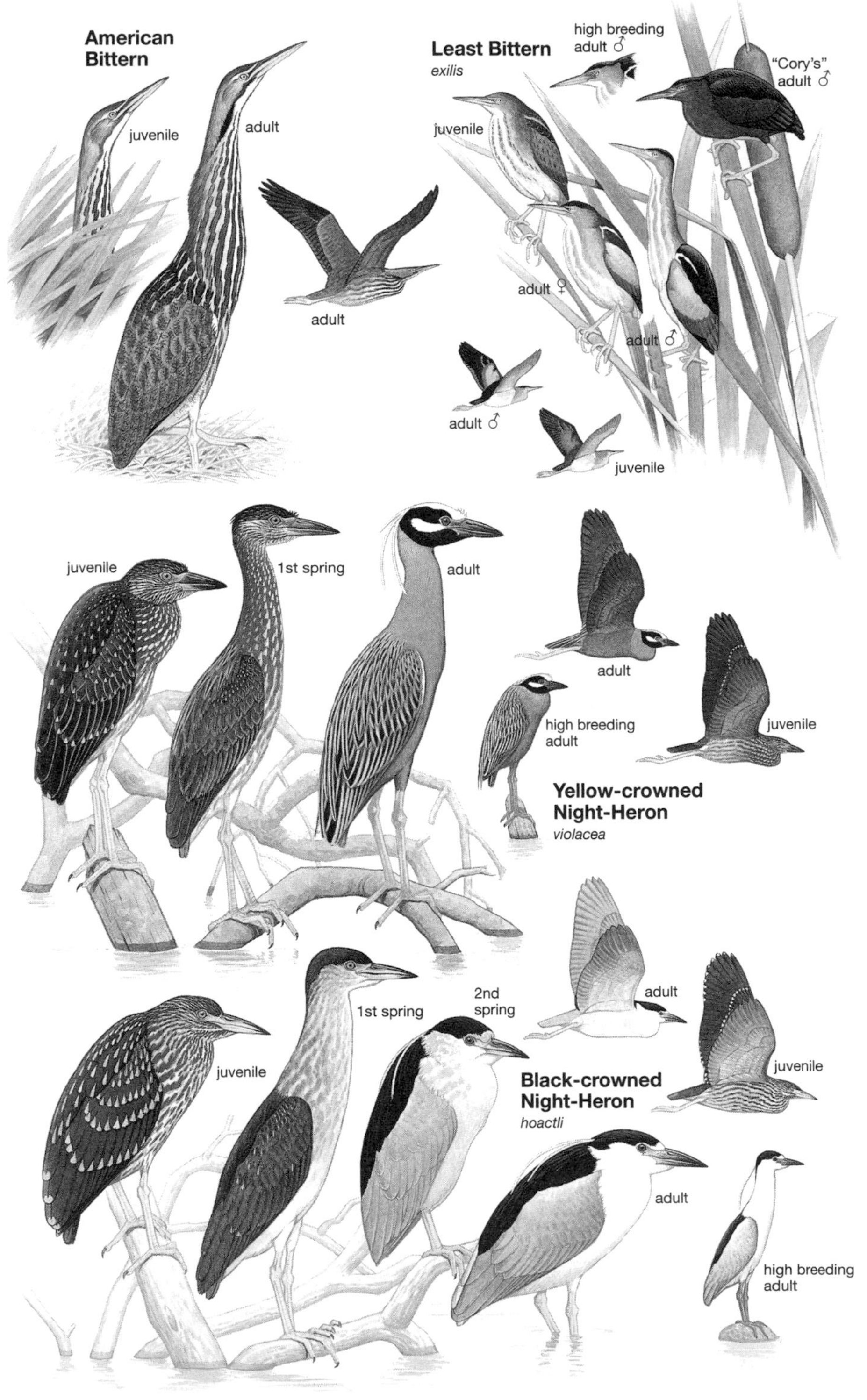
American Bittern
juvenile
adult
adult
Least Bittern
exilis
high breeding adult ♂
"Cory's" adult ♂
juvenile
adult ♀
adult ♂
adult ♂
juvenile
juvenile
1st spring
adult
adult
high breeding adult
juvenile
Yellow-crowned Night-Heron
violacea
juvenile
1st spring
2nd spring
adult
juvenile
Black-crowned Night-Heron
hoactli
adult
high breeding adult

Green Heron *Butorides virescens*

DATE LOCATION

Tricolored Heron *Egretta tricolor*

DATE LOCATION

Little Blue Heron *Egretta caerulea*

DATE LOCATION

Reddish Egret *Egretta rufescens*

DATE LOCATION

juvenile
adult
adult
Green Heron
virescens
juvenile
Tricolored Heron
ruficollis
breeding adult
molting immature
Little Blue Heron
breeding adult
juvenile
nonbreeding adult
canopy feeding
white-morph breeding adult
dark-morph juvenile
dark-morph breeding adult
Reddish Egret
rufescens

Cattle Egret *Bubulcus ibis*

DATE LOCATION

Little Egret *Egretta garzetta*

DATE LOCATION

Snowy Egret *Egretta thula*

DATE LOCATION

Great Egret *Ardea alba*

DATE LOCATION

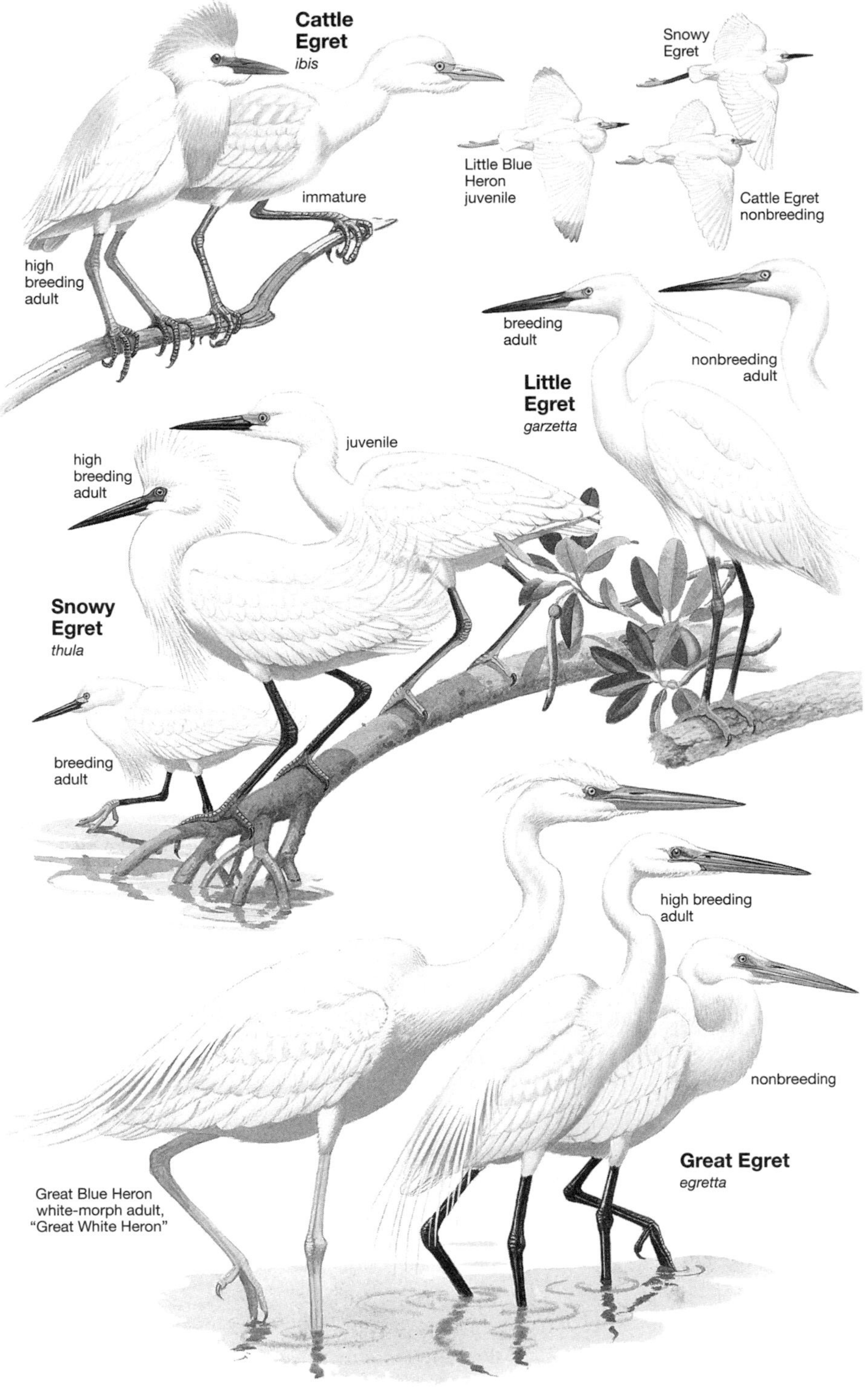
Cattle Egret
ibis
immature
high breeding adult
Snowy Egret
Little Blue Heron juvenile
Cattle Egret nonbreeding
breeding adult
nonbreeding adult
Little Egret
garzetta
juvenile
high breeding adult
Snowy Egret
thula
breeding adult
high breeding adult
nonbreeding
Great Egret
egretta
Great Blue Heron white-morph adult, "Great White Heron"

Great Blue Heron *Ardea herodias*

DATE LOCATION

Storks (Family Ciconiidae)

Wood Stork *Mycteria americana*

DATE LOCATION

Jabiru *Jabiru mycteria*

DATE LOCATION

Flamingos (Family Phoenicopteridae)

Greater Flamingo *Phoenicopterus ruber*

DATE LOCATION

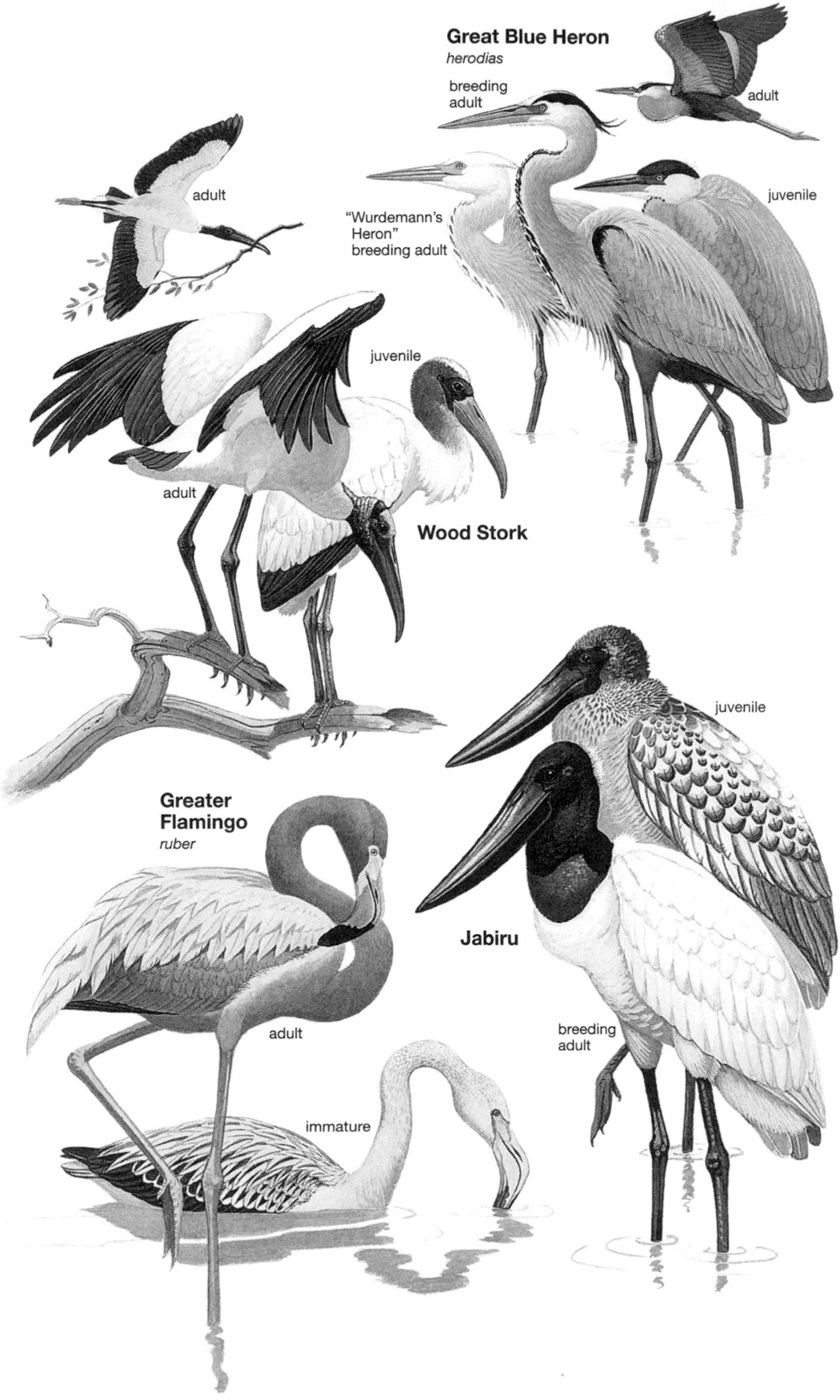
Great Blue Heron
herodias
breeding adult
adult
juvenile
"Wurdemann's Heron" breeding adult
adult
juvenile
adult
Wood Stork
juvenile
Greater Flamingo
ruber
Jabiru
breeding adult
adult
immature

Ibises, Spoonbills (Family Threskiornithidae)

Glossy Ibis *Plegadis falcinellus*

DATE LOCATION

White-faced Ibis *Plegadis chihi*

DATE LOCATION

White Ibis *Eudocimus albus*

DATE LOCATION

Roseate Spoonbill *Platalea ajaja*

DATE LOCATION

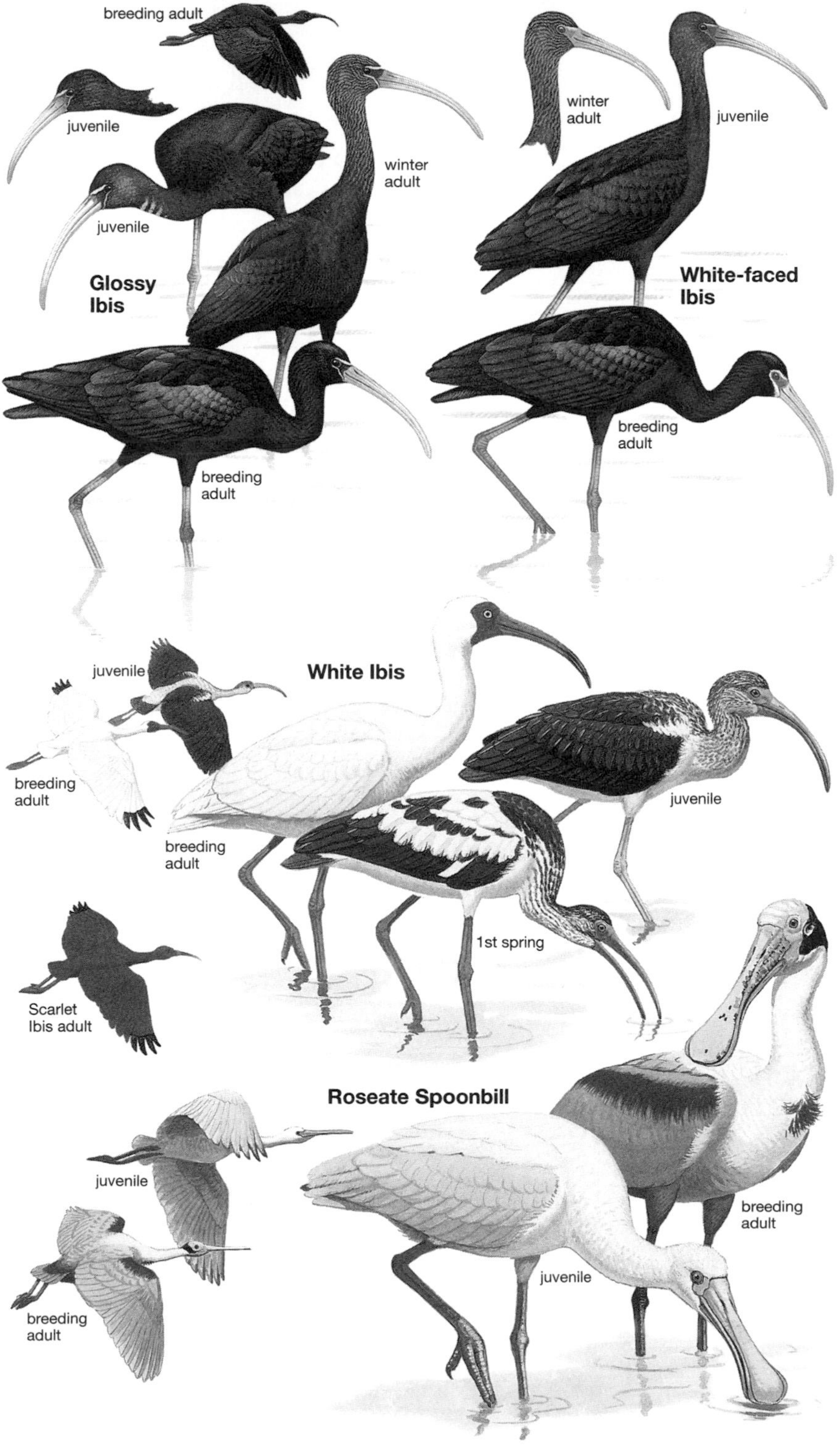

breeding adult
juvenile
juvenile
winter adult
Glossy Ibis
breeding adult
winter adult
juvenile
White-faced Ibis
breeding adult
juvenile
White Ibis
breeding adult
breeding adult
juvenile
1st spring
Scarlet Ibis adult
Roseate Spoonbill
juvenile
breeding adult
breeding adult
juvenile

New World Vultures (Family Cathartidae)

Turkey Vulture *Cathartes aura*

DATE LOCATION

Black Vulture *Coragyps atratus*

DATE LOCATION

California Condor *Gymnogyps californianus*

DATE LOCATION

Hawks, Kites, Eagles, Allies (Family Accipitridae)

Osprey *Pandion haliaetus*

DATE LOCATION

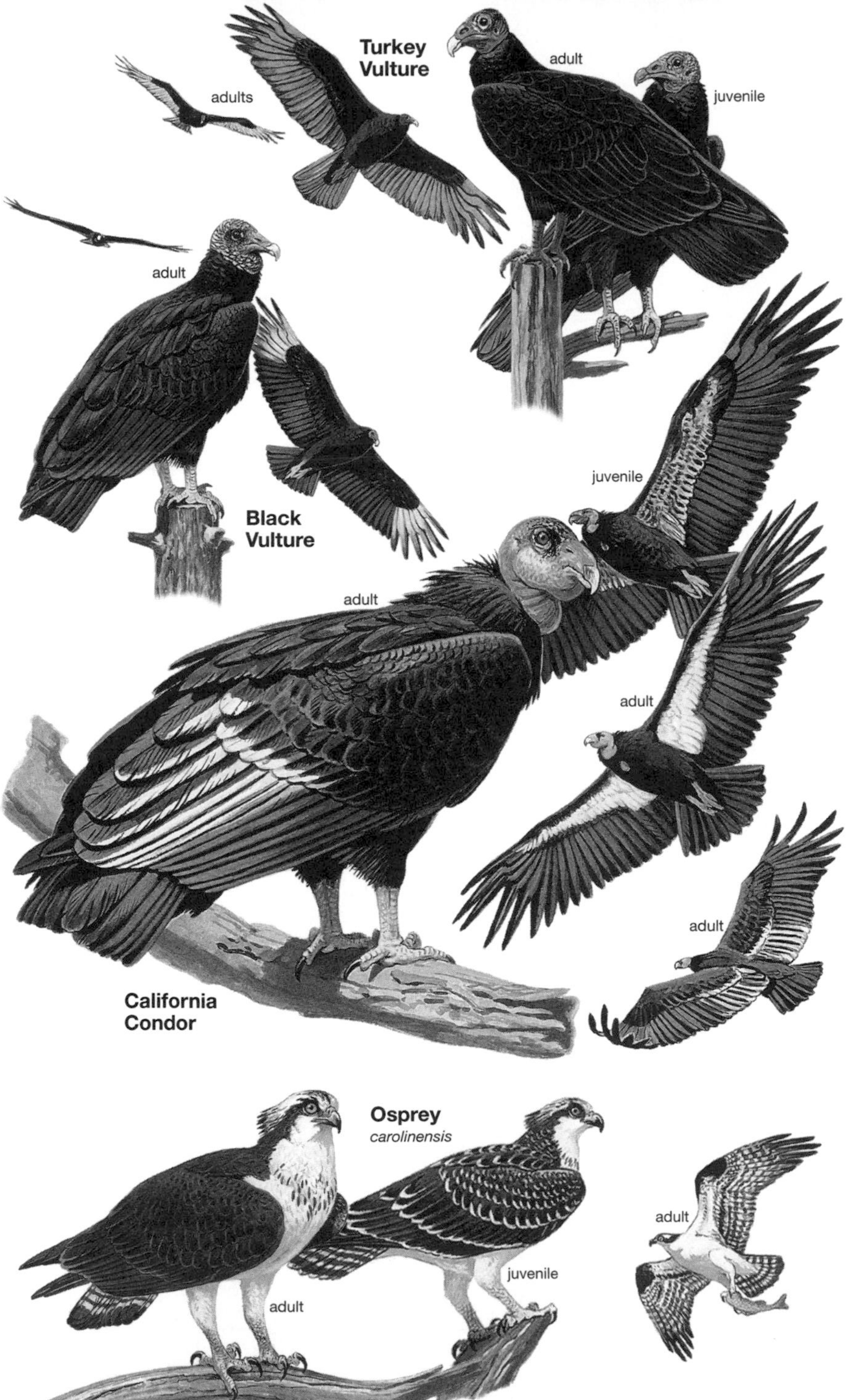
Turkey Vulture
adults
adult
juvenile
adult
Black Vulture
juvenile
adult
adult
adult
California Condor
Osprey
carolinensis
adult
adult
juvenile

Mississippi Kite *Ictinia mississippiensis*

DATE LOCATION

White-tailed Kite *Elanus leucurus*

DATE LOCATION

Swallow-tailed Kite *Elanoides forficatus*

DATE LOCATION

Mississippi Kite
adult ♂
juvenile
adult ♀
adult ♂
Swallow-tailed Kite
adults
adults
juvenile
adult
White-tailed Kite
majusculus

Snail Kite *Rostrhamus sociabilis*

DATE LOCATION

Hook-billed Kite *Chondrohierax uncinatus*

DATE LOCATION

Northern Harrier *Circus cyaneus*

DATE LOCATION

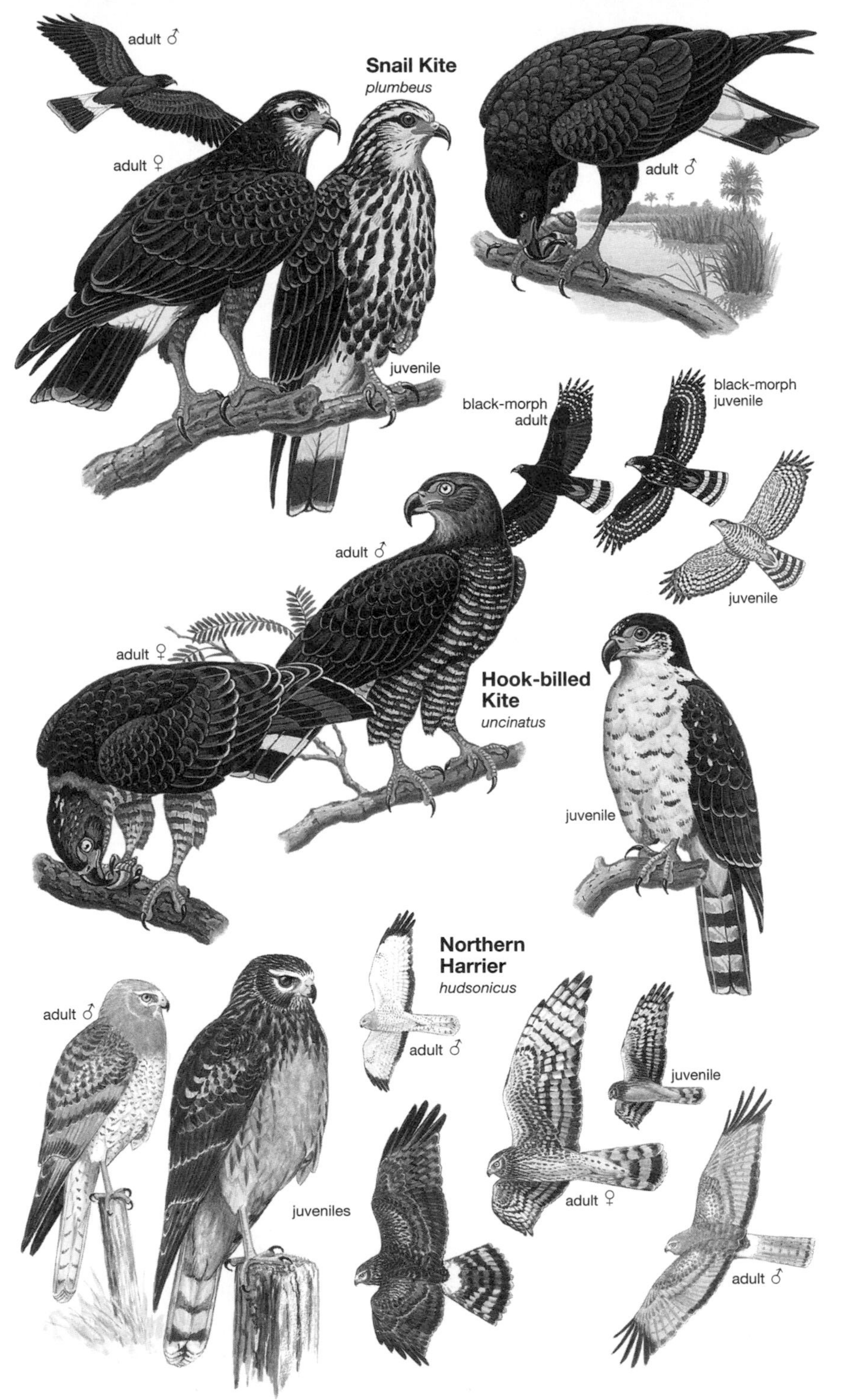

adult ♂
Snail Kite
plumbeus
adult ♀
adult ♂
juvenile
black-morph adult
black-morph juvenile
adult ♂
juvenile
adult ♀
Hook-billed Kite
uncinatus
juvenile
Northern Harrier
hudsonicus
adult ♂
adult ♂
juvenile
juveniles
adult ♀
adult ♂

Golden Eagle *Aquila chrysaetos*

DATE LOCATION

White-tailed Eagle *Haliaeetus albicilla*

DATE LOCATION

Steller's Sea-Eagle *Haliaeetus pelagicus*

DATE LOCATION

Bald Eagle *Haliaeetus leucocephalus*

DATE LOCATION

Golden Eagle
canadensis
juvenile
adult
adult
White-tailed Eagle
juvenile
adult
Steller's Sea-Eagle
adult
juvenile
Bald Eagle
juvenile
2nd year
3rd year
juvenile
adults

Accipiters

Sharp-shinned Hawk *Accipiter striatus*

DATE LOCATION

Cooper's Hawk *Accipiter cooperii*

DATE LOCATION

Northern Goshawk *Accipiter gentilis*

DATE LOCATION

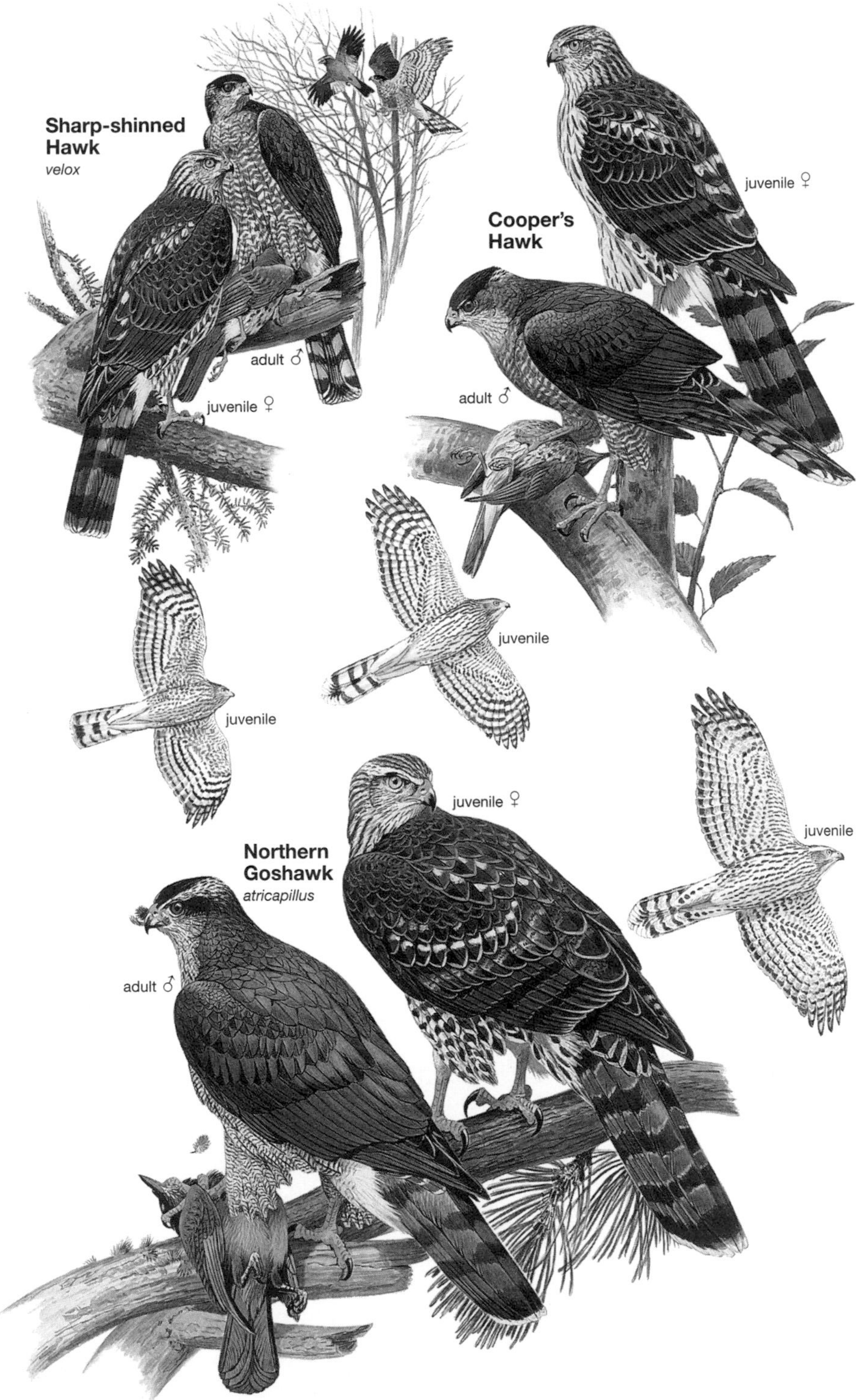
Sharp-shinned Hawk
velox
adult ♂
juvenile ♀
juvenile
Cooper's Hawk
juvenile ♀
adult ♂
juvenile
Northern Goshawk
atricapillus
juvenile ♀
juvenile
adult ♂

Buteos

Common Black-Hawk *Buteogallus anthracinus*

DATE LOCATION

Harris's Hawk *Parabuteo unicinctus*

DATE LOCATION

Zone-tailed Hawk *Buteo albonotatus*

DATE LOCATION

Short-tailed Hawk *Buteo brachyurus*

DATE LOCATION

Roadside Hawk *Buteo magnirostris*

DATE LOCATION

Common Black-Hawk
anthracinus
adult
juvenile
juvenile
adult
Turkey Vulture for comparison
juvenile
Harris's Hawk
harrisi
adult
adult
juvenile
adult
Zone-tailed Hawk
adult ♂
dark-morph adult
Short-tailed Hawk
fuliginosus
light-morph adults
adult
adult
Roadside Hawk
juvenile

Broad-winged Hawk *Buteo platypterus*

DATE LOCATION

Gray Hawk *Buteo nitidus*

DATE LOCATION

Red-shouldered Hawk *Buteo lineatus*

DATE LOCATION

juveniles
juveniles
juveniles
dark-morph adult
adult
Broad-winged Hawk
platypterus
juvenile
adult
adult
Gray Hawk
plagiata
adult
juvenile
adult lineatus
juvenile lineatus
California adult elegans
juvenile elegans
juvenile lineatus
Red-shouldered Hawk
Florida adult extimus
Eastern adult lineatus
juvenile lineatus
juvenile elegans

Red-tailed Hawk *Buteo jamaicensis*

DATE LOCATION

Swainson's Hawk *Buteo swainsoni*

DATE LOCATION

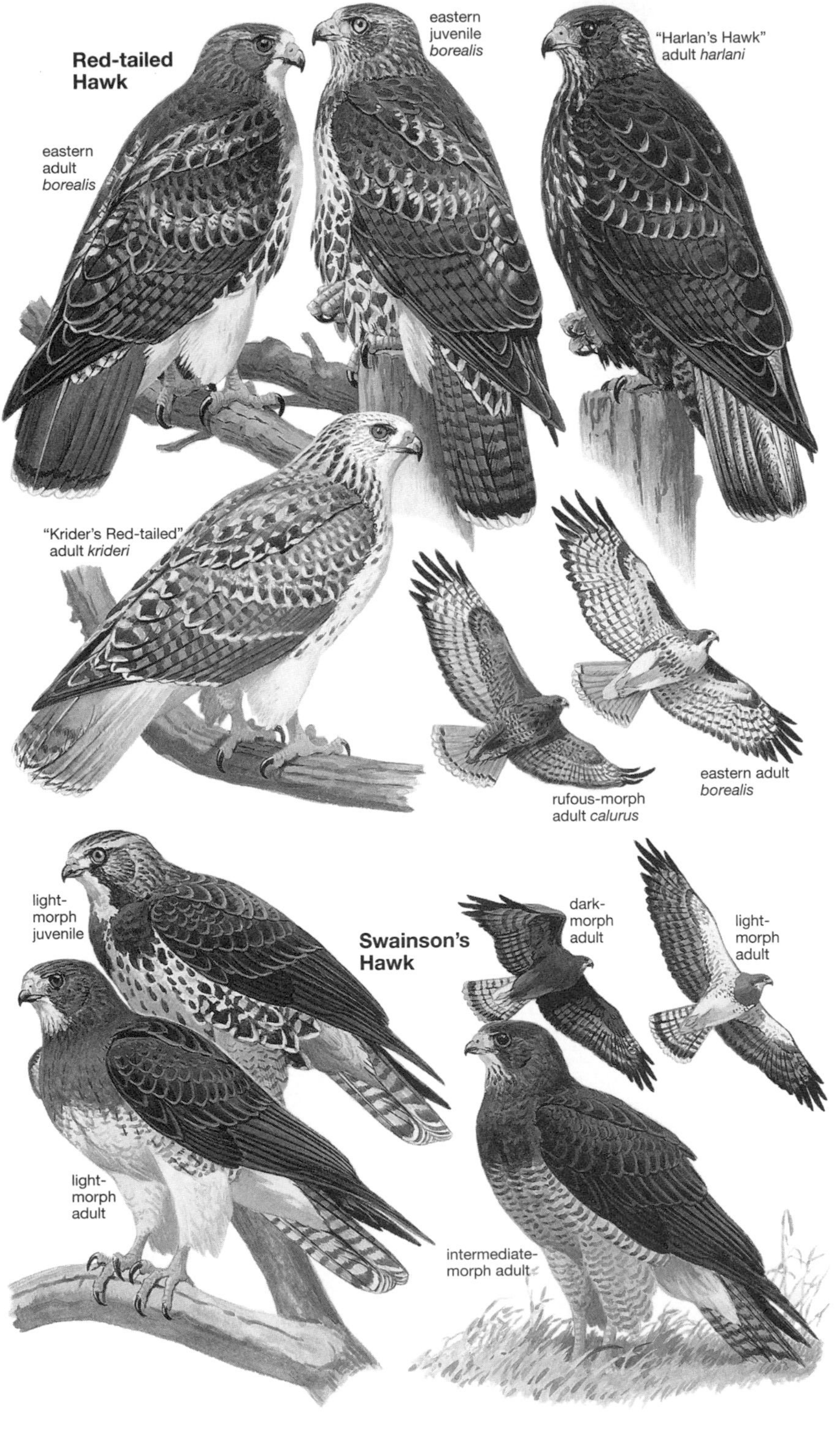

Red-tailed Hawk
eastern adult *borealis*
eastern juvenile *borealis*
"Harlan's Hawk" adult *harlani*
"Krider's Red-tailed" adult *krideri*
rufous-morph adult *calurus*
eastern adult *borealis*
Swainson's Hawk
light-morph juvenile
light-morph adult
dark-morph adult
light-morph adult
intermediate-morph adult

Rough-legged Hawk *Buteo lagopus*

DATE LOCATION

Ferruginous Hawk *Buteo regalis*

DATE LOCATION

White-tailed Hawk *Buteo albicaudatus*

DATE LOCATION

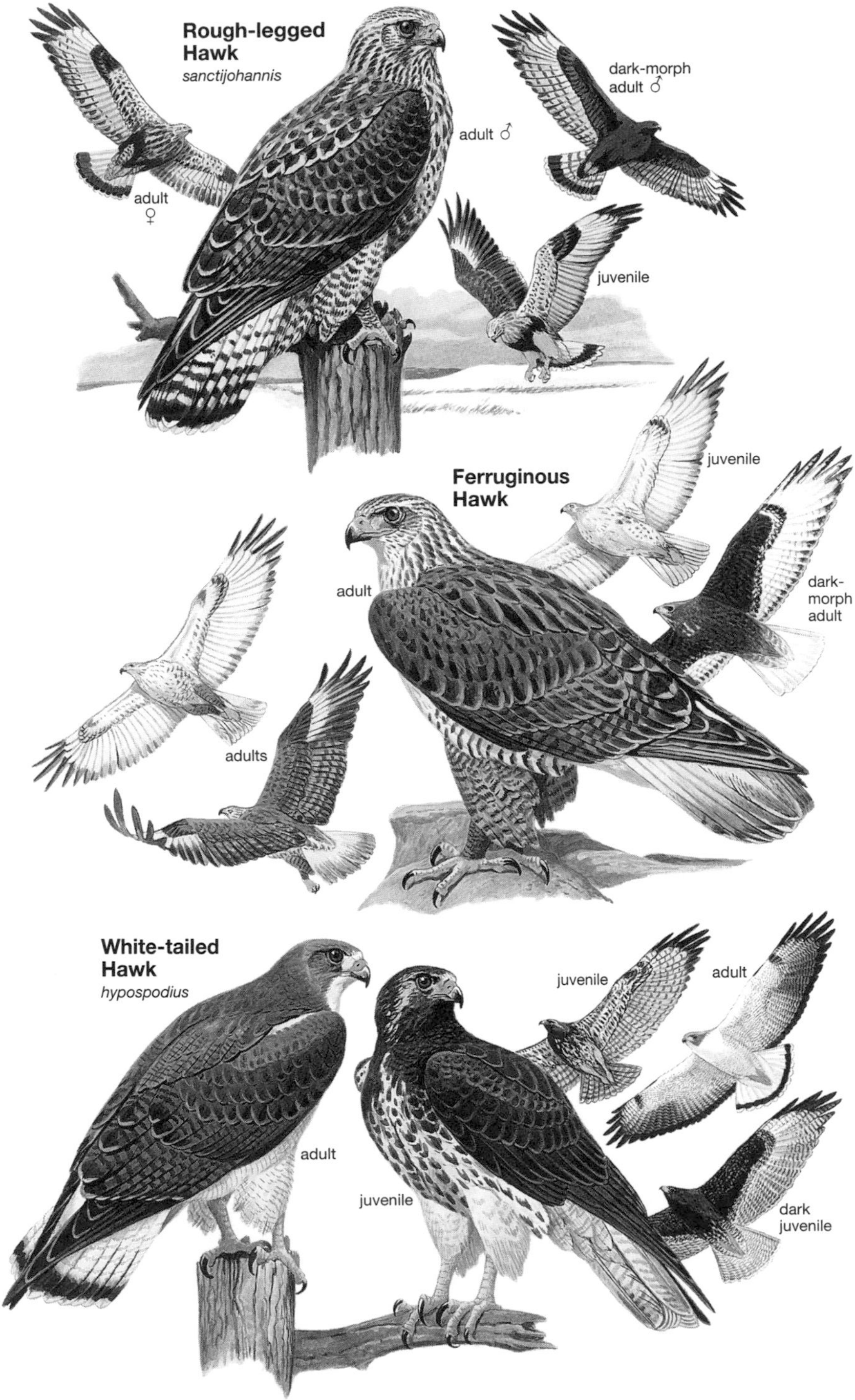

Rough-legged Hawk
sanctijohannis
adult ♀
adult ♂
dark-morph adult ♂
juvenile
Ferruginous Hawk
juvenile
adult
dark-morph adult
adults
White-tailed Hawk
hypospodius
juvenile
adult
adult
juvenile
dark juvenile

Caracaras, Falcons (Family Falconidae)

Eurasian Hobby *Falco subbuteo*

DATE LOCATION

Aplomado Falcon *Falco femoralis*

DATE LOCATION

Crested Caracara *Caracara cheriway*

DATE LOCATION

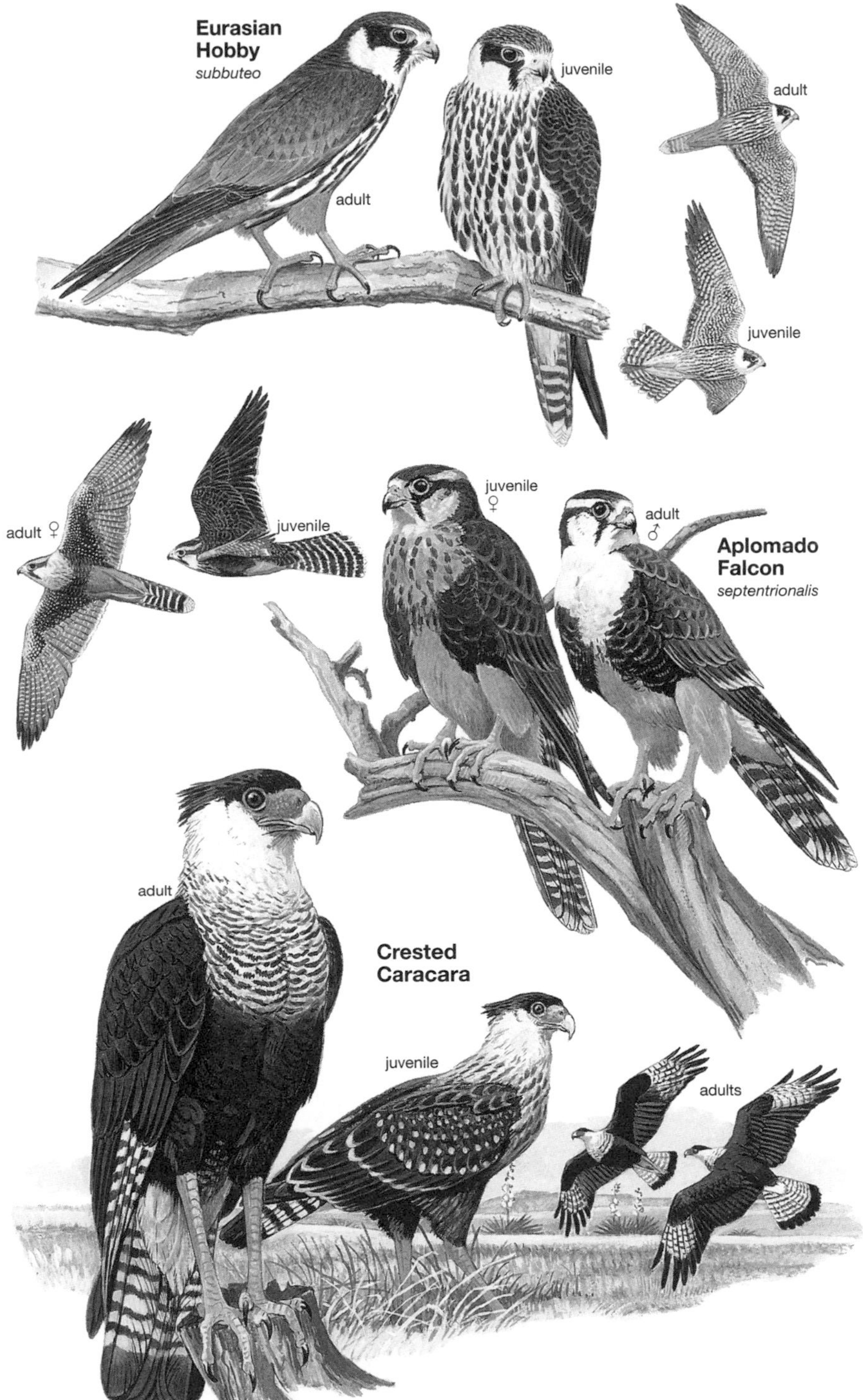
Eurasian Hobby
subbuteo
adult
juvenile
adult
juvenile
adult ♀
juvenile
juvenile ♀
adult ♂
Aplomado Falcon
septentrionalis
adult
Crested Caracara
juvenile
adults

American Kestrel *Falco sparverius*

DATE LOCATION

Eurasian Kestrel *Falco tinnunculus*

DATE LOCATION

Merlin *Falco columbarius*

DATE LOCATION

adult ♀
adult ♂
American Kestrel
adult ♂
juvenile ♂
adult ♂
adult ♂
juvenile
Eurasian Kestrel
adult ♀
adult ♂
♀
adult ♂
Merlin
columbarius
♀
♀ *suckleyi*
adult ♂
adult ♂ *suckleyi*
♀ *richardsonii*
adult ♂ *richardsonii*

Prairie Falcon *Falco mexicanus*

DATE	LOCATION

Peregrine Falcon *Falco peregrinus*

DATE	LOCATION

Gyrfalcon *Falco rusticolus*

DATE	LOCATION

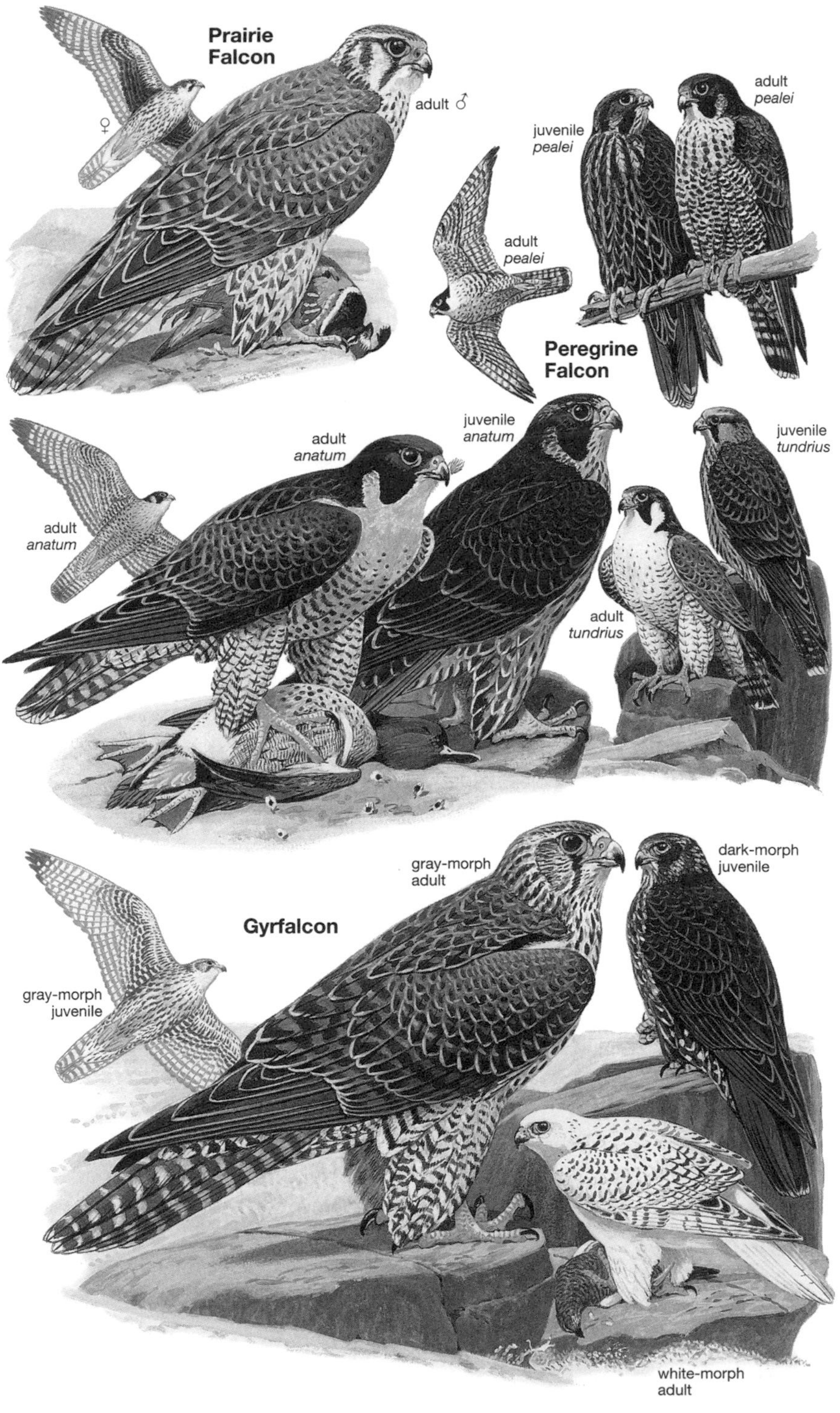

Prairie Falcon
♀
adult ♂
juvenile pealei
adult pealei
adult pealei
Peregrine Falcon
adult anatum
juvenile anatum
juvenile tundrius
adult anatum
adult tundrius
Gyrfalcon
gray-morph adult
dark-morph juvenile
gray-morph juvenile
white-morph adult

Female Hawks in Flight

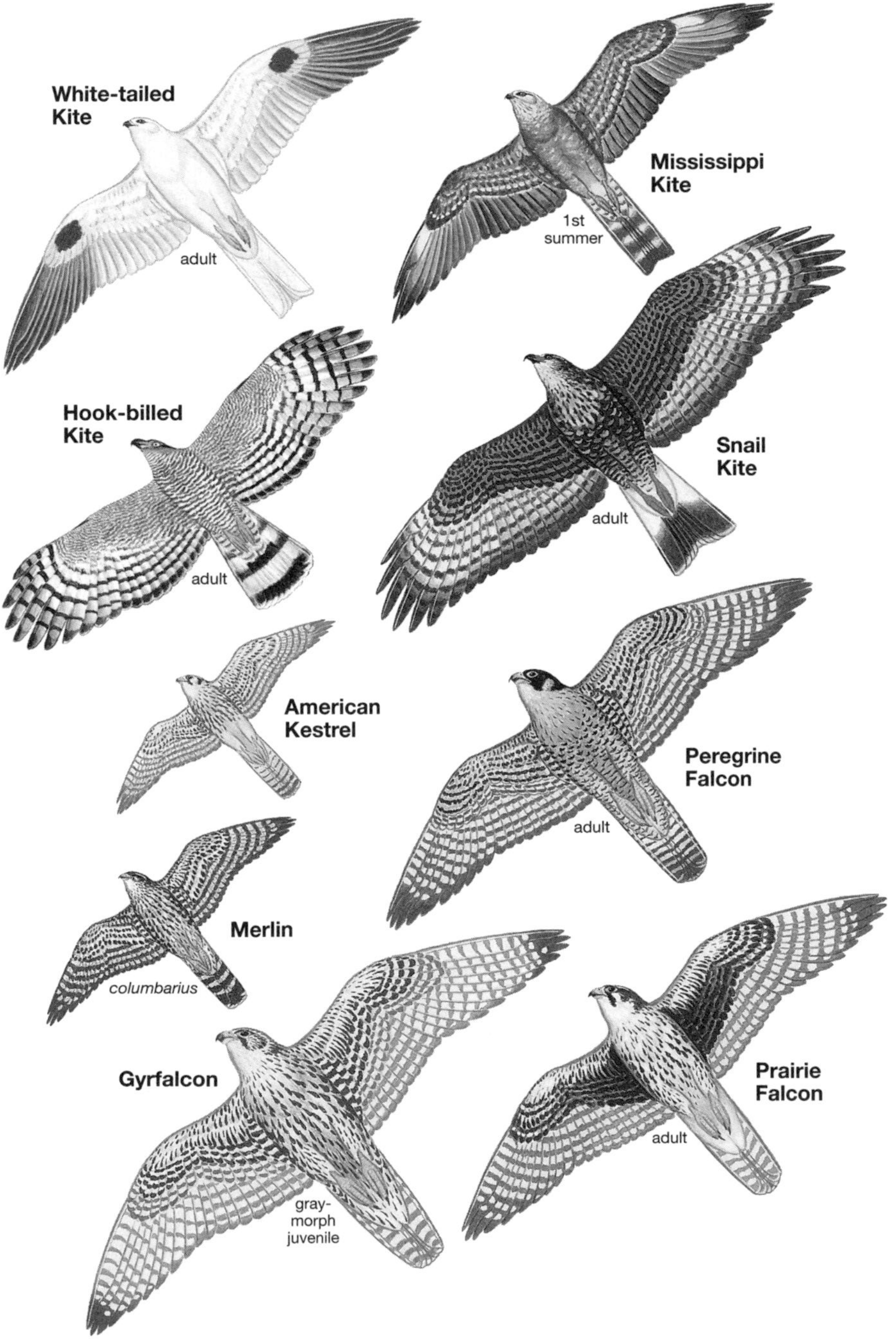
White-tailed Kite
adult
Mississippi Kite
1st summer
Hook-billed Kite
adult
Snail Kite
adult
American Kestrel
Peregrine Falcon
adult
Merlin
columbarius
Gyrfalcon
gray-morph juvenile
Prairie Falcon
adult

Sharp-shinned Hawk
adult

Cooper's Hawk
adult

Northern Goshawk
adult

Northern Harrier
adult

Gray Hawk
adult

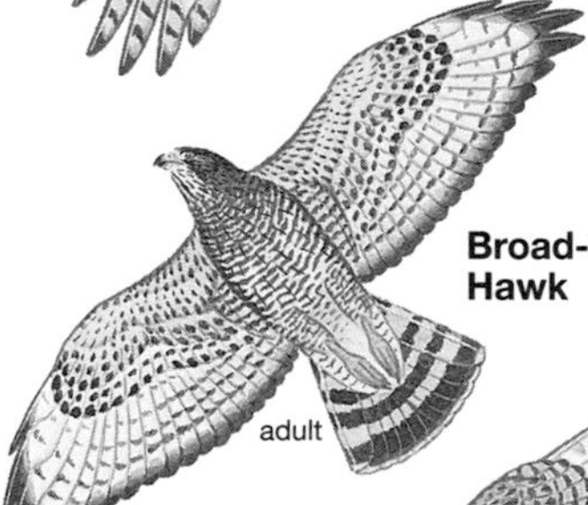

Broad-winged Hawk
adult

Broad-winged Hawk
dark-morph adult

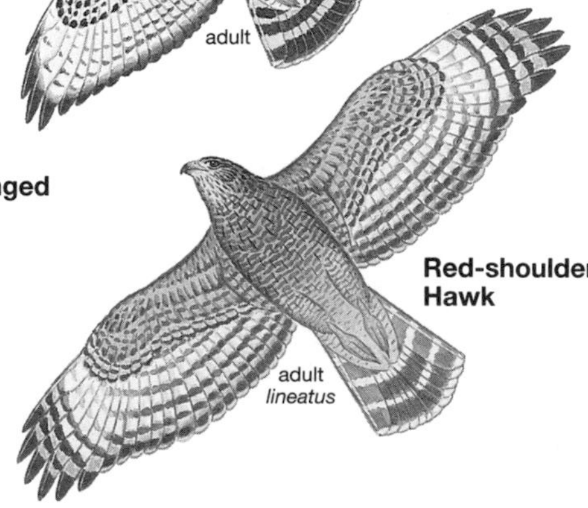

Red-shouldered Hawk
adult *lineatus*

Female Hawks in Flight

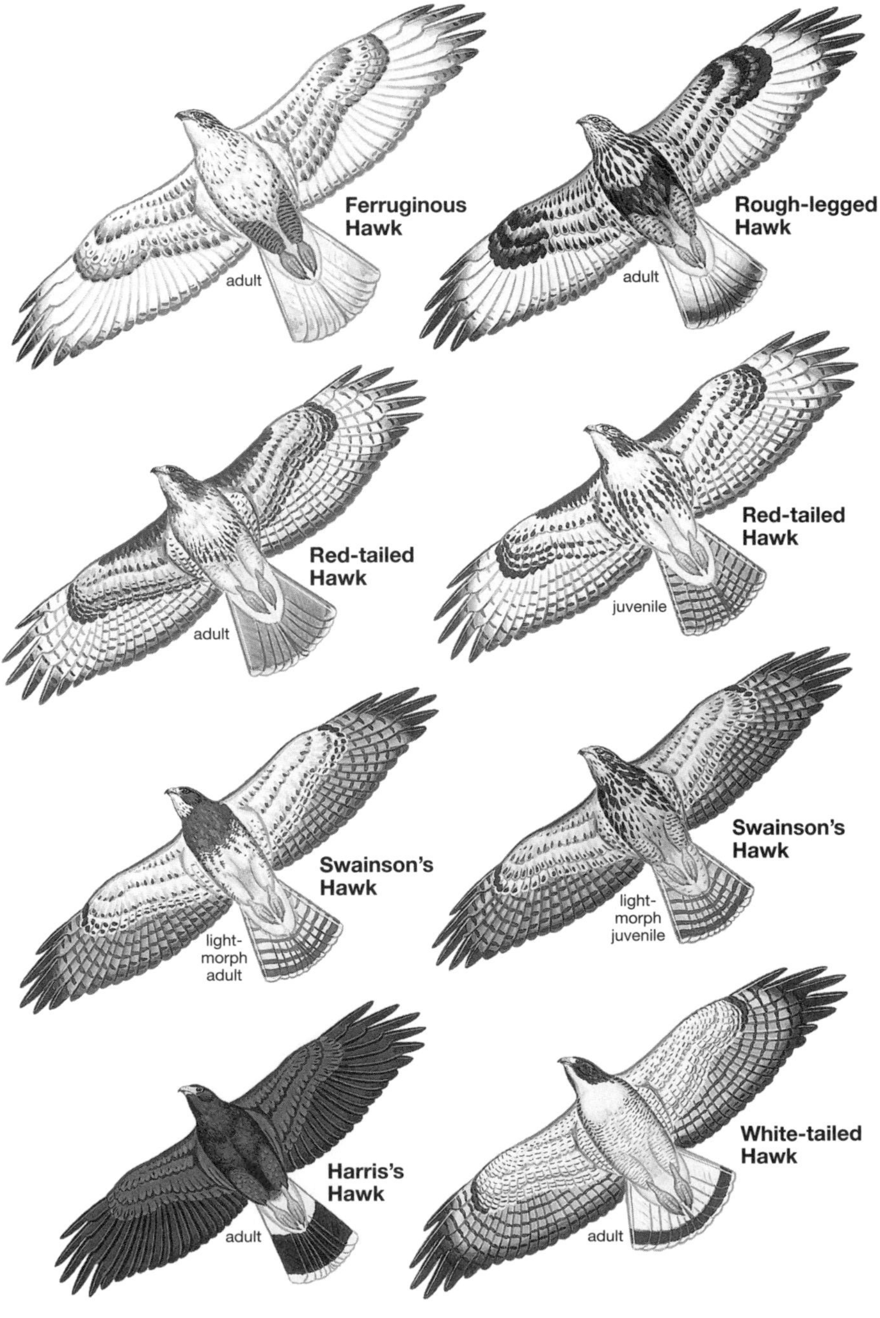
Ferruginous Hawk
adult
Rough-legged Hawk
adult
Red-tailed Hawk
adult
Red-tailed Hawk
juvenile
Swainson's Hawk
light-morph adult
Swainson's Hawk
light-morph juvenile
Harris's Hawk
adult
White-tailed Hawk
adult

Crested Caracara
adult
Osprey
adult
Bald Eagle
2nd year
Zone-tailed Hawk
juvenile
Common Black-Hawk
adult
Golden Eagle
adult
Turkey Vulture
adult
Black Vulture
adult

Limpkins (Family Aramidae)

Limpkin *Aramus guarauna*

DATE	LOCATION

Rails, Gallinules, Coots (Family Rallidae)

King Rail *Rallus elegans*

DATE	LOCATION

Clapper Rail *Rallus longirostris*

DATE	LOCATION

Limpkin
pictus
adult
King Rail
elegans
adult
juvenile
crepitans
yumanensis
Clapper
Rail
scottii
"Light-footed"
levipes

Virginia Rail *Rallus limicola*

DATE LOCATION

Sora *Porzana carolina*

DATE LOCATION

Yellow Rail *Coturnicops noveboracensis*

DATE LOCATION

Black Rail *Laterallus jamaicensis*

DATE LOCATION

Corn Crake *Crex crex*

DATE LOCATION

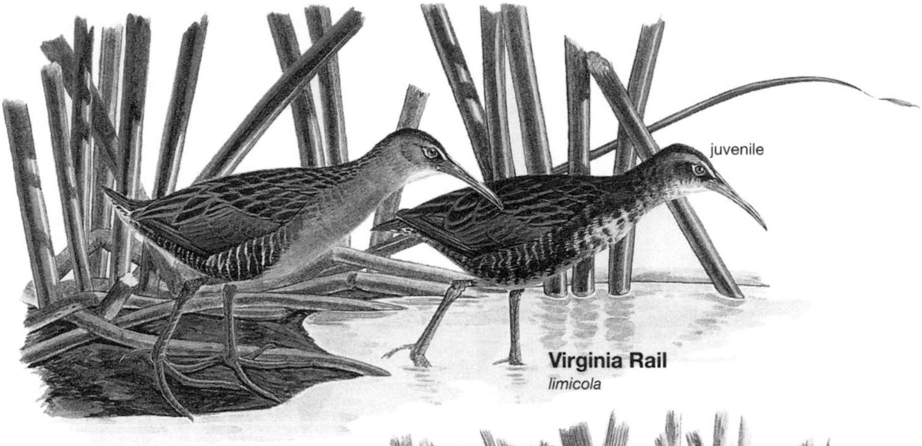
juvenile
Virginia Rail
limicola

Sora
winter ♀
juvenile
breeding adult ♂

juvenile
Yellow Rail
noveboracensis

Black Rail
jamaicensis

Corn Crake

Purple Gallinule *Porphyrio martinica*

DATE LOCATION

Purple Swamphen *Porphyrio porphyrio*

DATE LOCATION

Common Moorhen *Gallinula chloropus*

DATE LOCATION

American Coot *Fulica americana*

DATE LOCATION

Eurasian Coot *Fulica atra*

DATE LOCATION

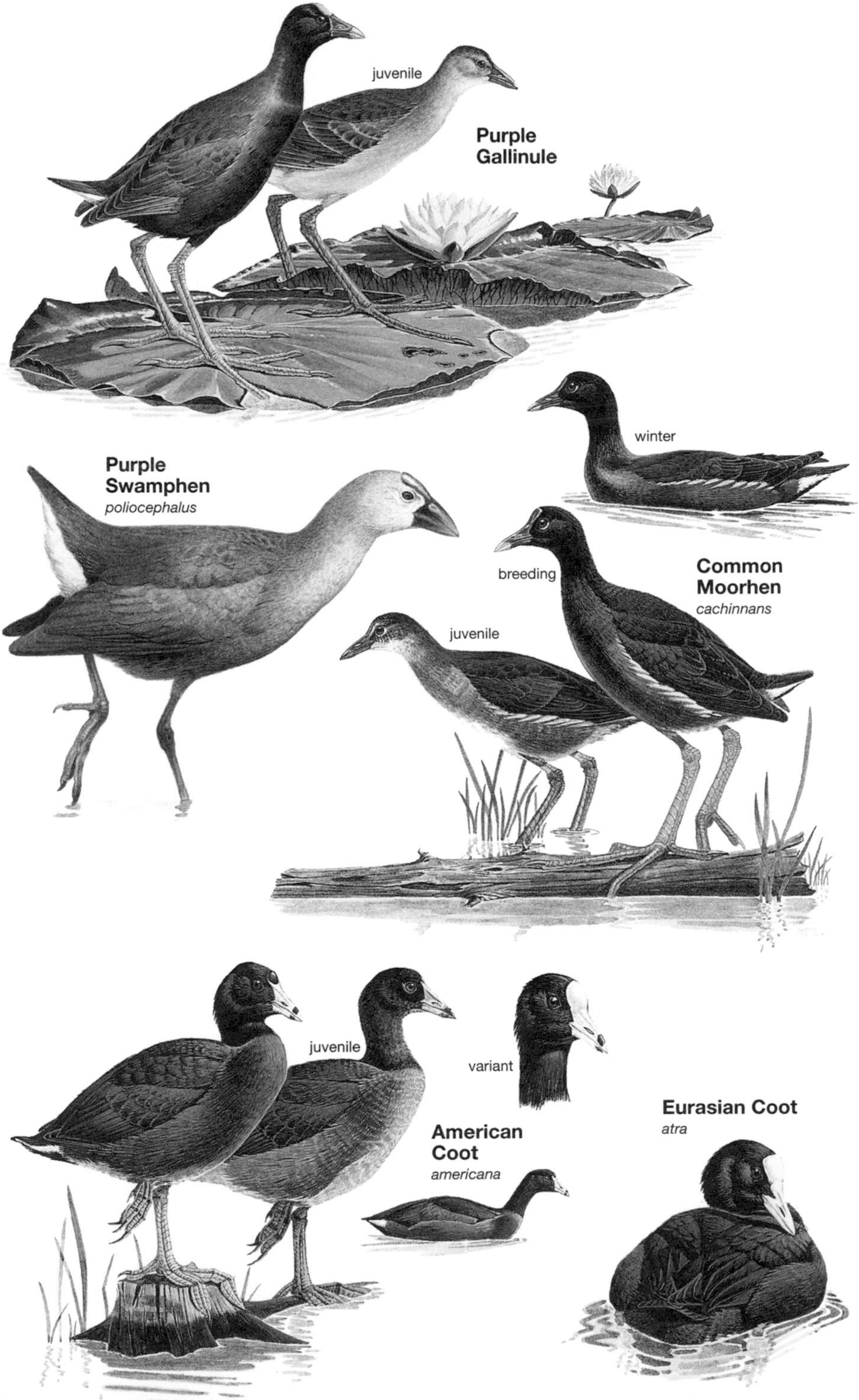

juvenile
Purple Gallinule
winter
Purple Swamphen
poliocephalus
breeding
Common Moorhen
cachinnans
juvenile
juvenile
variant
Eurasian Coot
atra
American Coot
americana

Cranes (Family Gruidae)

Sandhill Crane *Grus canadensis*

DATE LOCATION

Common Crane *Grus grus*

DATE LOCATION

Whooping Crane *Grus americana*

DATE LOCATION

juvenile
adult
Sandhill Crane
rowani
stained adult
adult
juvenile
adult
adult
Common Crane
lilfordi
adult
adult
juvenile
Whooping Crane

Lapwings, Plovers (Family Charadriidae)

Black-bellied Plover *Pluvialis squatarola*

DATE LOCATION

American Golden-Plover *Pluvialis dominica*

DATE LOCATION

Pacific Golden-Plover *Pluvialis fulva*

DATE LOCATION

European Golden-Plover *Pluvialis apricaria*

DATE LOCATION

juveniles in flight
European
Pacific
American
Black-bellied
bright juvenile
winter
breeding ♀
breeding ♂
Black-bellied Plover
juvenile
bright juvenile
juvenile
April ♂
breeding ♀
breeding ♂
American Golden-Plover
juveniles
winter
breeding ♂
breeding ♀
breeding ♂
Pacific Golden-Plover
juveniles
breeding ♂
breeding ♀
European Golden-Plover
altifrons

Snowy Plover *Charadrius alexandrinus*

DATE LOCATION

Piping Plover *Charadrius melodus*

DATE LOCATION

Wilson's Plover *Charadrius wilsonia*

DATE LOCATION

Semipalmated Plover *Charadrius semipalmatus*

DATE LOCATION

Common Ringed Plover *Charadrius hiaticula*

DATE LOCATION

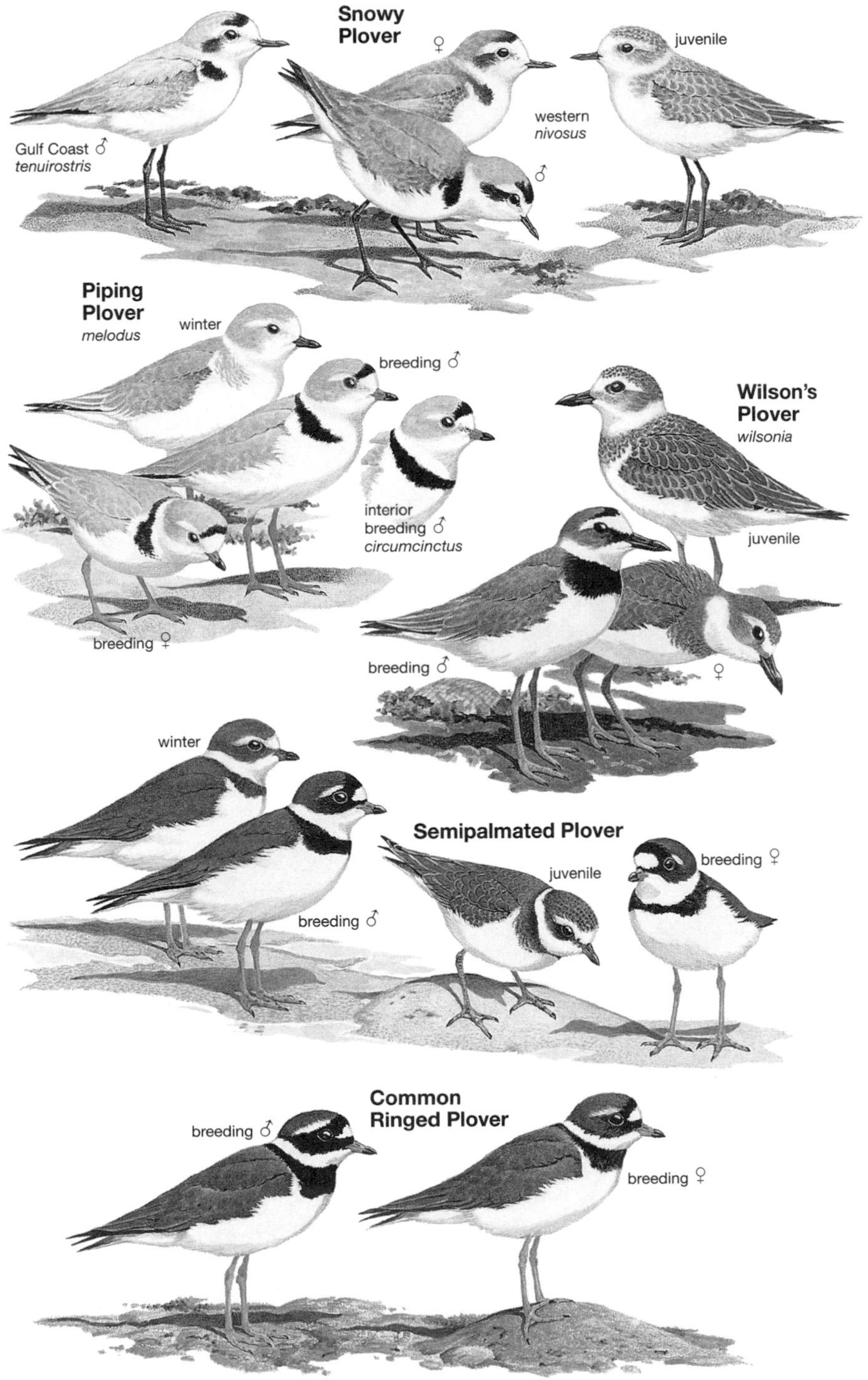
Snowy Plover
Gulf Coast ♂
tenuirostris
♀
western
nivosus
♂
juvenile
Piping Plover
melodus
winter
breeding ♂
interior
breeding ♂
circumcinctus
breeding ♀
Wilson's Plover
wilsonia
juvenile
breeding ♂
♀
winter
Semipalmated Plover
breeding ♀
juvenile
breeding ♂
Common Ringed Plover
breeding ♂
breeding ♀

Lesser Sand-Plover *Charadrius mongolus*

DATE LOCATION

Little Ringed Plover *Charadrius dubius*

DATE LOCATION

Killdeer *Charadrius vociferus*

DATE LOCATION

Mountain Plover *Charadrius montanus*

DATE LOCATION

Northern Lapwing *Vanellus vanellus*

DATE LOCATION

Eurasian Dotterel *Charadrius morinellus*

DATE LOCATION

breeding ♀
Lesser Sand-Plover
stegmanni
breeding ♂
winter
juvenile
winter
Little Ringed Plover
curonicus
juvenile
breeding ♂
Killdeer
Mountain Plover
breeding
winter
juvenile
Eurasian Dotterel
breeding ♂
breeding ♀
winter
juvenile
Northern Lapwing
winter
winter
winter

Jacanas (Family Jacanidae)

Northern Jacana *Jacana spinosa*

DATE LOCATION

Oystercatchers (Family Haematopodidae)

Black Oystercatcher *Haematopus bachmani*

DATE LOCATION

American Oystercatcher *Haematopus palliatus*

DATE LOCATION

Stilts, Avocets (Family Recurvirostridae)

American Avocet *Recurvirostra americana*

DATE LOCATION

Black-necked Stilt *Himantopus mexicanus*

DATE LOCATION

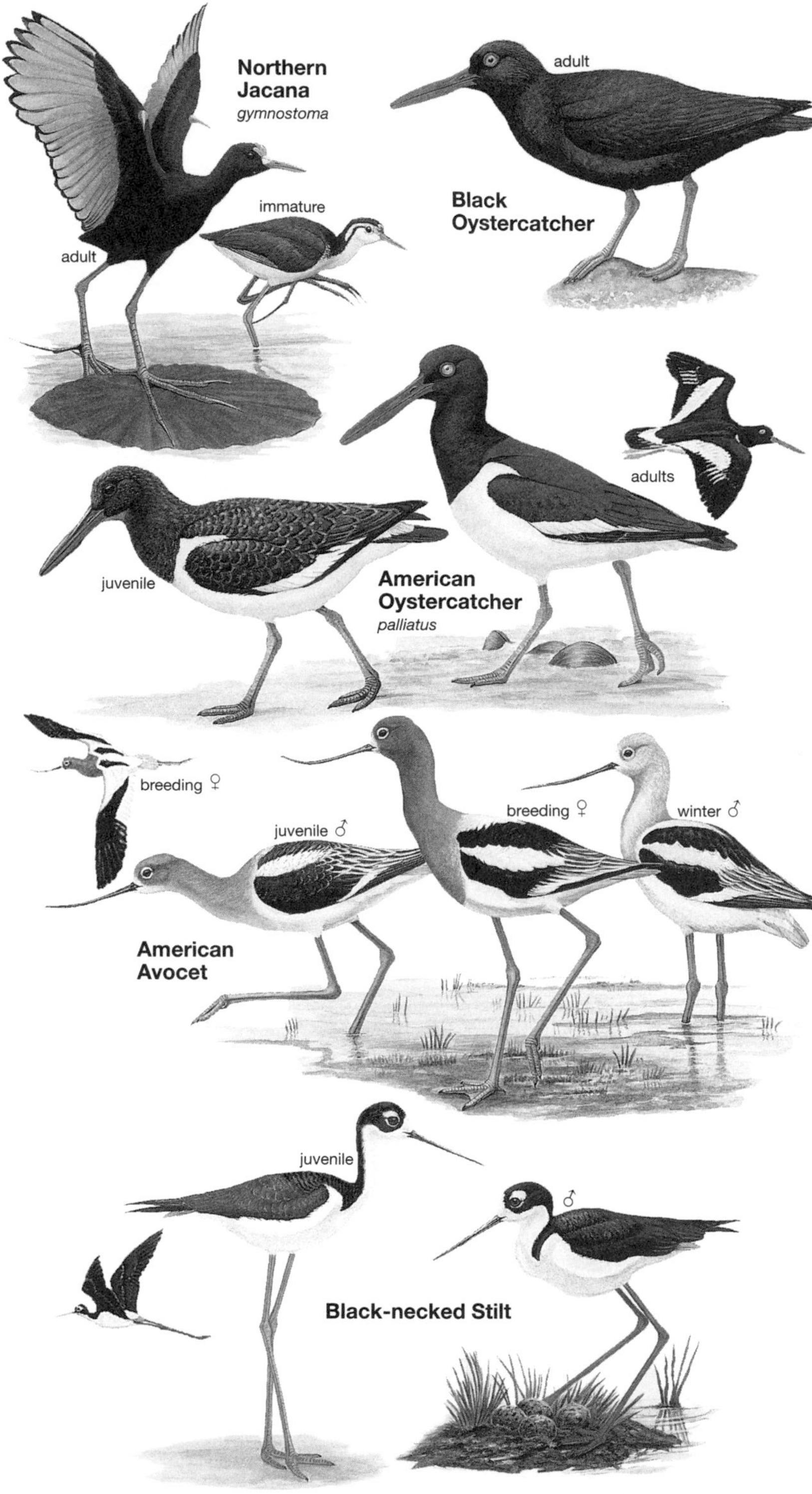
Northern
Jacana
gymnostoma
adult
immature
adult
Black
Oystercatcher
adults
juvenile
American
Oystercatcher
palliatus
breeding ♀
juvenile ♂
breeding ♀
winter ♂
American
Avocet
juvenile
♂
Black-necked Stilt

Sandpipers, Phalaropes, Allies (Family Scolopacidae)

illet *Tringa semipalmata*

DATE LOCATION

Lesser Yellowlegs *Tringa flavipes*

DATE LOCATION

Greater Yellowlegs *Tringa melanoleuca*

DATE LOCATION

Willet
early March
in molt
western
eastern
breeding
eastern
semipalmata
juvenile
winter
worn
breeding
western
inornata
winter
breeding
juvenile
Lesser
Yellowlegs
breeding
winter
juvenile
winter
winter
breeding
winter
juvenile
Greater
Yellowlegs

Common Greenshank *Tringa nebularia*

DATE LOCATION

Marsh Sandpiper *Tringa stagnatilis*

DATE LOCATION

Common Redshank *Tringa totanus*

DATE LOCATION

Spotted Redshank *Tringa erythropus*

DATE LOCATION

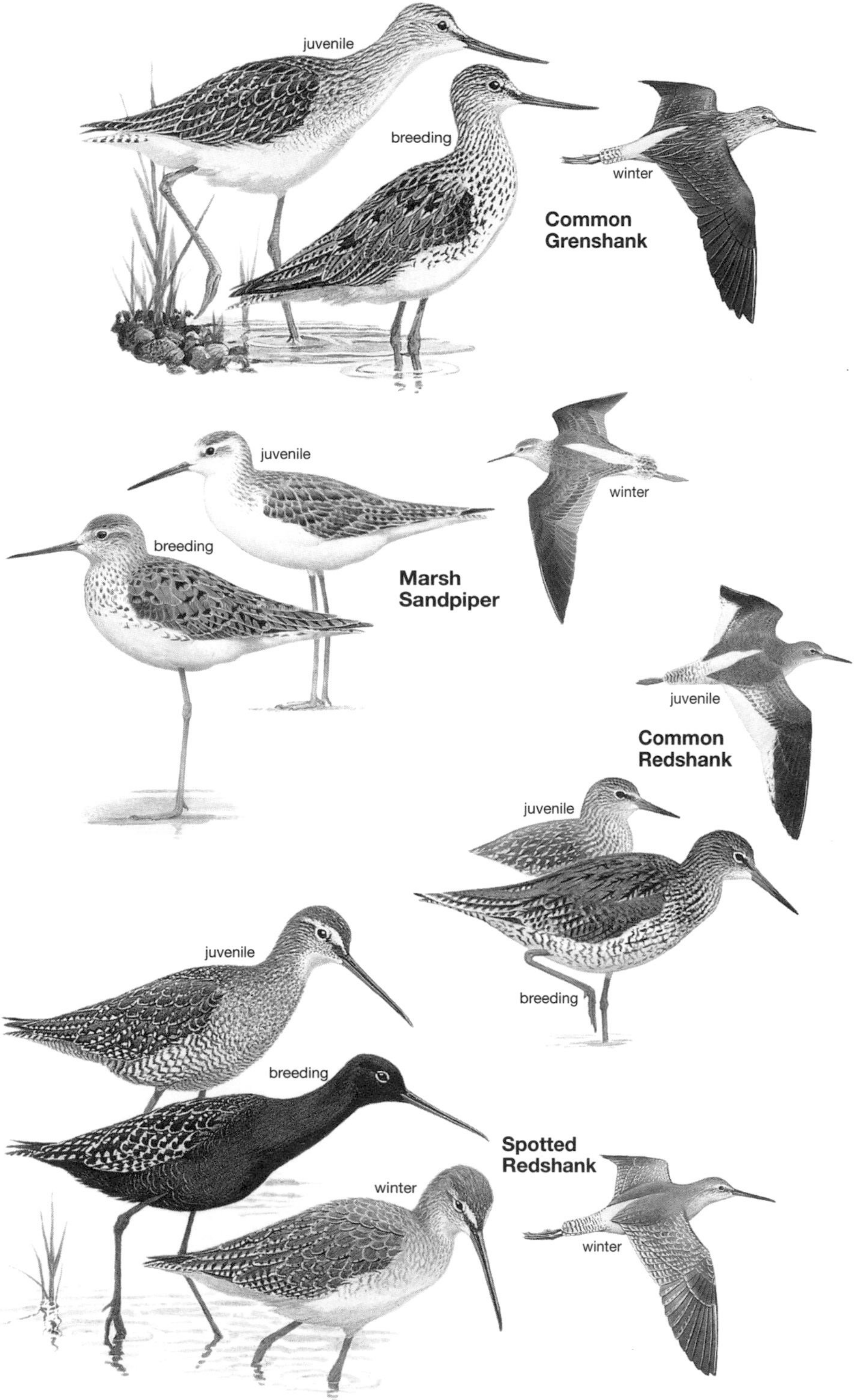
juvenile
breeding
winter
Common Grenshank
juvenile
winter
breeding
Marsh Sandpiper
juvenile
Common Redshank
juvenile
breeding
juvenile
breeding
Spotted Redshank
winter
winter

Wood Sandpiper *Tringa glareola*

DATE LOCATION

Green Sandpiper *Tringa ochropus*

DATE LOCATION

Solitary Sandpiper *Tringa solitaria*

DATE LOCATION

Terek Sandpiper *Xenus cinereus*

DATE LOCATION

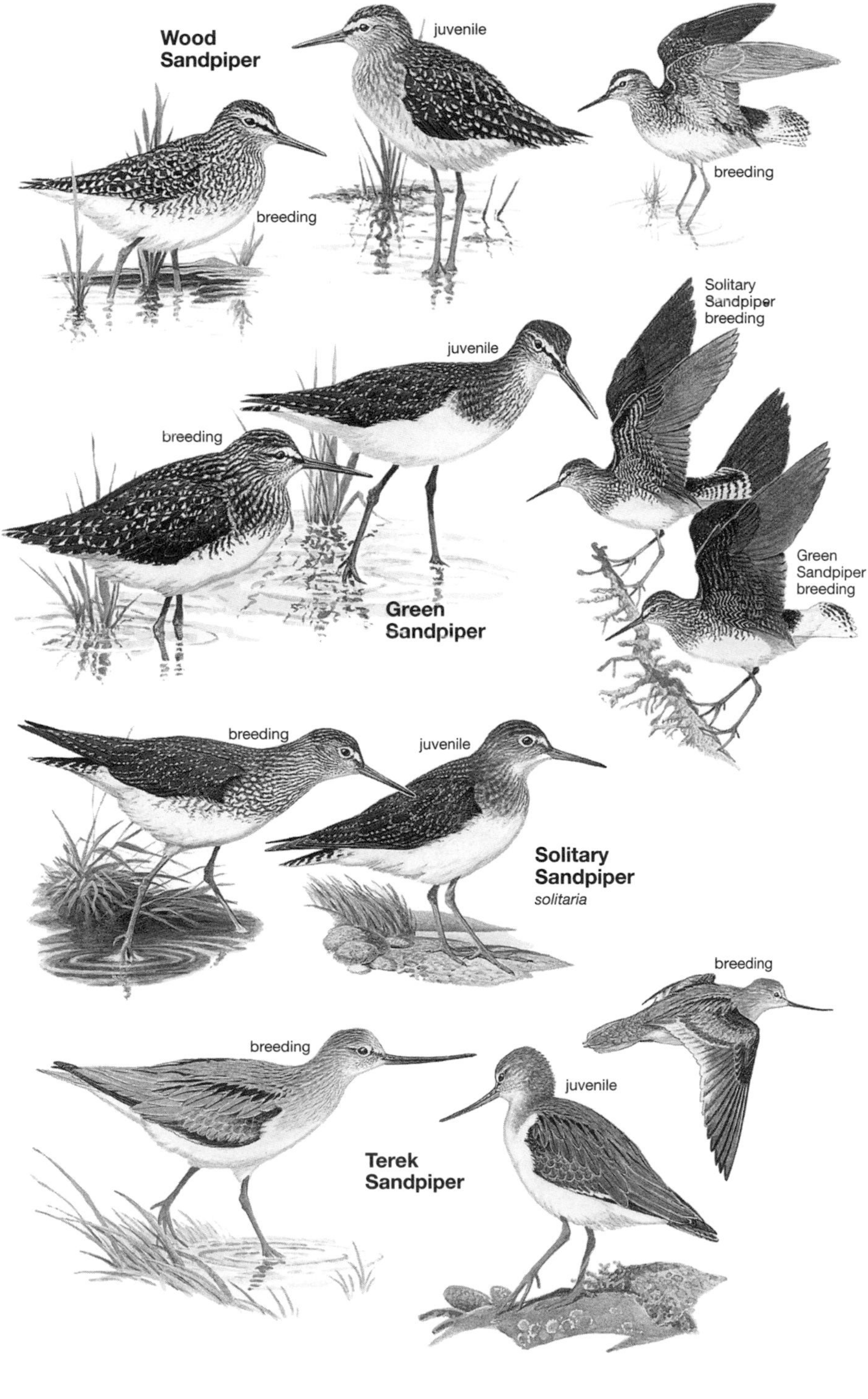
Wood Sandpiper
juvenile
breeding
breeding
Solitary Sandpiper breeding
juvenile
breeding
Green Sandpiper
Green Sandpiper breeding
breeding
juvenile
Solitary Sandpiper
solitaria
breeding
breeding
juvenile
Terek Sandpiper

Wandering Tattler *Tringa incana*

DATE LOCATION

Gray-tailed Tattler *Tringa brevipes*

DATE LOCATION

Common Sandpiper *Actitis hypoleucos*

DATE LOCATION

Spotted Sandpiper *Actitis macularius*

DATE LOCATION

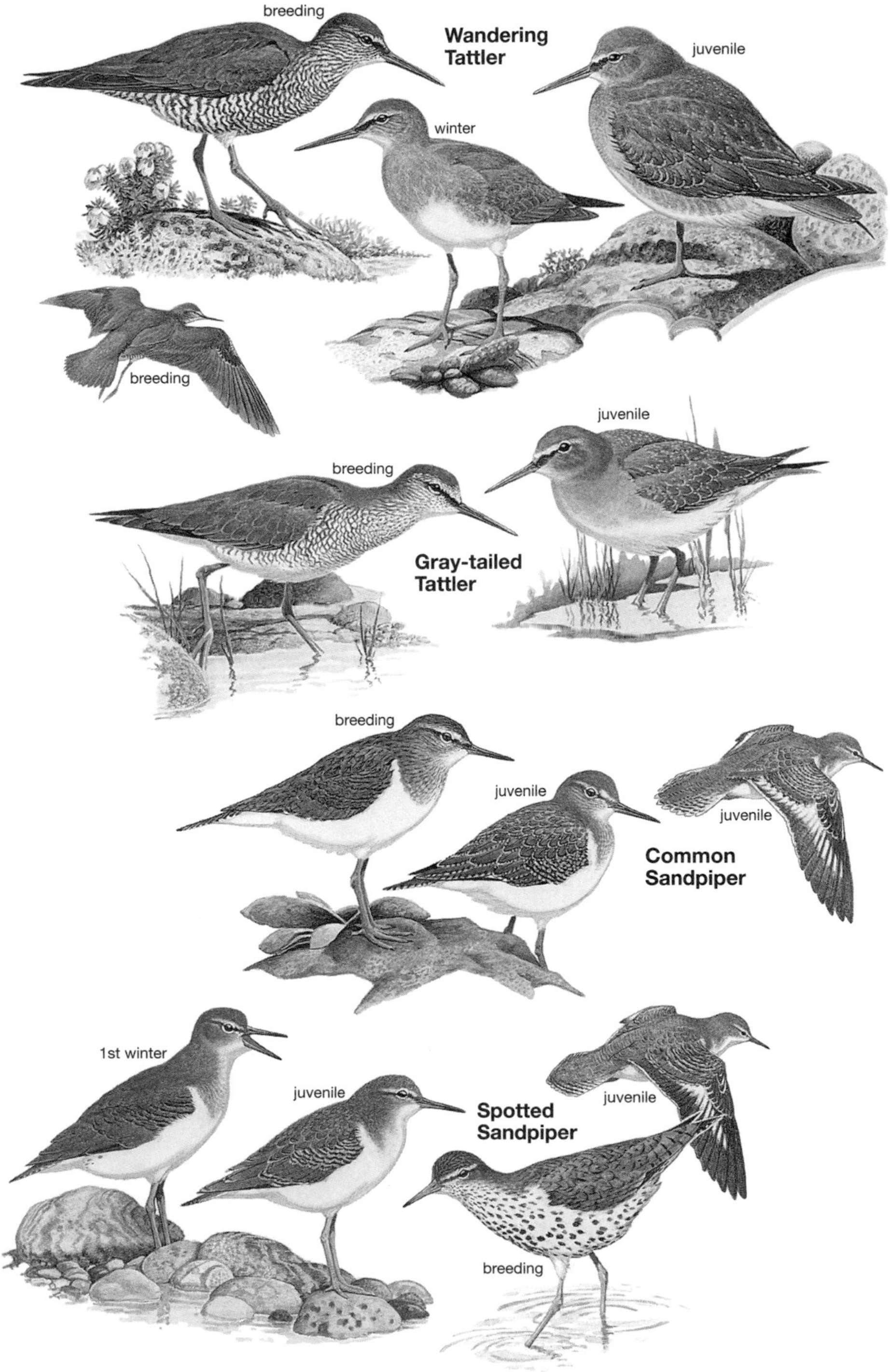

Wandering Tattler
breeding
winter
juvenile
breeding
Gray-tailed Tattler
breeding
juvenile
Common Sandpiper
breeding
juvenile
juvenile
Spotted Sandpiper
1st winter
juvenile
juvenile
breeding

Little Curlew *Numenius minutus*

DATE LOCATION

Eskimo Curlew *Numenius borealis*

DATE LOCATION

Whimbrel *Numenius phaeopus*

DATE LOCATION

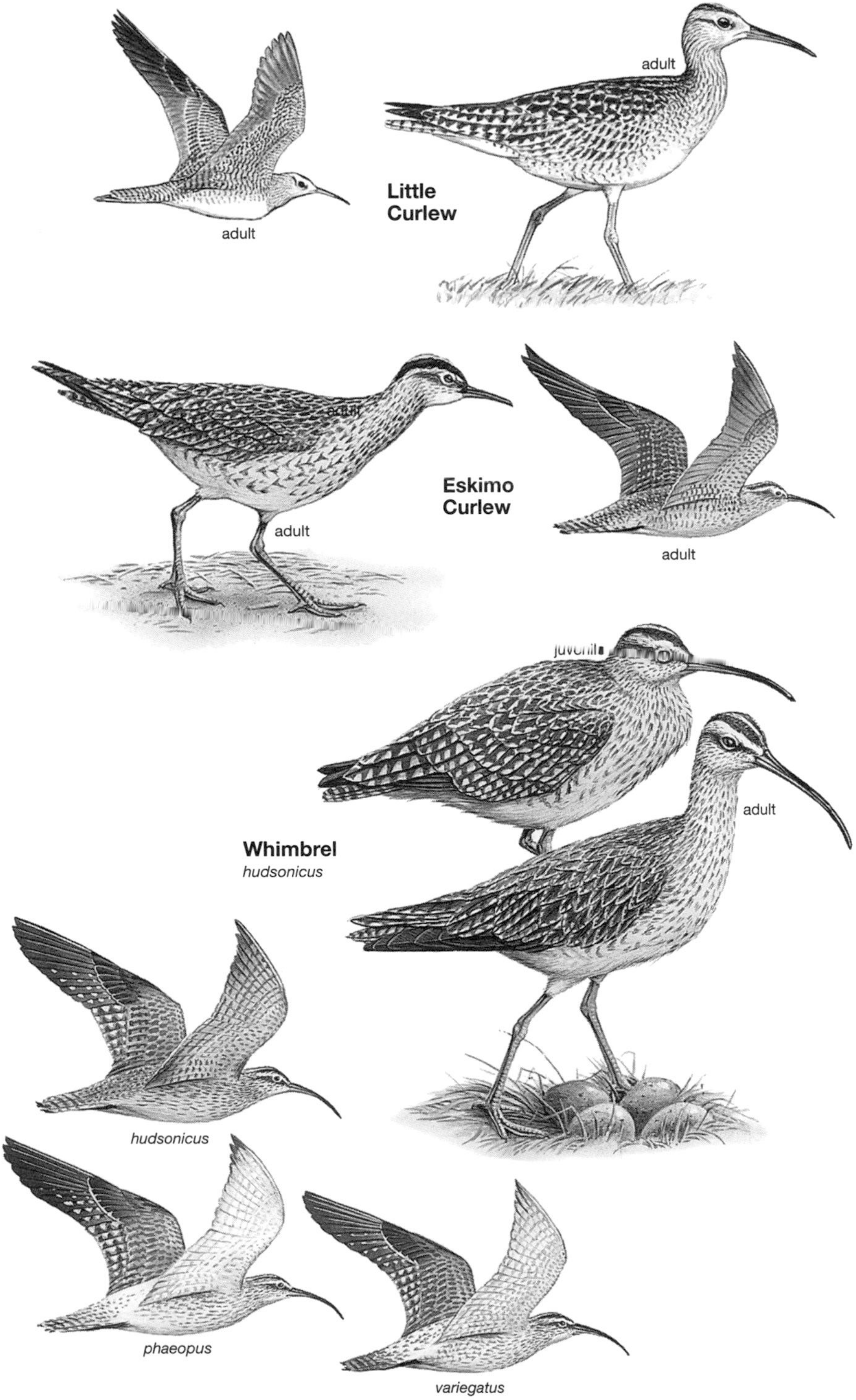

adult
Little Curlew
adult
adult
Eskimo Curlew
adult
Whimbrel
hudsonicus
adult
hudsonicus
phaeopus
variegatus

Bristle-thighed Curlew *Numenius tahitiensis*

DATE LOCATION

Long-billed Curlew *Numenius americanus*

DATE LOCATION

Eurasian Curlew *Numenius arquata*

DATE LOCATION

Far Eastern Curlew *Numenius madagascariensis*

DATE LOCATION

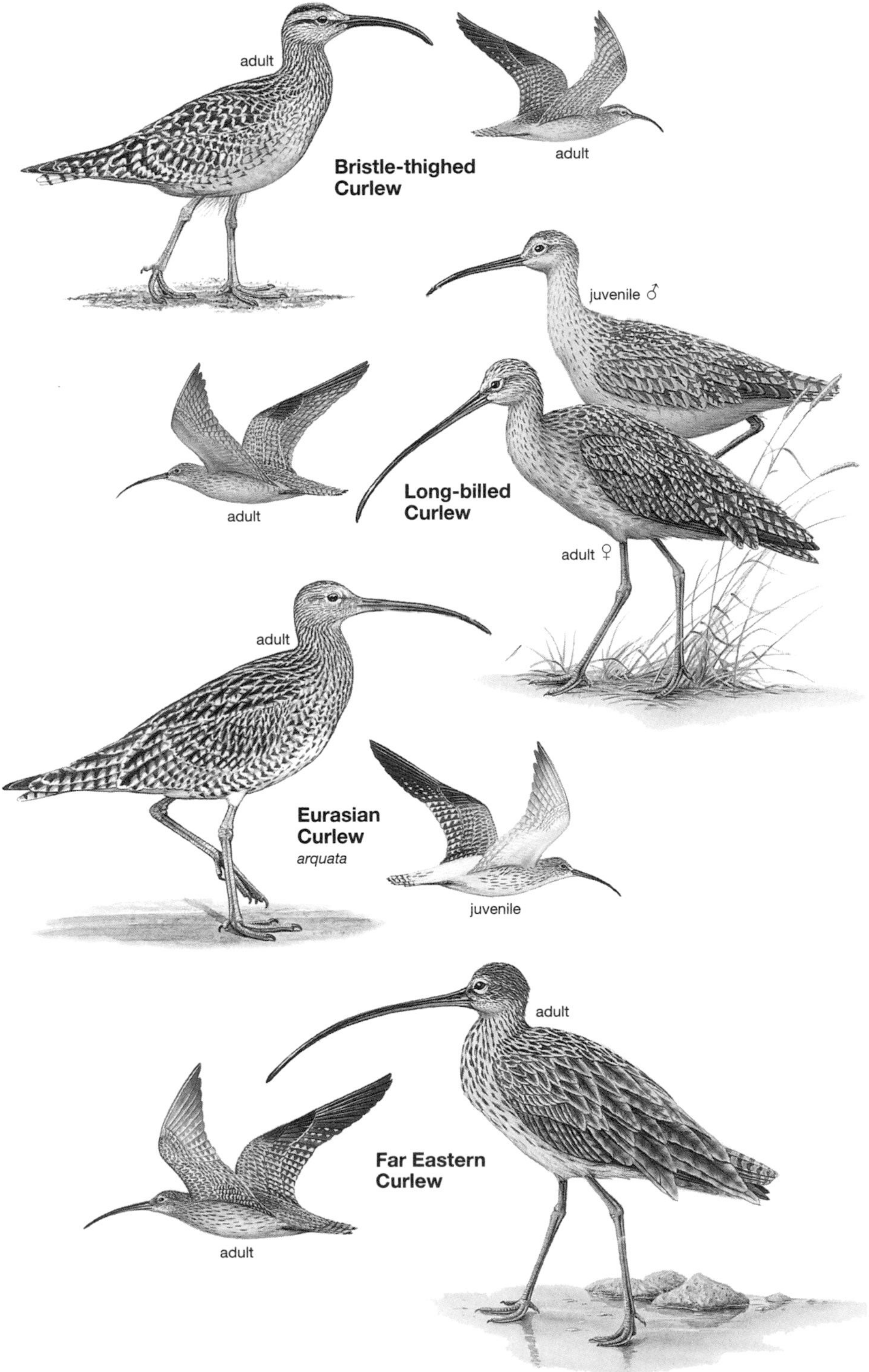
adult
adult
Bristle-thighed Curlew
juvenile ♂
adult
Long-billed Curlew
adult ♀
adult
Eurasian Curlew
arquata
juvenile
adult
Far Eastern Curlew
adult

Black-tailed Godwit *Limosa limosa*

DATE LOCATION

Hudsonian Godwit *Limosa haemastica*

DATE LOCATION

Bar-tailed Godwit *Limosa lapponica*

DATE LOCATION

Marbled Godwit *Limosa fedoa*

DATE LOCATION

Black-tailed Godwit
melanuroides
juvenile
juvenile
winter
breeding ♂
islandica
breeding ♂
breeding ♀
juvenile
Hudsonian
Godwit
juvenile
molting fall
adult ♂
breeding ♀
breeding ♂
juvenile
winter
breeding ♀
Bar-tailed
Godwit
baueri
breeding ♂
Marbled
Godwit
fedoa
juvenile Hudsonian,
Bar-tailed, and Marbled
(left to right)
breeding ♂
winter ♀

Ruddy Turnstone *Arenaria interpres*

DATE LOCATION

Black Turnstone *Arenaria melanocephala*

DATE LOCATION

Surfbird *Aphriza virgata*

DATE LOCATION

Rock Sandpiper *Calidris ptilocnemis*

DATE LOCATION

Purple Sandpiper *Calidris maritima*

DATE LOCATION

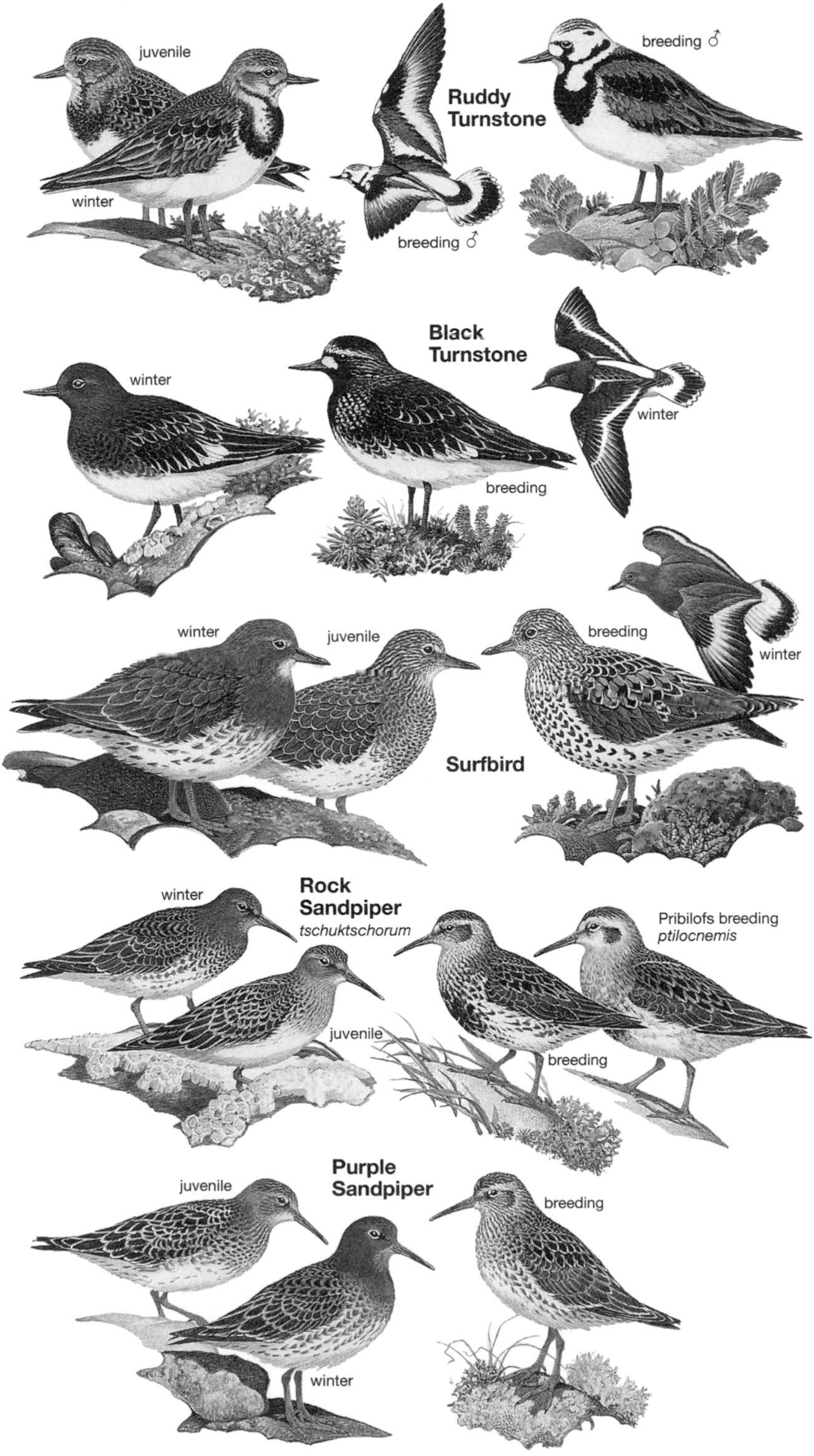
juvenile
winter
Ruddy Turnstone
breeding ♂
breeding ♂
Black Turnstone
winter
breeding
winter
winter
winter
juvenile
breeding
Surfbird
winter
Rock Sandpiper
tschuktschorum
juvenile
breeding
Pribilofs breeding
ptilocnemis
Purple Sandpiper
juvenile
winter
breeding

Great Knot *Calidris tenuirostris*

DATE LOCATION

Red Knot *Calidris canutus*

DATE LOCATION

Sanderling *Calidris alba*

DATE LOCATION

Dunlin *Calidris alpina*

DATE LOCATION

Curlew Sandpiper *Calidris ferruginea*

DATE LOCATION

Great Knot
juvenile
breeding
Red Knot
juvenile
winter
breeding
Sanderling
winter
breeding
juvenile
breeding
sakhalina
breeding
pacifica
breeding
schinzii
Dunlin
hudsonia
juvenile
breeding
winter
Curlew Sandpiper
juvenile
breeding ♂
winter

Peeps

Semipalmated Sandpiper *Calidris pusilla*

DATE LOCATION

Western Sandpiper *Calidris mauri*

DATE LOCATION

Least Sandpiper *Calidris minutilla*

DATE LOCATION

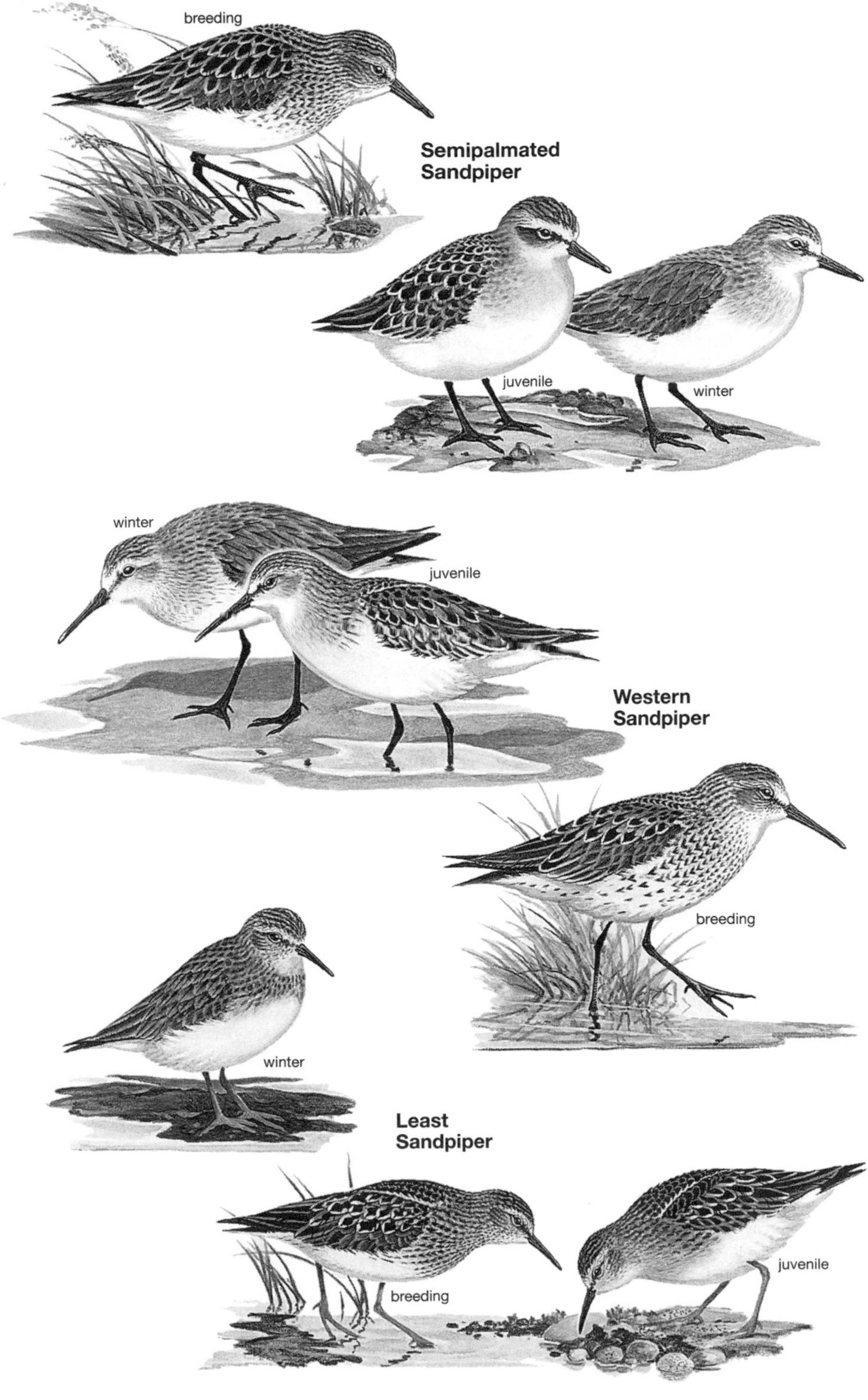

breeding
Semipalmated Sandpiper
juvenile
winter
winter
juvenile
Western Sandpiper
breeding
winter
Least Sandpiper
breeding
juvenile

Rare Stints

Red-necked Stint *Calidris ruficollis*

DATE LOCATION

Little Stint *Calidris minuta*

DATE LOCATION

Long-toed Stint *Calidris subminuta*

DATE LOCATION

Temminck's Stint *Calidris temminckii*

DATE LOCATION

juvenile
breeding
breeding
Red-necked Stint
Little Stint
breeding
juvenile
juvenile
Long-toed Stint
breeding
Temminck's Stint
juvenile
breeding

White-rumped Sandpiper *Calidris fuscicollis*

DATE LOCATION

Baird's Sandpiper *Calidris bairdii*

DATE LOCATION

Spoon-billed Sandpiper *Eurynorhynchus pygmeus*

DATE LOCATION

Broad-billed Sandpiper *Limicola falcinellus*

DATE LOCATION

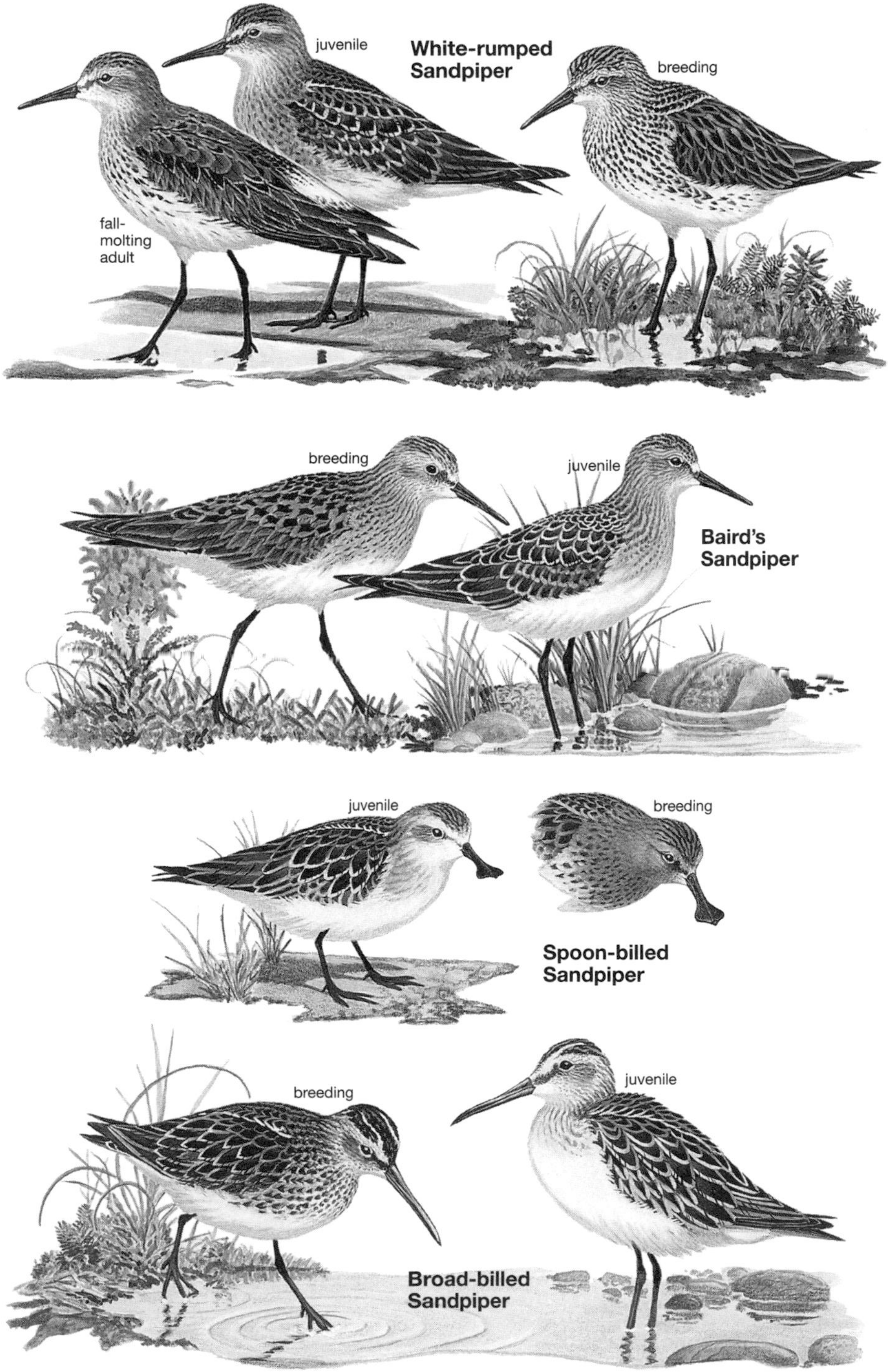
White-rumped Sandpiper
juvenile
breeding
fall-molting adult
Baird's Sandpiper
breeding
juvenile
Spoon-billed Sandpiper
juvenile
breeding
Broad-billed Sandpiper
breeding
juvenile

Pectoral Sandpiper *Calidris melanotos*

DATE LOCATION

Sharp-tailed Sandpiper *Calidris acuminata*

DATE LOCATION

Upland Sandpiper *Bartramia longicauda*

DATE LOCATION

Buff-breasted Sandpiper *Tryngites subruficollis*

DATE LOCATION

Ruff *Philomachus pugnax*

DATE LOCATION

Pectoral Sandpiper
breeding ♂
breeding ♀
juvenile
juvenile Sharp-tailed (center) with juvenile Pectorals
breeding adult
Sharp-tailed Sandpiper
juvenile
Upland Sandpiper
adult
juvenile
displaying adult
juvenile
Buff-breasted Sandpiper
breeding adult
breeding males
♀
summer molting ♂
juvenile ♀
Ruff
summer molting ♀
winter ♂

Dowitchers

Short-billed Dowitcher *Limnodromus griseus*

DATE LOCATION

Long-billed Dowitcher *Limnodromus scolopaceus*

DATE LOCATION

Short-billed Dowitcher
worn breeding *griseus*
breeding *caurinus*
breeding *griseus*
breeding *hendersoni*
molting juvenile
winter
juvenile
griseus
winter *hendersoni*
juvenile tertials
Long-billed Dowitcher
molting juvenile
winter
juvenile
winter
juvenile tertials
worn breeding ♀
fresh breeding ♂

Stilt Sandpiper *Calidris himantopus*

DATE LOCATION

Wilson's Snipe *Gallinago delicata*

DATE LOCATION

Common Snipe *Gallinago gallinago*

DATE LOCATION

Pin-tailed Snipe *Gallinago stenura*

DATE LOCATION

American Woodcock *Scolopax minor*

DATE LOCATION

Jack Snipe *Lymnocryptes minimus*

DATE LOCATION

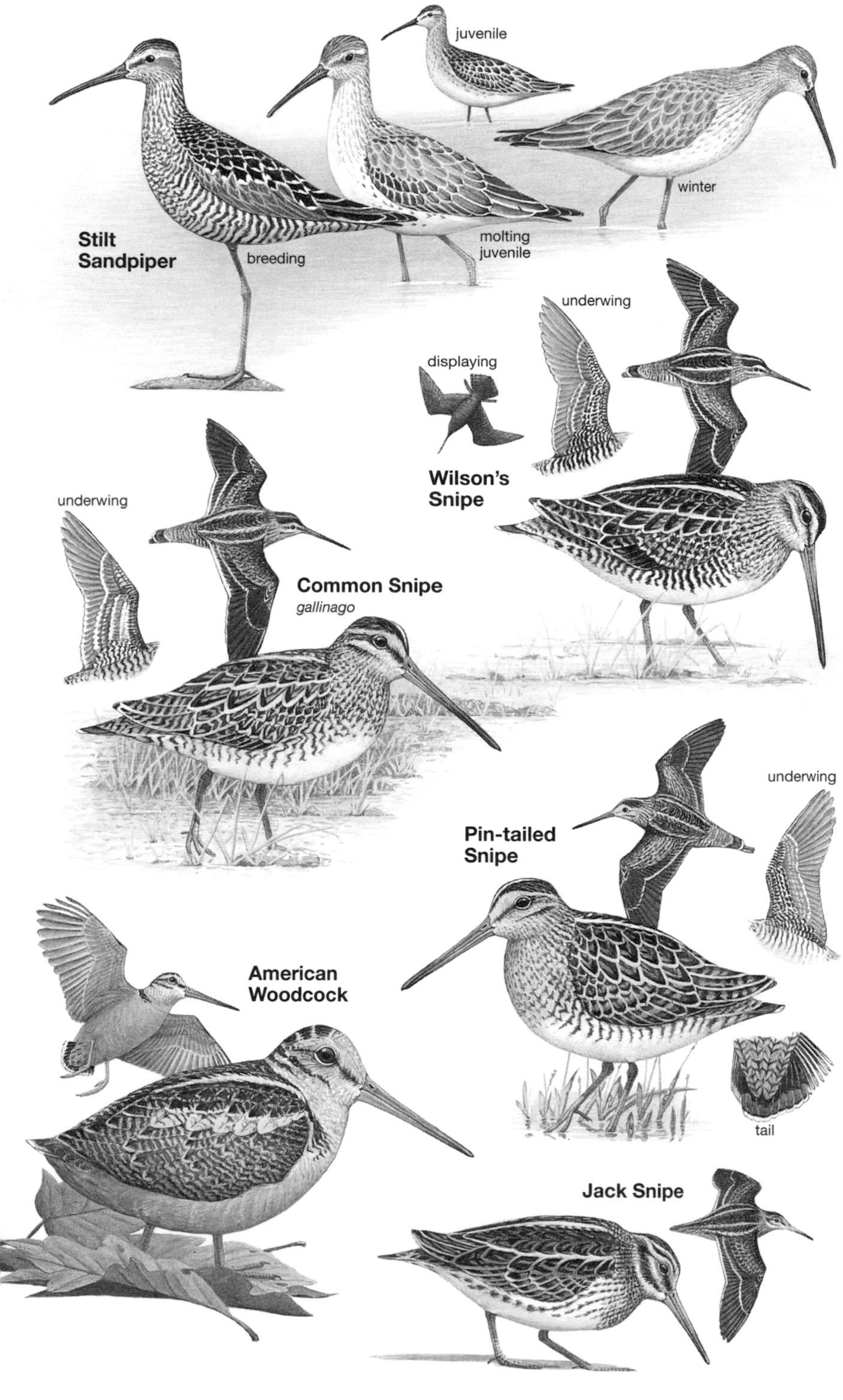

juvenile
winter
Stilt Sandpiper
breeding
molting juvenile
underwing
displaying
Wilson's Snipe
underwing
Common Snipe
gallinago
underwing
Pin-tailed Snipe
American Woodcock
tail
Jack Snipe

Phalaropes

Wilson's Phalarope *Phalaropus tricolor*

DATE LOCATION

Red-necked Phalarope *Phalaropus lobatus*

DATE LOCATION

Red Phalarope *Phalaropus fulicarius*

DATE LOCATION

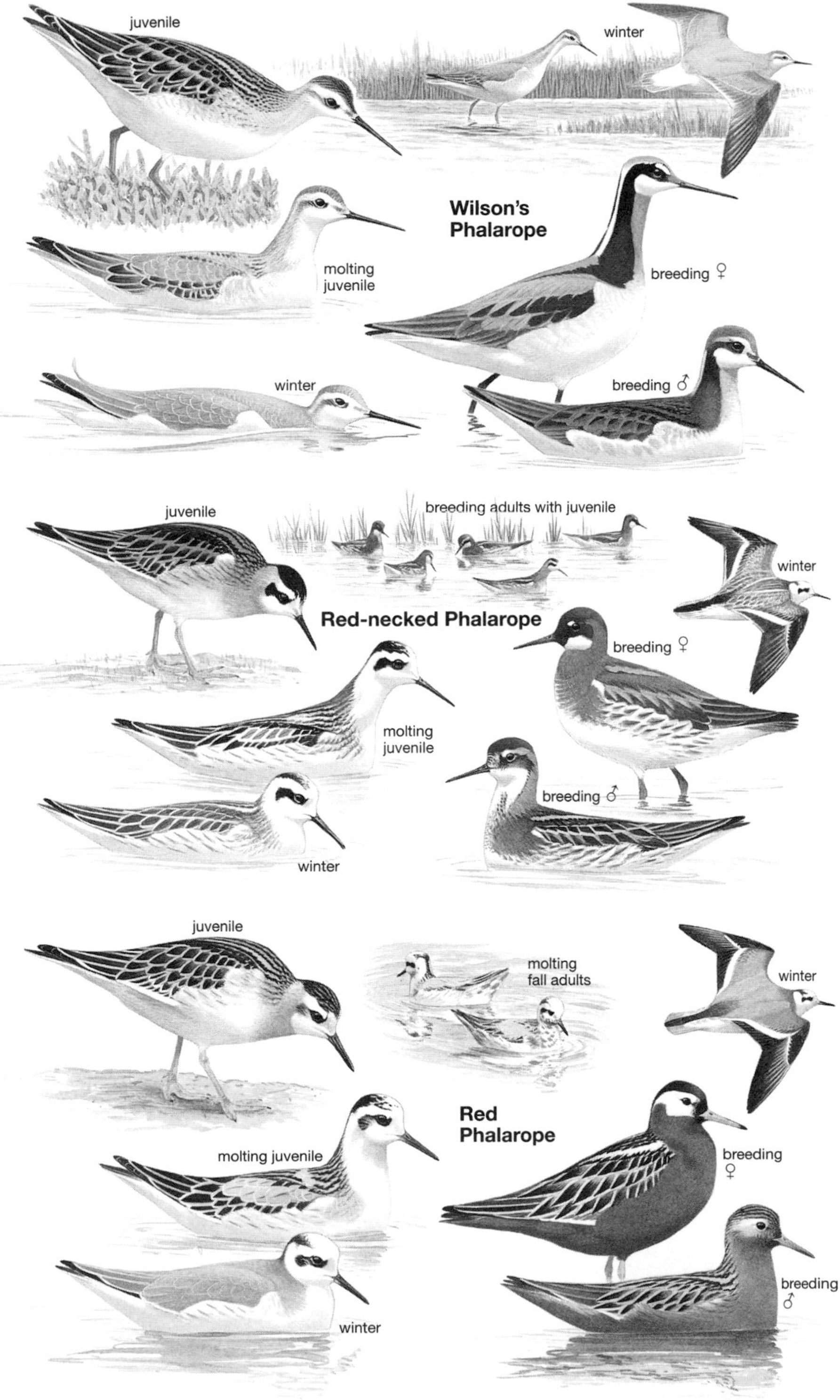
juvenile
winter
Wilson's Phalarope
molting juvenile
breeding ♀
winter
breeding ♂
juvenile
breeding adults with juvenile
winter
Red-necked Phalarope
breeding ♀
molting juvenile
breeding ♂
winter
juvenile
molting fall adults
winter
Red Phalarope
molting juvenile
breeding ♀
winter
breeding ♂

Shorebirds in Flight

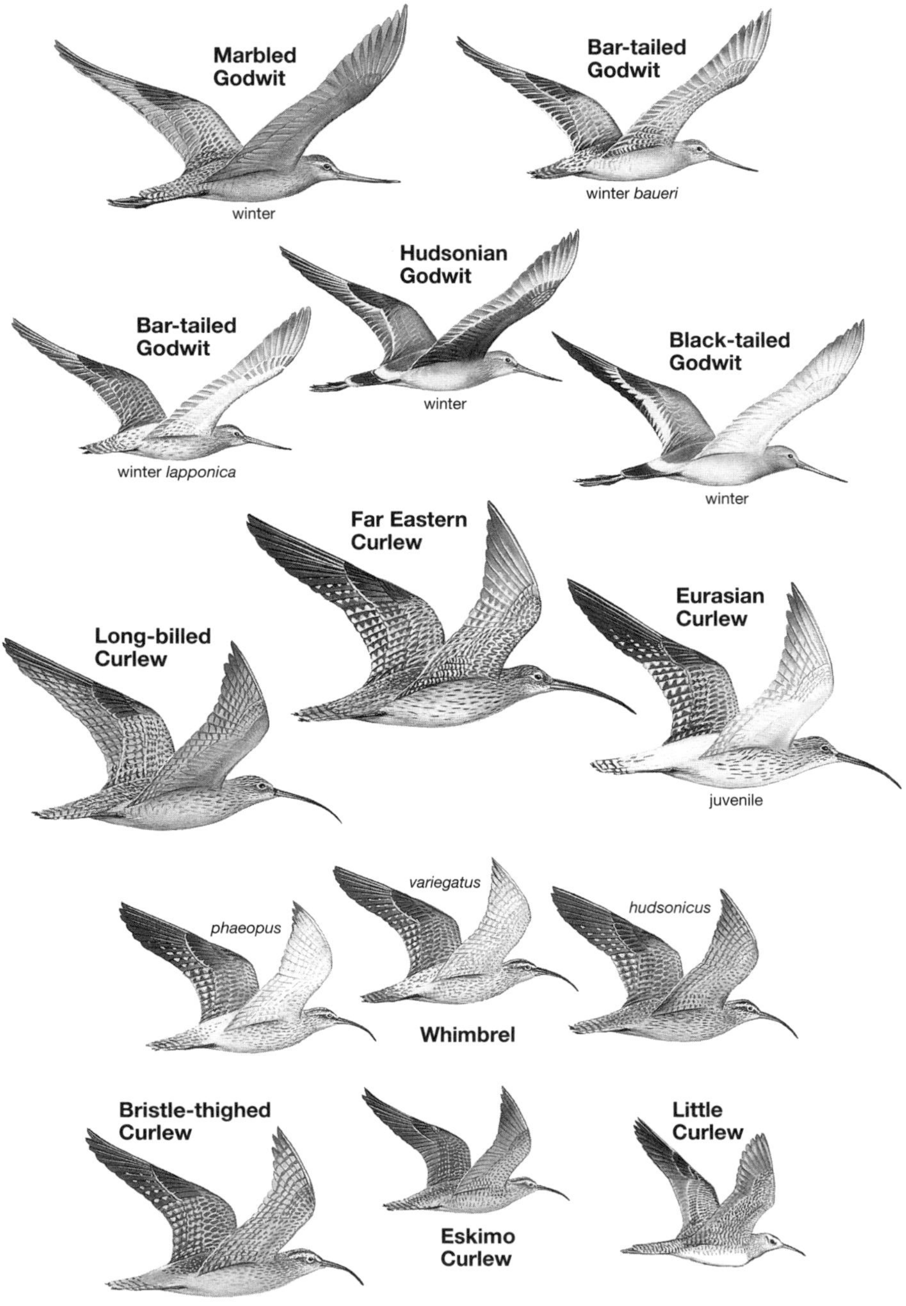
Marbled Godwit
winter
Bar-tailed Godwit
winter baueri
Hudsonian Godwit
winter
Bar-tailed Godwit
winter lapponica
Black-tailed Godwit
winter
Far Eastern Curlew
Eurasian Curlew
juvenile
Long-billed Curlew
variegatus
phaeopus
hudsonicus
Whimbrel
Bristle-thighed Curlew
Eskimo Curlew
Little Curlew

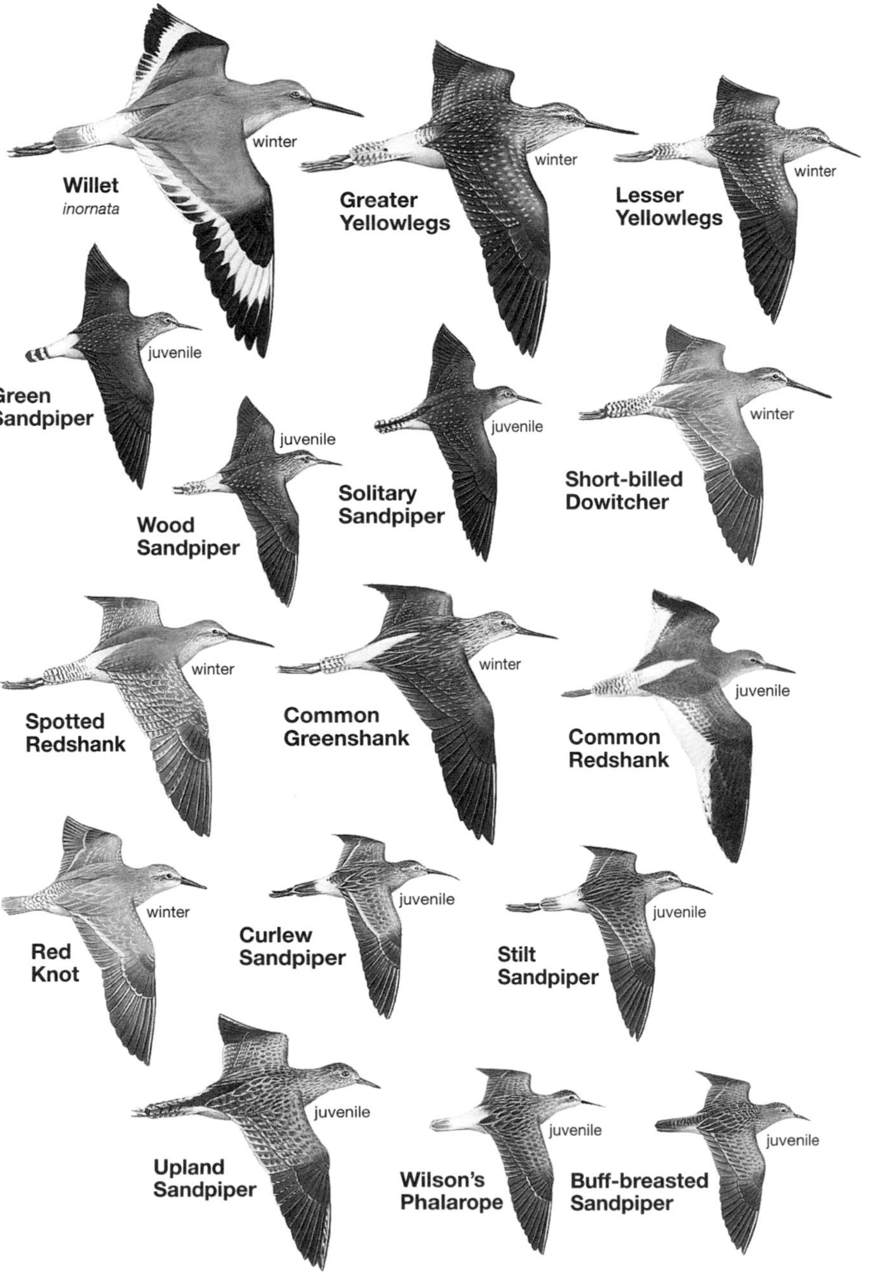
Willet
inornata
winter
Greater Yellowlegs
winter
Lesser Yellowlegs
winter
Green Sandpiper
juvenile
Wood Sandpiper
juvenile
Solitary Sandpiper
juvenile
Short-billed Dowitcher
winter
Spotted Redshank
winter
Common Greenshank
winter
Common Redshank
juvenile
Red Knot
winter
Curlew Sandpiper
juvenile
Stilt Sandpiper
juvenile
Upland Sandpiper
juvenile
Wilson's Phalarope
juvenile
Buff-breasted Sandpiper
juvenile

Shorebirds in Flight

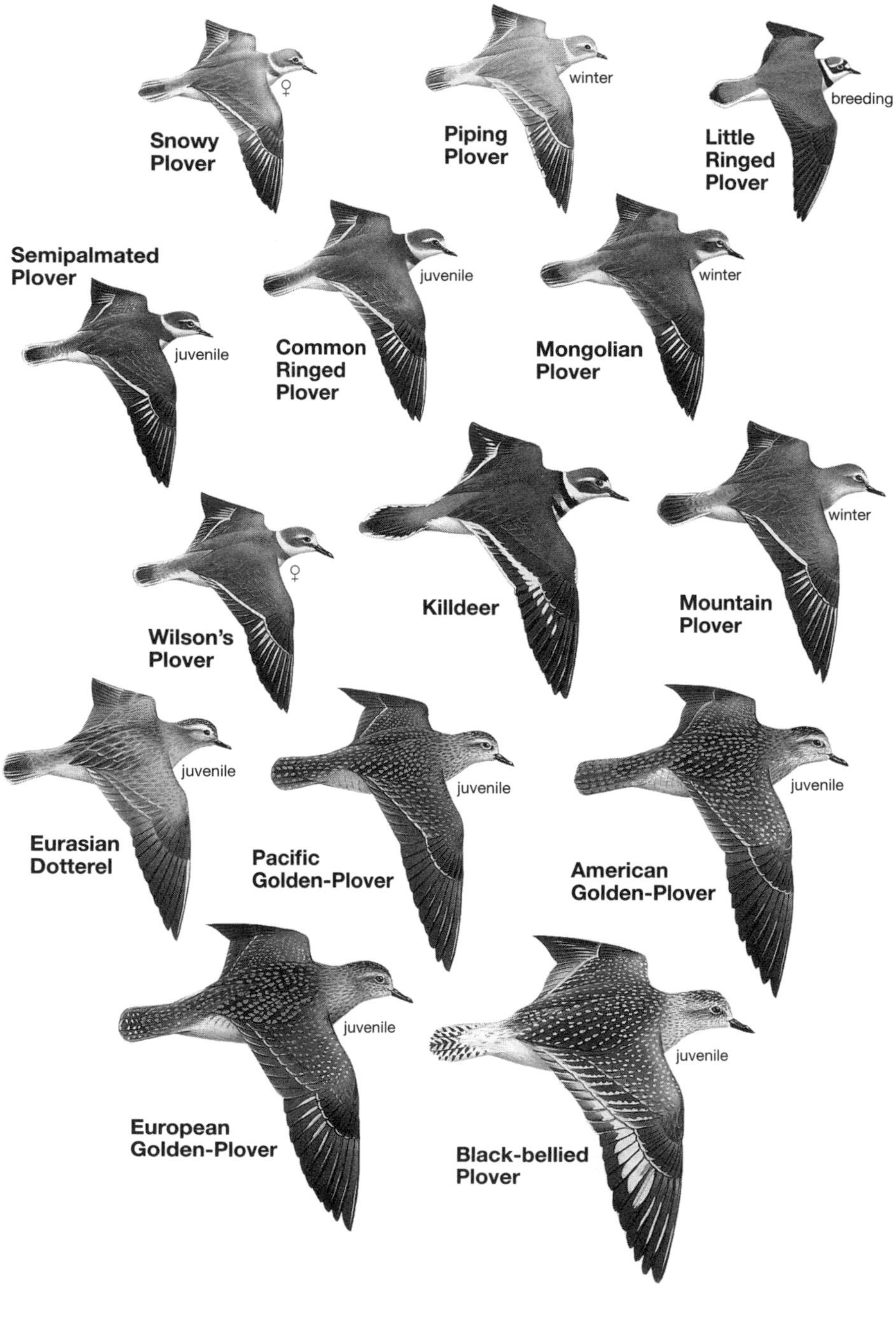
Snowy Plover
♀
Piping Plover
winter
Little Ringed Plover
breeding
Semipalmated Plover
juvenile
Common Ringed Plover
juvenile
Mongolian Plover
winter
Wilson's Plover
♀
Killdeer
Mountain Plover
winter
Eurasian Dotterel
juvenile
Pacific Golden-Plover
juvenile
American Golden-Plover
juvenile
European Golden-Plover
juvenile
Black-bellied Plover
juvenile

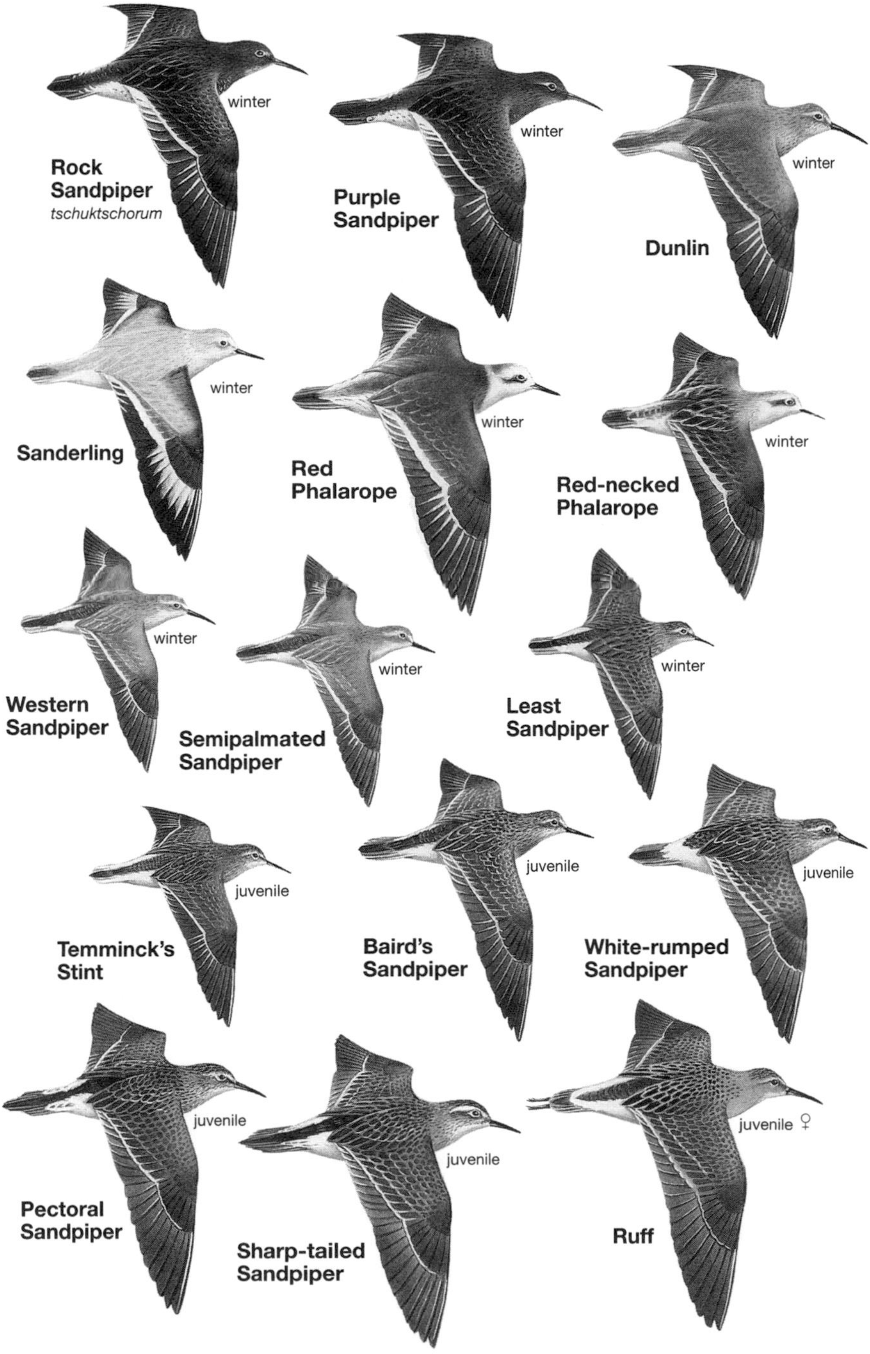
Rock Sandpiper
tschuktschorum
winter
Purple Sandpiper
winter
Dunlin
winter
Sanderling
winter
Red Phalarope
winter
Red-necked Phalarope
winter
Western Sandpiper
winter
Semipalmated Sandpiper
winter
Least Sandpiper
winter
Temminck's Stint
juvenile
Baird's Sandpiper
juvenile
White-rumped Sandpiper
juvenile
Pectoral Sandpiper
juvenile
Sharp-tailed Sandpiper
juvenile
Ruff
juvenile ♀

Gulls, Terns, Skimmers (Family Laridae)

Heermann's Gull *Larus heermanni*

DATE LOCATION

Franklin's Gull *Larus pipixcan*

DATE LOCATION

Laughing Gull *Larus atricilla*

DATE LOCATION

Heermann's Gull
breeding adult
winter adult
2nd winter
1st winter
breeding adult
breeding adult
winter adult
1st winter
breeding adult
1st summer
Franklin's Gull
breeding adult
2nd winter
breeding adult
winter adult
1st winter
Laughing Gull
juvenile

Bonaparte's Gull *Larus philadelphia*

DATE LOCATION

Black-headed Gull *Larus ridibundus*

DATE LOCATION

Little Gull *Larus minutus*

DATE LOCATION

Ross's Gull *Rhodostethia rosea*

DATE LOCATION

Bonaparte's Gull
breeding adult
winter adult
1st winter
winter adult
breeding adult
1st summer
winter adult
1st winter
winter adult
Black-headed Gull
breeding adult
1st winter
Little Gull
breeding adult
winter adult
winter adult
Ross's Gull
1st winter
breeding adult

Ring-billed Gull *Larus delawarensis*

DATE LOCATION

Mew Gull *Larus canus*

DATE LOCATION

Ring-billed Gull
breeding adult
2nd winter
winter adult
breeding adult
1st winter tail
juvenile
1st winter
1st winter tail
winter adult
2nd winter
breeding adults
juvenile
Mew Gull
brachyrhynchus
1st winter
kamtschatschensis
winter adult
1st winter
winter adult
canus
1st winter
adult kamtschatschensis
adult canus

California Gull *Larus californicus*

DATE LOCATION

Black-tailed Gull *Larus crassirostris*

DATE LOCATION

Belcher's Gull *Larus belcheri*

DATE LOCATION

Kelp Gull *Larus dominicanus*

DATE LOCATION

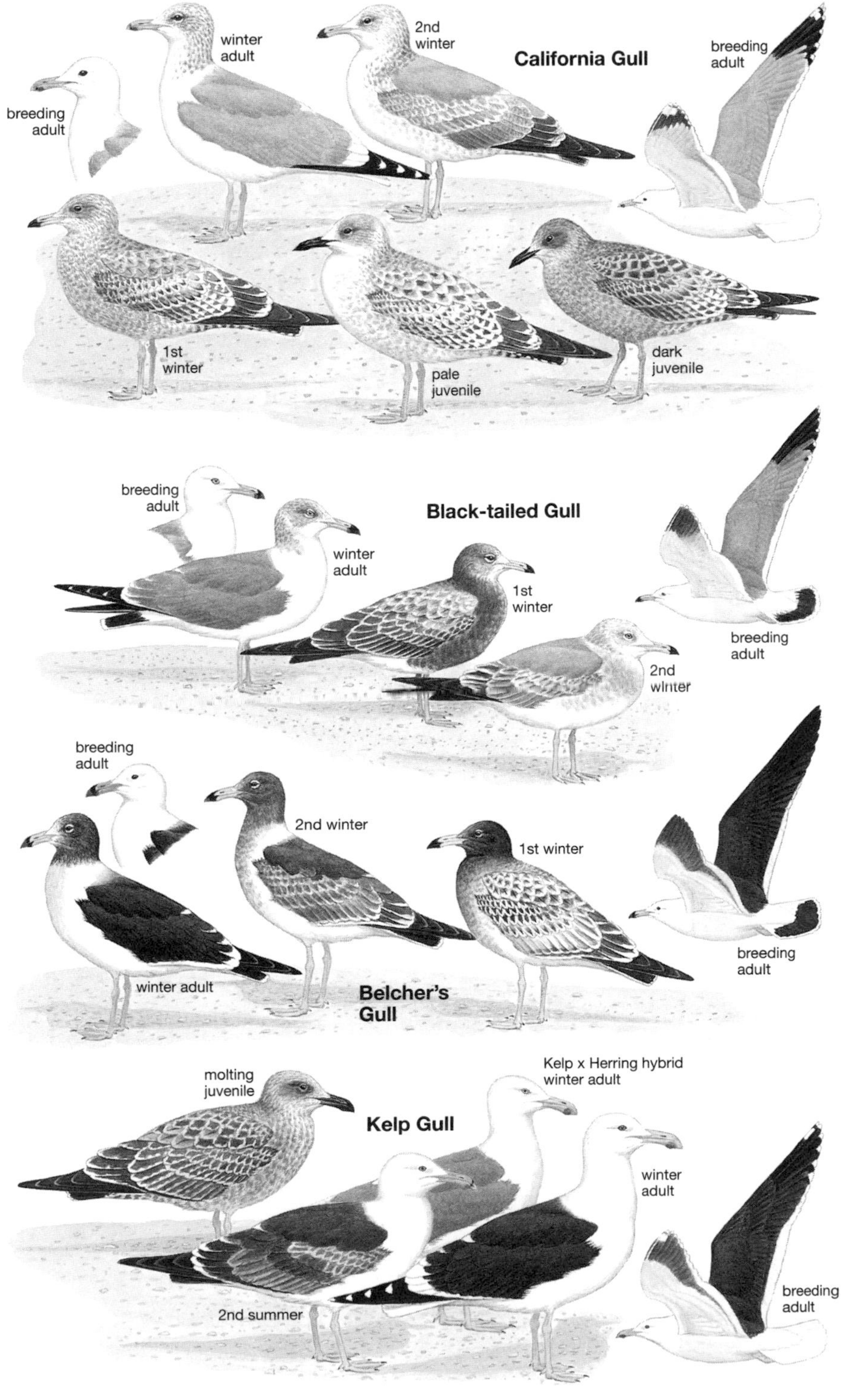
California Gull
breeding adult
winter adult
2nd winter
breeding adult
1st winter
pale juvenile
dark juvenile
Black-tailed Gull
breeding adult
winter adult
1st winter
breeding adult
2nd winter
breeding adult
2nd winter
1st winter
breeding adult
winter adult
Belcher's Gull
Kelp Gull
molting juvenile
Kelp x Herring hybrid winter adult
winter adult
breeding adult
2nd summer

Herring Gull *Larus argentatus*

DATE LOCATION

Yellow-legged Gull *Larus cachinnans*

DATE LOCATION

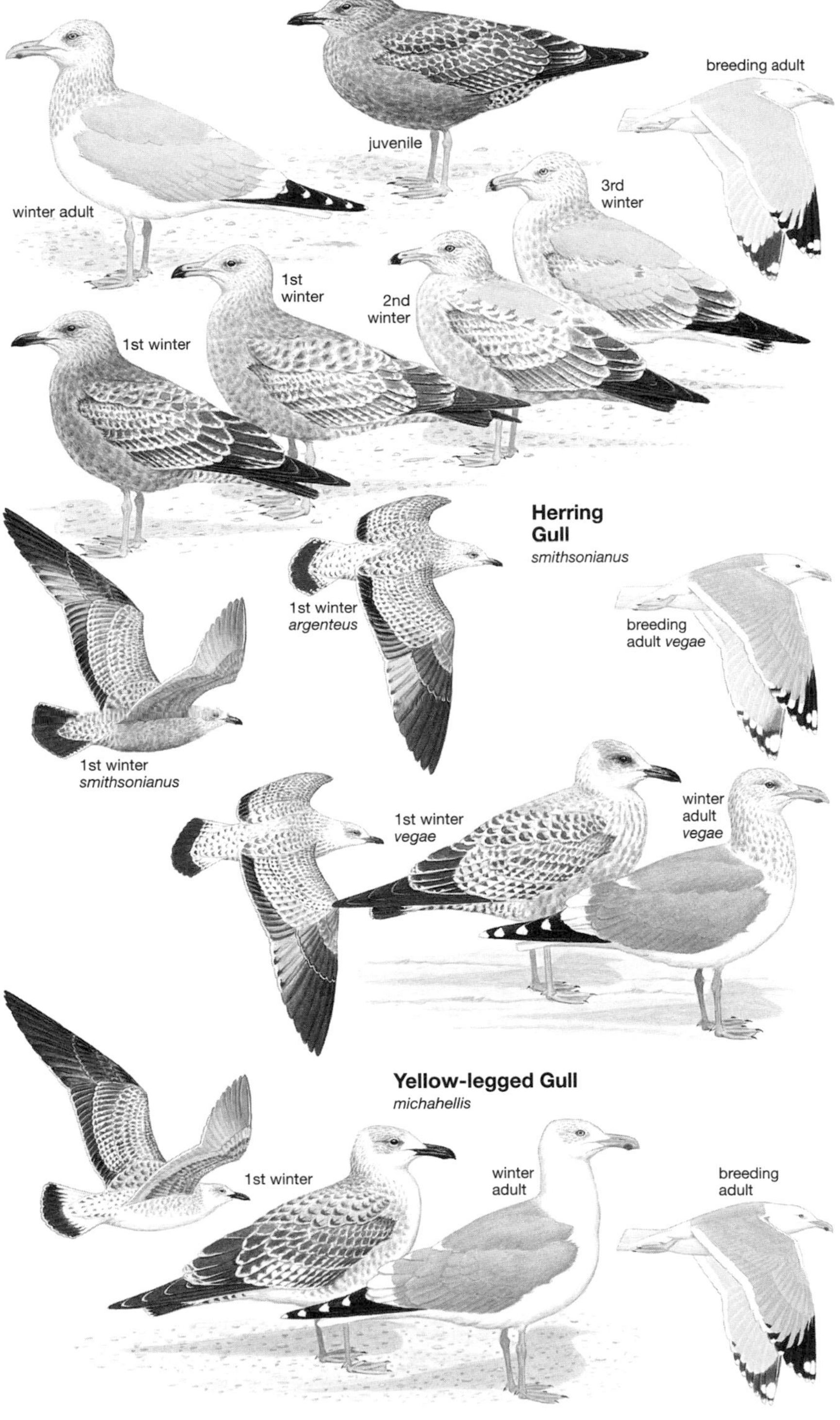
winter adult
juvenile
breeding adult
3rd winter
1st winter
2nd winter
1st winter
Herring Gull
smithsonianus
1st winter argenteus
breeding adult vegae
1st winter smithsonianus
1st winter vegae
winter adult vegae
Yellow-legged Gull
michahellis
1st winter
winter adult
breeding adult

Glaucous Gull *Larus hyperboreus*

DATE LOCATION

Iceland Gull *Larus glaucoides*

DATE LOCATION

Thayer's Gull *Larus thayeri*

DATE LOCATION

winter adult
winter
adult
2nd
winter
breeding
adult
1st winter
Glaucous Gull
1st winter

Iceland
Gull
kumlieni
breeding
adult ♂
glaucoides
winter
adult ♀
winter adult
1st winter ♂
1st winter ♀
glaucoides
2nd winter ♀

winter adult
2nd
winter
winter
adult
breeding
adult
Thayer's
Gull
1st winter
1st winter

Yellow-footed Gull *Larus livens*

DATE LOCATION

Western Gull *Larus occidentalis*

DATE LOCATION

Glaucous-winged Gull *Larus glaucescens*

DATE LOCATION

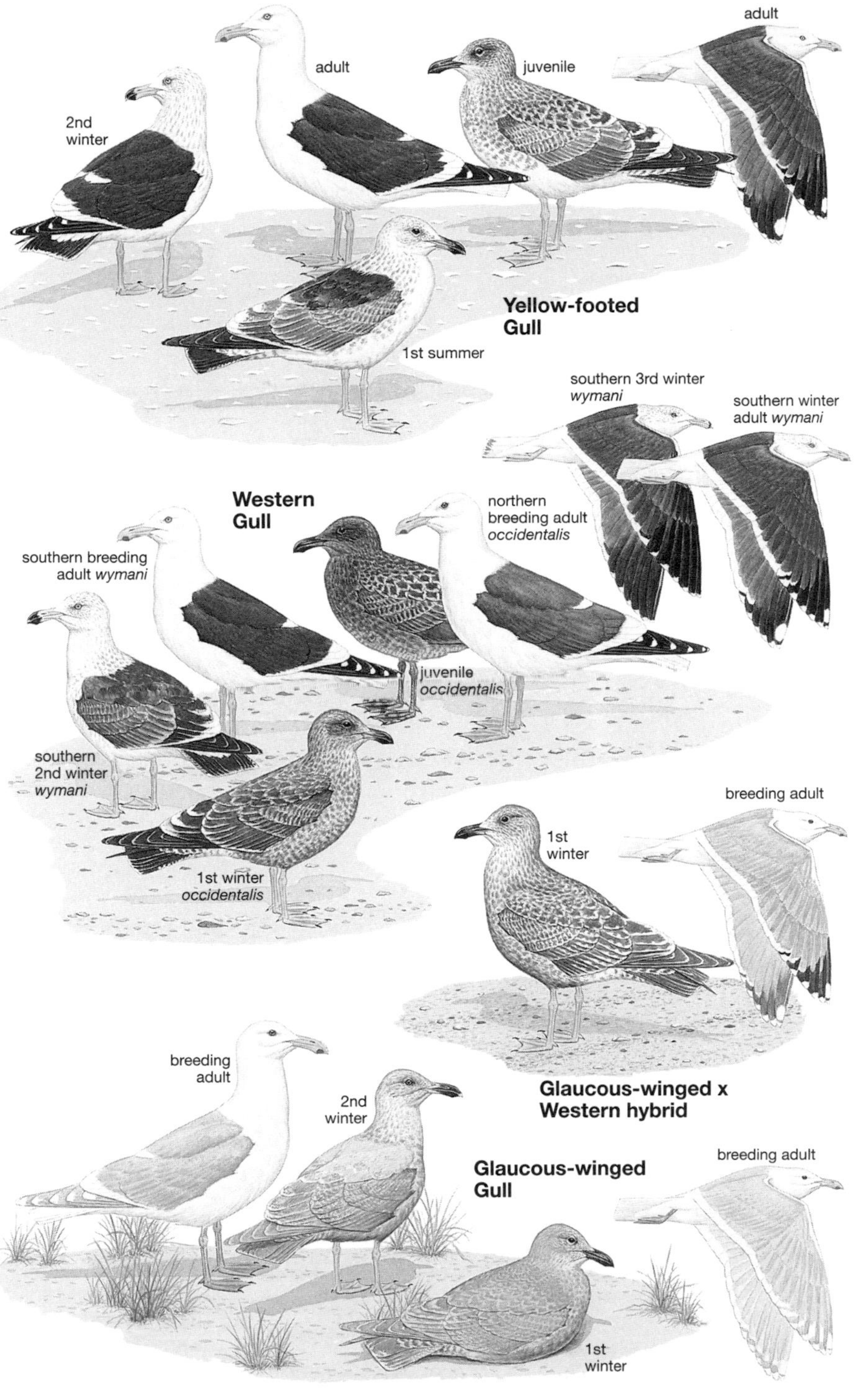

adult
juvenile
adult
2nd winter
Yellow-footed Gull
1st summer
southern 3rd winter *wymani*
southern winter adult *wymani*
Western Gull
northern breeding adult *occidentalis*
southern breeding adult *wymani*
juvenile *occidentalis*
southern 2nd winter *wymani*
1st winter *occidentalis*
breeding adult
1st winter
Glaucous-winged x Western hybrid
breeding adult
2nd winter
Glaucous-winged Gull
breeding adult
1st winter

Slaty-backed Gull *Larus schistisagus*

DATE LOCATION

Lesser Black-backed Gull *Larus fuscus*

DATE LOCATION

Great Black-backed Gull *Larus marinus*

DATE LOCATION

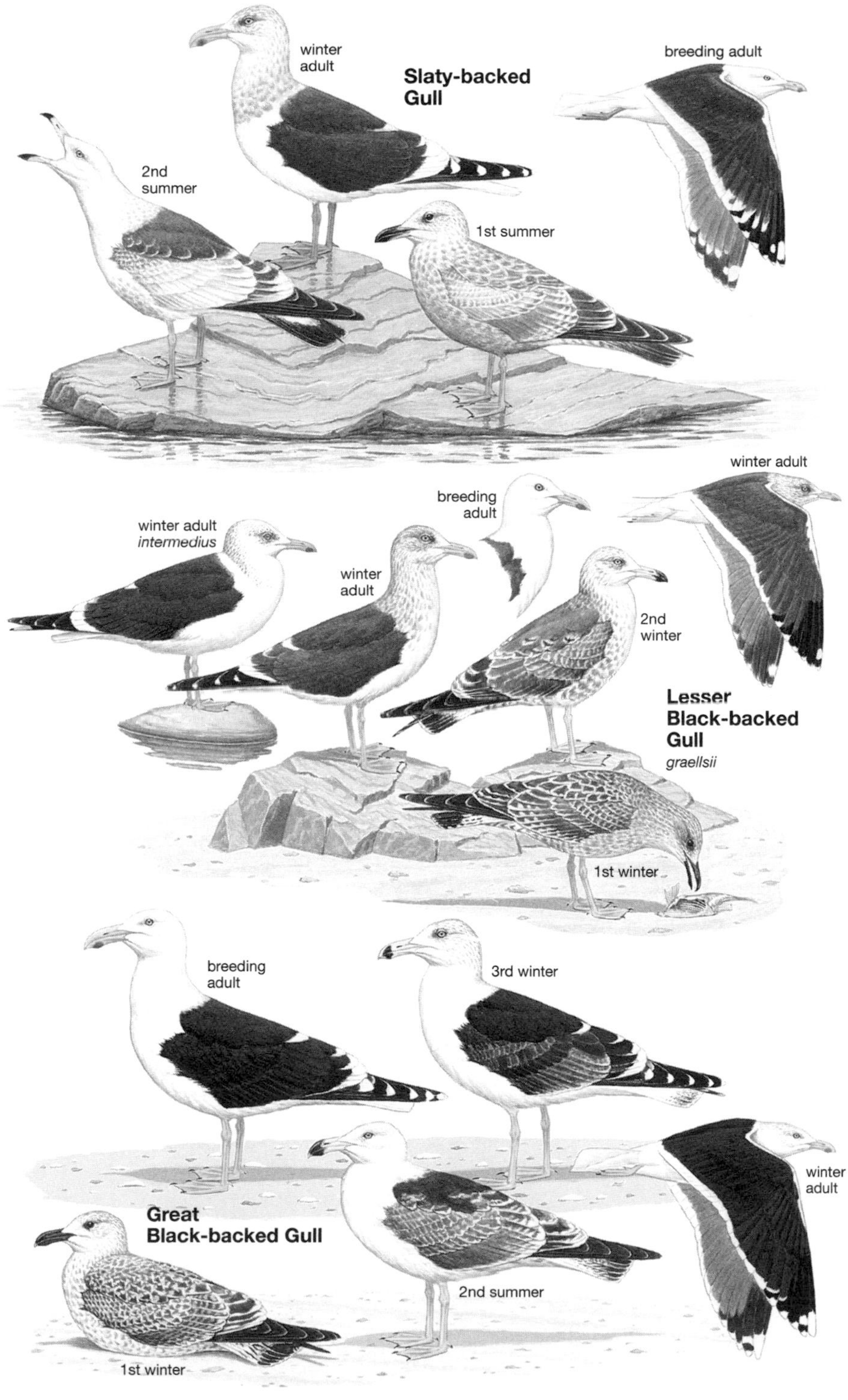

Slaty-backed Gull
winter adult
breeding adult
2nd summer
1st summer
winter adult
breeding adult
winter adult
intermedius
winter adult
2nd winter
Lesser Black-backed Gull
graellsii
1st winter
breeding adult
3rd winter
winter adult
Great Black-backed Gull
2nd summer
1st winter

Black-legged Kittiwake *Rissa tridactyla*

DATE LOCATION

Red-legged Kittiwake *Rissa brevirostris*

DATE LOCATION

Sabine's Gull *Xema sabini*

DATE LOCATION

Ivory Gull *Pagophila eburnea*

DATE LOCATION

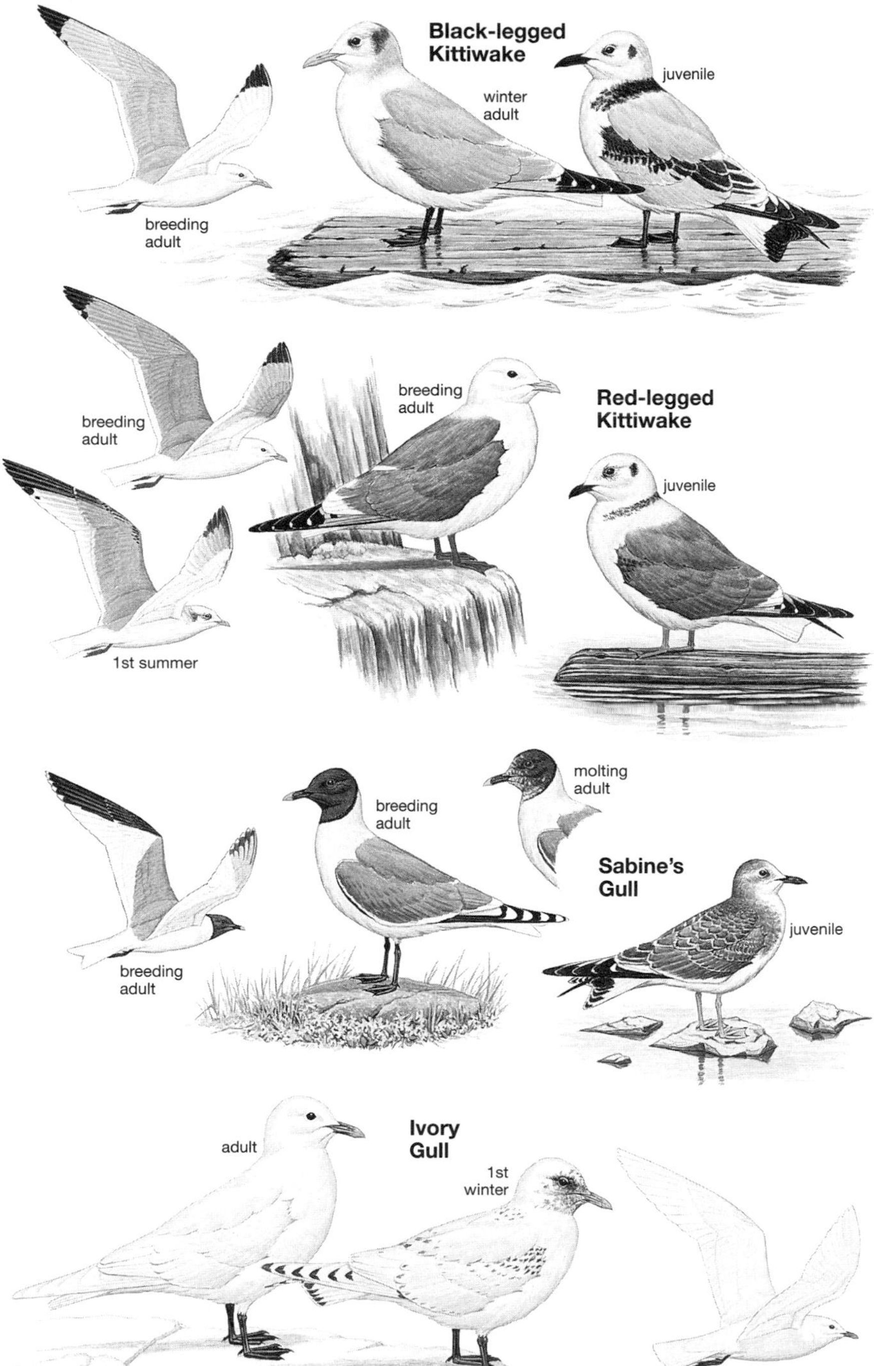
Black-legged Kittiwake
breeding adult
winter adult
juvenile
Red-legged Kittiwake
breeding adult
breeding adult
1st summer
juvenile
Sabine's Gull
breeding adult
breeding adult
molting adult
juvenile
Ivory Gull
adult
1st winter
adult

Immature Gulls in Flight

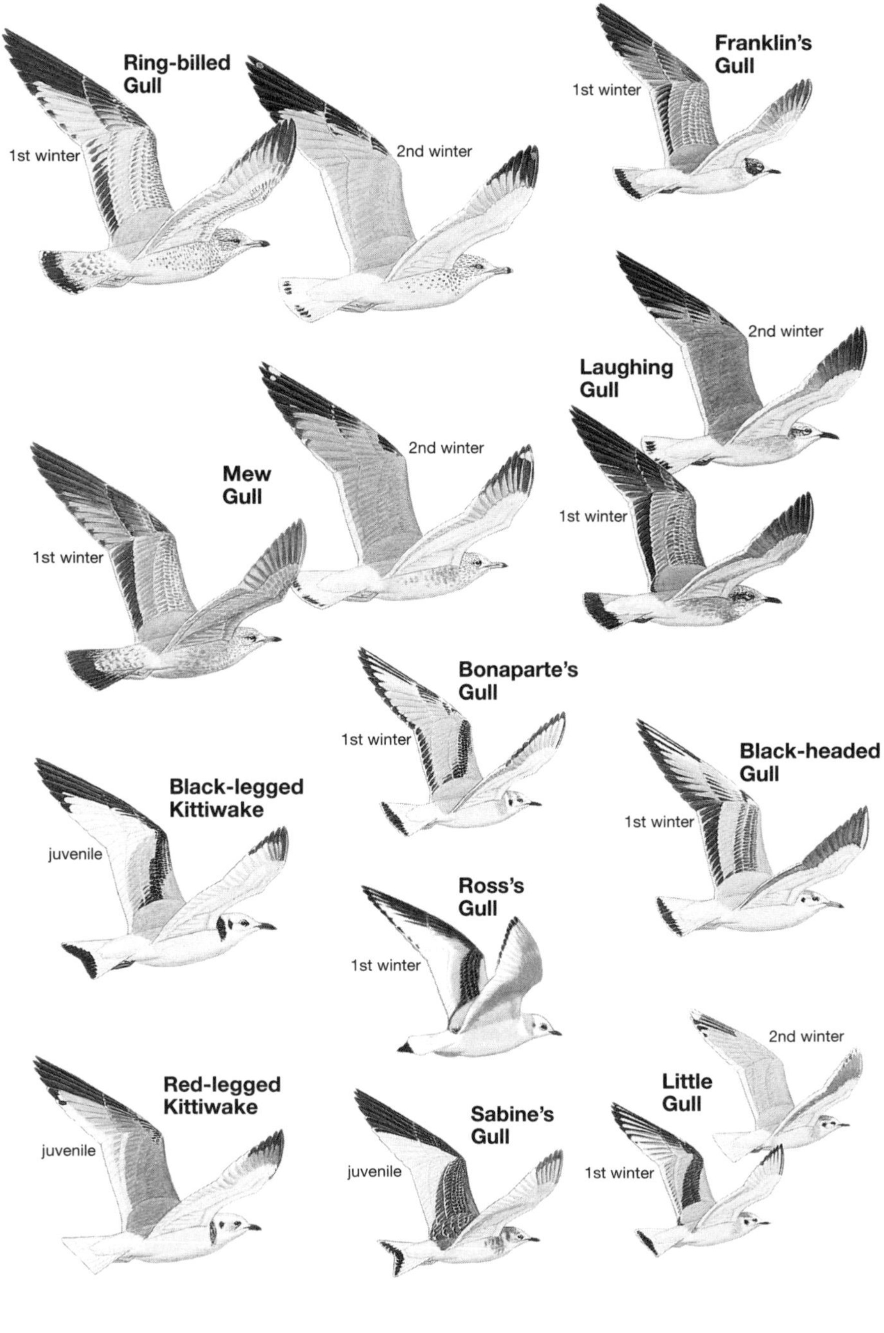

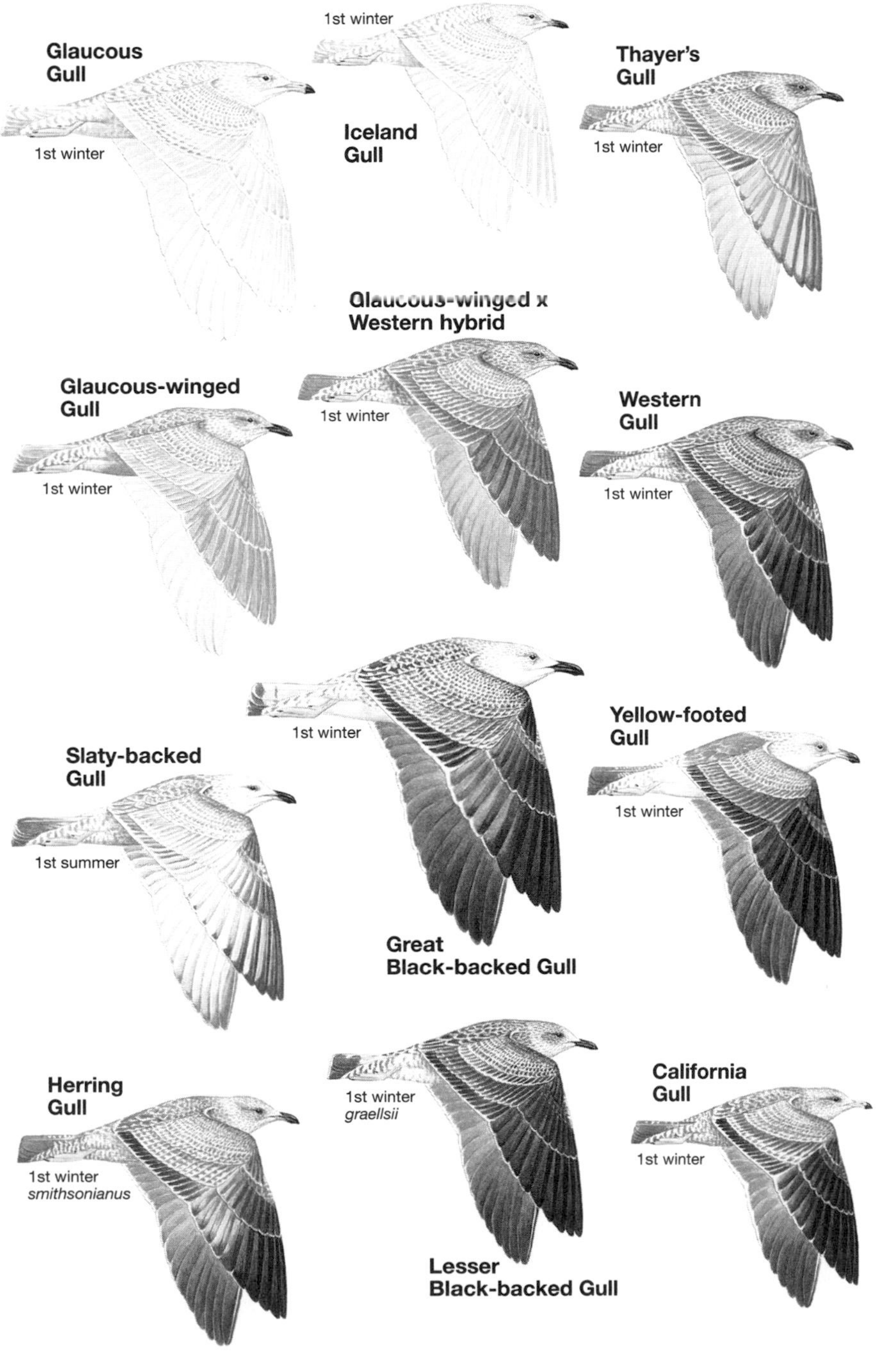
1st winter
Glaucous Gull
1st winter
Iceland Gull
Thayer's Gull
1st winter
Glaucous-winged x Western hybrid
1st winter
Glaucous-winged Gull
1st winter
Western Gull
1st winter
1st winter
Yellow-footed Gull
1st winter
Slaty-backed Gull
1st summer
Great Black-backed Gull
Herring Gull
1st winter
smithsonianus
1st winter
graellsii
Lesser Black-backed Gull
California Gull
1st winter

Terns

Sandwich Tern *Thalasseus sandvicensis*

DATE LOCATION

Elegant Tern *Thalasseus elegans*

DATE LOCATION

Royal Tern *Thalasseus maximus*

DATE LOCATION

Caspian Tern *Hydroprogne caspia*

DATE LOCATION

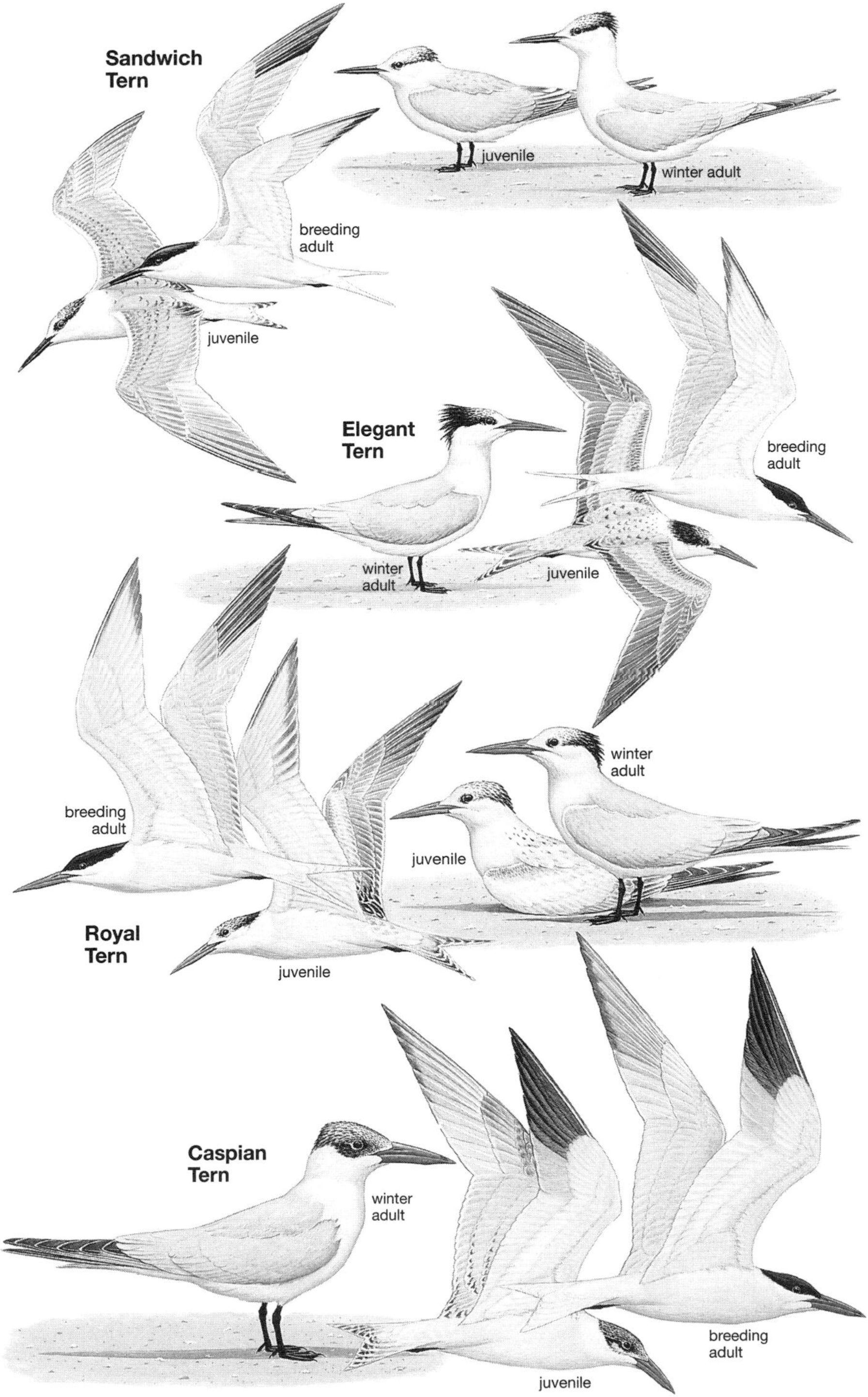
Sandwich Tern
juvenile
winter adult
breeding adult
juvenile
Elegant Tern
breeding adult
winter adult
juvenile
winter adult
breeding adult
juvenile
Royal Tern
juvenile
Caspian Tern
winter adult
breeding adult
juvenile

Roseate Tern *Sterna dougallii*

DATE LOCATION

Forster's Tern *Sterna forsteri*

DATE LOCATION

Gull-billed Tern *Gelochelidon nilotica*

DATE LOCATION

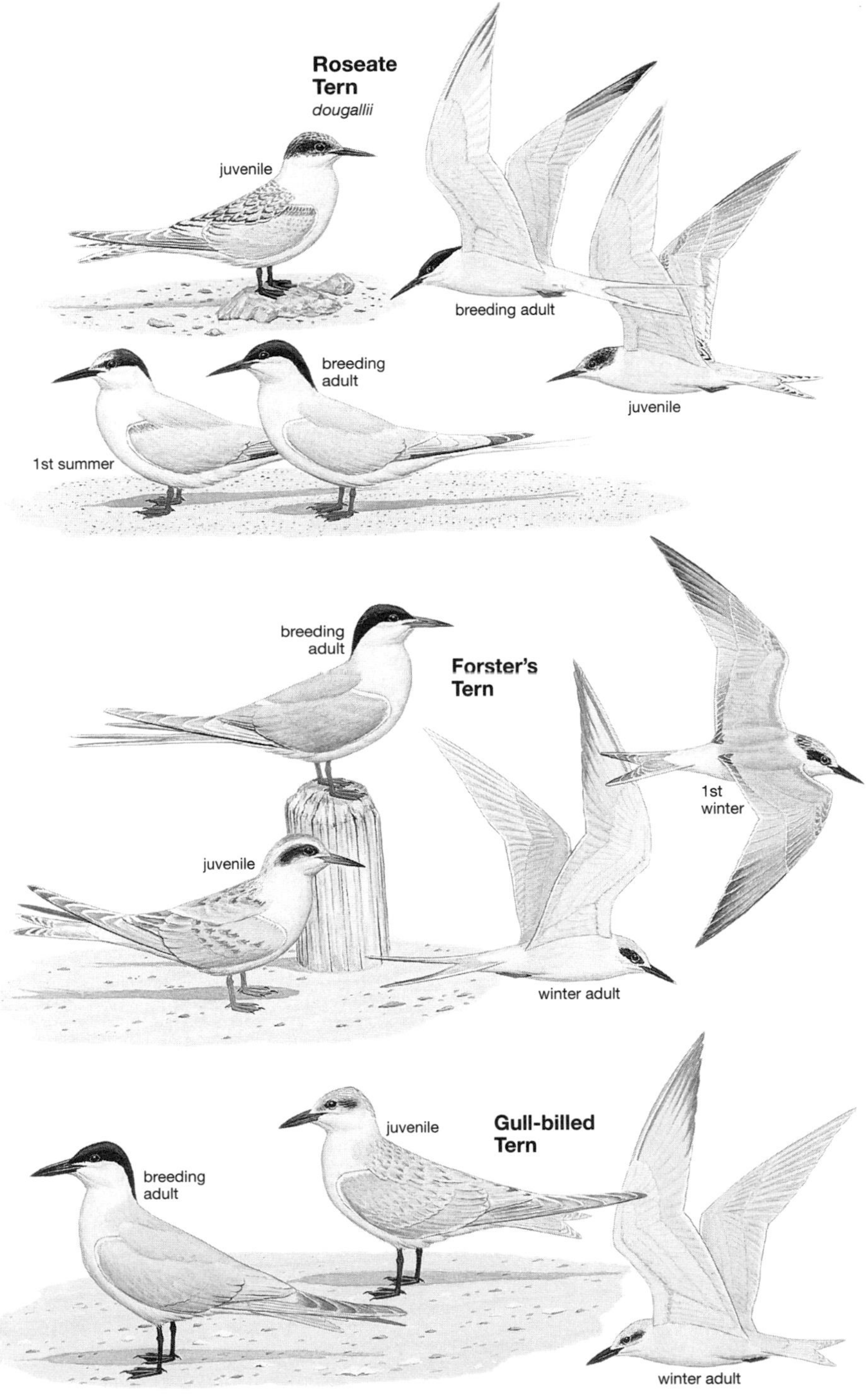
Roseate Tern
dougallii
juvenile
breeding adult
breeding adult
1st summer
juvenile
breeding adult
Forster's Tern
1st winter
juvenile
winter adult
juvenile
Gull-billed Tern
breeding adult
winter adult

Common Tern *Sterna hirundo*

DATE LOCATION

Arctic Tern *Sterna paradisaea*

DATE LOCATION

Aleutian Tern *Onychoprion aleuticus*

DATE LOCATION

Common Tern
hirundo
breeding adult
1st summer
juvenile
2nd summer
breeding adult
longipennis
1st fall
breeding adult
Arctic Tern
juvenile
1st summer
breeding adult
breeding adult
juvenile
Aleutian Tern
juvenile
breeding adult

Least Tern *Sternula antillarum*

DATE LOCATION

Black Tern *Chlidonias niger*

DATE LOCATION

White-winged Tern *Chlidonias leucopterus*

DATE LOCATION

Least
Tern
antillarum
breeding
adult
juvenile
breeding adult
1st summer

breeding adult
molting
fall adult
juvenile
Black
Tern
surinamensis
breeding adult
juvenile

White-winged
Tern
winter
adult
juvenile
breeding adult
molting
adult

Bridled Tern *Onychoprion anaethetus*

DATE LOCATION

Sooty Tern *Onychoprion fuscata*

DATE LOCATION

Black Noddy *Anous minutus*

DATE LOCATION

Brown Noddy *Anous stolidus*

DATE LOCATION

Large-billed Tern *Phaetusa simplex*

DATE LOCATION

Black Skimmer *Rynchops niger*

DATE LOCATION

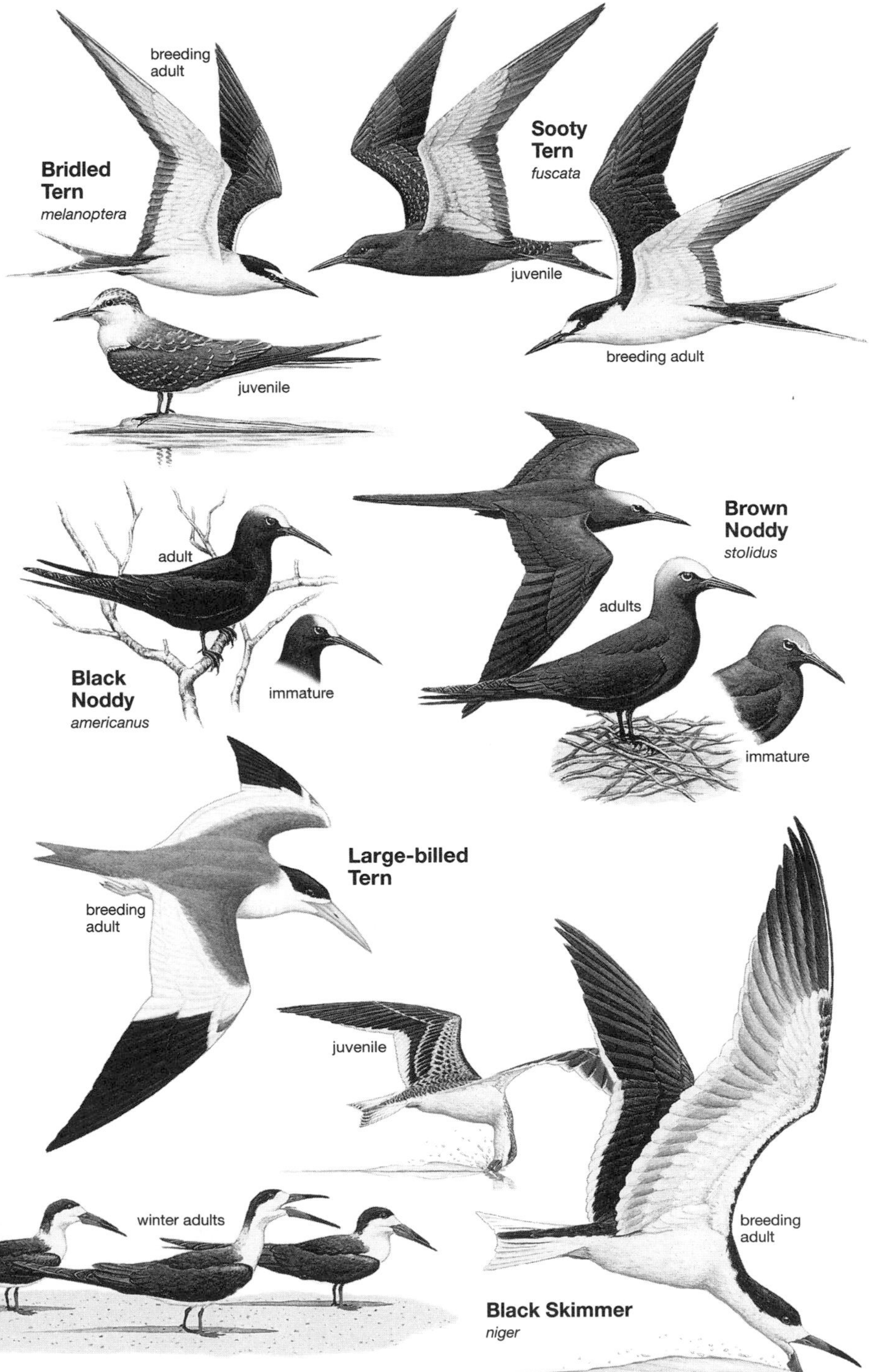

Bridled Tern
melanoptera
breeding adult
juvenile
Sooty Tern
fuscata
juvenile
breeding adult
Black Noddy
americanus
adult
immature
Brown Noddy
stolidus
adults
immature
Large-billed Tern
breeding adult
juvenile
Black Skimmer
niger
winter adults
breeding adult

Skuas, Jaegers (Family Stercorariidae)

Great Skua *Stercorarius skua*

DATE LOCATION

South Polar Skua *Stercorarius maccormicki*

DATE LOCATION

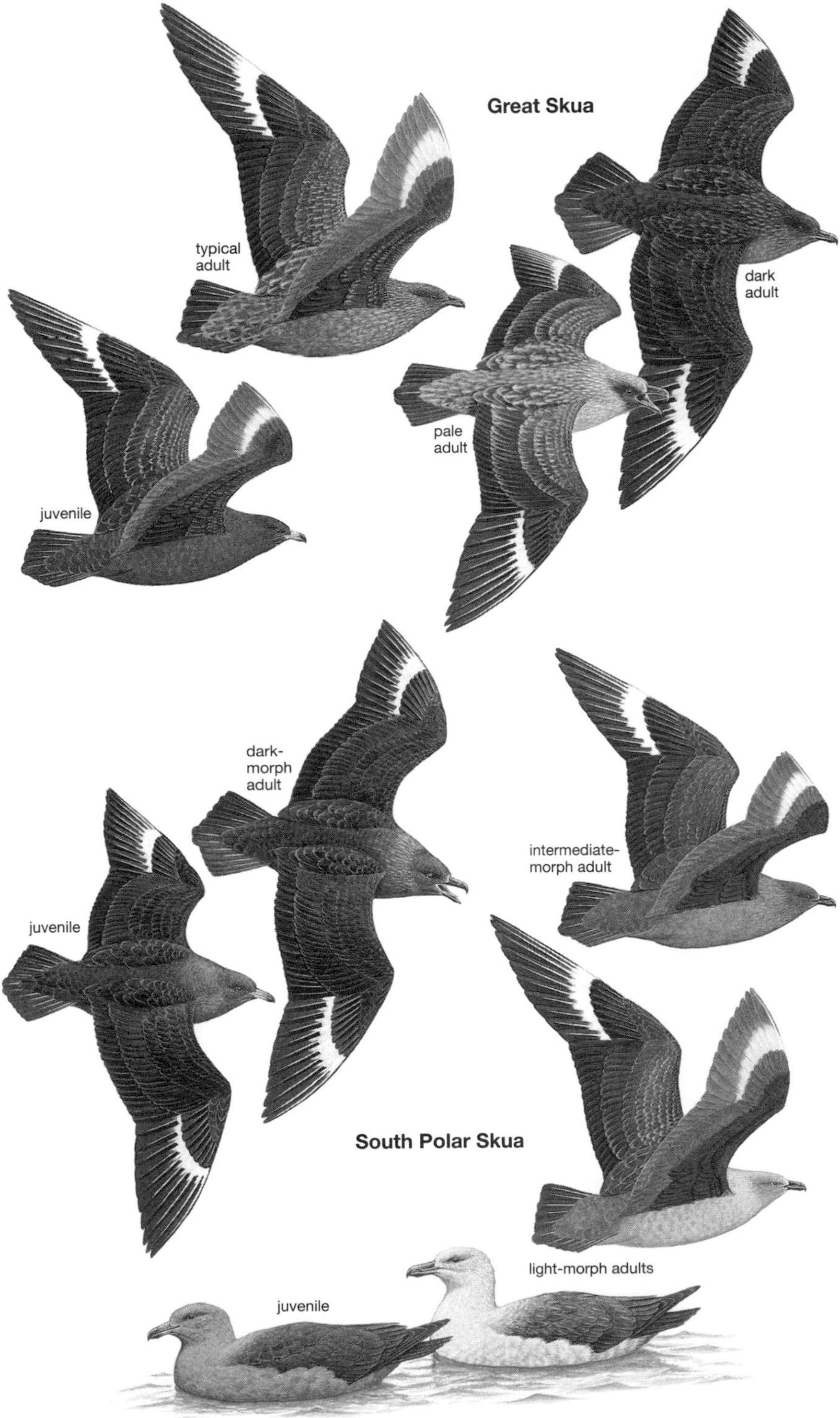

Great Skua
typical adult
dark adult
pale adult
juvenile
dark-morph adult
intermediate-morph adult
juvenile
South Polar Skua
light-morph adults
juvenile

Jaegers

Pomarine Jaeger *Stercorarius pomarinus*

DATE LOCATION

Parasitic Jaeger *Stercorarius parasiticus*

DATE LOCATION

Long-tailed Jaeger *Stercorarius longicaudus*

DATE LOCATION

Pomarine Jaeger
dark-morph breeding adult
light-morph breeding adult
light-morph 1st summer
juvenile
Parasitic Jaeger
dark-morph breeding adult
light-morph breeding adult
light-morph juveniles
light-morph 1st summer
Long-tailed Jaeger
light-morph juvenile
dark-morph juvenile
breeding adult
1st summer

Auks, Murres, Puffins (Family Alcidae)

Dovekie *Alle alle*

DATE LOCATION

Common Murre *Uria aalge*

DATE LOCATION

Thick-billed Murre *Uria lomvia*

DATE LOCATION

Razorbill *Alca torda*

DATE LOCATION

Dovekie
breeding adult
winter
breeding adult
winter
Common Murre
bridled breeding adult
breeding adult
breeding adult
winter
juvenile
Thick-billed Murre
Pacific winter *arra*
Atlantic breeding adults *lomvia*
Razorbill
immature
breeding adult
winter adult
breeding adult

Black Guillemot *Cepphus grylle*

DATE LOCATION

Pigeon Guillemot *Cepphus columba*

DATE LOCATION

Long-billed Murrelet *Brachyramphus perdix*

DATE LOCATION

Marbled Murrelet *Brachyramphus marmoratus*

DATE LOCATION

Kittlitz's Murrelet *Brachyramphus brevirostris*

DATE LOCATION

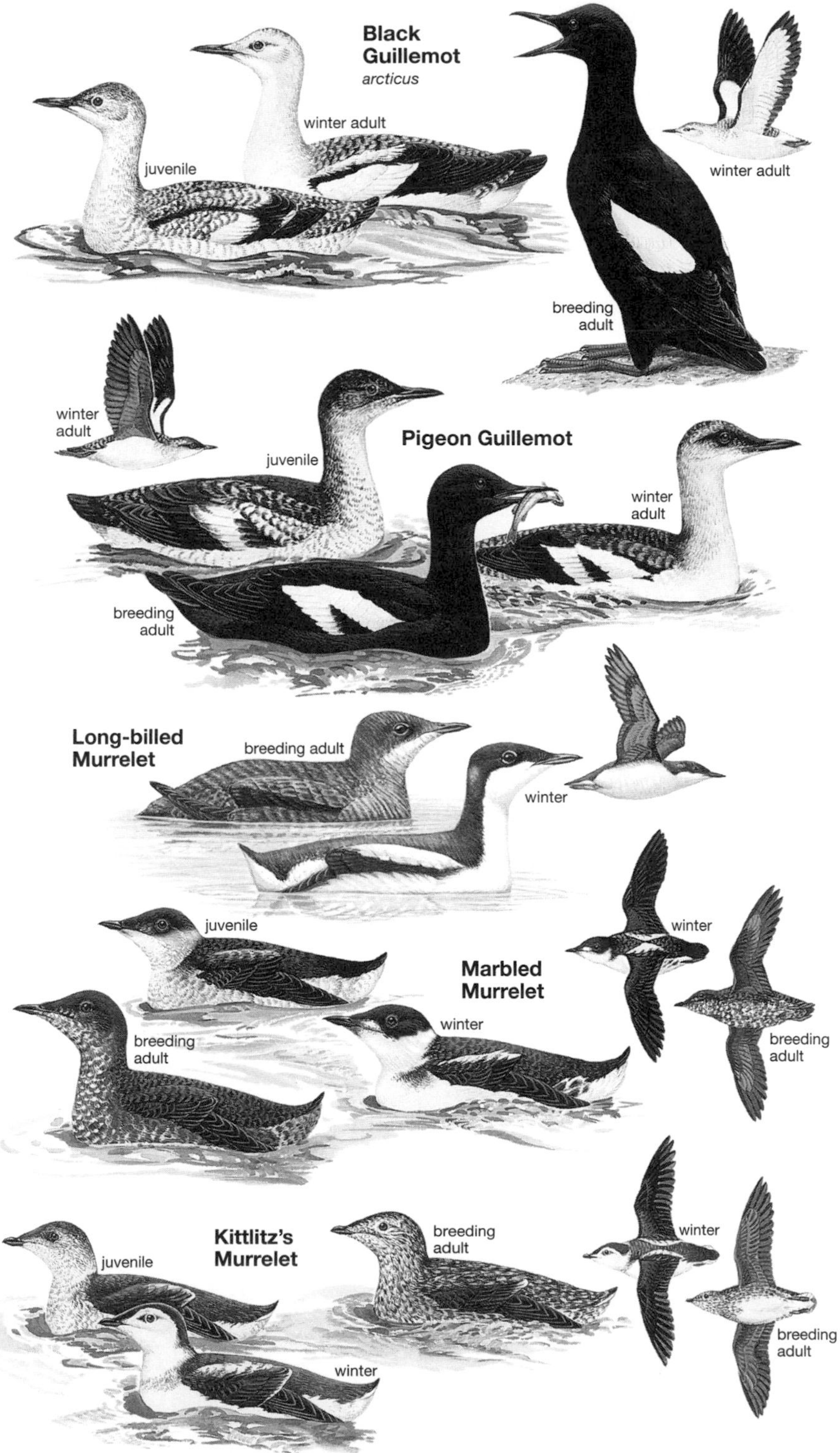

Black Guillemot
arcticus
winter adult
juvenile
winter adult
breeding adult
winter adult
Pigeon Guillemot
juvenile
winter adult
breeding adult
Long-billed Murrelet
breeding adult
winter
juvenile
winter
Marbled Murrelet
winter
breeding adult
breeding adult
Kittlitz's Murrelet
juvenile
breeding adult
winter
breeding adult
winter

Xantus's Murrelet *Synthliboramphus hypoleucus*

DATE LOCATION

Craveri's Murrelet *Synthliboramphus craveri*

DATE LOCATION

Ancient Murrelet *Synthliboramphus antiquus*

DATE LOCATION

Cassin's Auklet *Ptychoramphus aleuticus*

DATE LOCATION

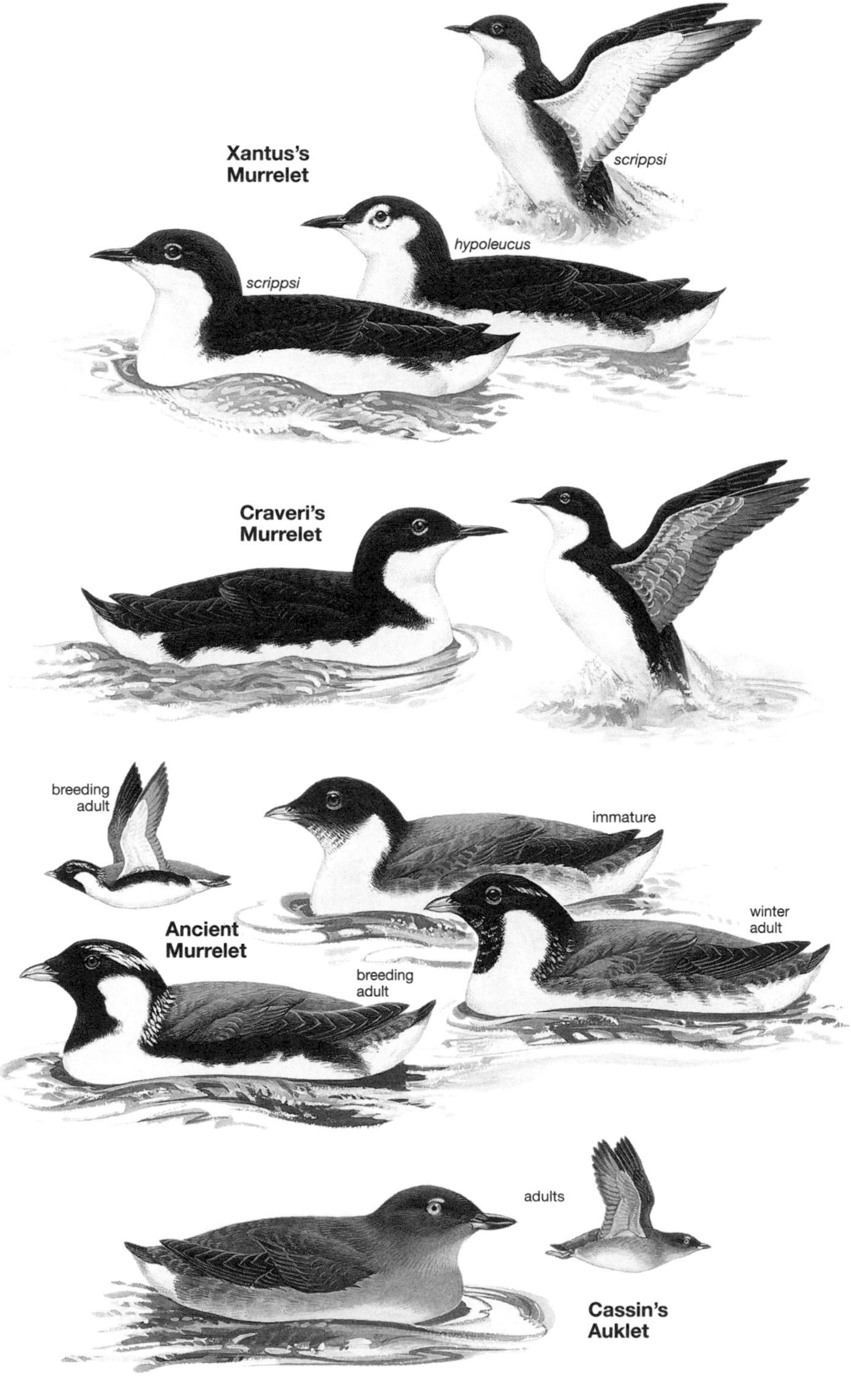
Xantus's Murrelet
scrippsi
hypoleucus
scrippsi
Craveri's Murrelet
breeding adult
immature
Ancient Murrelet
winter adult
breeding adult
adults
Cassin's Auklet

Least Auklet *Aethia pusilla*

DATE LOCATION

Parakeet Auklet *Aethia psittacula*

DATE LOCATION

Whiskered Auklet *Aethia pygmaea*

DATE LOCATION

Crested Auklet *Aethia cristatella*

DATE LOCATION

Least Auklet
light
breeding adults
dark
breeding adults
winter adults
juvenile
Parakeet Auklet
breeding adults
dark
breeding adult
juvenile
winter adults
Whiskered Auklet
breeding adult
winter adult
breeding adults
juvenile
winter adult
Crested Auklet
breeding adult
breeding adult
winter adult
1st summer
juvenile
winter adult

Rhinoceros Auklet *Cerorhinca monocerata*

DATE LOCATION

Atlantic Puffin *Fratercula arctica*

DATE LOCATION

Horned Puffin *Fratercula corniculata*

DATE LOCATION

Tufted Puffin *Fratercula cirrhata*

DATE LOCATION

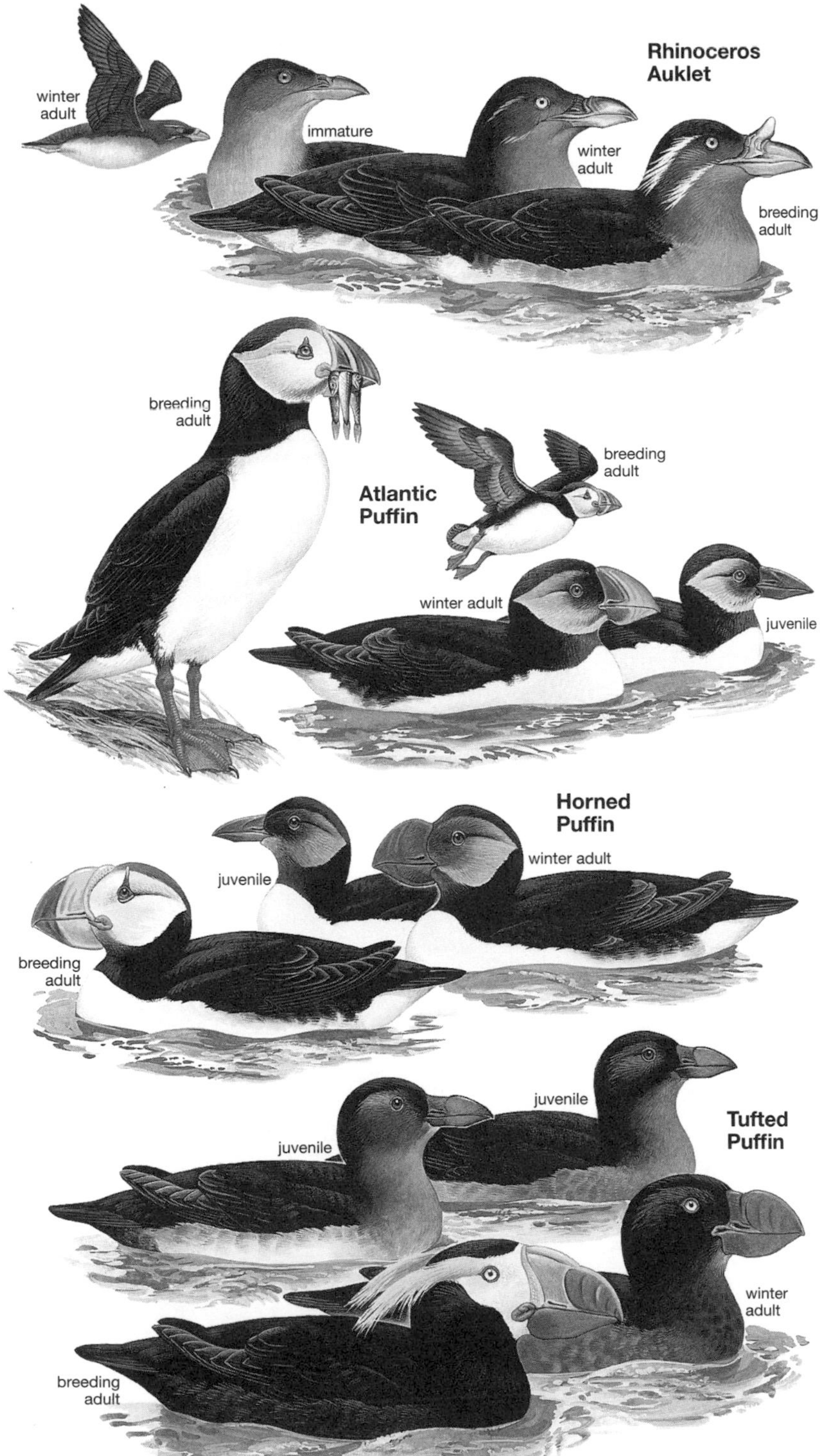

Rhinoceros Auklet
winter adult
immature
winter adult
breeding adult
breeding adult
Atlantic Puffin
breeding adult
winter adult
juvenile
Horned Puffin
juvenile
winter adult
breeding adult
juvenile
juvenile
Tufted Puffin
winter adult
breeding adult

Pigeons, Doves (Family Columbidae)

Band-tailed Pigeon *Patagioenas fasciata*

DATE LOCATION

Red-billed Pigeon *Patagioenas flavirostris*

DATE LOCATION

White-crowned Pigeon *Patagioenas leucocephala*

DATE LOCATION

Rock Pigeon *Columba livia*

DATE LOCATION

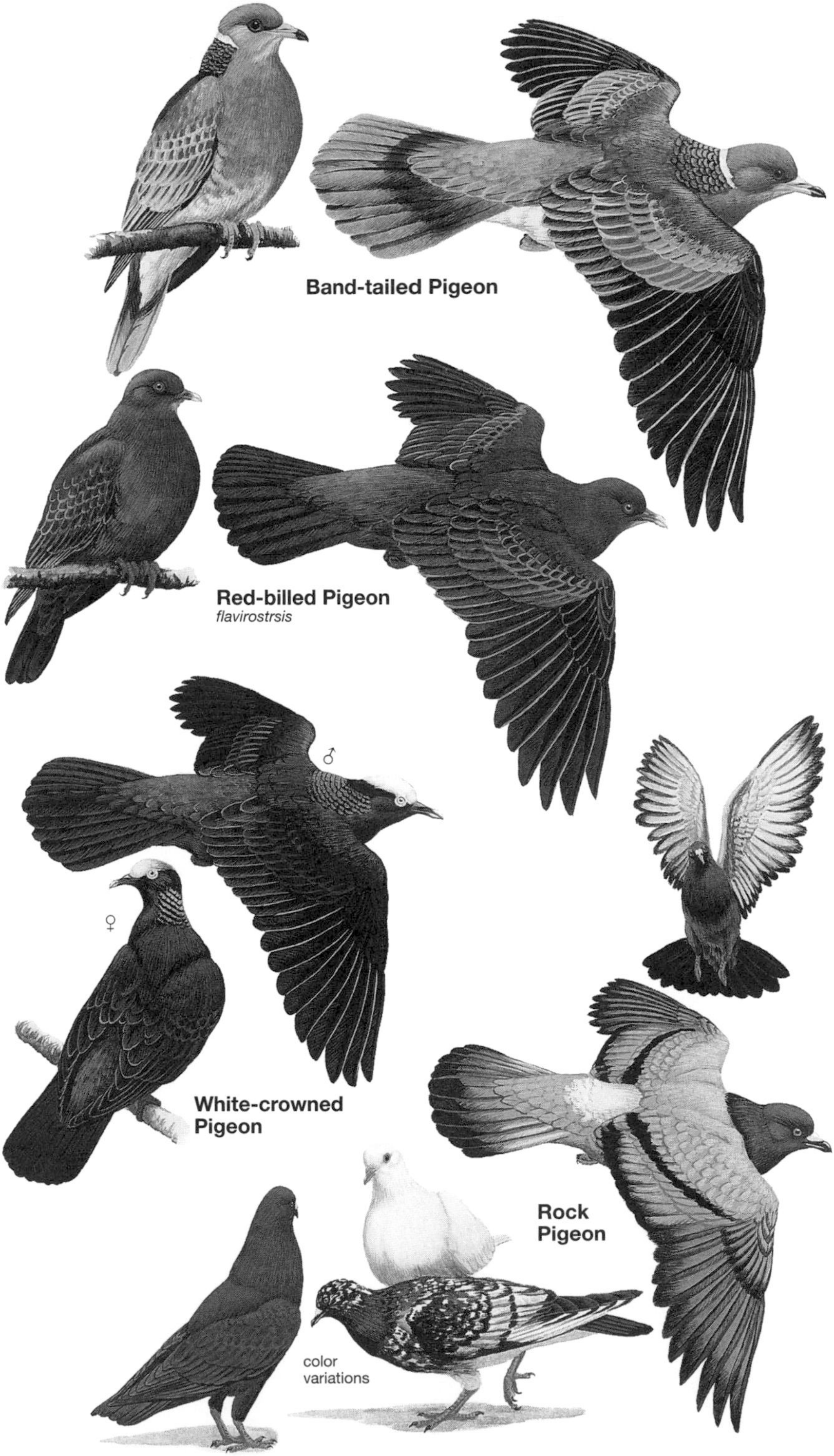
Band-tailed Pigeon
Red-billed Pigeon
flavirostrsis
♂
♀
White-crowned Pigeon
Rock Pigeon
color variations

Zenaida Dove *Zenaida aurita*

DATE LOCATION

Mourning Dove *Zenaida macroura*

DATE LOCATION

Spotted Dove *Streptopelia chinensis*

DATE LOCATION

Eurasian Collared-Dove *Streptopelia decaocto*

DATE LOCATION

White-winged Dove *Zenaida asiatica*

DATE LOCATION

Oriental Turtle-Dove *Streptopelia orientalis*

DATE LOCATION

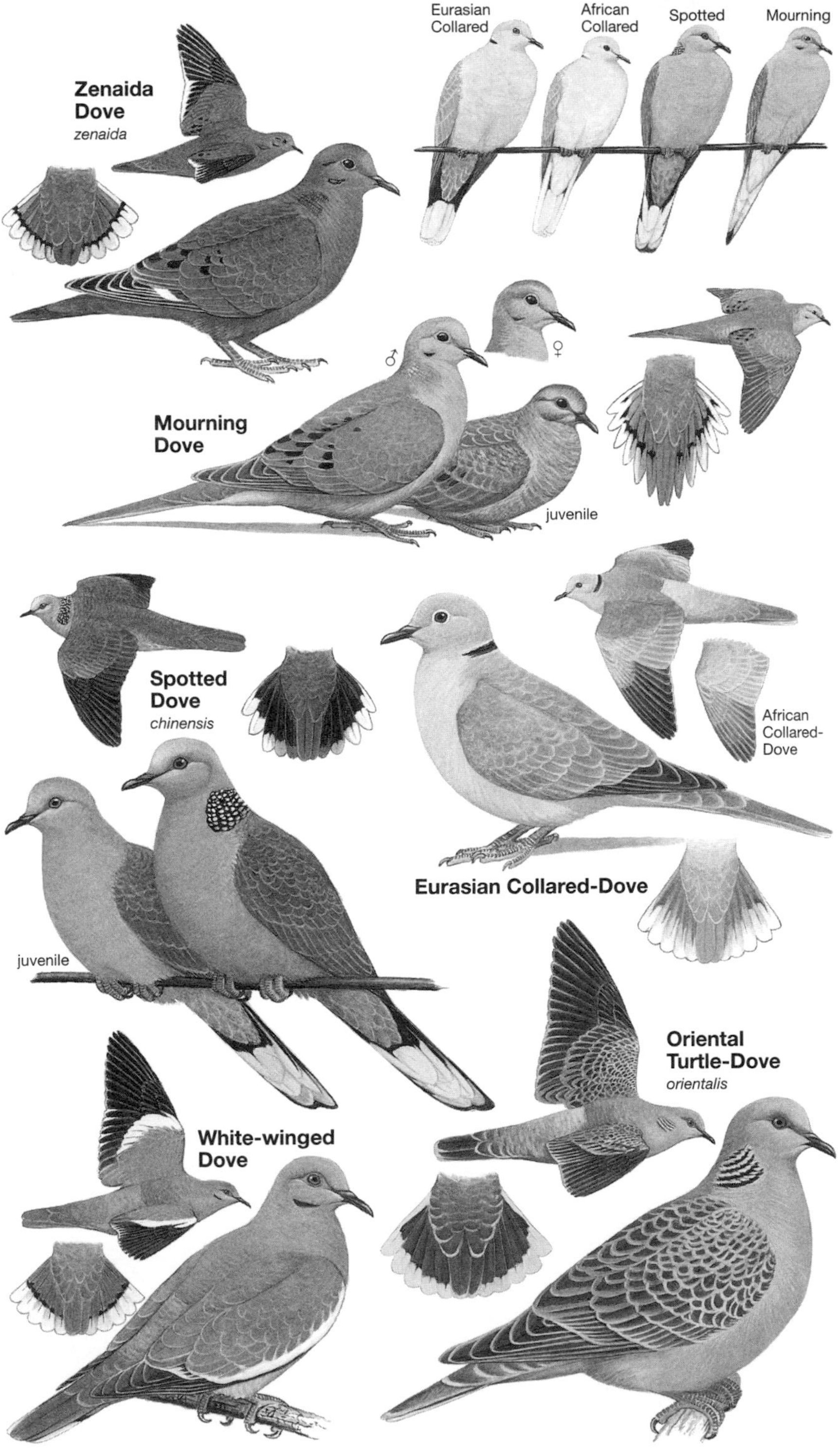
Eurasian Collared
African Collared
Spotted
Mourning
Zenaida Dove
zenaida
Mourning Dove
♂
♀
juvenile
Spotted Dove
chinensis
African Collared-Dove
juvenile
Eurasian Collared-Dove
Oriental Turtle-Dove
orientalis
White-winged Dove

Common Ground-Dove *Columbina passerina*

DATE LOCATION

Ruddy Ground-Dove *Columbina talpacoti*

DATE LOCATION

Inca Dove *Columbina inca*

DATE LOCATION

White-tipped Dove *Leptotila verreauxi*

DATE LOCATION

Key West Quail-Dove *Geotrygon chrysia*

DATE LOCATION

Ruddy Quail-Dove *Geotrygon montana*

DATE LOCATION

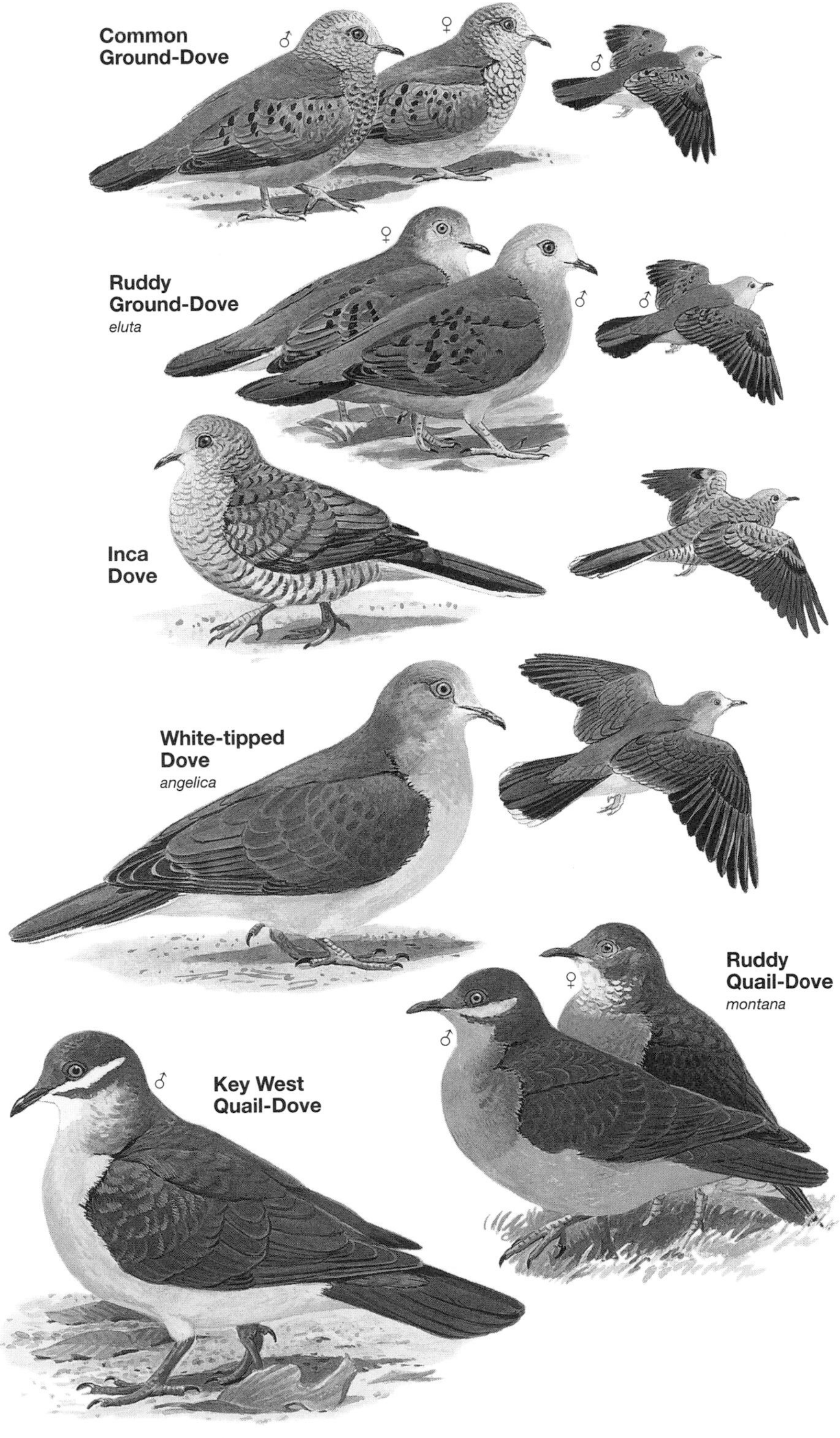
Common Ground-Dove
♂
♀
♂
Ruddy Ground-Dove
eluta
♀
♂
♂
Inca Dove
White-tipped Dove
angelica
Ruddy Quail-Dove
montana
♀
♂
Key West Quail-Dove
♂

Lories, Parakeets, Macaws, Parrots (Family Psittacidae)

White-winged Parakeet *Brotogeris versicolurus*

DATE LOCATION

Yellow-chevroned Parakeet *Brotogeris chiriri*

DATE LOCATION

Monk Parakeet *Myiopsitta monachus*

DATE LOCATION

Dusky-headed Parakeet *Aratinga weddellii*

DATE LOCATION

Black-hooded Parakeet *Nandayus nenday*

DATE LOCATION

Green Parakeet *Aratinga holochlora*

DATE LOCATION

Blue-crowned Parakeet *Aratinga acuticaudata*

DATE LOCATION

Mitred Parakeet *Aratinga mitrata*

DATE LOCATION

Red-masked Parakeet *Aratinga erythrogenys*

DATE LOCATION

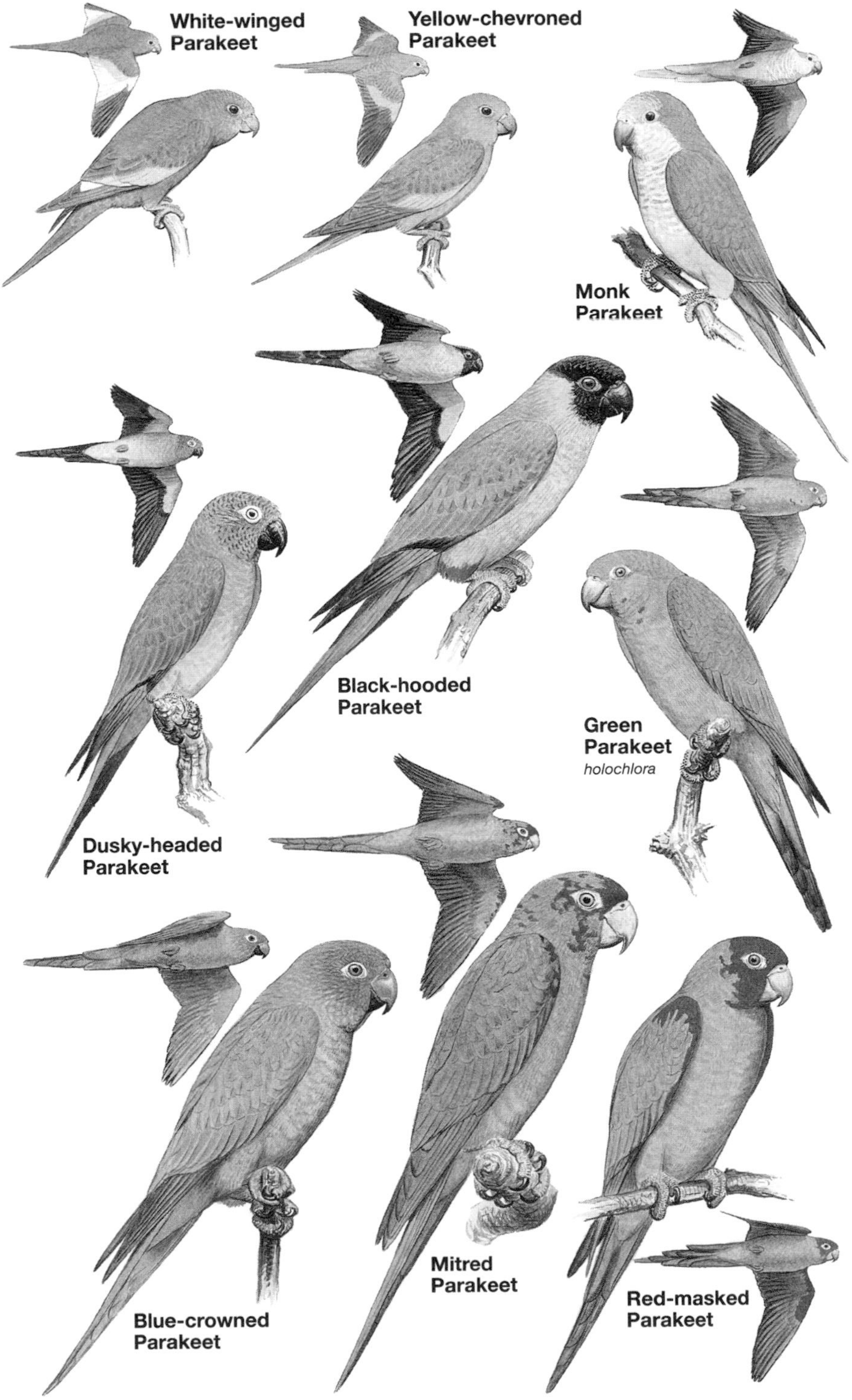
White-winged Parakeet
Yellow-chevroned Parakeet
Monk Parakeet
Black-hooded Parakeet
Dusky-headed Parakeet
Green Parakeet
holochlora
Blue-crowned Parakeet
Mitred Parakeet
Red-masked Parakeet

Thick-billed Parrot *Rhynchopsitta pachyrhyncha*

DATE LOCATION

Rose-ringed Parakeet *Psittacula krameri*

DATE LOCATION

Red-crowned Parrot *Amazona viridigenalis*

DATE LOCATION

Orange-winged Parrot *Amazona amazonica*

DATE LOCATION

Lilac-crowned Parrot *Amazona finschi*

DATE LOCATION

Yellow-headed Parrot *Amazona oratrix*

DATE LOCATION

Budgerigar *Melopsittacus undulatus*

DATE LOCATION

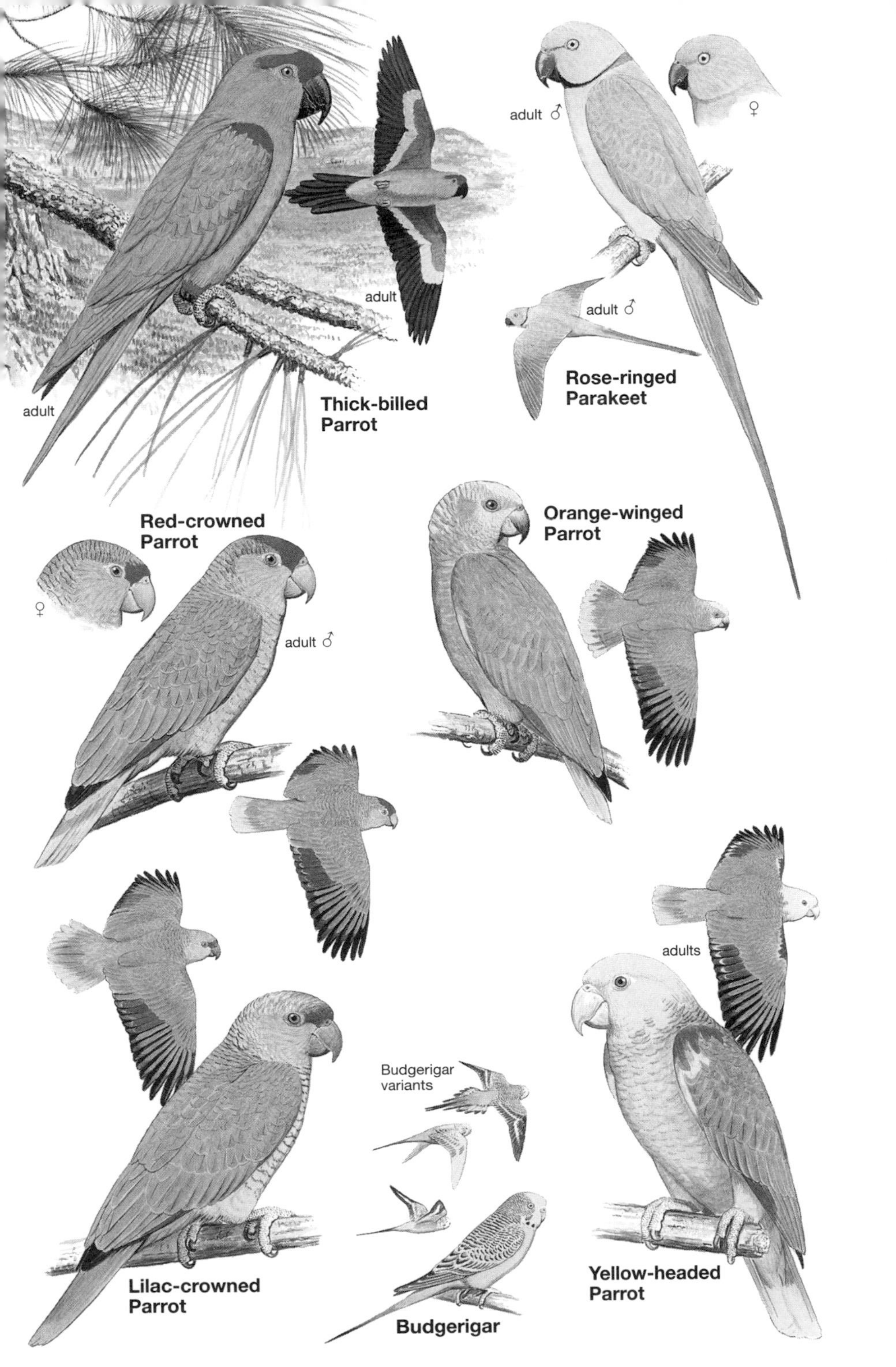
adult
adult
Thick-billed Parrot
adult ♂
♀
adult ♂
Rose-ringed Parakeet
Red-crowned Parrot
♀
adult ♂
Orange-winged Parrot
adults
Budgerigar variants
Lilac-crowned Parrot
Budgerigar
Yellow-headed Parrot

Cuckoos, Roadrunners, Anis (Family Cuculidae)

Mangrove Cuckoo *Coccyzus minor*

DATE LOCATION

Yellow-billed Cuckoo *Coccyzus americanus*

DATE LOCATION

Black-billed Cuckoo *Coccyzus erythropthalmus*

DATE LOCATION

Greater Roadrunner *Geococcyx californianus*

DATE LOCATION

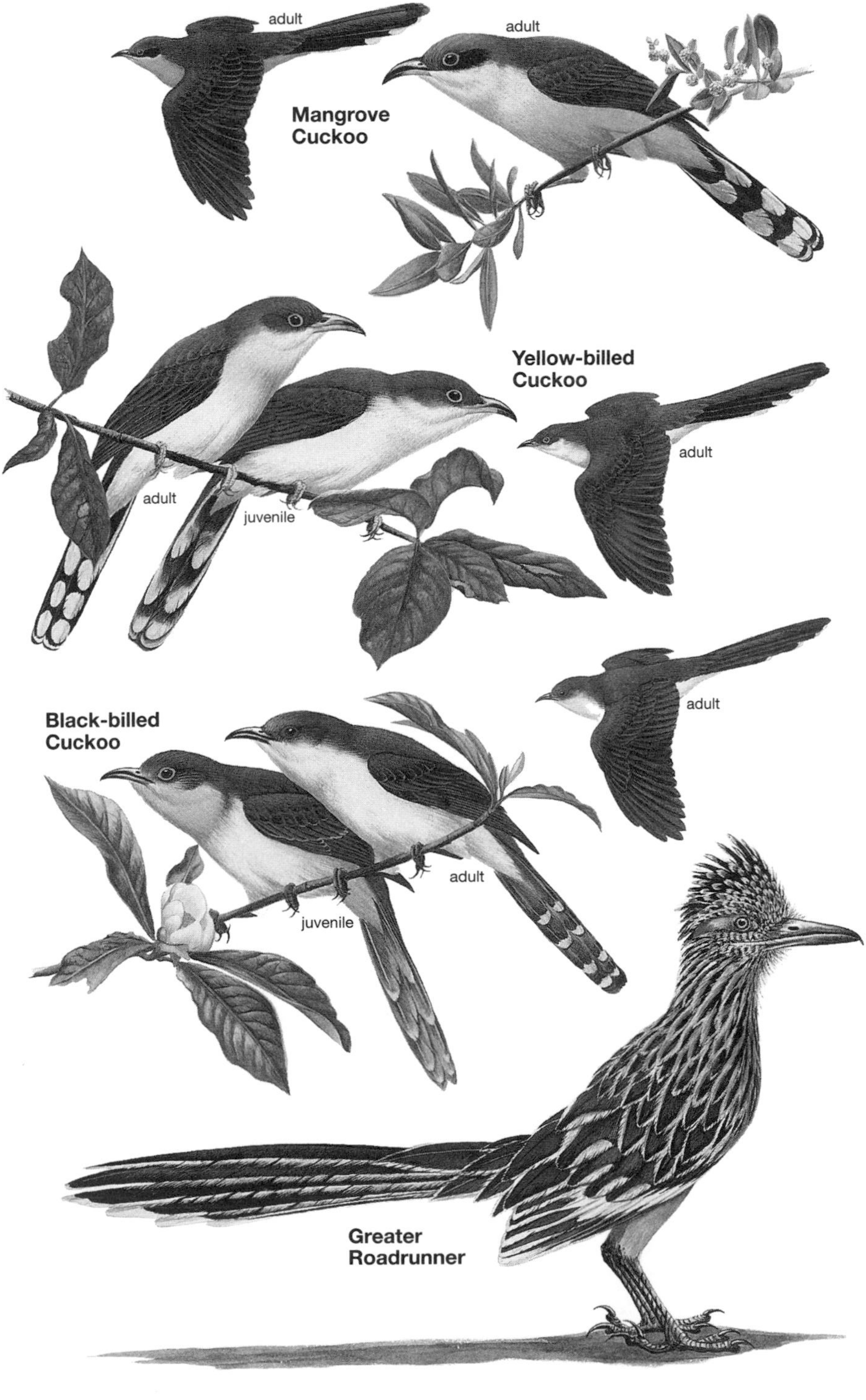
adult
adult
Mangrove
Cuckoo
Yellow-billed
Cuckoo
adult
adult
juvenile
adult
Black-billed
Cuckoo
adult
juvenile
Greater
Roadrunner

Common Cuckoo *Cuculus canorus*

DATE LOCATION

Oriental Cuckoo *Cuculus optatus*

DATE LOCATION

Smooth-billed Ani *Crotophaga ani*

DATE LOCATION

Groove-billed Ani *Crotophaga sulcirostris*

DATE LOCATION

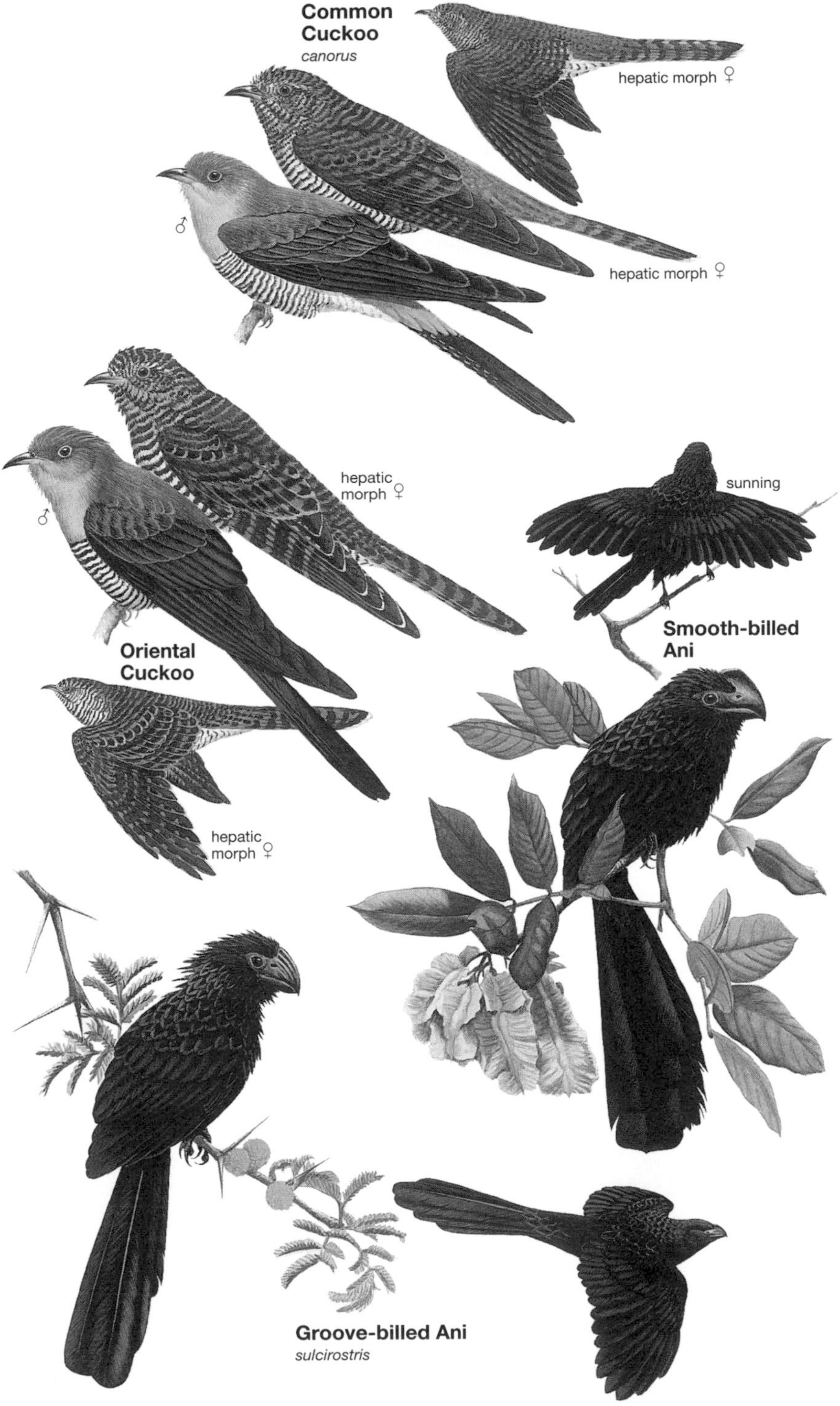

Common Cuckoo
canorus
hepatic morph ♀
♂
hepatic morph ♀
hepatic morph ♀
♂
Oriental Cuckoo
hepatic morph ♀
sunning
Smooth-billed Ani
Groove-billed Ani
sulcirostris

Owls (Families Tytonidae and Strigidae)

Barn Owl *Tyto alba*

DATE LOCATION

Short-eared Owl *Asio flammeus*

DATE LOCATION

Long-eared Owl *Asio otus*

DATE LOCATION

Great Horned Owl *Bubo virginianus*

DATE LOCATION

♂
♀
Barn
Owl
pratincola
Long-eared
Owl
Short-eared
Owl
flammeus
Great
Horned
Owl
subarcticus

Barred Owl *Strix varia*

DATE LOCATION

Great Gray Owl *Strix nebulosa*

DATE LOCATION

Spotted Owl *Strix occidentalis*

DATE LOCATION

Snowy Owl *Bubo scandiacus*

DATE LOCATION

Barred Owl
Great Gray Owl
nebulosa
Spotted Owl
immature
Snowy Owl

Eastern Screech-Owl *Megascops asio*

DATE LOCATION

Western Screech-Owl *Megascops kennicottii*

DATE LOCATION

Whiskered Screech-Owl *Megascops trichopsis*

DATE LOCATION

Eastern Screech-Owl
rufous morph
gray morph
gray-morph juvenile
maxwelliae
northwest coast kennicottii
Western Screech-Owl
Whiskered Screech-Owl
aspersus

Flammulated Owl *Otus flammeolus*

DATE LOCATION

Ferruginous Pygmy-Owl *Glaucidium brasilianum*

DATE LOCATION

Elf Owl *Micrathene whitneyi*

DATE LOCATION

Northern Pygmy-Owl *Glaucidium gnoma*

DATE LOCATION

Flammulated Owl
reddish type
grayish type
Elf Owl
whitneyi
Ferruginous Pygmy-Owl
cactorum
Northern Pygmy-Owl
Rockies type
Pacific coast type

Northern Saw-whet Owl *Aegolius acadicus*

DATE LOCATION

Northern Hawk Owl *Surnia ulula*

DATE LOCATION

Boreal Owl *Aegolius funereus*

DATE LOCATION

Burrowing Owl *Athene cunicularia*

DATE LOCATION

Northern Saw-whet Owl
acadicus
juvenile
Northern Hawk Owl
caparoch
Boreal Owl
richardsoni
juvenile
Burrowing Owl
western hypugaea
juvenile

Goatsuckers (Family Caprimulgidae)

Lesser Nighthawk *Chordeiles acutipennis*

DATE LOCATION

Common Nighthawk *Chordeiles minor*

DATE LOCATION

Antillean Nighthawk *Chordeiles gundlachii*

DATE LOCATION

Common Pauraque *Nyctidromus albicollis*

DATE LOCATION

Lesser Nighthawk
texensis
♂
♀
♂
♀
Common Nighthawk
minor
♂
juvenile
sennetti
♂
Antillean Nighthawk
♂
♂
Common Pauraque
merrilli
♂
♀
♂

Chuck-will's-widow *Caprimulgus carolinensis*

DATE LOCATION

Whip-poor-will *Caprimulgus vociferus*

DATE LOCATION

Buff-collared Nightjar *Caprimulgus ridgwayi*

DATE LOCATION

Common Poorwill *Phalaenoptilus nuttallii*

DATE LOCATION

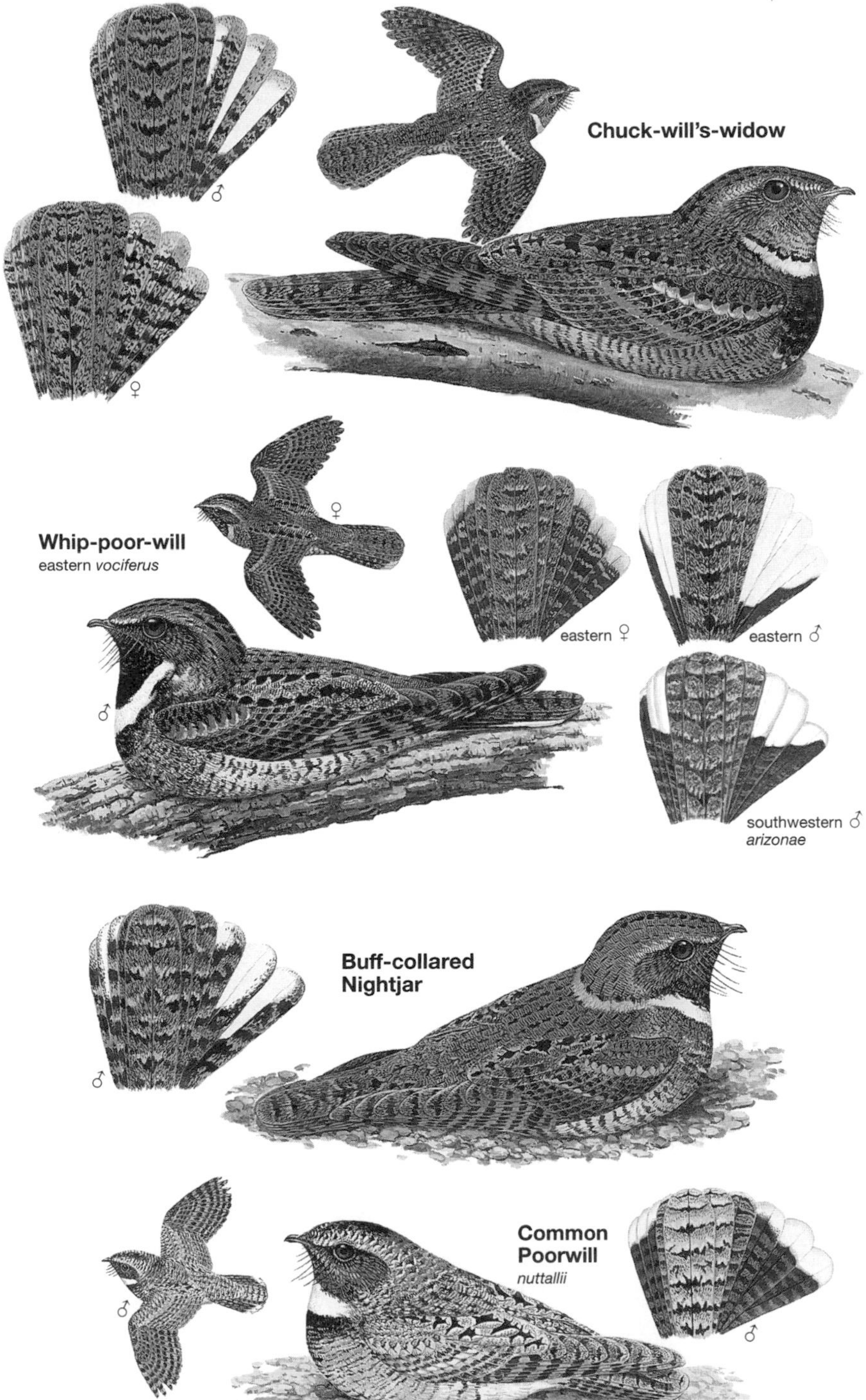

Chuck-will's-widow
♂
♀
Whip-poor-will
eastern *vociferus*
♀
eastern ♀
eastern ♂
♂
southwestern ♂
arizonae
Buff-collared
Nightjar
♂
Common
Poorwill
nuttallii
♂
♂

Swifts (Family Apodidae)

Black Swift *Cypseloides niger*

DATE LOCATION

Vaux's Swift *Chaetura vauxi*

DATE LOCATION

Chimney Swift *Chaetura pelagica*

DATE LOCATION

Common Swift *Apus apus*

DATE LOCATION

White-collared Swift *Streptoprocne zonaris*

DATE LOCATION

White-throated Swift *Aeronautes saxatalis*

DATE LOCATION

White-throated Needletail *Hirundapus caudacutus*

DATE LOCATION

Fork-tailed Swift *Apus pacificus*

DATE LOCATION

Black Swift
borealis
juvenile
adult
Vaux's Swift
vauxi
soaring
Chimney Swift
White-collared Swift
Common Swift
pekinensis
soaring
White-throated Swift
saxatalis
immature
soaring
Fork-tailed Swift
pacificus
White-throated Needletail
caudacutus

Hummingbirds (Family Trochilidae)

Green Violet-ear *Colibri thalassinus*

DATE LOCATION

Green-breasted Mango *Anthracothorax prevostii*

DATE LOCATION

Buff-bellied Hummingbird *Amazilia yucatanensis*

DATE LOCATION

Berylline Hummingbird *Amazilia beryllina*

DATE LOCATION

Bahama Woodstar *Calliphlox evelynae*

DATE LOCATION

Violet-crowned Hummingbird *Amazilia violiceps*

DATE LOCATION

Lucifer Hummingbird *Calothorax lucifer*

DATE LOCATION

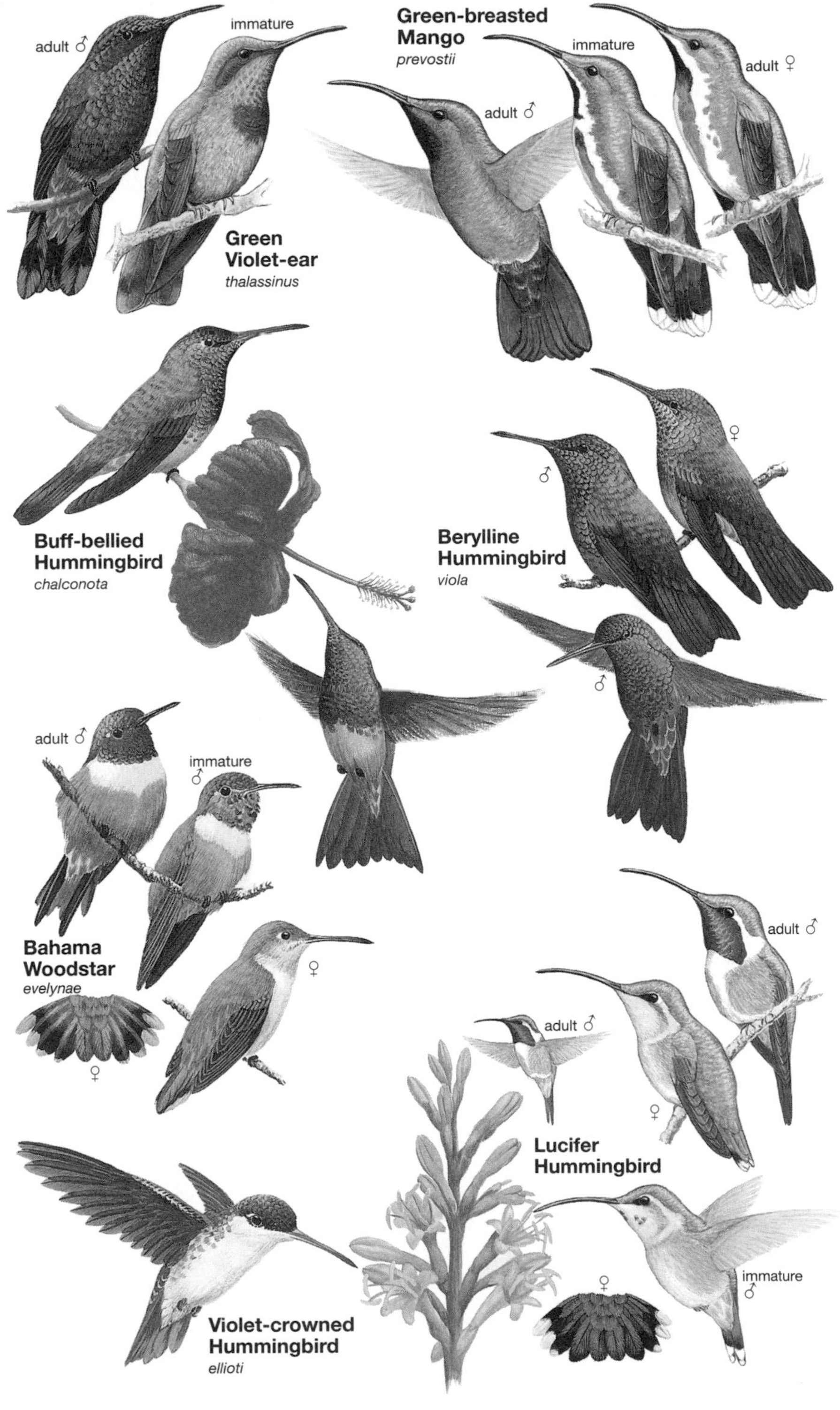
adult ♂
immature
Green Violet-ear
thalassinus
Green-breasted Mango
prevostii
immature
adult ♀
adult ♂
♀
♂
Buff-bellied Hummingbird
chalconota
Berylline Hummingbird
viola
♂
adult ♂
immature ♂
Bahama Woodstar
evelynae
♀
♀
adult ♂
adult ♂
♀
Lucifer Hummingbird
Violet-crowned Hummingbird
ellioti
♀
immature ♂

Broad-billed Hummingbird *Cynanthus latirostris*

DATE LOCATION

White-eared Hummingbird *Hylocharis leucotis*

DATE LOCATION

Blue-throated Hummingbird *Lampornis clemenciae*

DATE LOCATION

Xantus's Hummingbird *Hylocharis xantusii*

DATE LOCATION

Magnificent Hummingbird *Eugenes fulgens*

DATE LOCATION

Plain-capped Starthroat *Heliomaster constantii*

DATE LOCATION

Broad-billed Hummingbird
magicus
♀
immature ♂
adult ♂
♂
White-eared Hummingbird
borealis
adult ♀
adult ♂
♂
Blue-throated Hummingbird
bessophilus
♀
♂
♂
♀
Xantus's Hummingbird
♀
Magnificent Hummingbird
fulgens
adult ♂
Plain-capped Starthroat
pinicola

Ruby-throated Hummingbird *Archilochus colubris*

DATE LOCATION

Black-chinned Hummingbird *Archilochus alexandri*

DATE LOCATION

Costa's Hummingbird *Calypte costae*

DATE LOCATION

Anna's Hummingbird *Calypte anna*

DATE LOCATION

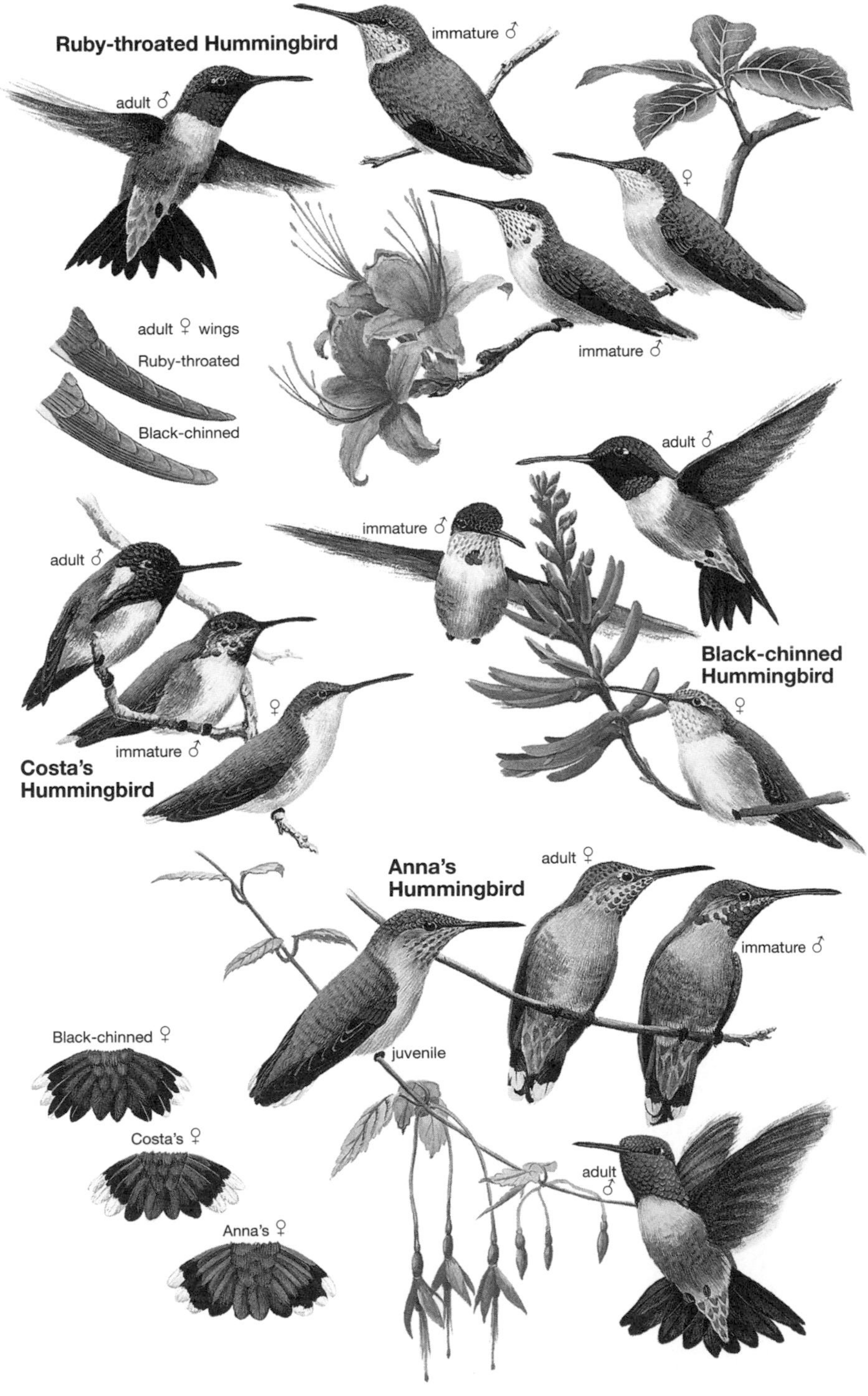

Ruby-throated Hummingbird
immature ♂
adult ♂
♀
immature ♂
adult ♀ wings
Ruby-throated
Black-chinned
adult ♂
immature ♂
adult ♂
Black-chinned Hummingbird
♀
immature ♂
♀
Costa's Hummingbird
Anna's Hummingbird
adult ♀
immature ♂
Black-chinned ♀
juvenile
Costa's ♀
adult ♂
Anna's ♀

Broad-tailed Hummingbird *Selasphorus platycercus*

DATE LOCATION

Calliope Hummingbird *Stellula calliope*

DATE LOCATION

Rufous Hummingbird *Selasphorus rufus*

DATE LOCATION

Allen's Hummingbird *Selasphorus sasin*

DATE LOCATION

Trogons (Family Trogonidae)

Elegant Trogon *Trogon elegans*

DATE LOCATION

Eared Quetzal *Euptilotis neoxenus*

DATE LOCATION

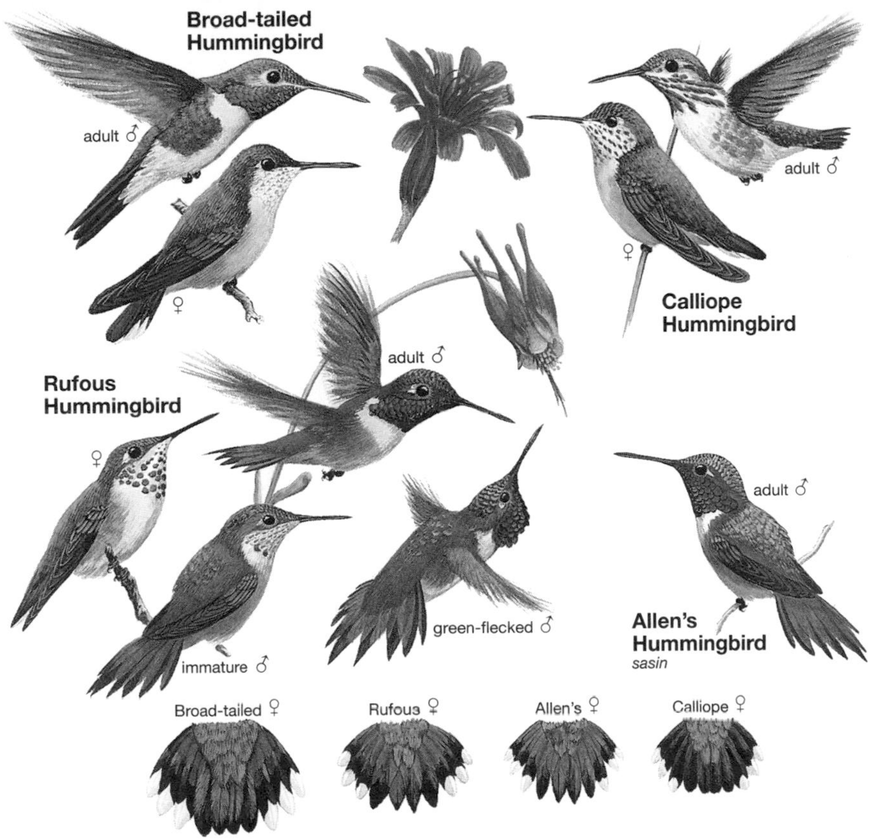
Broad-tailed Hummingbird
adult ♂
♀
Calliope Hummingbird
adult ♂
♀
Rufous Hummingbird
♀
adult ♂
immature ♂
green-flecked ♂
Allen's Hummingbird
sasin
adult ♂
Broad-tailed ♀
Rufous ♀
Allen's ♀
Calliope ♀

Eared Quetzal
♀
♂
Elegant Trogan
canescens
♀
♂
♂
♀

Kingfishers (Family Alcedinidae)

Belted Kingfisher *Ceryle alcyon*

DATE LOCATION

Ringed Kingfisher *Ceryle torquatus*

DATE LOCATION

Green Kingfisher *Chloroceryle americana*

DATE LOCATION

Belted
Kingfisher
♀
♂
♀
♂
♀
♂
Ringed
Kingfisher
torquatus
♂
♀
Green
Kingfisher

Woodpeckers, Allies (Family Picidae)

Red-headed Woodpecker *Melanerpes erythrocephalus*

DATE LOCATION

Acorn Woodpecker *Melanerpes formicivorus*

DATE LOCATION

White-headed Woodpecker *Picoides albolarvatus*

DATE LOCATION

Lewis's Woodpecker *Melanerpes lewis*

DATE LOCATION

Red-headed Woodpecker
juvenile
adults
♂
♀
♂
Acorn Woodpecker
White-headed Woodpecker
♂
♂
♀
juvenile
Lewis's Woodpecker
adults

Golden-fronted Woodpecker *Melanerpes aurifrons*

DATE LOCATION

Red-bellied Woodpecker *Melanerpes carolinus*

DATE LOCATION

Gila Woodpecker *Melanerpes uropygialis*

DATE LOCATION

Northern Flicker *Colaptes auratus*

DATE LOCATION

Gilded Flicker *Colaptes chrysoides*

DATE LOCATION

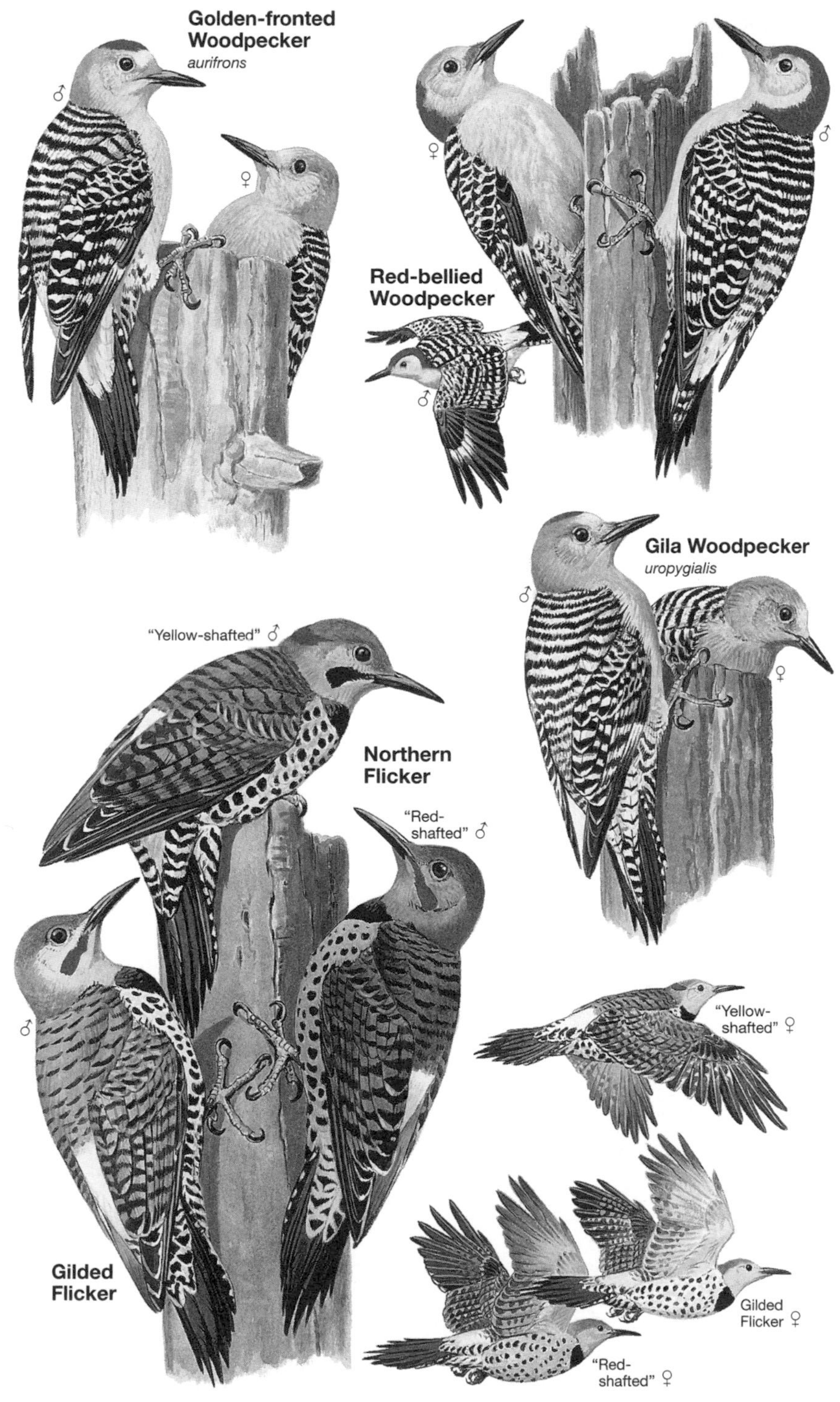
Golden-fronted Woodpecker
aurifrons
♂
♀
Red-bellied Woodpecker
♀
♂
♂
Gila Woodpecker
uropygialis
♂
♀
"Yellow-shafted" ♂
Northern Flicker
"Red-shafted" ♂
♂
Gilded Flicker
"Yellow-shafted" ♀
Gilded Flicker ♀
"Red-shafted" ♀

Sapsuckers

Williamson's Sapsucker *Sphyrapicus thyroideus*

DATE LOCATION

Red-breasted Sapsucker *Sphyrapicus ruber*

DATE LOCATION

Yellow-bellied Sapsucker *Sphyrapicus varius*

DATE LOCATION

Red-naped Sapsucker *Sphyrapicus nuchalis*

DATE LOCATION

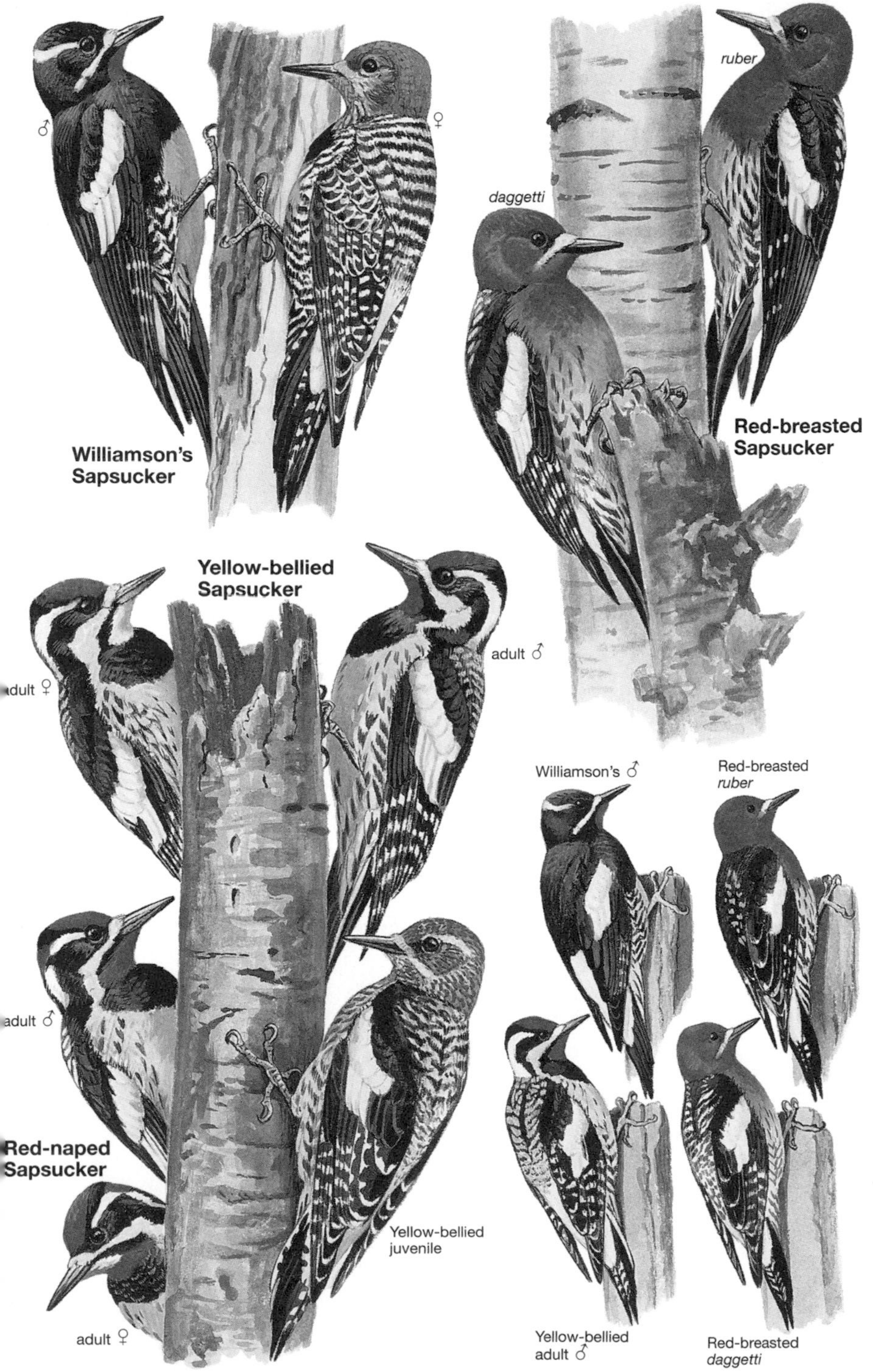

♂
♀
Williamson's Sapsucker
ruber
daggetti
Red-breasted Sapsucker
Yellow-bellied Sapsucker
adult ♀
adult ♂
adult ♂
Red-naped Sapsucker
adult ♀
Yellow-bellied juvenile
Williamson's ♂
Red-breasted ruber
Yellow-bellied adult ♂
Red-breasted daggetti

Ladder-backed Woodpecker *Picoides scalaris*

DATE LOCATION

Red-cockaded Woodpecker *Picoides borealis*

DATE LOCATION

Arizona Woodpecker *Picoides arizonae*

DATE LOCATION

Nuttall's Woodpecker *Picoides nuttallii*

DATE LOCATION

Great Spotted Woodpecker *Dendrocopos major*

DATE LOCATION

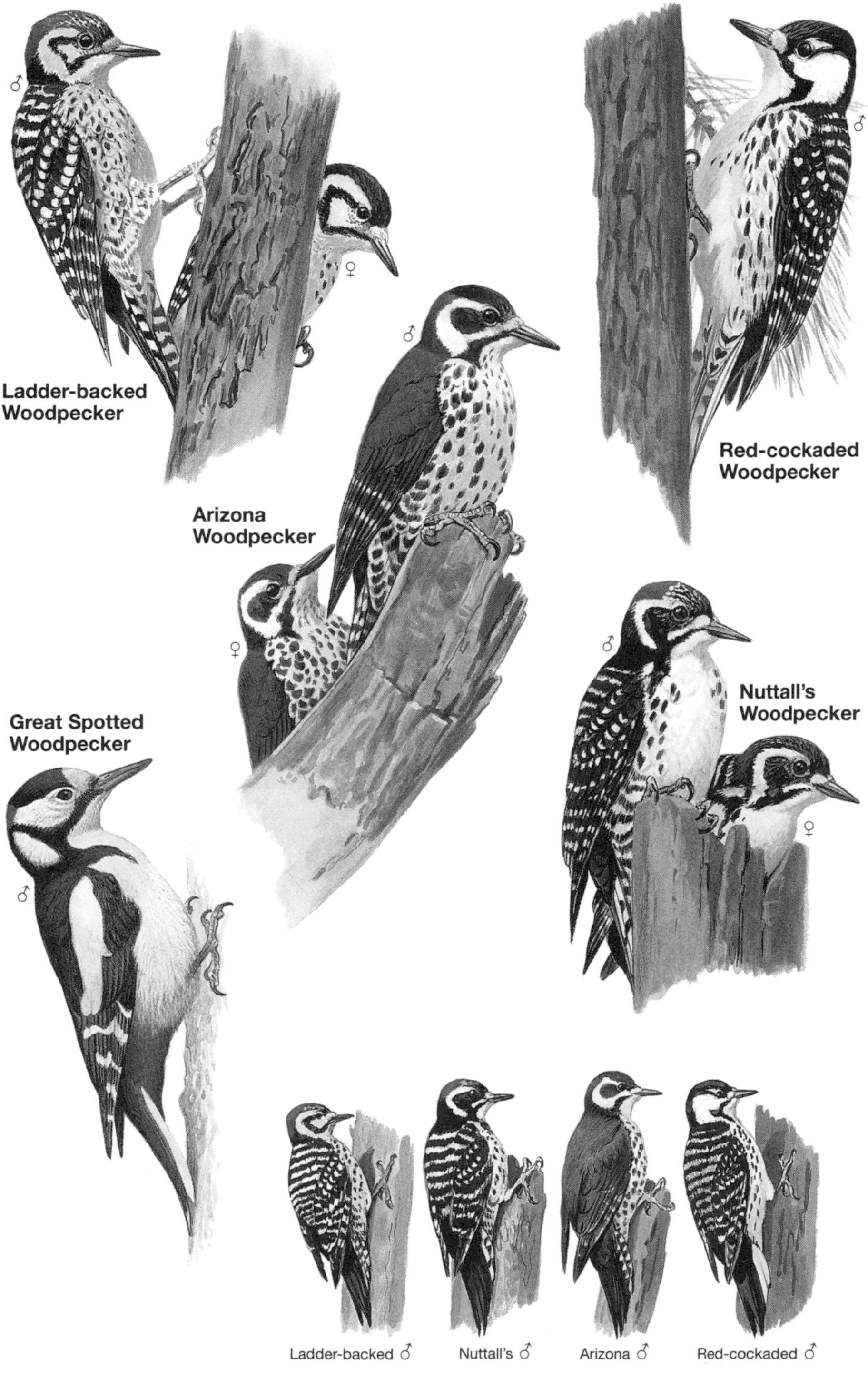

Ladder-backed Woodpecker
Arizona Woodpecker
Red-cockaded Woodpecker
Nuttall's Woodpecker
Great Spotted Woodpecker
Ladder-backed ♂
Nuttall's ♂
Arizona ♂
Red-cockaded ♂

Downy Woodpecker *Picoides pubescens*

DATE LOCATION

Hairy Woodpecker *Picoides villosus*

DATE LOCATION

American Three-toed Woodpecker *Picoides dorsalis*

DATE LOCATION

Black-backed Woodpecker *Picoides arcticus*

DATE LOCATION

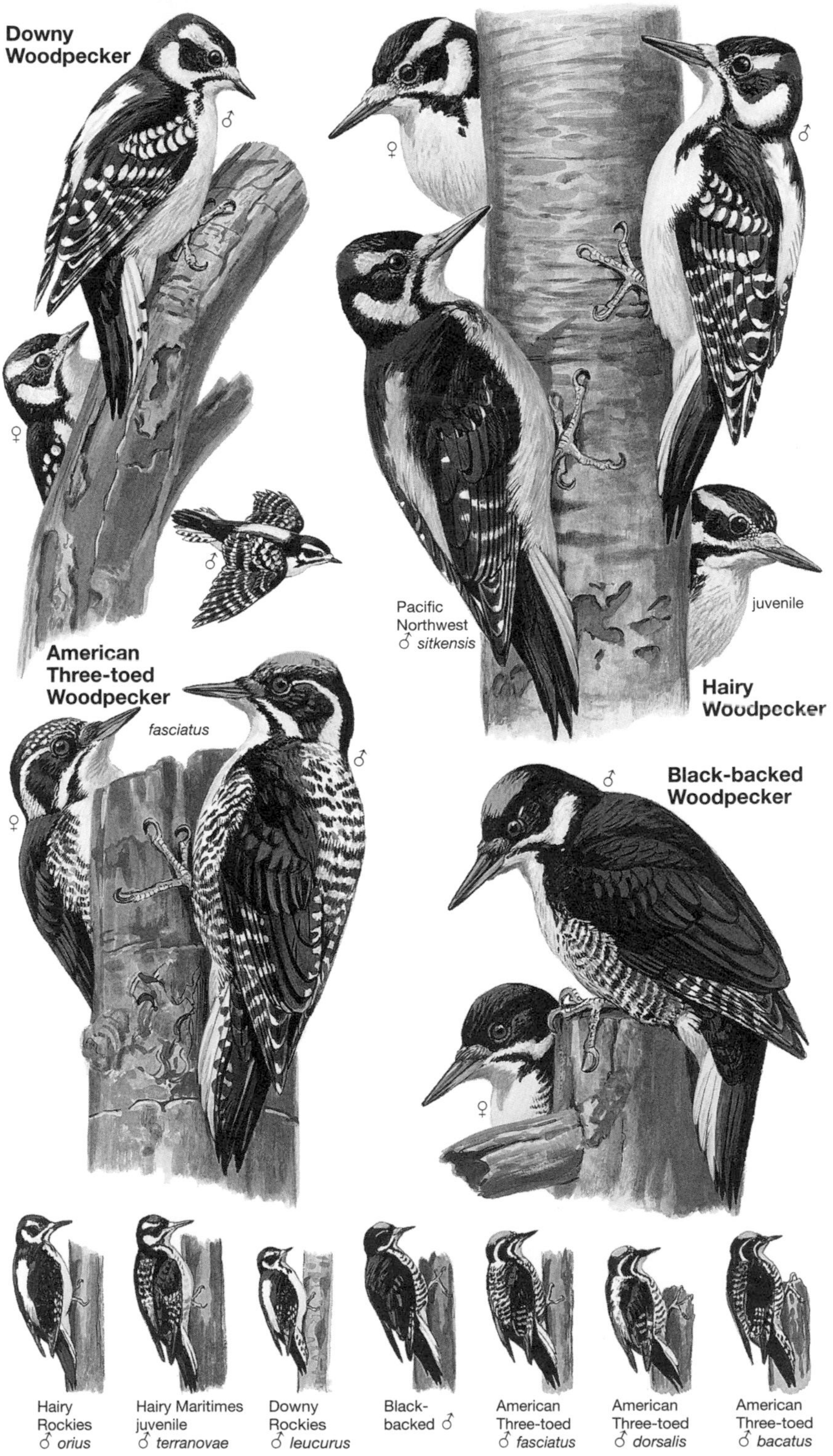

Downy Woodpecker
♂
♀
♂
♀
♂
Pacific Northwest
♂ *sitkensis*
juvenile
Hairy Woodpecker
American Three-toed Woodpecker
fasciatus
♀
♂
♂
Black-backed Woodpecker
♀
Hairy Rockies
♂ *orius*
Hairy Maritimes juvenile
♂ *terranovae*
Downy Rockies
♂ *leucurus*
Black-backed ♂
American Three-toed
♂ *fasciatus*
American Three-toed
♂ *dorsalis*
American Three-toed
♂ *bacatus*

Ivory-billed Woodpecker *Campephilus principalis*

DATE	LOCATION

Pileated Woodpecker *Dryocopus pileatus*

DATE	LOCATION

Ivory-billed Woodpecker
♀
♀
♂
♂
♀
♂
♀
Pileated Woodpecker
♂

Tyrant Flycatchers (Family Tyrannidae)

Greater Pewee *Contopus pertinax*

DATE LOCATION

Olive-sided Flycatcher *Contopus cooperi*

DATE LOCATION

Eastern Wood-Pewee *Contopus virens*

DATE LOCATION

Western Wood-Pewee *Contopus sordidulus*

DATE LOCATION

Cuban Pewee *Contopus caribaeus*

DATE LOCATION

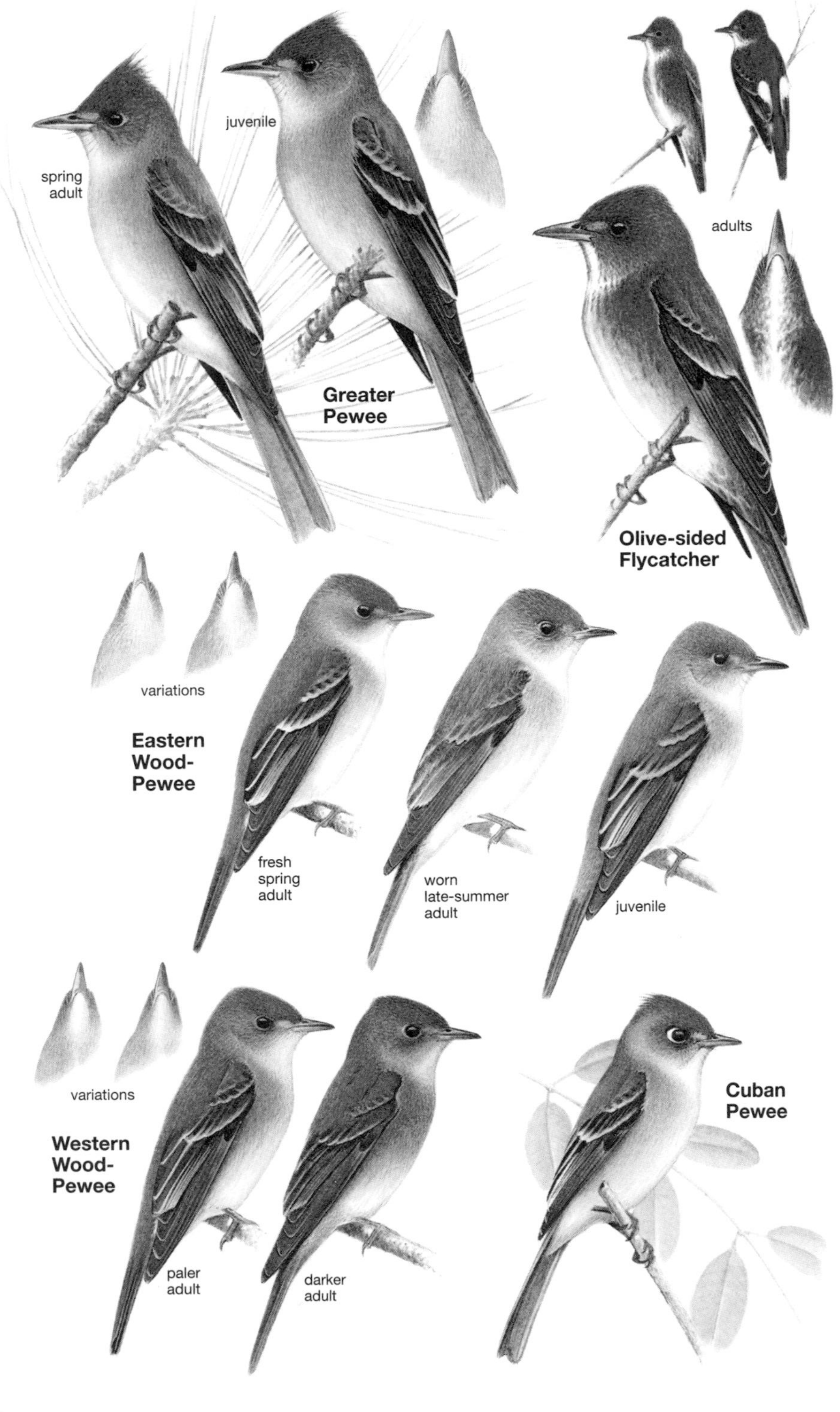
spring adult
juvenile
Greater Pewee
adults
Olive-sided Flycatcher
variations
Eastern Wood-Pewee
fresh spring adult
worn late-summer adult
juvenile
variations
Western Wood-Pewee
paler adult
darker adult
Cuban Pewee

Empidonax Flycatchers

Acadian Flycatcher *Empidonax virescens*

DATE LOCATION

Yellow-bellied Flycatcher *Empidonax flaviventris*

DATE LOCATION

Alder Flycatcher *Empidonax alnorum*

DATE LOCATION

Willow Flycatcher *Empidonax traillii*

DATE LOCATION

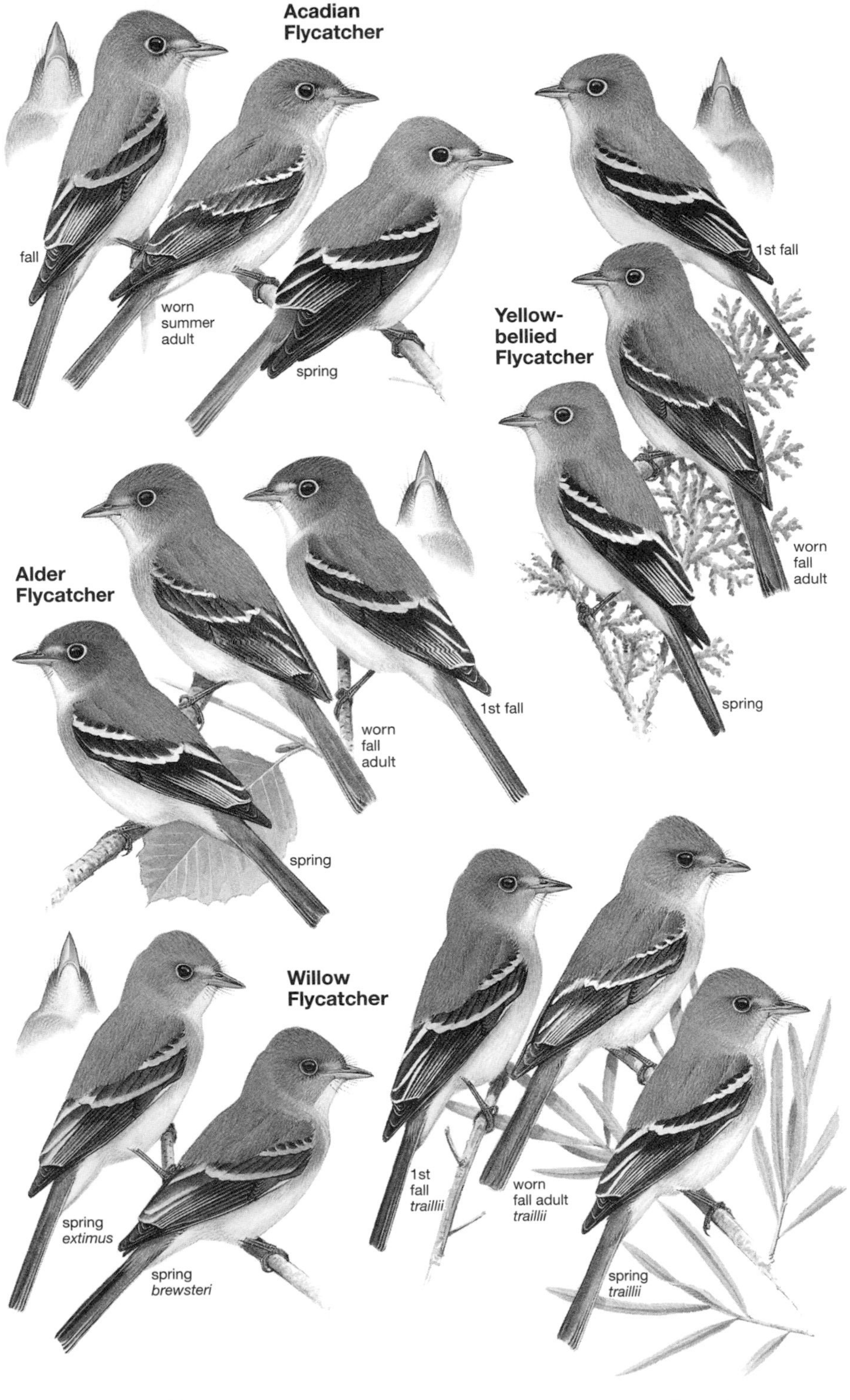

Acadian Flycatcher
fall
worn summer adult
spring
Yellow-bellied Flycatcher
1st fall
worn fall adult
spring
Alder Flycatcher
1st fall
worn fall adult
spring
Willow Flycatcher
spring *extimus*
spring *brewsteri*
1st fall *traillii*
worn fall adult *traillii*
spring *traillii*

Least Flycatcher *Empidonax minimus*

DATE LOCATION

Hammond's Flycatcher *Empidonax hammondii*

DATE LOCATION

Gray Flycatcher *Empidonax wrightii*

DATE LOCATION

Dusky Flycatcher *Empidonax oberholseri*

DATE LOCATION

Least Flycatcher
1st fall
worn fall adult
spring
Hammond's Flycatcher
fall
spring
Gray Flycatcher
winter
spring
Dusky Flycatcher
1st fall
worn fall adult
winter
spring

Pacific-slope Flycatcher *Empidonax difficilis*

DATE LOCATION

Cordilleran Flycatcher *Empidonax occidentalis*

DATE LOCATION

Buff-breasted Flycatcher *Empidonax fulvifrons*

DATE LOCATION

Northern Beardless-Tyrannulet *Camptostoma imberbe*

DATE LOCATION

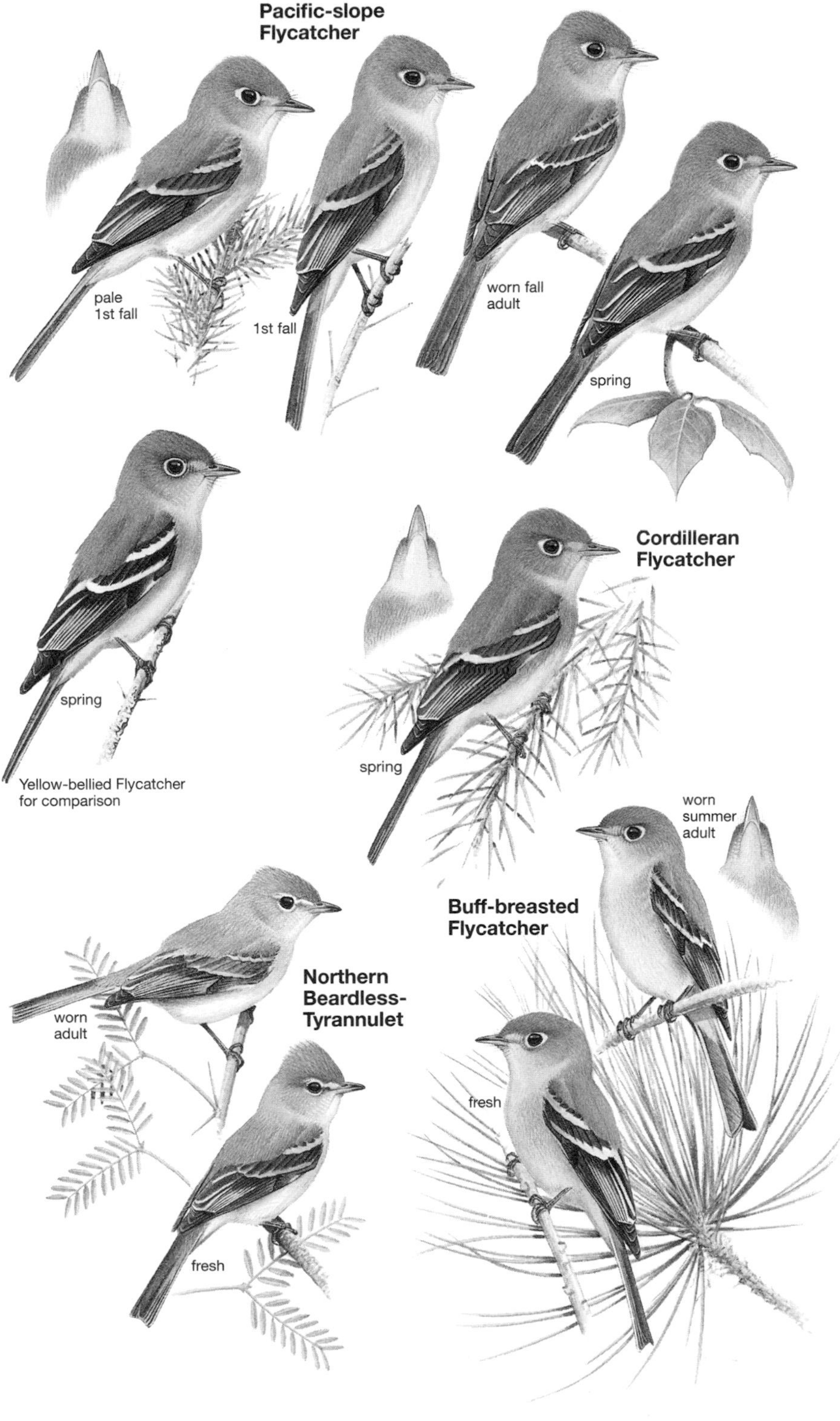
Pacific-slope Flycatcher
pale 1st fall
1st fall
worn fall adult
spring
spring
Yellow-bellied Flycatcher for comparison
Cordilleran Flycatcher
spring
worn summer adult
Buff-breasted Flycatcher
fresh
Northern Beardless-Tyrannulet
worn adult
fresh

Tufted Flycatcher *Mitrephanes phaeocercus*

DATE LOCATION

Eastern Phoebe *Sayornis phoebe*

DATE LOCATION

Black Phoebe *Sayornis nigricans*

DATE LOCATION

Say's Phoebe *Sayornis saya*

DATE LOCATION

Vermilion Flycatcher *Pyrocephalus rubinus*

DATE LOCATION

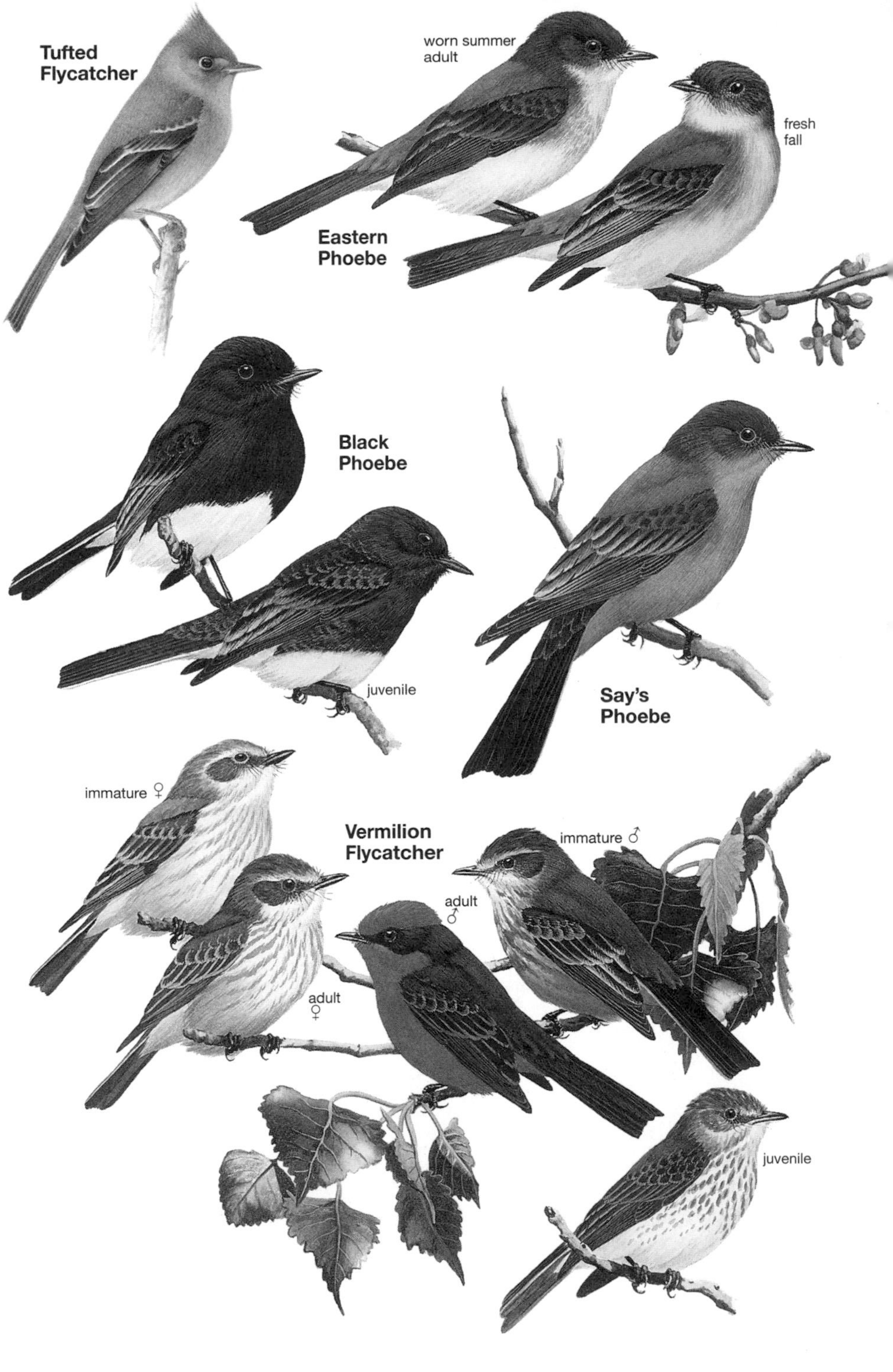
Tufted Flycatcher
worn summer adult
fresh fall
Eastern Phoebe
Black Phoebe
juvenile
Say's Phoebe
immature ♀
Vermilion Flycatcher
immature ♂
adult ♂
adult ♀
juvenile

Brown-crested Flycatcher *Myiarchus tyrannulus*

DATE LOCATION

Great Crested Flycatcher *Myiarchus crinitus*

DATE LOCATION

Nutting's Flycatcher *Myiarchus nuttingi*

DATE LOCATION

Ash-throated Flycatcher *Myiarchus cinerascens*

DATE LOCATION

La Sagra's Flycatcher *Myiarchus sagrae*

DATE LOCATION

Dusky-capped Flycatcher *Myiarchus tuberculifer*

DATE LOCATION

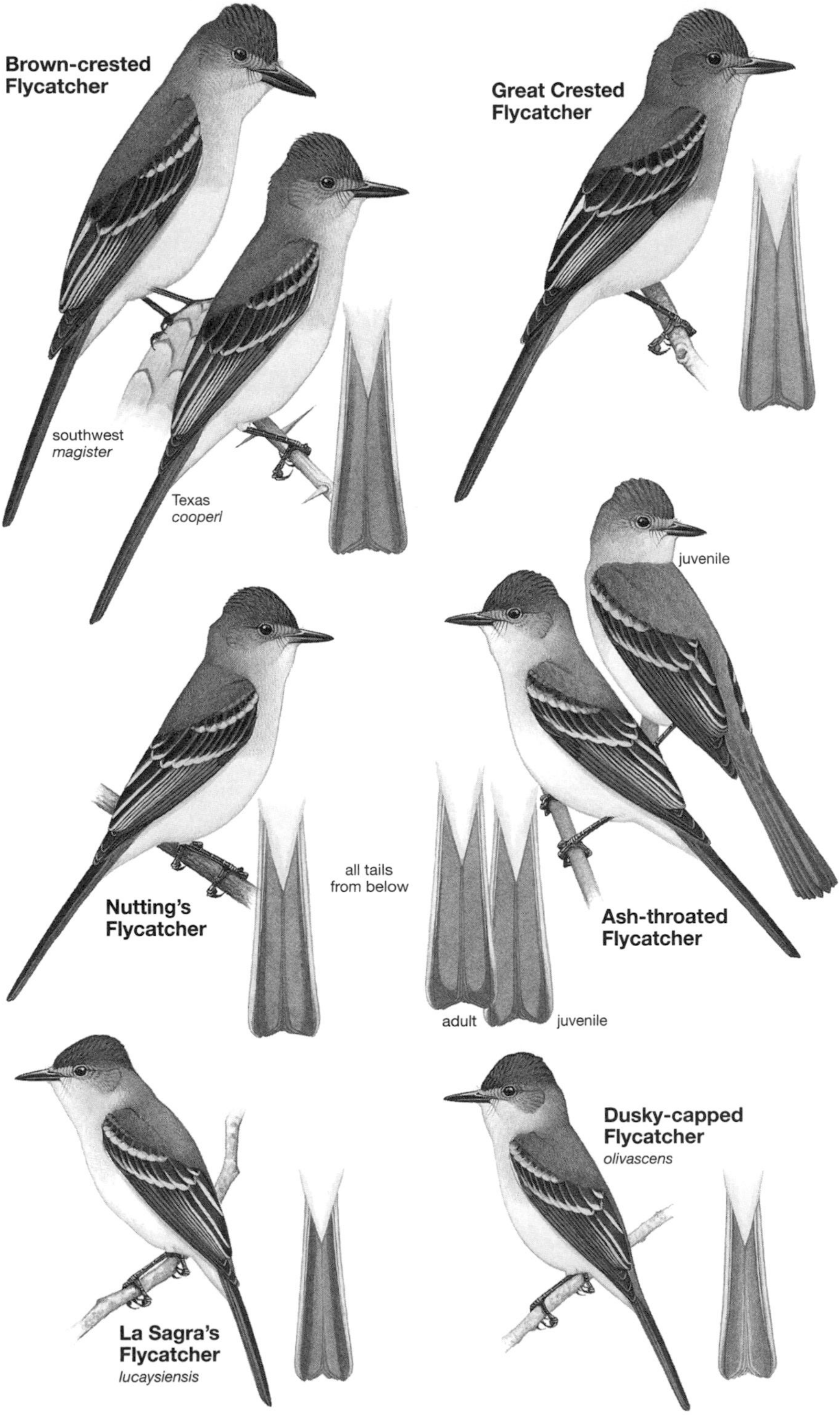
Brown-crested Flycatcher
southwest
magister
Texas
cooperi
Great Crested Flycatcher
juvenile
Nutting's Flycatcher
all tails from below
Ash-throated Flycatcher
adult
juvenile
La Sagra's Flycatcher
lucaysiensis
Dusky-capped Flycatcher
olivascens

Cassin's Kingbird *Tyrannus vociferans*

DATE LOCATION

Western Kingbird *Tyrannus verticalis*

DATE LOCATION

Couch's Kingbird *Tyrannus couchii*

DATE LOCATION

Tropical Kingbird *Tyrannus melancholicus*

DATE LOCATION

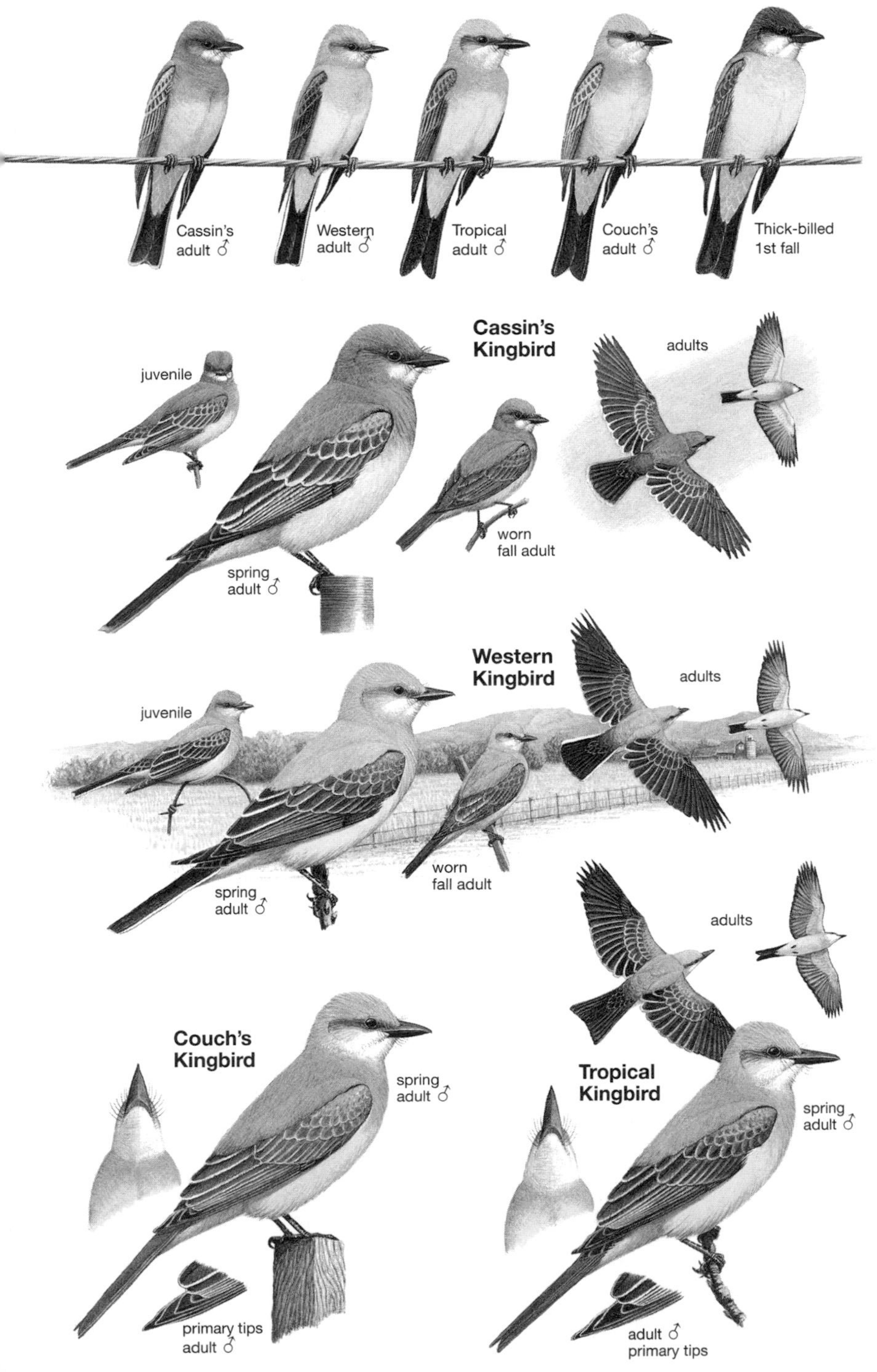
Cassin's
adult ♂
Western
adult ♂
Tropical
adult ♂
Couch's
adult ♂
Thick-billed
1st fall
Cassin's Kingbird
juvenile
adults
worn
fall adult
spring
adult ♂
Western Kingbird
juvenile
adults
worn
fall adult
spring
adult ♂
adults
Couch's Kingbird
spring
adult ♂
primary tips
adult ♂
Tropical Kingbird
spring
adult ♂
adult ♂
primary tips

Fork-tailed Flycatcher *Tyrannus savana*

DATE LOCATION

Eastern Kingbird *Tyrannus tyrannus*

DATE LOCATION

Gray Kingbird *Tyrannus dominicensis*

DATE LOCATION

Thick-billed Kingbird *Tyrannus crassirostris*

DATE LOCATION

Fork-tailed Flycatcher
adult
juvenile
Eastern Kingbird
juvenile
Gray Kingbird
1st fall
worn summer adult
Thick-billed Kingbird
pompalis

Scissor-tailed Flycatcher *Tyrannus forficatus*

DATE LOCATION

Piratic Flycatcher *Legatus leucophaius*

DATE LOCATION

Variegated Flycatcher *Empidonomus varius*

Great Kiskadee *Pitangus sulphuratus*

DATE LOCATION

Sulphur-bellied Flycatcher *Myiodynastes luteiventris*

DATE LOCATION

Rose-throated Becard (*Incertae Sedis*)

Rose-throated Becard *Pachyramphus aglaiae*

DATE LOCATION

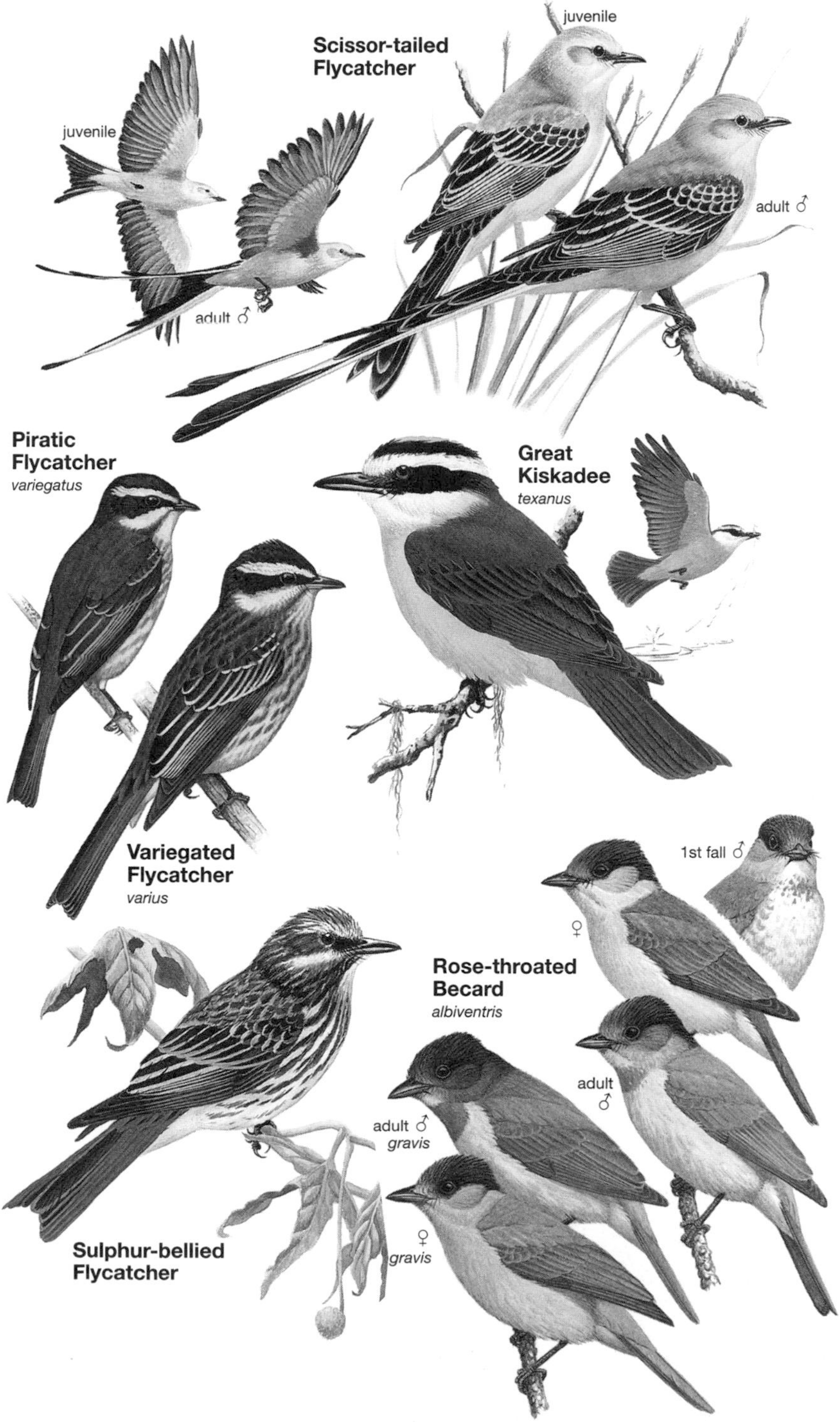
Scissor-tailed Flycatcher
juvenile
juvenile
adult ♂
adult ♂
Piratic Flycatcher
variegatus
Great Kiskadee
texanus
Variegated Flycatcher
varius
1st fall ♂
♀
Rose-throated Becard
albiventris
adult ♂
adult ♂
gravis
♀
gravis
Sulphur-bellied Flycatcher

Shrikes (Family Laniidae)

Brown Shrike *Lanius cristatus*

DATE LOCATION

Loggerhead Shrike *Lanius ludovicianus*

DATE LOCATION

Northern Shrike *Lanius excubitor*

DATE LOCATION

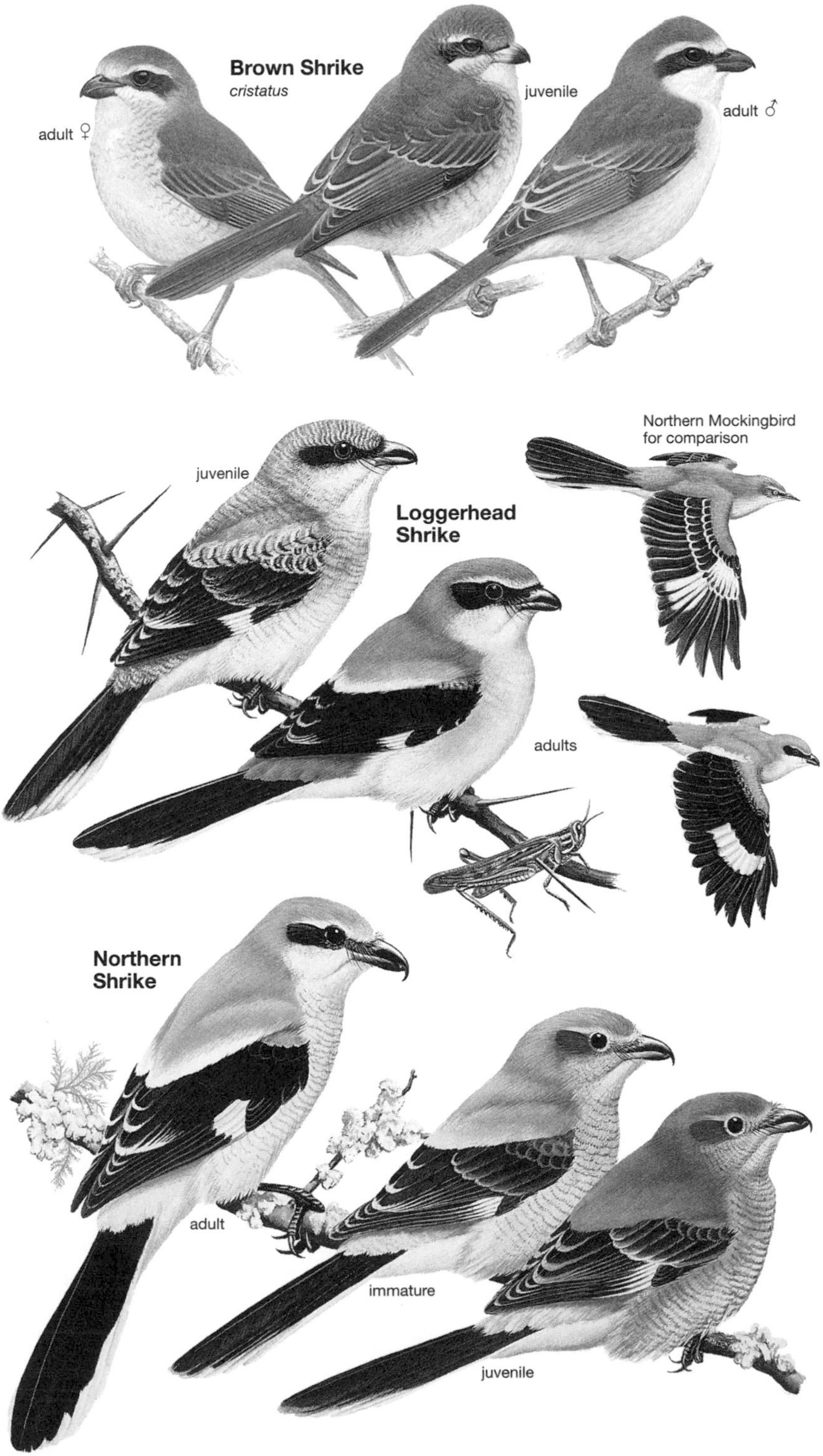
Brown Shrike
cristatus
adult ♀
juvenile
adult ♂
Northern Mockingbird
for comparison
juvenile
Loggerhead
Shrike
adults
Northern
Shrike
adult
immature
juvenile

Vireos (Family Vireonidae)

Black-capped Vireo *Vireo atricapilla*

DATE LOCATION

White-eyed Vireo *Vireo griseus*

DATE LOCATION

Thick-billed Vireo *Vireo crassirostris*

DATE LOCATION

Yellow-throated Vireo *Vireo flavifrons*

DATE LOCATION

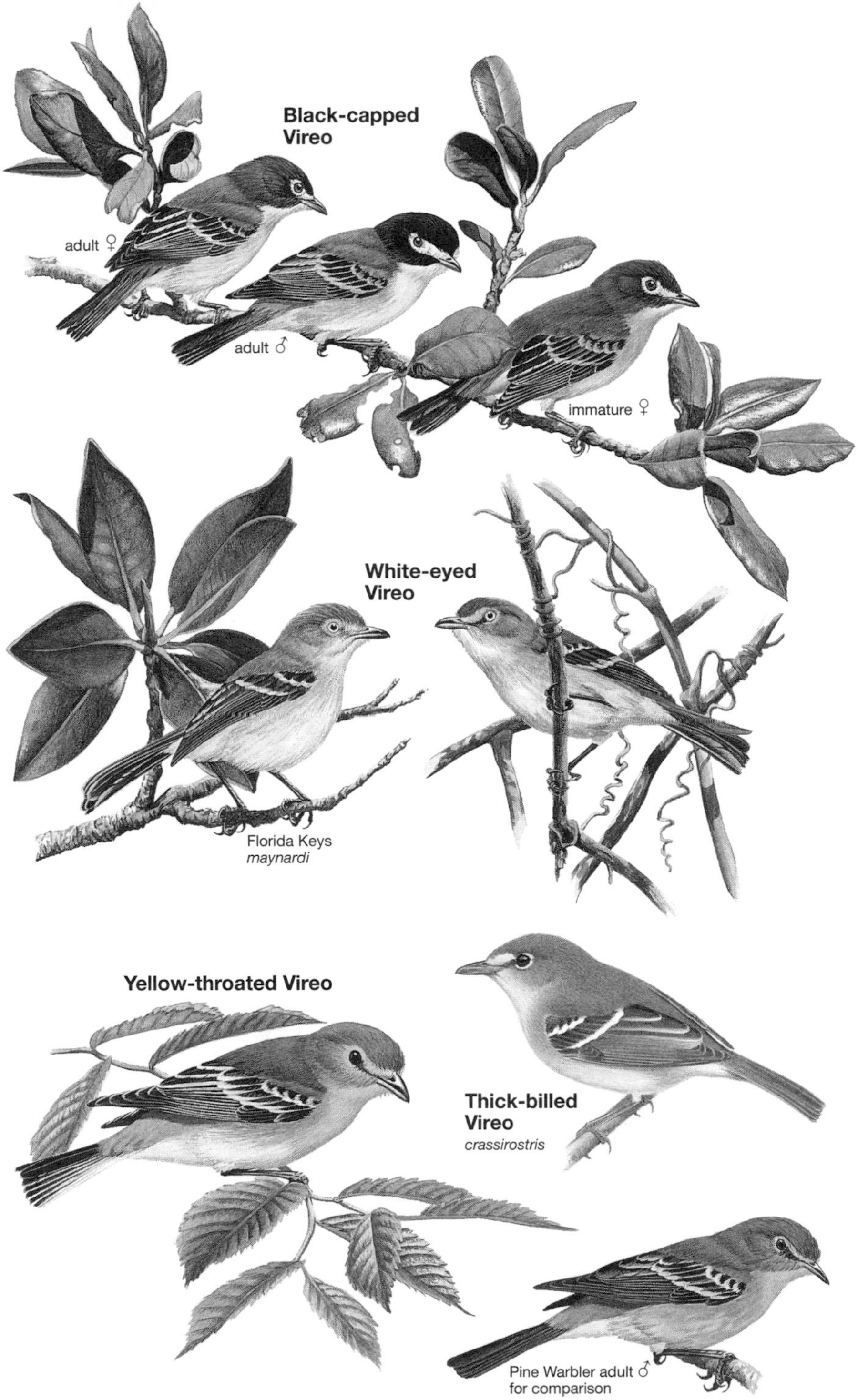
Black-capped Vireo
adult ♀
adult ♂
immature ♀
White-eyed Vireo
Florida Keys
maynardi
Yellow-throated Vireo
Thick-billed Vireo
crassirostris
Pine Warbler adult ♂
for comparison

Bell's Vireo *Vireo bellii*

DATE LOCATION

Hutton's Vireo *Vireo huttoni*

DATE LOCATION

Gray Vireo *Vireo vicinior*

DATE LOCATION

Blue-headed Vireo *Vireo solitarius*

DATE LOCATION

Plumbeous Vireo *Vireo plumbeus*

DATE LOCATION

Cassin's Vireo *Vireo cassinii*

DATE LOCATION

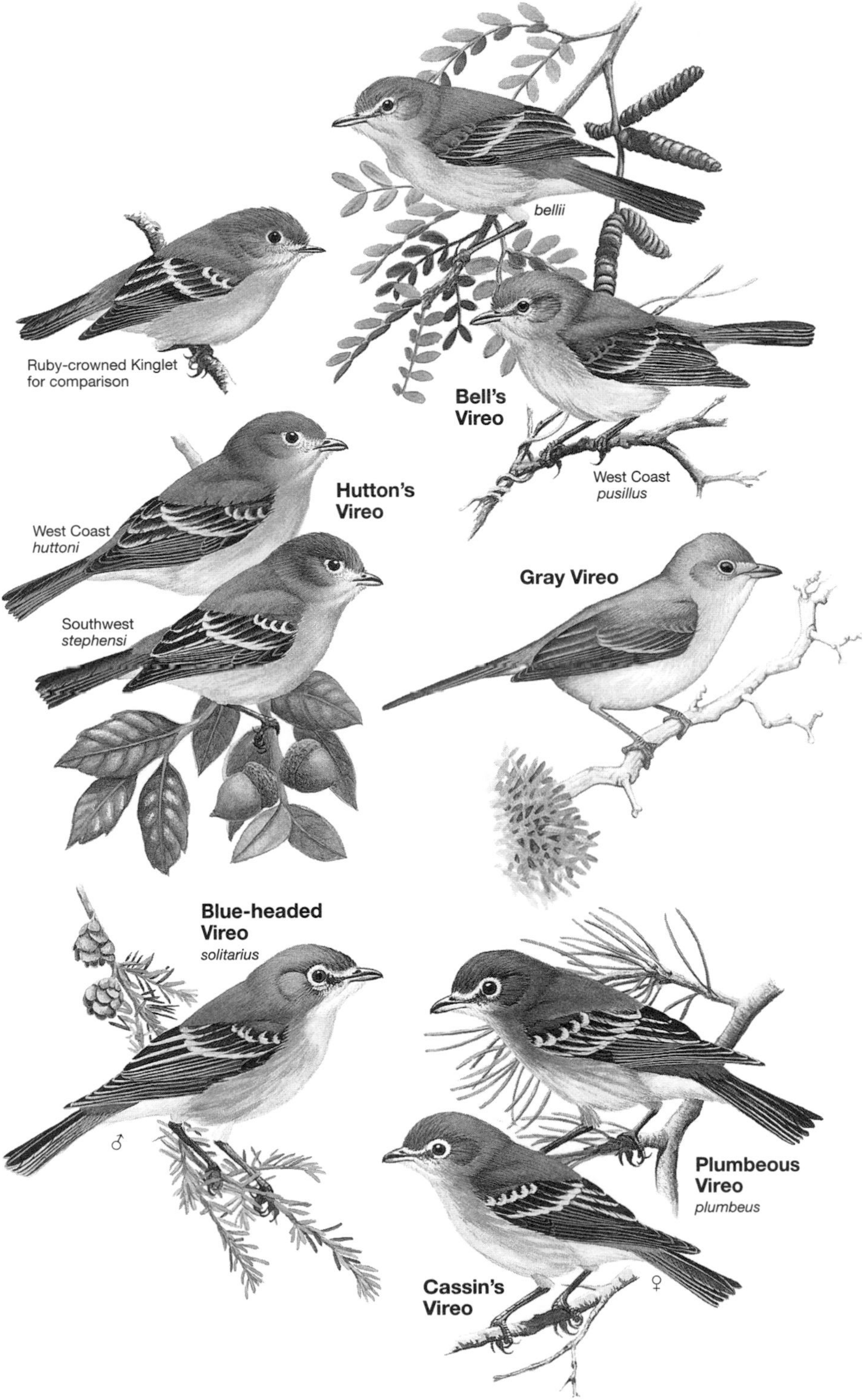

bellii
Ruby-crowned Kinglet
for comparison
Bell's
Vireo
West Coast
pusillus
Hutton's
Vireo
West Coast
huttoni
Southwest
stephensi
Gray Vireo
Blue-headed
Vireo
solitarius
♂
Plumbeous
Vireo
plumbeus
Cassin's
Vireo
♀

Yellow-green Vireo *Vireo flavoviridis*

DATE LOCATION

Red-eyed Vireo *Vireo olivaceus*

DATE LOCATION

Black-whiskered Vireo *Vireo altiloquus*

DATE LOCATION

Philadelphia Vireo *Vireo philadelphicus*

DATE LOCATION

Warbling Vireo *Vireo gilvus*

DATE LOCATION

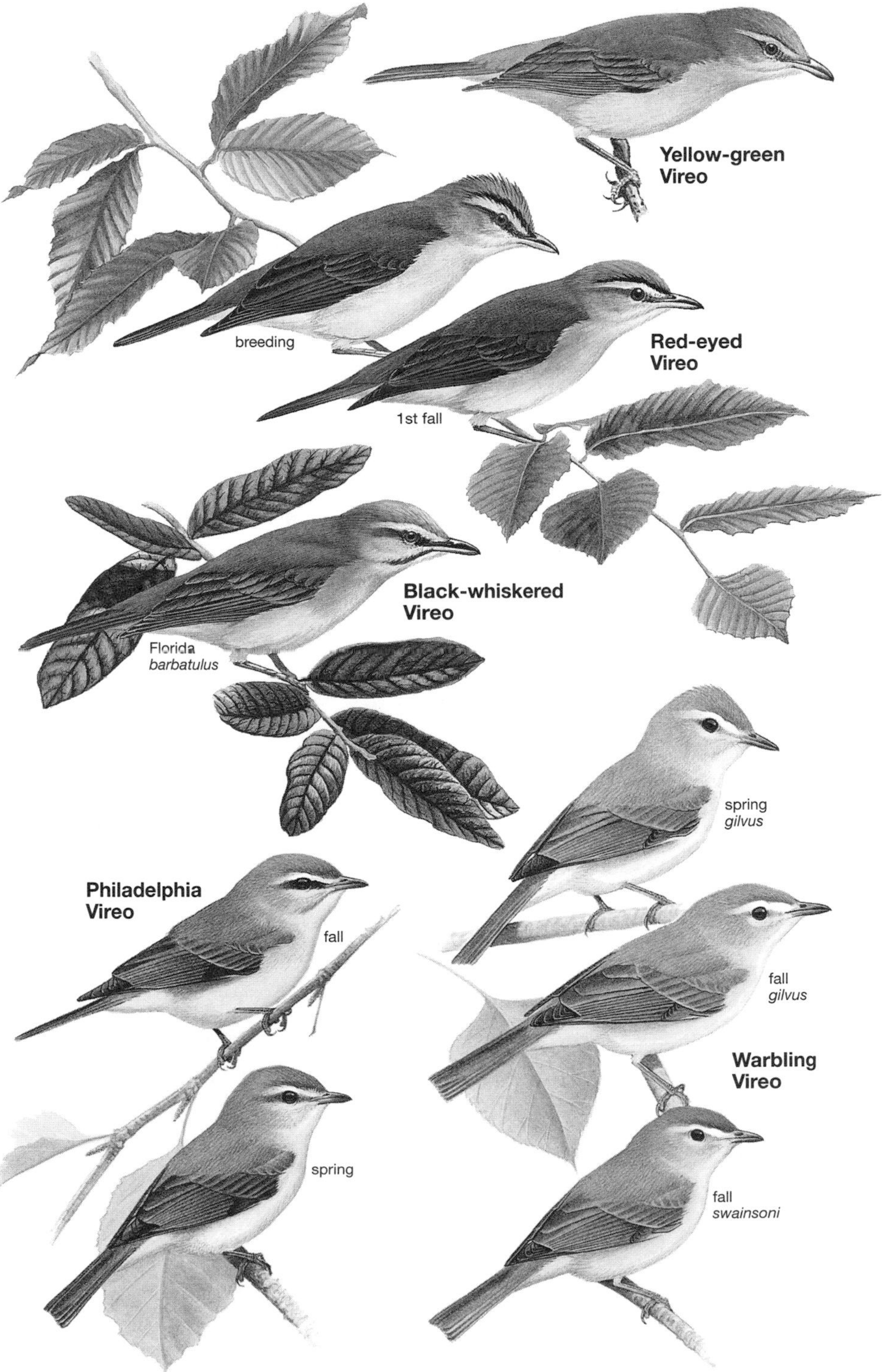
Yellow-green Vireo
breeding
Red-eyed Vireo
1st fall
Black-whiskered Vireo
Florida *barbatulus*
spring *gilvus*
Philadelphia Vireo
fall
fall *gilvus*
Warbling Vireo
spring
fall *swainsoni*

Crows, Jays (Family Corvidae)

Blue Jay *Cyanocitta cristata*

DATE LOCATION

Steller's Jay *Cyanocitta stelleri*

DATE LOCATION

Gray Jay *Perisoreus canadensis*

DATE LOCATION

Clark's Nutcracker *Nucifraga columbiana*

DATE LOCATION

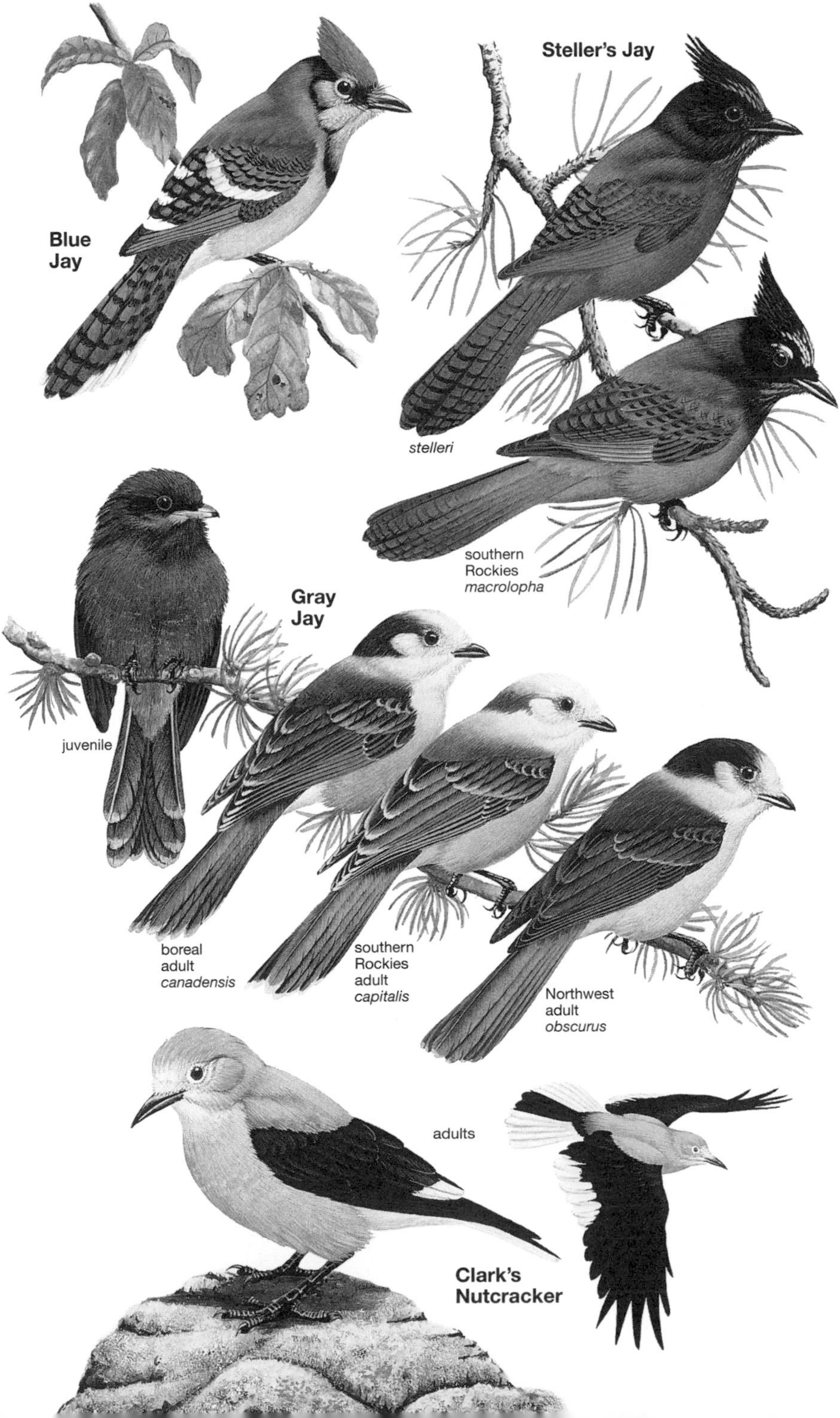
Blue Jay
Steller's Jay
stelleri
southern Rockies macrolopha
Gray Jay
juvenile
boreal adult canadensis
southern Rockies adult capitalis
Northwest adult obscurus
adults
Clark's Nutcracker

Western Scrub-Jay *Aphelocoma californica*

DATE LOCATION

Island Scrub-Jay *Aphelocoma insularis*

DATE LOCATION

Florida Scrub-Jay *Aphelocoma coerulescens*

DATE LOCATION

Mexican Jay *Aphelocoma ultramarina*

DATE LOCATION

Pinyon Jay *Gymnorhinus cyanocephalus*

DATE LOCATION

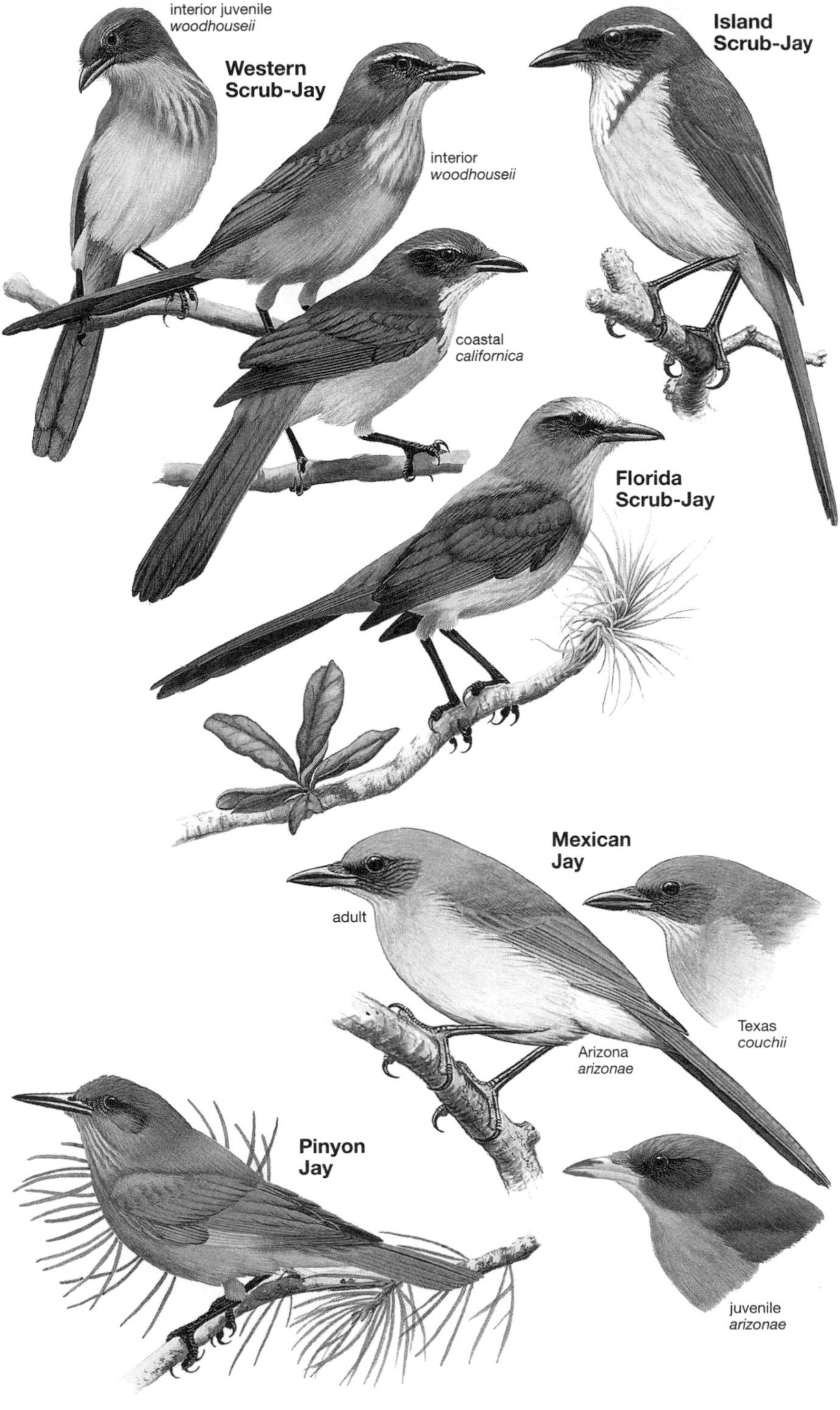

interior juvenile
woodhouseii
Western
Scrub-Jay
interior
woodhouseii
coastal
californica
Island
Scrub-Jay
Florida
Scrub-Jay
Mexican
Jay
adult
Texas
couchii
Arizona
arizonae
Pinyon
Jay
juvenile
arizonae

Brown Jay *Cyanocorax morio*

DATE LOCATION

Green Jay *Cyanocorax yncas*

DATE LOCATION

Black-billed Magpie *Pica hudsonia*

DATE LOCATION

Yellow-billed Magpie *Pica nuttalli*

DATE LOCATION

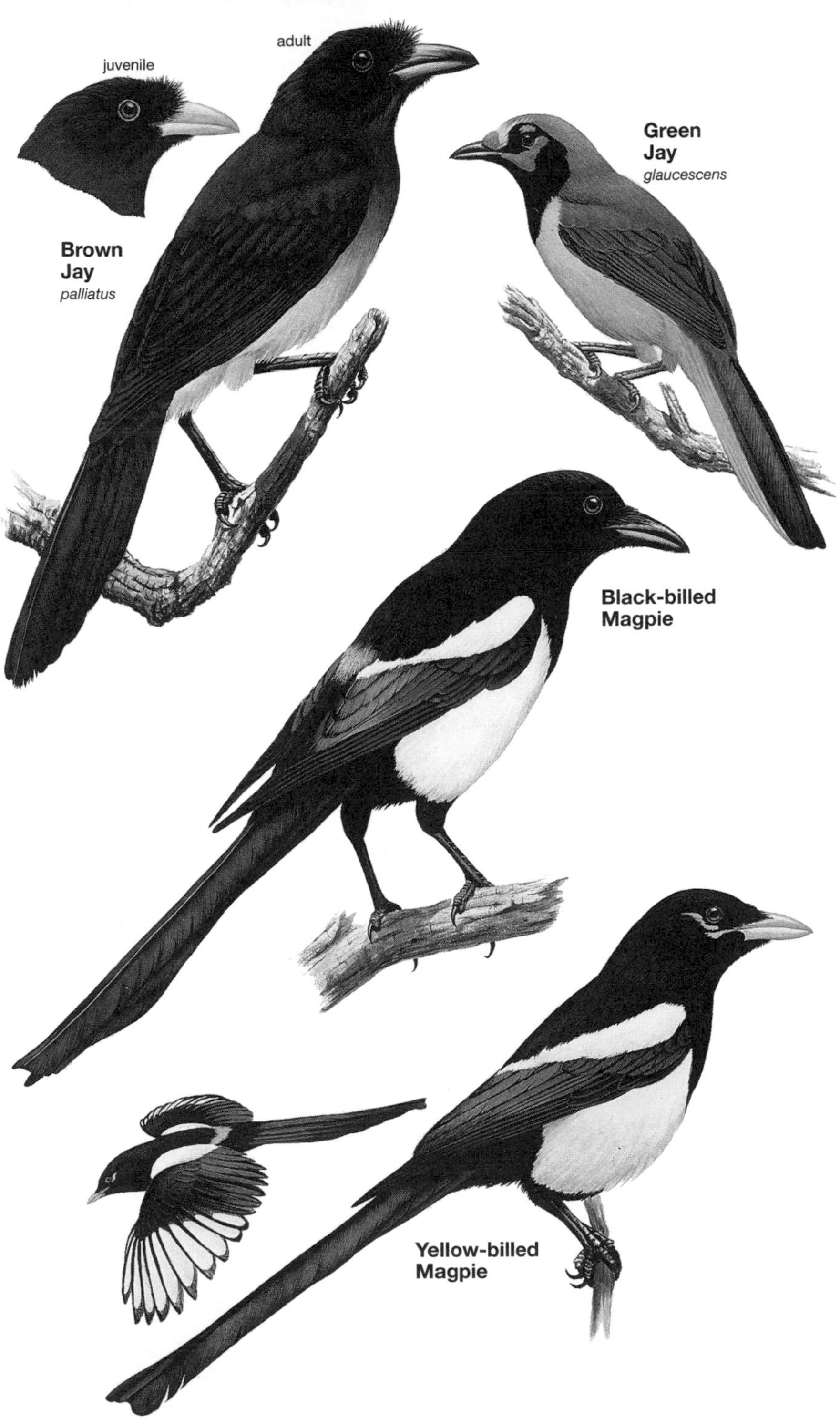

juvenile
adult
Brown
Jay
palliatus
Green
Jay
glaucescens
Black-billed
Magpie
Yellow-billed
Magpie

Eurasian Jackdaw *Corvus monedula*

DATE LOCATION

Tamaulipas Crow *Corvus imparatus*

DATE LOCATION

American Crow *Corvus brachyrhynchos*

DATE LOCATION

Northwestern Crow *Corvus caurinus* (not shown)

DATE LOCATION

Fish Crow *Corvus ossifragus*

DATE LOCATION

Chihuahuan Raven *Corvus cryptoleucus*

DATE LOCATION

Common Raven *Corvus cora*

DATE LOCATION

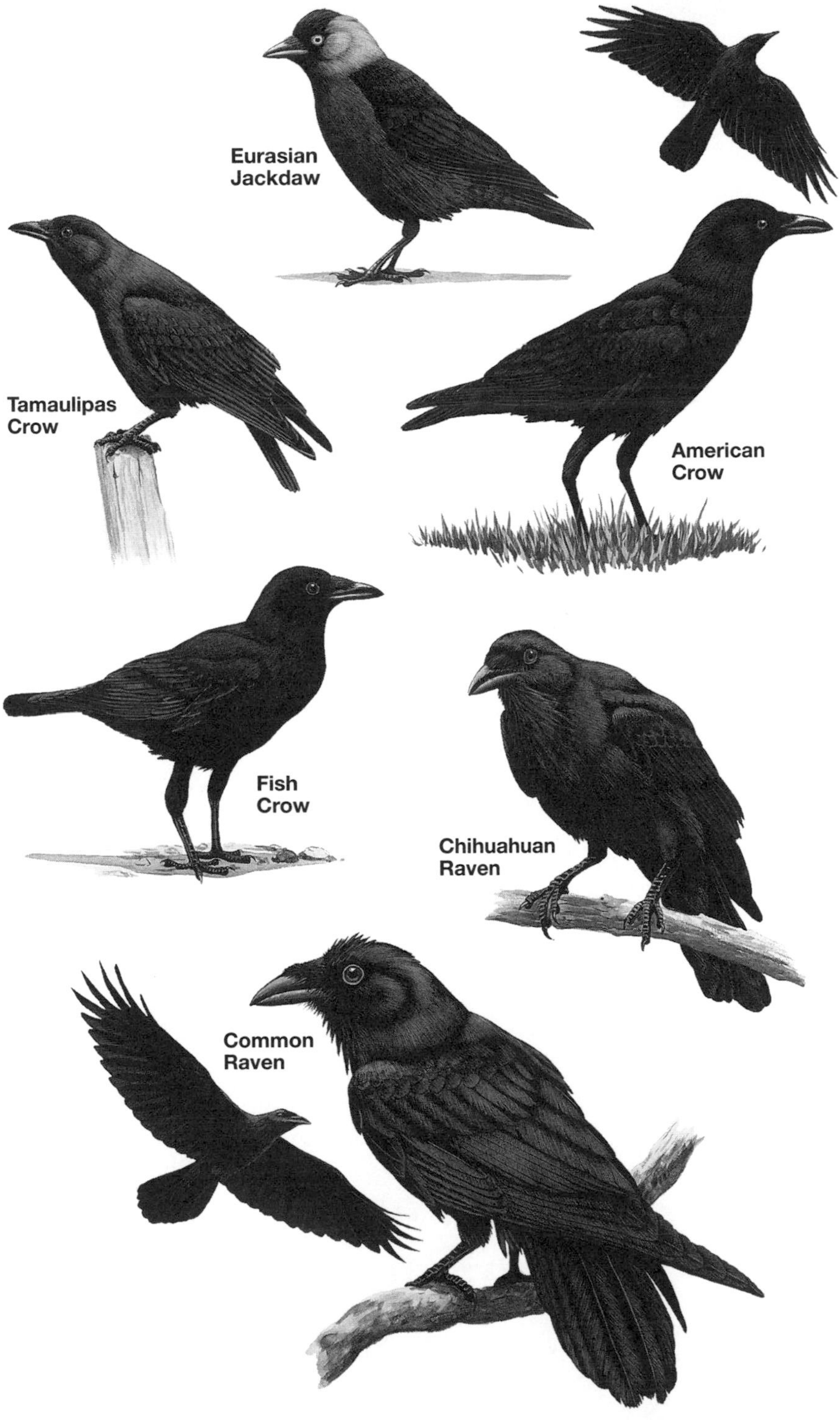

Eurasian
Jackdaw
Tamaulipas
Crow
American
Crow
Fish
Crow
Chihuahuan
Raven
Common
Raven

Larks (Family Alaudidae)

Sky Lark *Alauda arvensis*

DATE LOCATION

Horned Lark *Eremophila alpestris*

DATE LOCATION

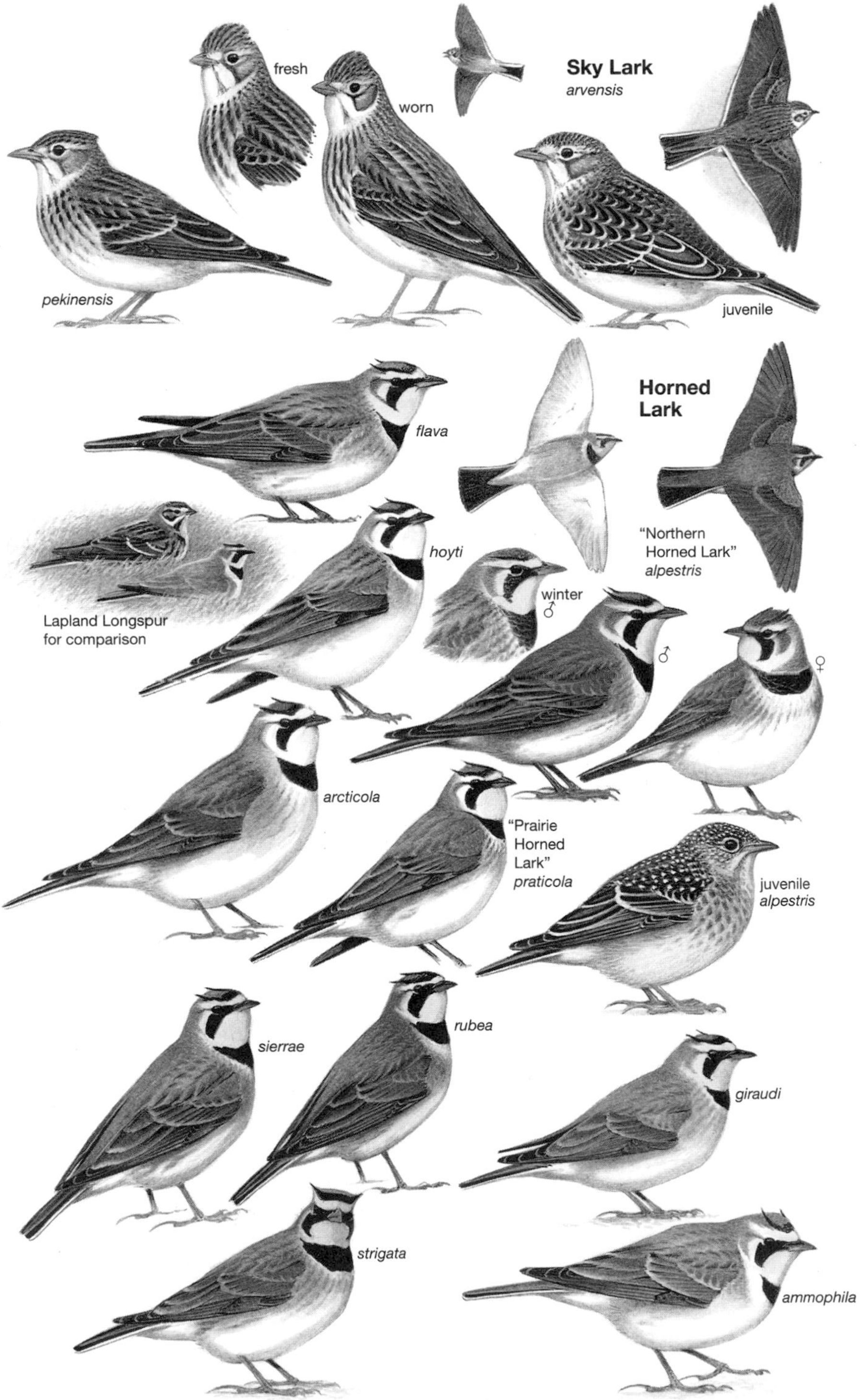
Sky Lark
arvensis
fresh
worn
pekinensis
juvenile
Horned Lark
flava
"Northern Horned Lark"
alpestris
Lapland Longspur for comparison
hoyti
winter ♂
♂
♀
arcticola
"Prairie Horned Lark"
praticola
juvenile
alpestris
sierrae
rubea
giraudi
strigata
ammophila

Swallows (Family Hirundinidae)

Tree Swallow *Tachycineta bicolor*

DATE LOCATION

Bahama Swallow *Tachycineta cyaneoviridis*

DATE LOCATION

Violet-green Swallow *Tachycineta thalassina*

DATE LOCATION

Purple Martin *Progne subis*

DATE LOCATION

Common House-Martin *Delichon urbicum*

DATE LOCATION

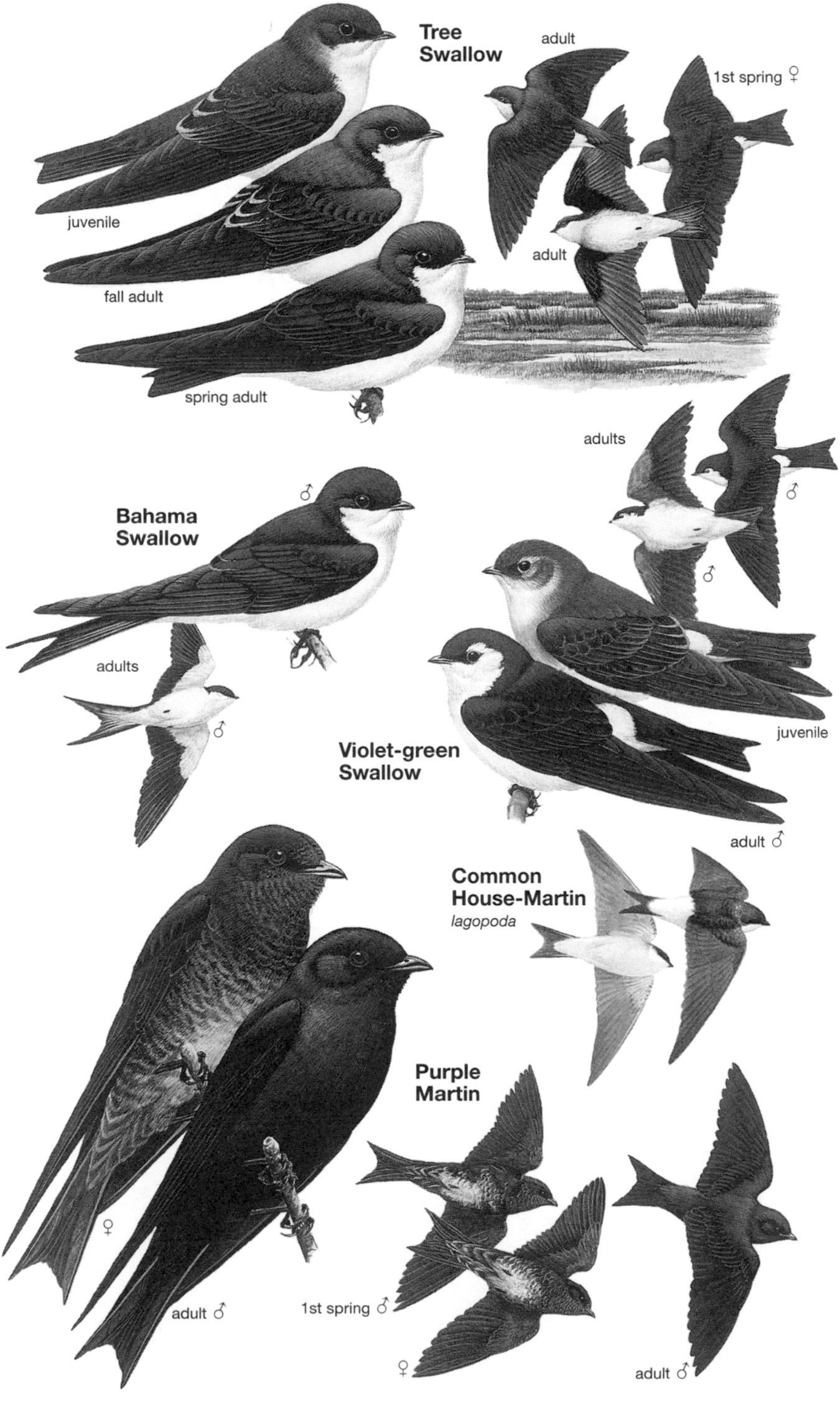
Tree Swallow
adult
1st spring ♀
juvenile
adult
fall adult
spring adult
Bahama Swallow
♂
adults
♂
adults
♂
♂
Violet-green Swallow
juvenile
adult ♂
Common House-Martin
lagopoda
Purple Martin
♀
adult ♂
1st spring ♂
♀
adult ♂

Bank Swallow *Riparia riparia*

DATE LOCATION

Cliff Swallow *Petrochelidon pyrrhonota*

DATE LOCATION

Northern Rough-winged Swallow *Stelgidopteryx serripennis*

DATE LOCATION

Barn Swallow *Hirundo rustica*

DATE LOCATION

Cave Swallow *Petrochelidon fulva*

DATE LOCATION

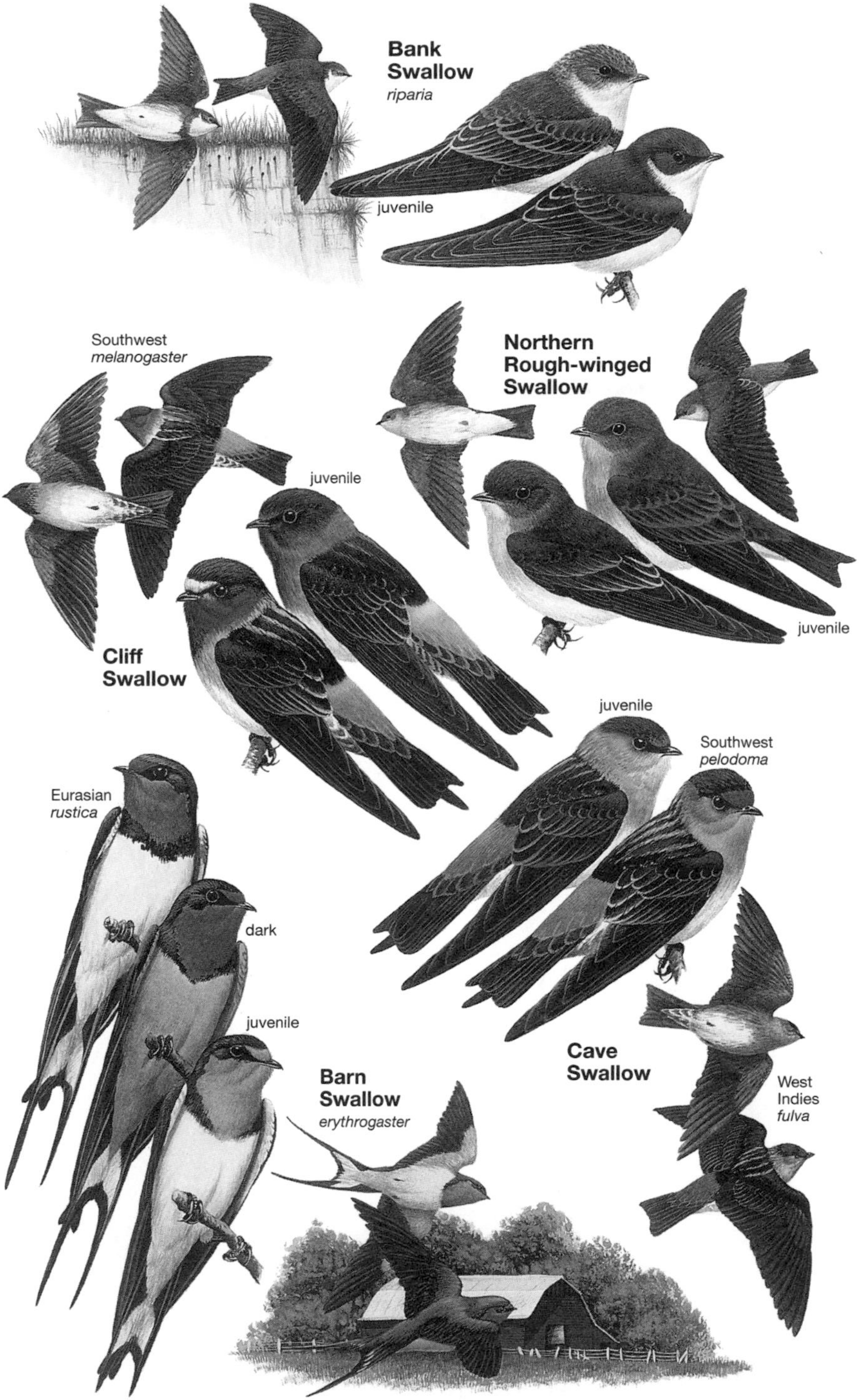

Bank
Swallow
riparia
juvenile
Southwest
melanogaster
Northern
Rough-winged
Swallow
juvenile
juvenile
Cliff
Swallow
juvenile
Southwest
pelodoma
Eurasian
rustica
dark
juvenile
Barn
Swallow
erythrogaster
Cave
Swallow
West
Indies
fulva

Babblers (Family Timaliidae)

Wrentit *Chamaea fasciata*

DATE LOCATION

Chickadees, Titmice (Family Paridae)

Bridled Titmouse *Baeolophus wollweberi*

Oak Titmouse *Baeolophus inornatus*

DATE LOCATION

Juniper Titmouse *Baeolophus ridgwayi*

DATE LOCATION

Tufted Titmouse *Baeolophus bicolor*

DATE LOCATION

Black-crested Titmouse *Baeolophus atricristatus*

DATE LOCATION

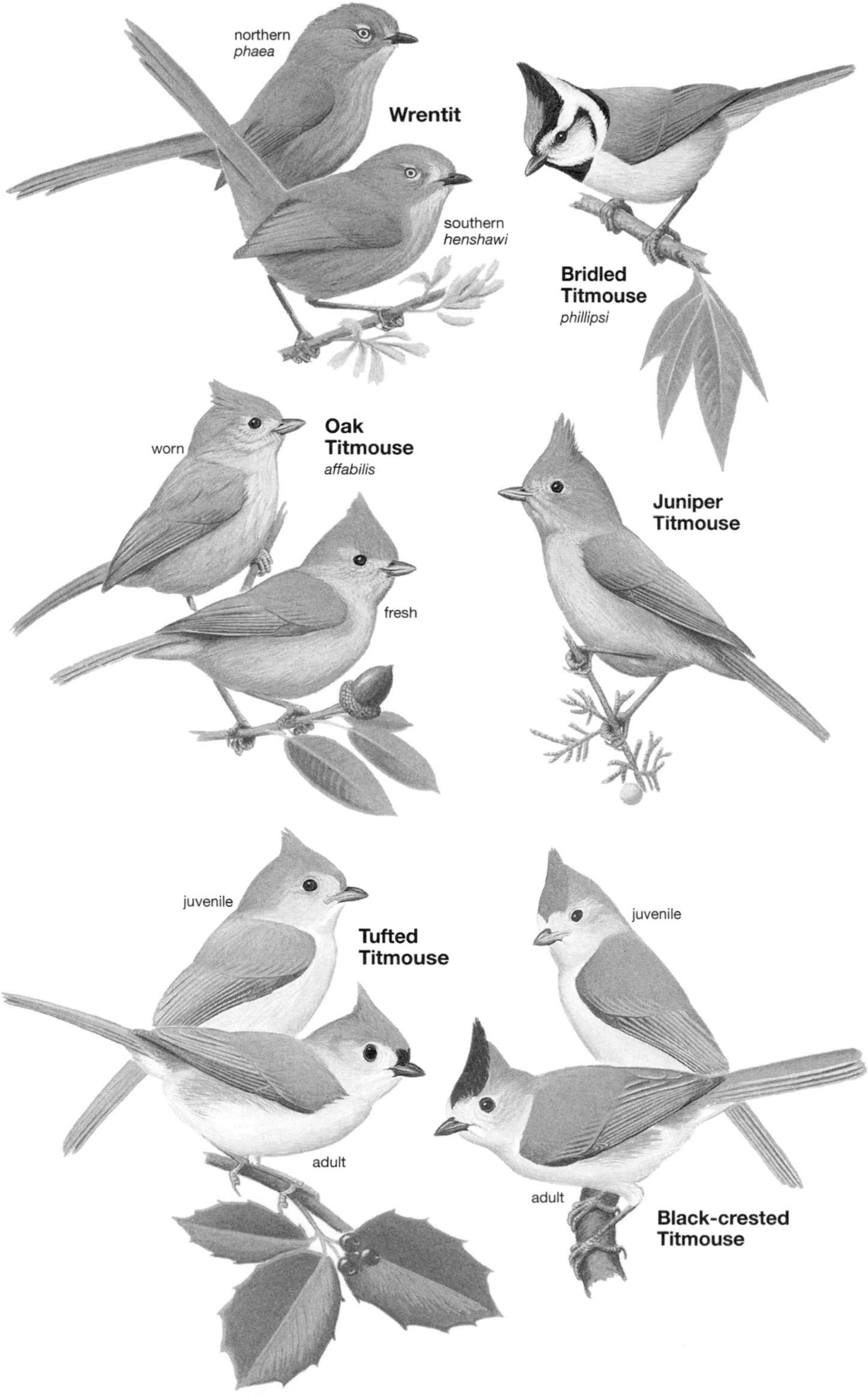
northern
phaea
Wrentit
southern
henshawi
Bridled
Titmouse
phillipsi
Oak
Titmouse
affabilis
worn
fresh
Juniper
Titmouse
juvenile
Tufted
Titmouse
adult
juvenile
adult
Black-crested
Titmouse

Black-capped Chickadee *Poecile atricapillus*

DATE LOCATION

Carolina Chickadee *Poecile carolinensis*

DATE LOCATION

Mexican Chickadee *Poecile sclateri*

DATE LOCATION

Mountain Chickadee *Poecile gambeli*

DATE LOCATION

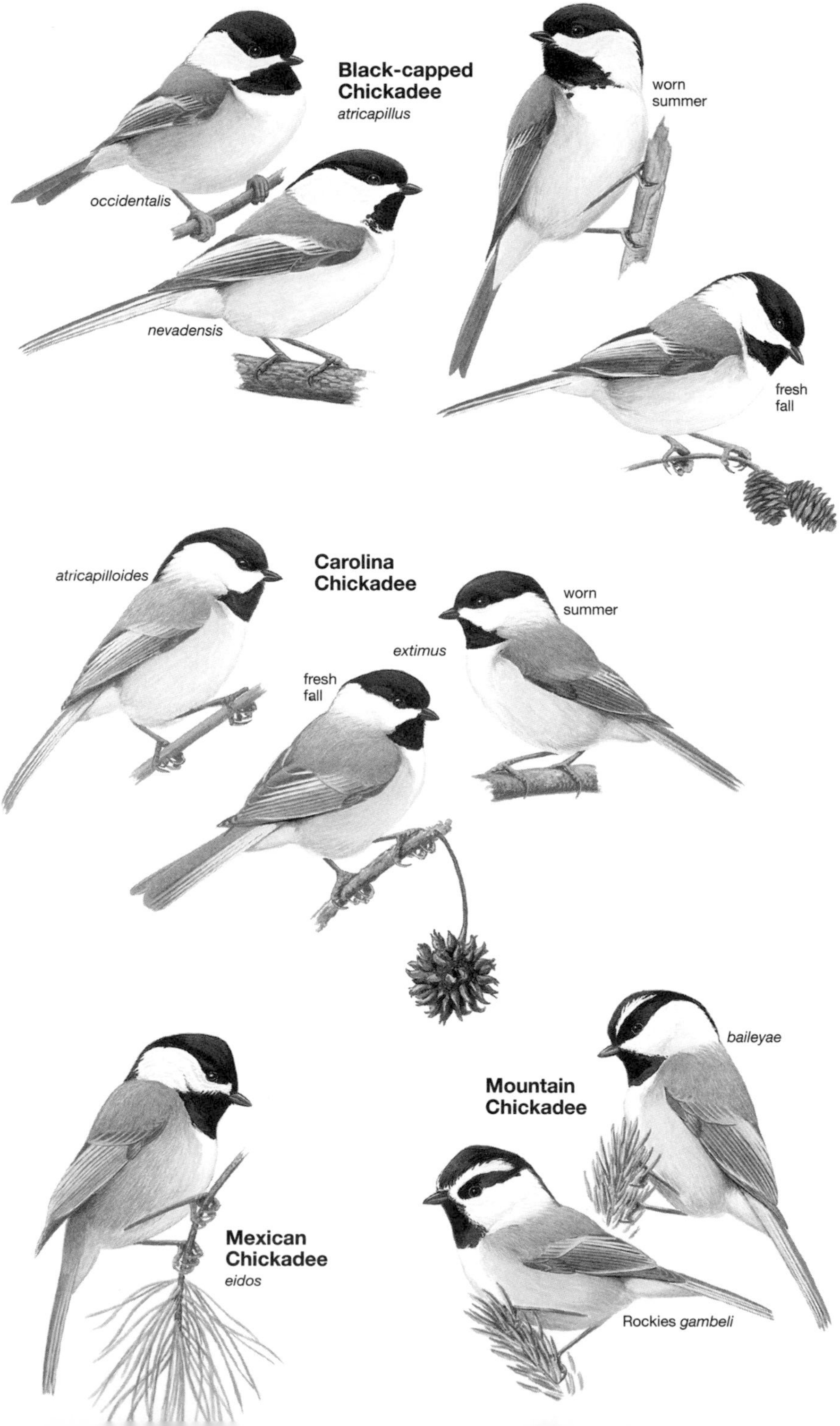
Black-capped
Chickadee
atricapillus
occidentalis
nevadensis
worn
summer
fresh
fall
Carolina
Chickadee
atricapilloides
worn
summer
extimus
fresh
fall
baileyae
Mountain
Chickadee
Mexican
Chickadee
eidos
Rockies gambeli

Chestnut-backed Chickadee *Poecile rufescens*

DATE LOCATION

Boreal Chickadee *Poecile hudsonica*

DATE LOCATION

Gray-headed Chickadee *Poecile cincta*

DATE LOCATION

Penduline Tits, Verdins (Family Remizidae)

Verdin *Auriparus flaviceps*

DATE LOCATION

Long-tailed Tits, Bushtits (Family Aegithalidae)

Bushtit *Psaltriparus minimus*

DATE LOCATION

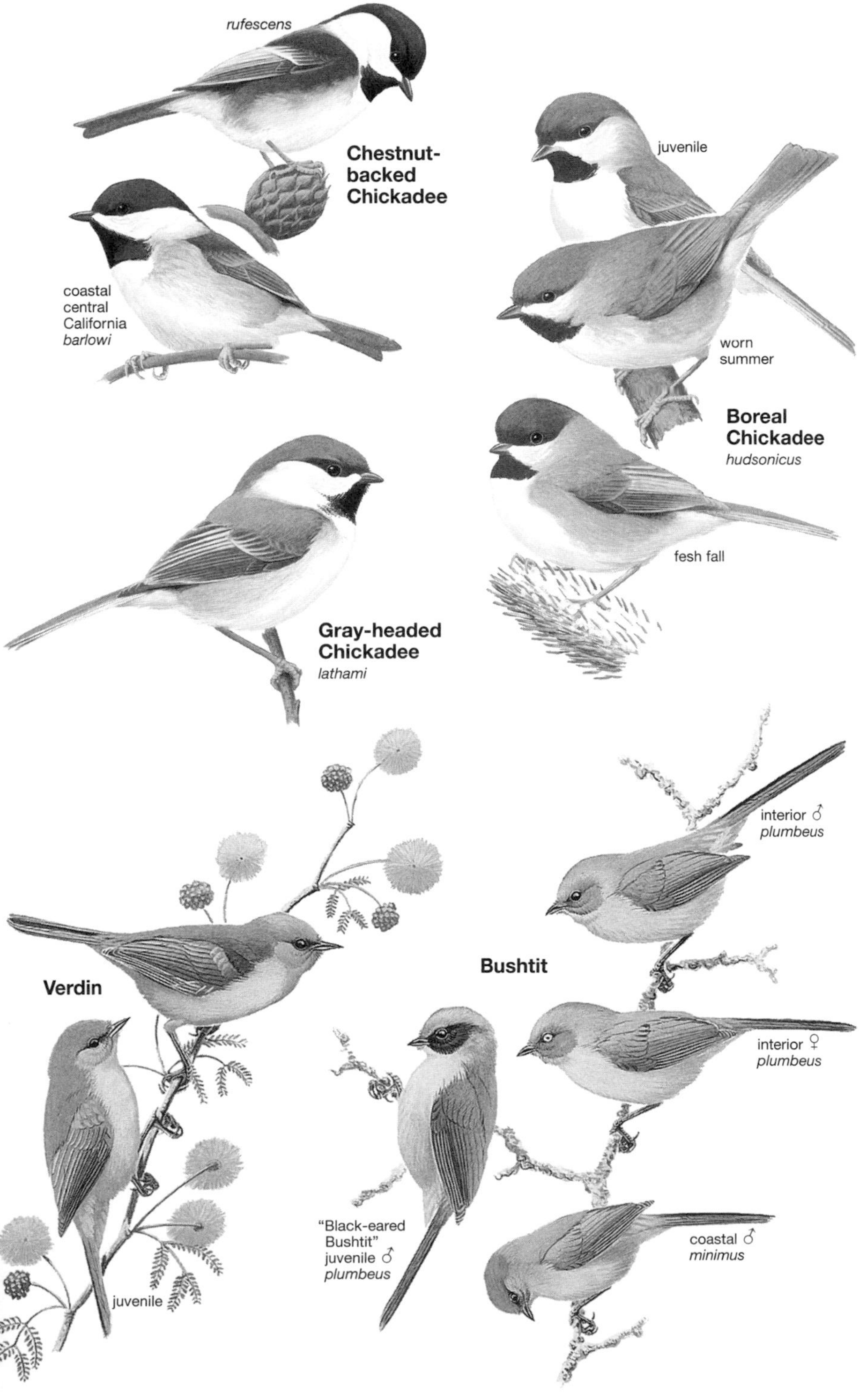
rufescens
Chestnut-backed Chickadee
coastal central California barlowi
juvenile
worn summer
Boreal Chickadee
hudsonicus
fesh fall
Gray-headed Chickadee
lathami
interior ♂ plumbeus
Bushtit
Verdin
interior ♀ plumbeus
"Black-eared Bushtit" juvenile ♂ plumbeus
coastal ♂ minimus
juvenile

Creepers (Family Certhiidae)

Brown Creeper *Certhia americana*

DATE LOCATION

Nuthatches (Family Sittidae)

White-breasted Nuthatch *Sitta carolinensis*

DATE LOCATION

Red-breasted Nuthatch *Sitta canadensis*

DATE LOCATION

Pygmy Nuthatch *Sitta pygmaea*

DATE LOCATION

Brown-headed Nuthatch *Sitta pusilla*

DATE LOCATION

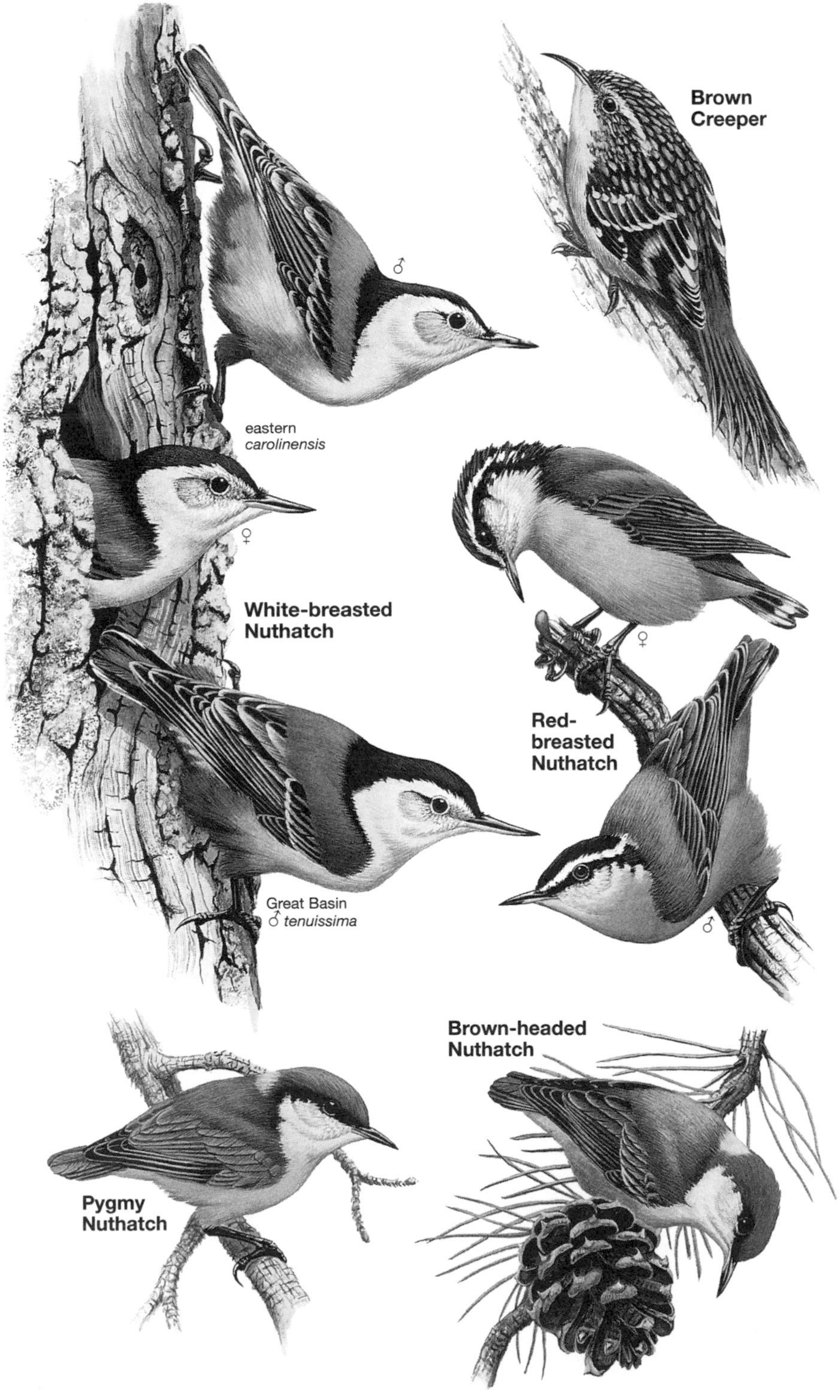
Brown
Creeper
eastern
carolinensis
♂
♀
White-breasted
Nuthatch
Great Basin
♂ tenuissima
Red-
breasted
Nuthatch
♀
♂
Brown-headed
Nuthatch
Pygmy
Nuthatch

Wrens (Family Troglodytidae)

House Wren *Troglodytes aedon*

DATE LOCATION

Winter Wren *Troglodytes troglodytes*

DATE LOCATION

Carolina Wren *Thryothorus ludovicianus*

DATE LOCATION

Bewick's Wren *Thryomanes bewickii*

DATE LOCATION

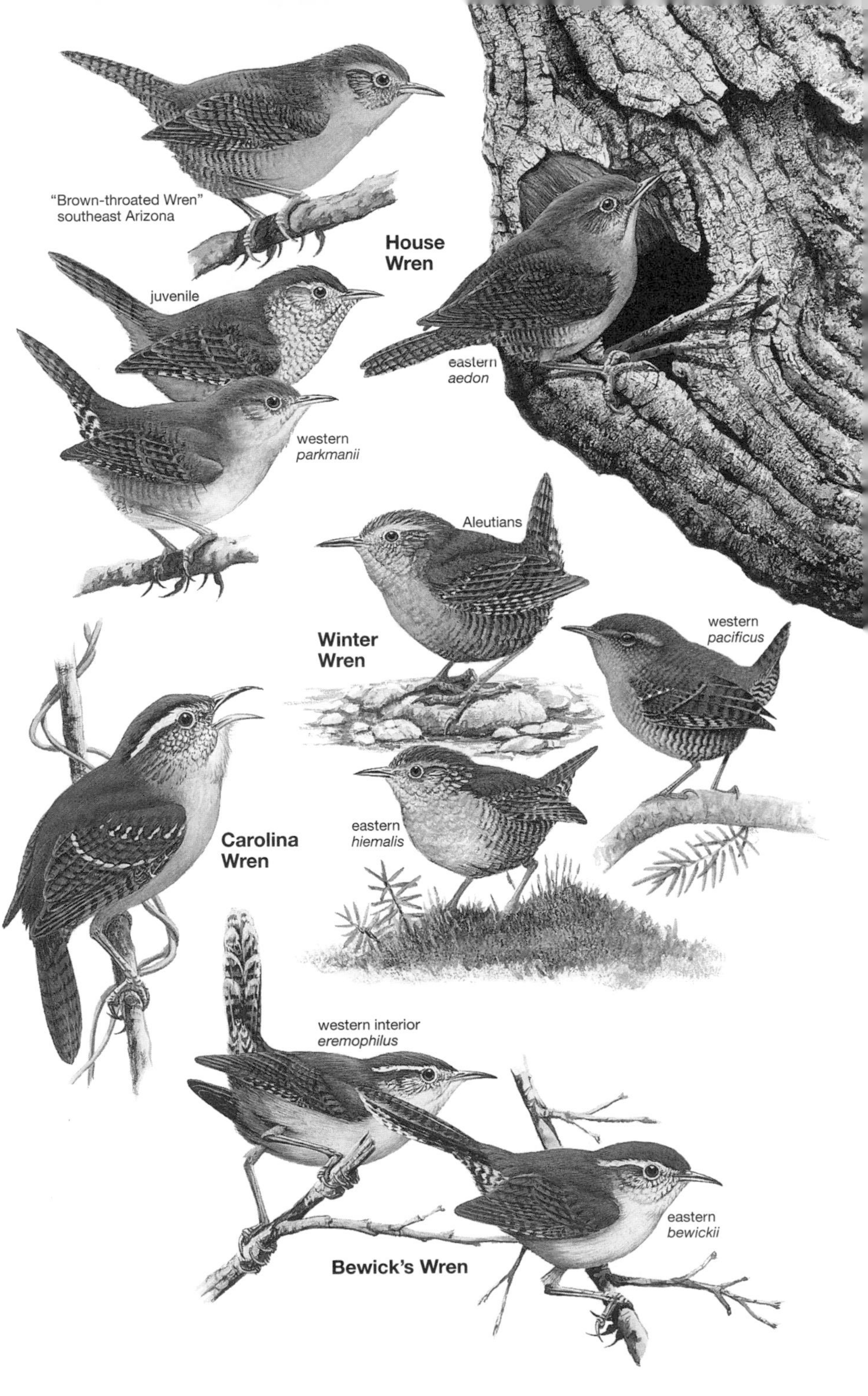
"Brown-throated Wren"
southeast Arizona
House
Wren
juvenile
eastern
aedon
western
parkmanii
Aleutians
Winter
Wren
western
pacificus
Carolina
Wren
eastern
hiemalis
western interior
eremophilus
eastern
bewickii
Bewick's Wren

Cactus Wren *Campylorhynchus brunneicapillus*

DATE LOCATION

Rock Wren *Salpinctes obsoletus*

DATE LOCATION

Canyon Wren *Catherpes mexicanus*

DATE LOCATION

Marsh Wren *Cistothorus palustris*

DATE LOCATION

Sedge Wren *Cistothorus platensis*

DATE LOCATION

Dippers (Family Cinclidae)

American Dipper *Cinclus mexicanus*

DATE LOCATION

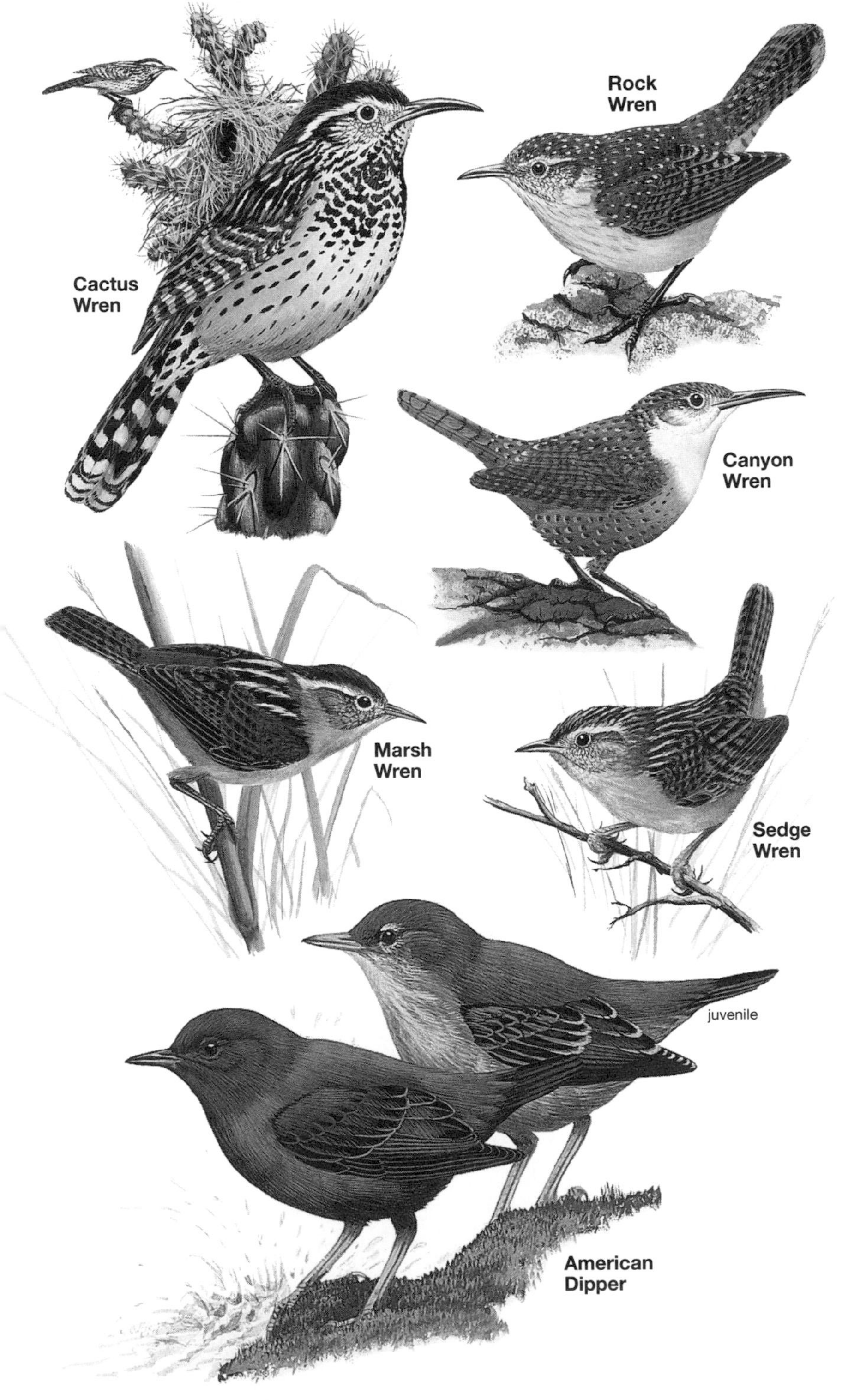
Cactus Wren
Rock Wren
Canyon Wren
Marsh Wren
Sedge Wren
juvenile
American Dipper

Kinglets (Family Regulidae)

Golden-crowned Kinglet *Regulus satrapa*

DATE LOCATION

Ruby-crowned Kinglet *Regulus calendula*

DATE LOCATION

Old World Warblers, Gnatcatchers (Family Sylviidae)

Blue-gray Gnatcatcher *Polioptila caerulea*

DATE LOCATION

Black-capped Gnatcatcher *Polioptila nigriceps*

DATE LOCATION

Black-tailed Gnatcatcher *Polioptila melanura*

DATE LOCATION

California Gnatcatcher *Polioptila californica*

DATE LOCATION

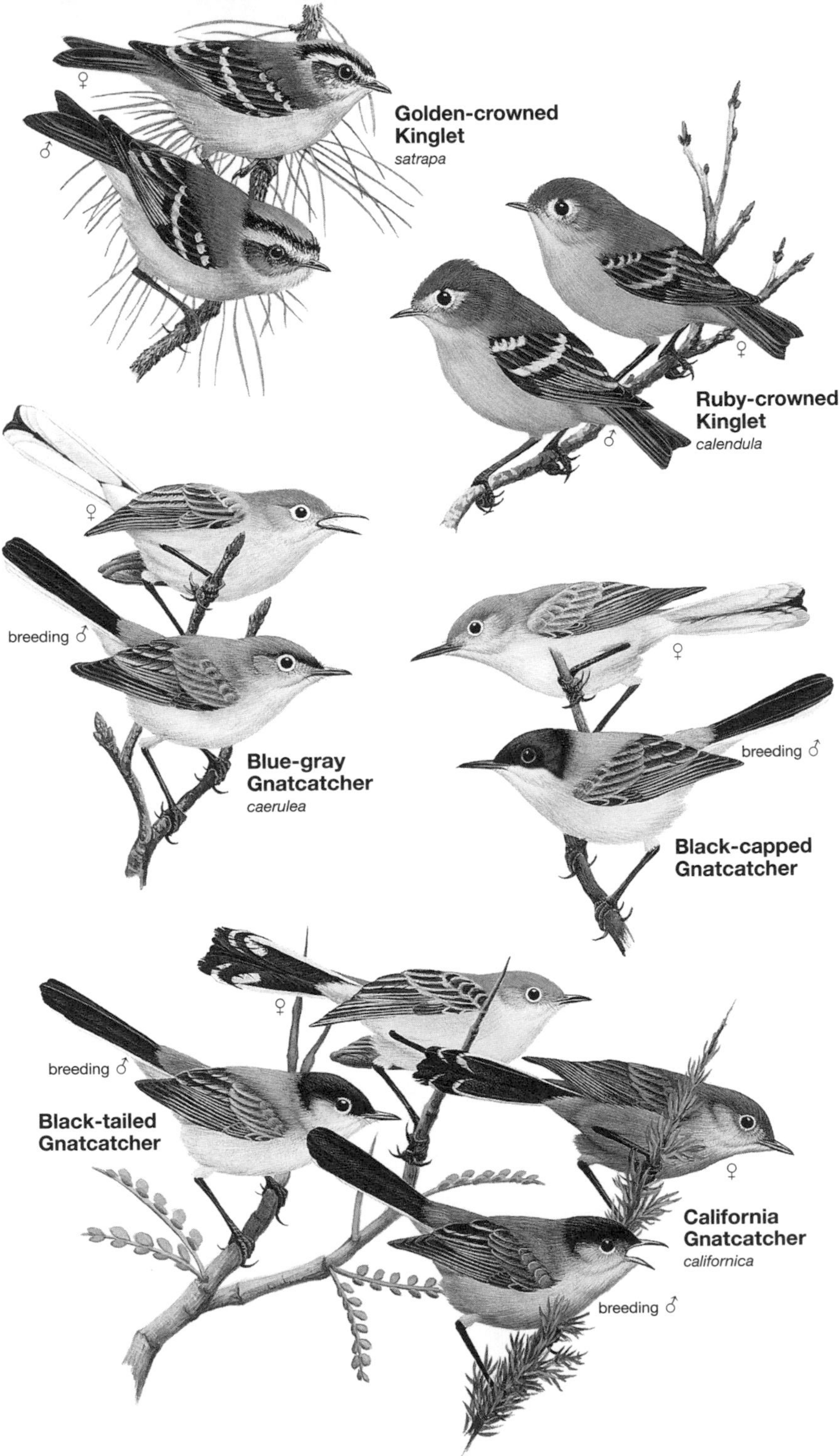

♀
♂
Golden-crowned Kinglet
satrapa
Ruby-crowned Kinglet
calendula
♀
♂
♀
breeding ♂
Blue-gray Gnatcatcher
caerulea
♀
breeding ♂
Black-capped Gnatcatcher
♀
breeding ♂
Black-tailed Gnatcatcher
♀
California Gnatcatcher
californica
breeding ♂

Lanceolated Warbler *Locustella lanceolata*

DATE LOCATION

Middendorff's Grasshopper-Warbler *Locustella ochotensis*

DATE LOCATION

Dusky Warbler *Phylloscopus fuscatus*

DATE LOCATION

Arctic Warbler *Phylloscopus borealis*

DATE LOCATION

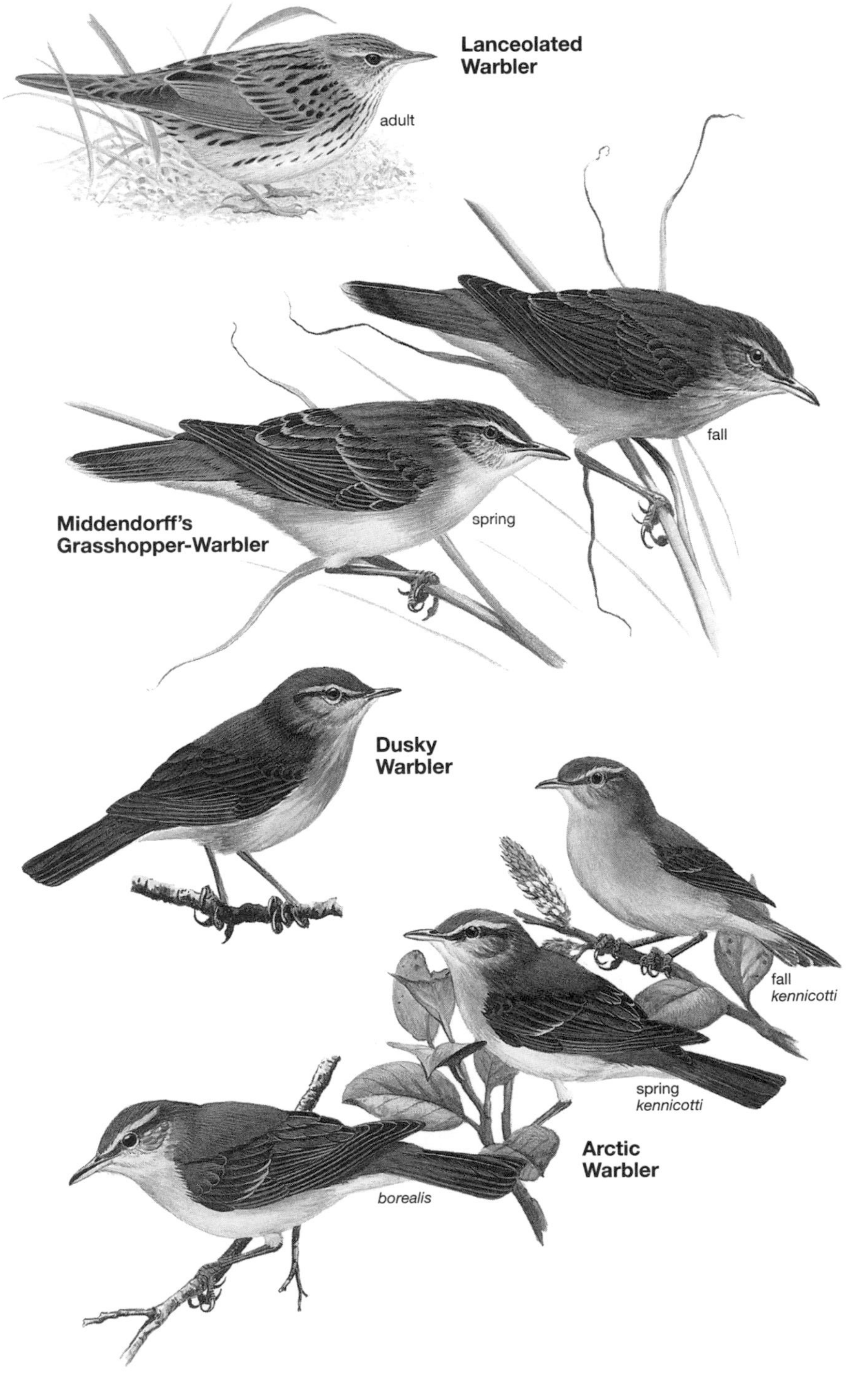
Lanceolated Warbler
adult
fall
Middendorff's Grasshopper-Warbler
spring
Dusky Warbler
fall
kennicotti
spring
kennicotti
Arctic Warbler
borealis

Old World Flycatchers (Family Muscicapidae)

Narcissus Flycatcher *Ficedula narcissina*

DATE LOCATION

Dark-sided Flycatcher *Muscicapa sibirica*

DATE LOCATION

Taiga Flycatcher *Ficedula albicilla*

DATE LOCATION

Gray-streaked Flycatcher *Muscicapa griseisticta*

DATE LOCATION

Asian Brown Flycatcher *Muscicapa dauurica*

DATE LOCATION

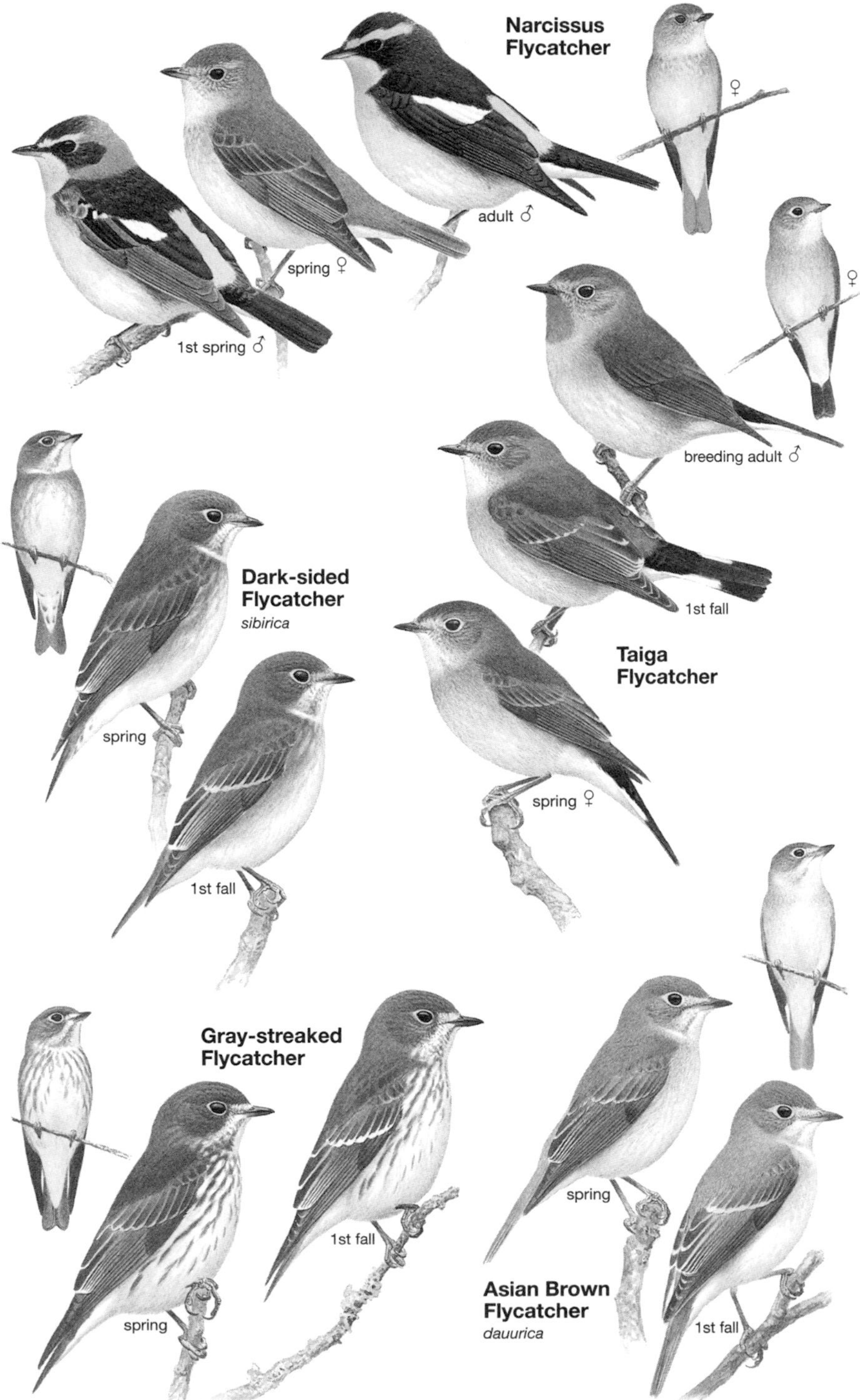

Narcissus Flycatcher
♀
adult ♂
spring ♀
1st spring ♂
♀
breeding adult ♂
Dark-sided Flycatcher
sibirica
spring
1st fall
1st fall
Taiga Flycatcher
spring ♀
Gray-streaked Flycatcher
spring
1st fall
spring
Asian Brown Flycatcher
dauurica
1st fall

Thrushes (Family Turdidae)

Siberian Rubythroat *Luscinia calliope*

DATE LOCATION

Bluethroat *Luscinia svecica*

DATE LOCATION

Red-flanked Bluetail *Tarsiger cyanurus*

DATE LOCATION

Northern Wheatear *Oenanthe oenanthe*

DATE LOCATION

Stonechat *Saxicola torquatus*

DATE LOCATION

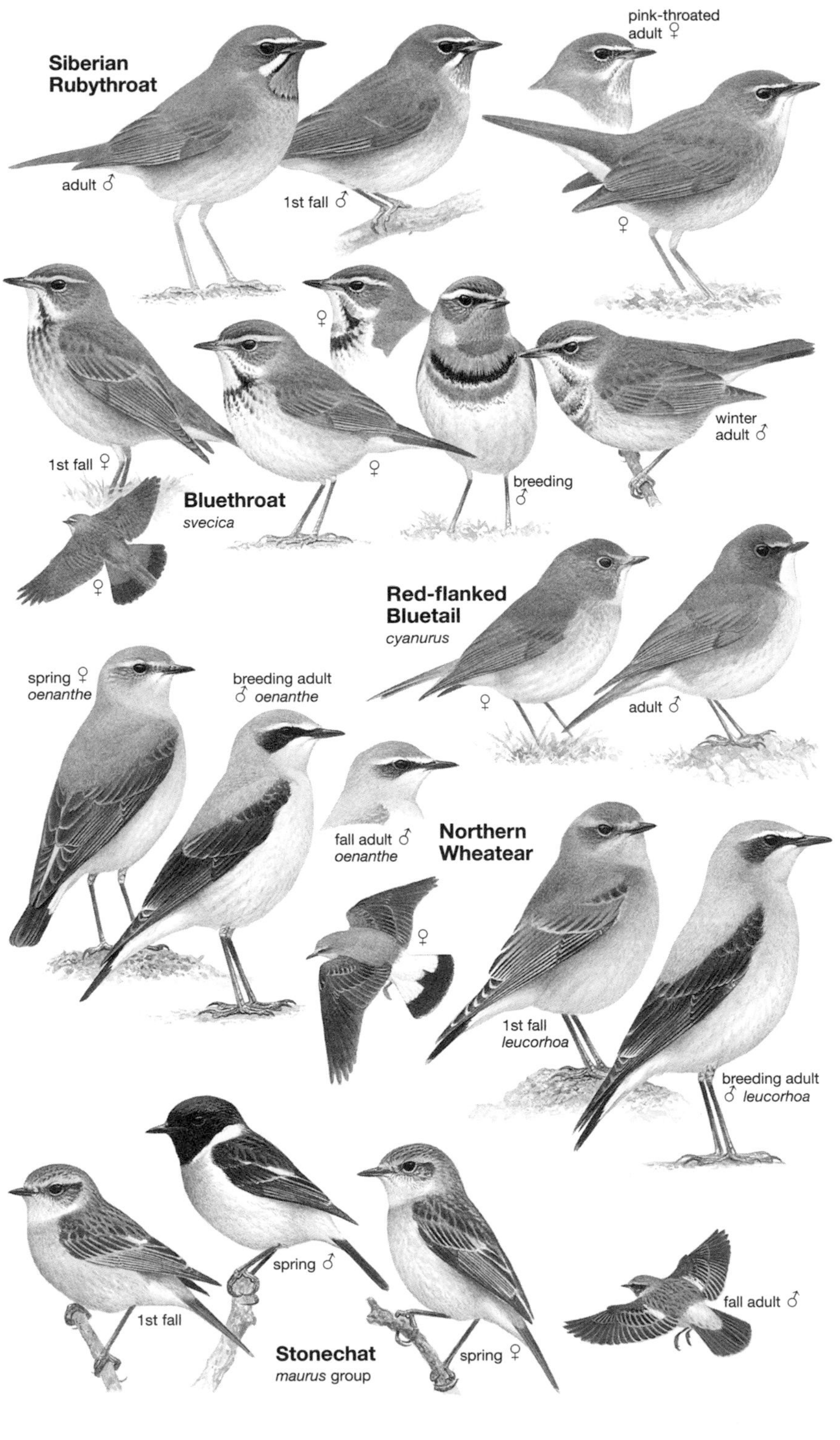
Siberian Rubythroat
adult ♂
1st fall ♂
pink-throated adult ♀
♀
1st fall ♀
♀
♀
breeding ♂
winter adult ♂
Bluethroat
svecica
♀
Red-flanked Bluetail
cyanurus
♀
adult ♂
spring ♀
oenanthe
breeding adult
♂ oenanthe
fall adult ♂
oenanthe
Northern Wheatear
♀
1st fall
leucorhoa
breeding adult
♂ leucorhoa
spring ♂
1st fall
Stonechat
maurus group
spring ♀
fall adult ♂

Eastern Bluebird *Sialia sialis*

DATE LOCATION

Western Bluebird *Sialia mexicana*

DATE LOCATION

Mountain Bluebird *Sialia currucoides*

DATE LOCATION

Townsend's Solitaire *Myadestes townsendi*

DATE LOCATION

juvenile
♀
♂
Eastern
Bluebird
sialis
southwestern
♂ fulva
Western
Bluebird
♀
♂
♀
♂
Mountain
Bluebird
juvenile
Townsend's
Solitaire

Wood Thrush *Hylocichla mustelina*

DATE LOCATION

Veery *Catharus fuscescens*

DATE LOCATION

Gray-cheeked Thrush *Catharus minimus*

DATE LOCATION

Bicknell's Thrush *Catharus bicknelli*

DATE LOCATION

Swainson's Thrush *Catharus ustulatus*

DATE LOCATION

Hermit Thrush *Catharus guttatus*

DATE LOCATION

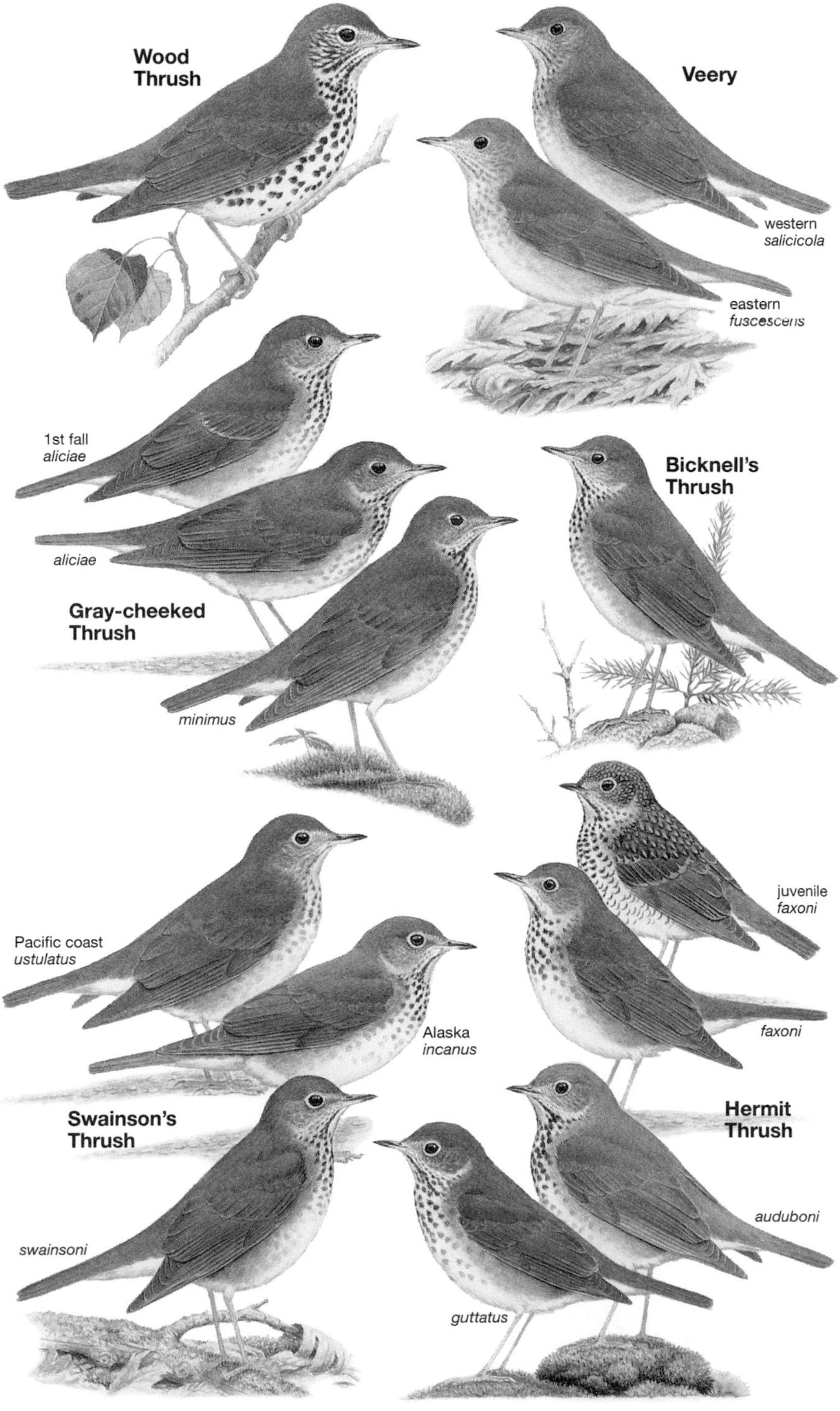

Wood Thrush

Veery

western
salicicola

eastern
fuscescens

1st fall
aliciae

aliciae

Bicknell's Thrush

Gray-cheeked Thrush

minimus

Pacific coast
ustulatus

juvenile
faxoni

Alaska
incanus

faxoni

Swainson's Thrush

Hermit Thrush

swainsoni

auduboni

guttatus

Varied Thrush *Ixoreus naevius*

DATE LOCATION

Eyebrowed Thrush *Turdus obscurus*

DATE LOCATION

Dusky Thrush *Turdus naumanni*

DATE LOCATION

Fieldfare *Turdus pilaris*

DATE LOCATION

Redwing *Turdus iliacus*

DATE LOCATION

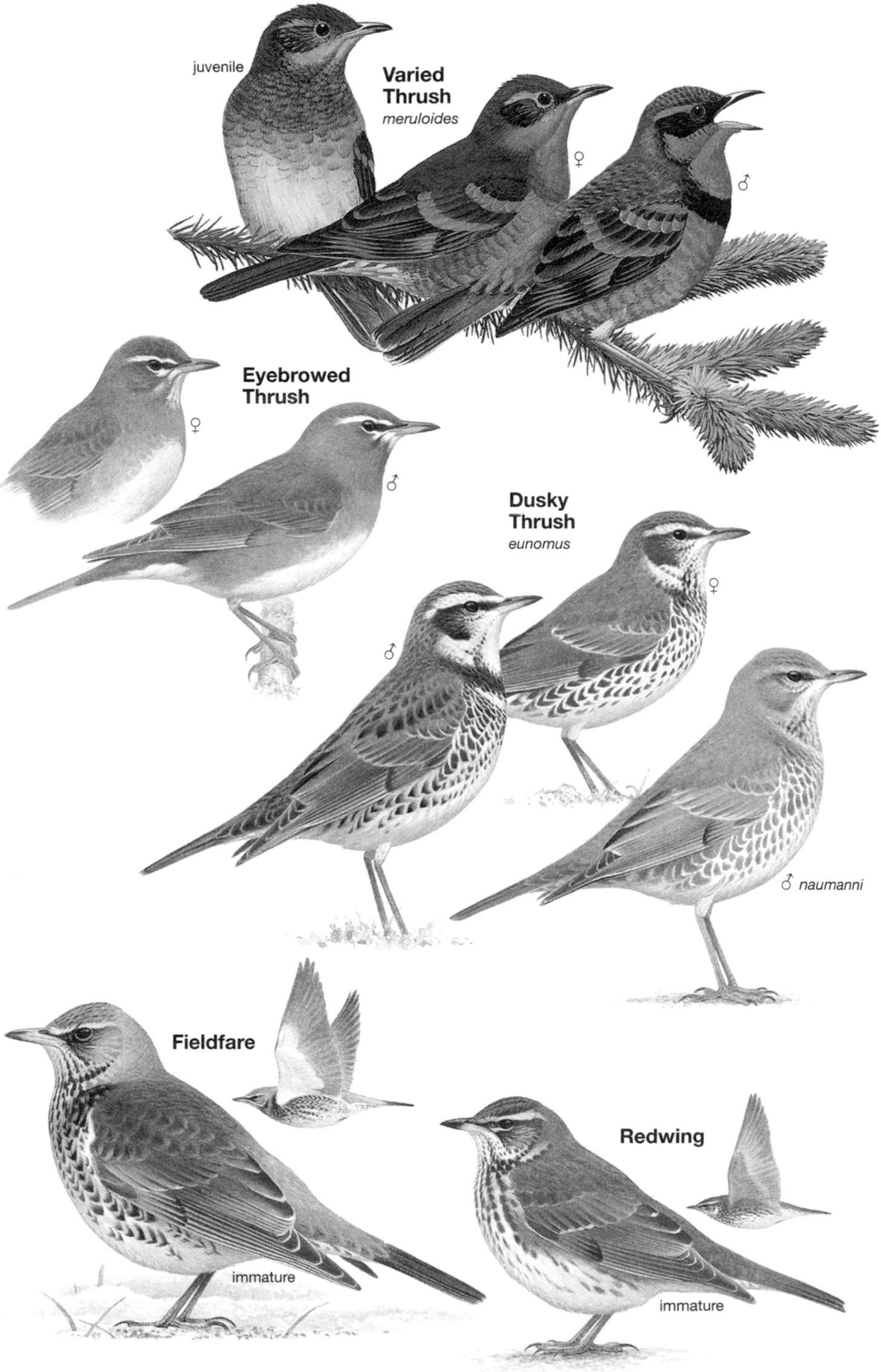

juvenile
Varied Thrush
meruloides
♀
♂
Eyebrowed Thrush
♀
♂
Dusky Thrush
eunomus
♀
♂
♂ naumanni
Fieldfare
immature
Redwing
immature

American Robin *Turdus migratorius*

DATE LOCATION

White-throated Robin *Turdus assimilis*

DATE LOCATION

Rufous-backed Robin *Turdus rufopalliatus*

DATE LOCATION

Clay-colored Robin *Turdus grayi*

DATE LOCATION

Aztec Thrush *Ridgwayia pinicola*

DATE LOCATION

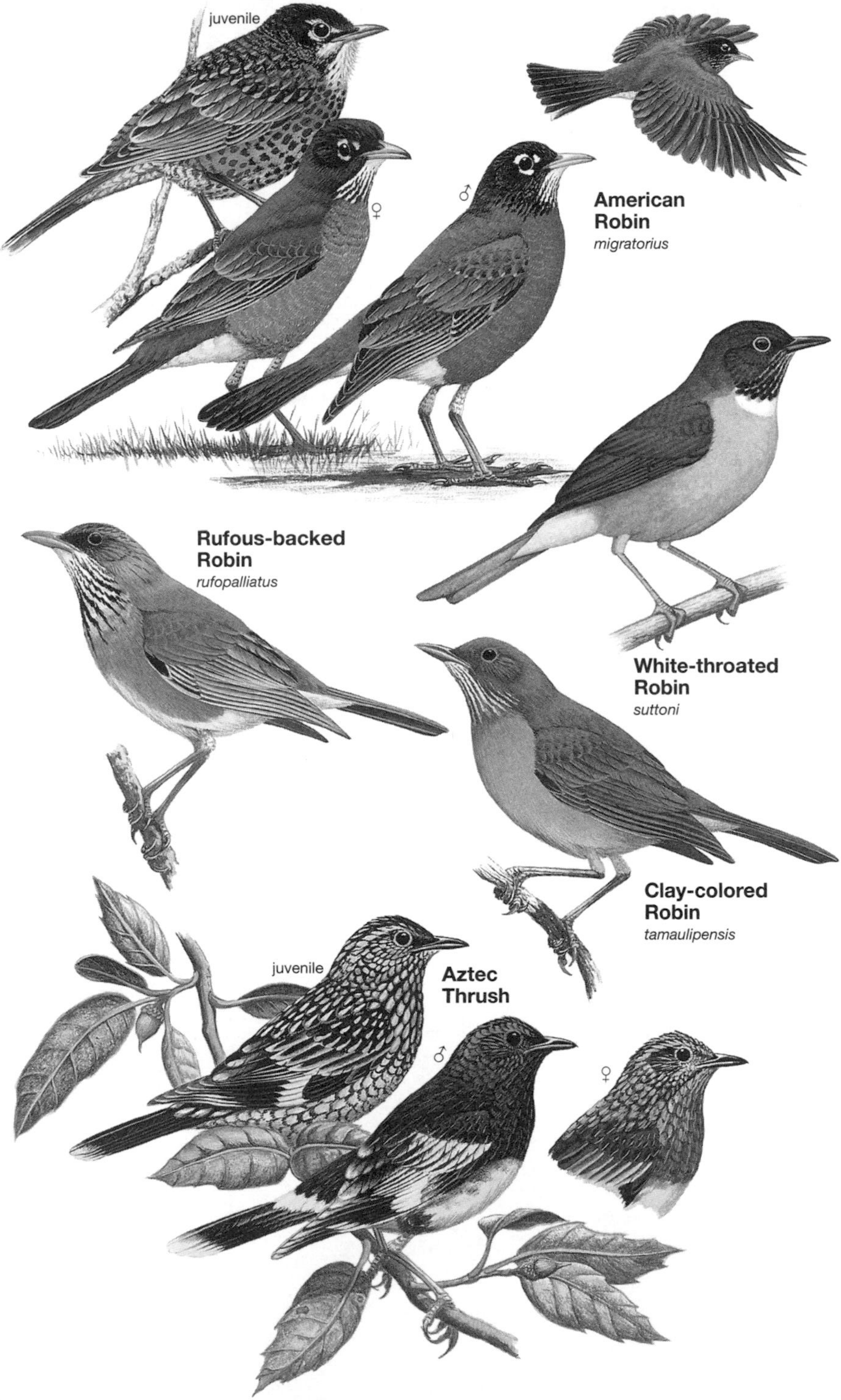
juvenile
♀
♂
American
Robin
migratorius
Rufous-backed
Robin
rufopalliatus
White-throated
Robin
suttoni
Clay-colored
Robin
tamaulipensis
juvenile
Aztec
Thrush
♂
♀

Mockingbirds, Thrashers (Family Mimidae)

Gray Catbird *Dumetella carolinensis*

DATE LOCATION

Northern Mockingbird *Mimus polyglottos*

DATE LOCATION

Bahama Mockingbird *Mimus gundlachii*

DATE LOCATION

Blue Mockingbird *Melanotis caerulescens*

DATE LOCATION

Brown Thrasher *Toxostoma rufum*

DATE LOCATION

Long-billed Thrasher *Toxostoma longirostre*

DATE LOCATION

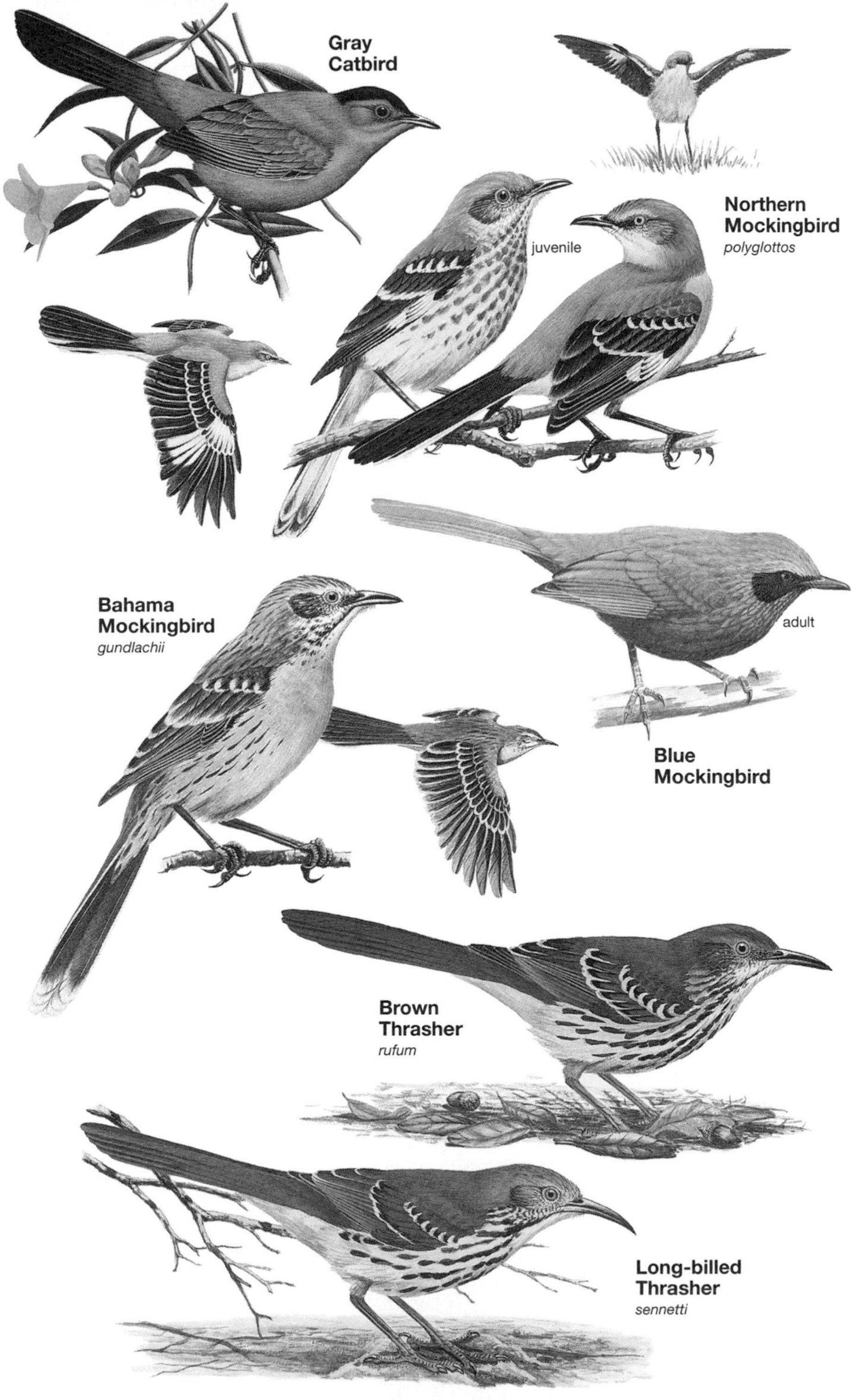
Gray
Catbird
Northern
Mockingbird
polyglottos
juvenile
Bahama
Mockingbird
gundlachii
adult
Blue
Mockingbird
Brown
Thrasher
rufum
Long-billed
Thrasher
sennetti

Sage Thrasher *Oreoscoptes montanus*

DATE LOCATION

Bendire's Thrasher *Toxostoma bendirei*

DATE LOCATION

Curve-billed Thrasher *Toxostoma curvirostre*

DATE LOCATION

California Thrasher *Toxostoma redivivum*

DATE LOCATION

Crissal Thrasher *Toxostoma crissale*

DATE LOCATION

Le Conte's Thrasher *Toxostoma lecontei*

DATE LOCATION

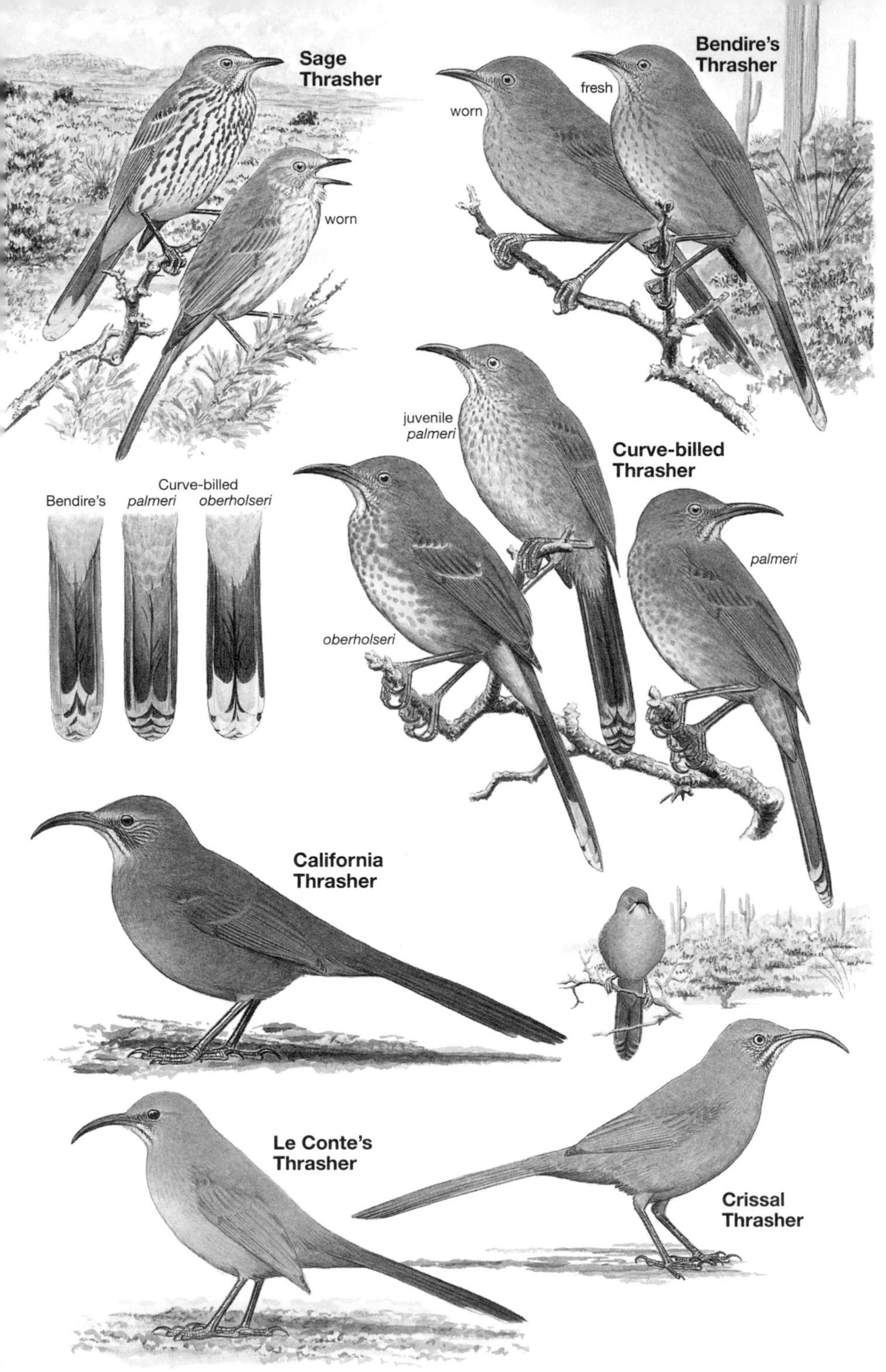
Sage Thrasher
worn
Bendire's Thrasher
fresh
worn
juvenile palmeri
Curve-billed Thrasher
Curve-billed
Bendire's
palmeri
oberholseri
palmeri
oberholseri
California Thrasher
Le Conte's Thrasher
Crissal Thrasher

Bulbuls (Family Pycnonotidae)

Red-whiskered Bulbul *Pycnonotus jocosus*

DATE LOCATION

Starlings (Family Sturnidae)

Crested Myna *Acridotheres cristatellus*

DATE LOCATION

Common Myna *Acridotheres tristis*

DATE LOCATION

Hill Myna *Gracula religiosa*

DATE LOCATION

European Starling *Sturnus vulgaris*

DATE LOCATION

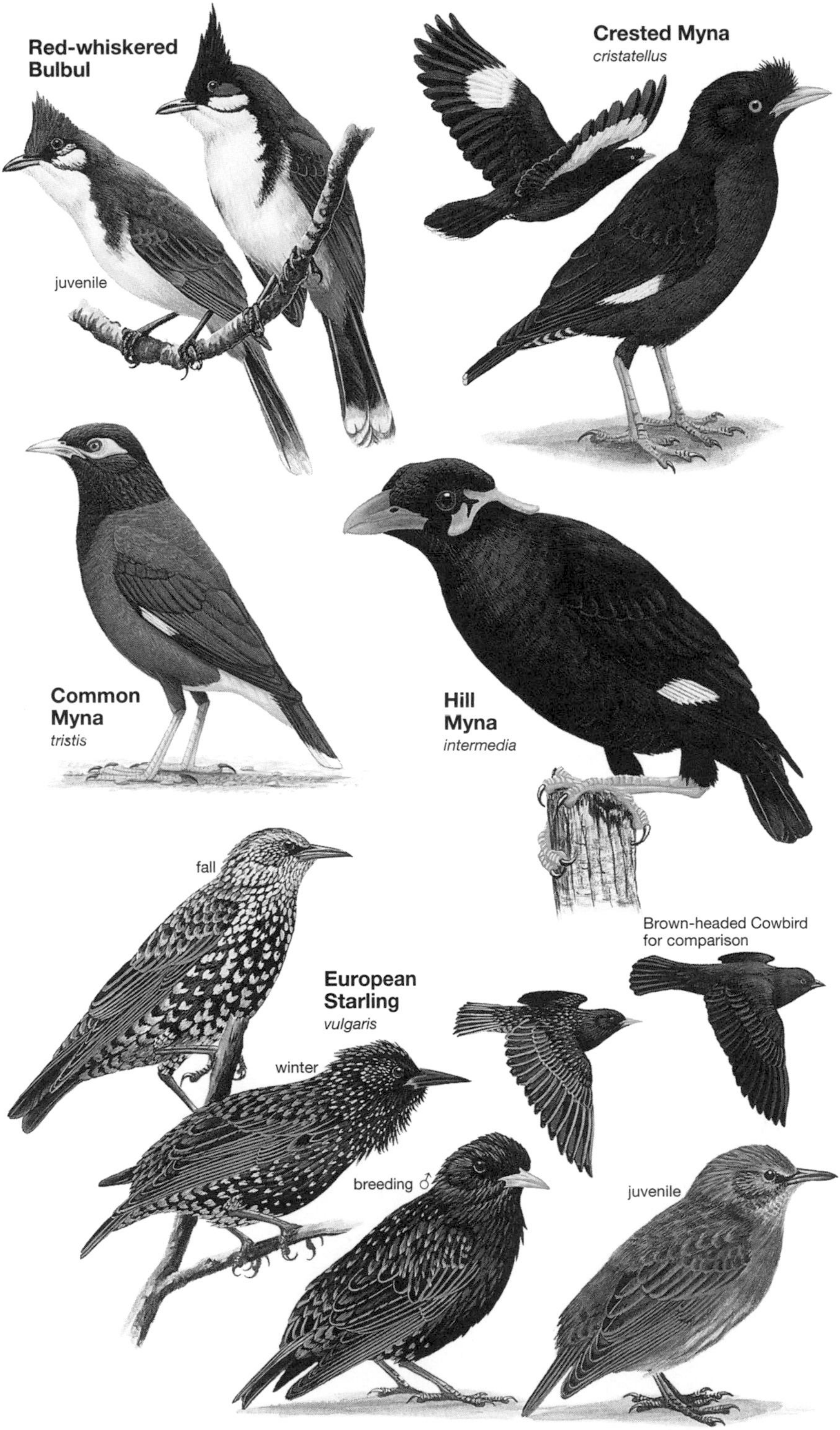
Red-whiskered Bulbul
juvenile
Crested Myna
cristatellus
Common Myna
tristis
Hill Myna
intermedia
fall
European Starling
vulgaris
winter
breeding ♂
juvenile
Brown-headed Cowbird for comparison

Accentors (Family Prunellidae)

Siberian Accentor *Prunella montanella*

DATE LOCATION

Wagtails, Pipits (Family Motacillidae)

Eastern Yellow Wagtail *Motacilla tschutschensis*

DATE LOCATION

Gray Wagtail *Motacilla cinerea*

DATE LOCATION

White Wagtail *Motacilla alba*

DATE LOCATION

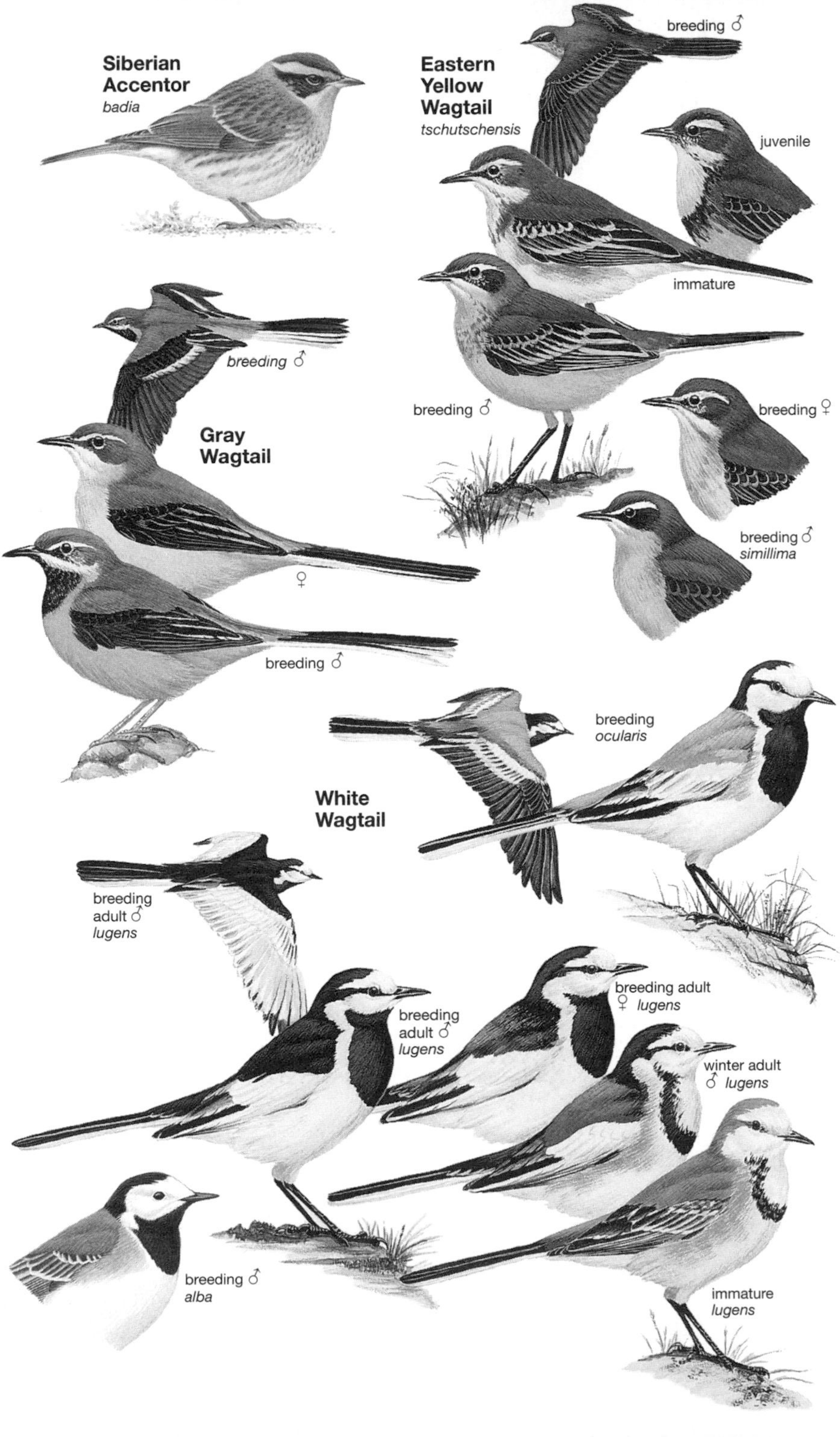
Siberian Accentor
badia
Eastern Yellow Wagtail
tschutschensis
breeding ♂
juvenile
immature
breeding ♂
breeding ♀
breeding ♂
simillima
breeding ♂
Gray Wagtail
♀
breeding ♂
breeding
ocularis
White Wagtail
breeding adult ♂
lugens
breeding adult ♀
lugens
breeding adult ♂
lugens
winter adult ♂ *lugens*
breeding ♂
alba
immature
lugens

American Pipit *Anthus rubescens*

DATE LOCATION

Sprague's Pipit *Anthus spragueii*

DATE LOCATION

Olive-backed Pipit *Anthus hodgsoni*

DATE LOCATION

Pechora Pipit *Anthus gustavi*

DATE LOCATION

Red-throated Pipit *Anthus cervinus*

DATE LOCATION

American Pipit
rubescens
breeding
winter
breeding
alticola
winter
japonicus
Sprague's Pipit
Olive-backed Pipit
yunnanensis
Pechora Pipit
gustavi
breeding ♀
Red-throated Pipit
breeding ♂
immature

Waxwings (Family Bombycillidae)

Bohemian Waxwing *Bombycilla garrulus*

DATE LOCATION

Cedar Waxwing *Bombycilla cedrorum*

DATE LOCATION

Silky-flycatchers (Family Ptilogonatidae)

Phainopepla *Phainopepla nitens*

DATE LOCATION

juvenile
Bohemian Waxwing
pallidiceps
juvenile
Cedar Waxwing
Phainopepla
♂
♀
♂

Wood-Warblers (Family Parulidae)

Prothonotary Warbler *Protonotaria citrea*

DATE LOCATION

Blue-winged Warbler *Vermivora pinus*

DATE LOCATION

Golden-winged Warbler *Vermivora chrysoptera*

DATE LOCATION

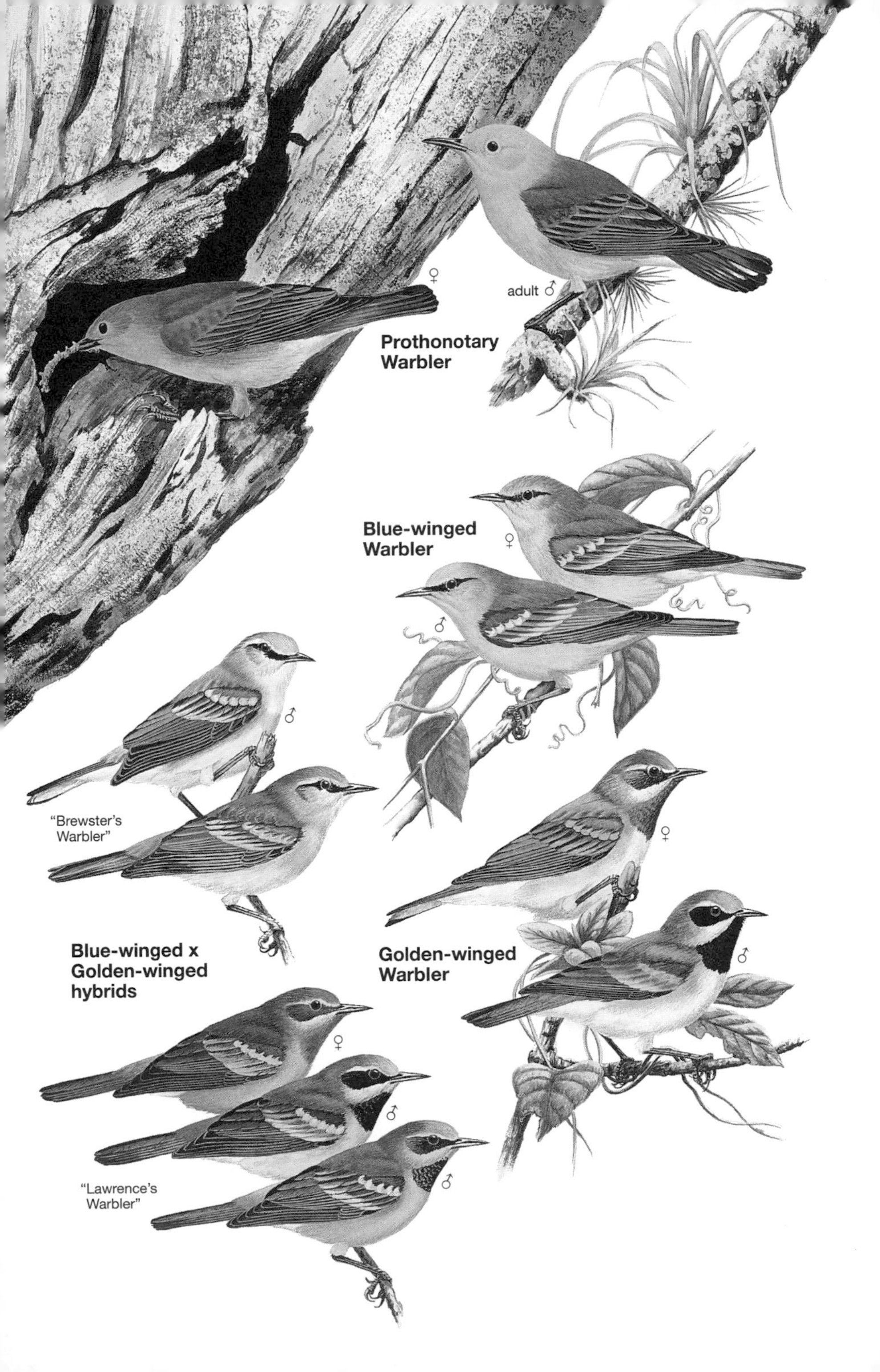

♀
adult ♂
Prothonotary Warbler
Blue-winged Warbler
♀
♂
♂
"Brewster's Warbler"
♀
Blue-winged x Golden-winged hybrids
Golden-winged Warbler
♂
♀
♂
"Lawrence's Warbler"
♂

Tennessee Warbler *Vermivora peregrina*

DATE LOCATION

Orange-crowned Warbler *Vermivora celata*

DATE LOCATION

Bachman's Warbler *Vermivora bachmanii*

DATE LOCATION

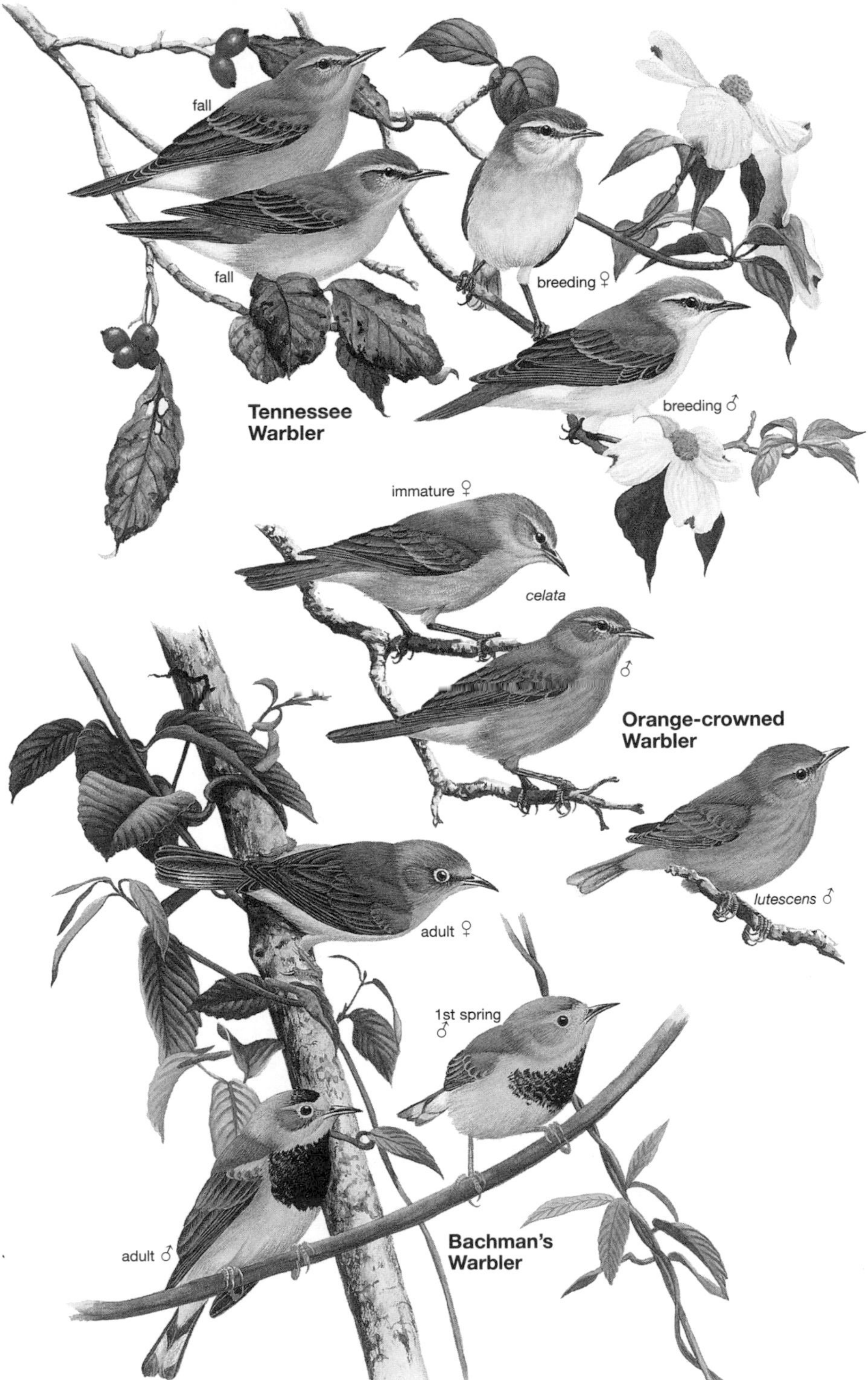
fall
fall
breeding ♀
breeding ♂
Tennessee Warbler
immature ♀
celata
♂
Orange-crowned Warbler
lutescens ♂
adult ♀
1st spring ♂
adult ♂
Bachman's Warbler

Nashville Warbler *Vermivora ruficapilla*

DATE LOCATION

Virginia's Warbler *Vermivora virginiae*

DATE LOCATION

Colima Warbler *Vermivora crissalis*

DATE LOCATION

Lucy's Warbler *Vermivora luciae*

DATE LOCATION

Crescent-chested Warbler *Parula superciliosa*

DATE LOCATION

Northern Parula *Parula americana*

DATE LOCATION

Tropical Parula *Parula pitiayumi*

DATE LOCATION

Nashville Warbler
ruficapilla
immature ♀
♂
immature
♂
Virginia's Warbler
Colima Warbler
immature ♀
Lucy's Warbler
♂
Crescent-chested Warbler
immature ♀
adult ♂
♀
adult ♂
Tropical Parula
nigrilora
immature ♀
adult ♂
Northern Parula

Chestnut-sided Warbler *Dendroica pensylvanica*

DATE LOCATION

Cape May Warbler *Dendroica tigrina*

DATE LOCATION

Magnolia Warbler *Dendroica magnolia*

DATE LOCATION

Yellow-rumped Warbler *Dendroica coronata*

DATE LOCATION

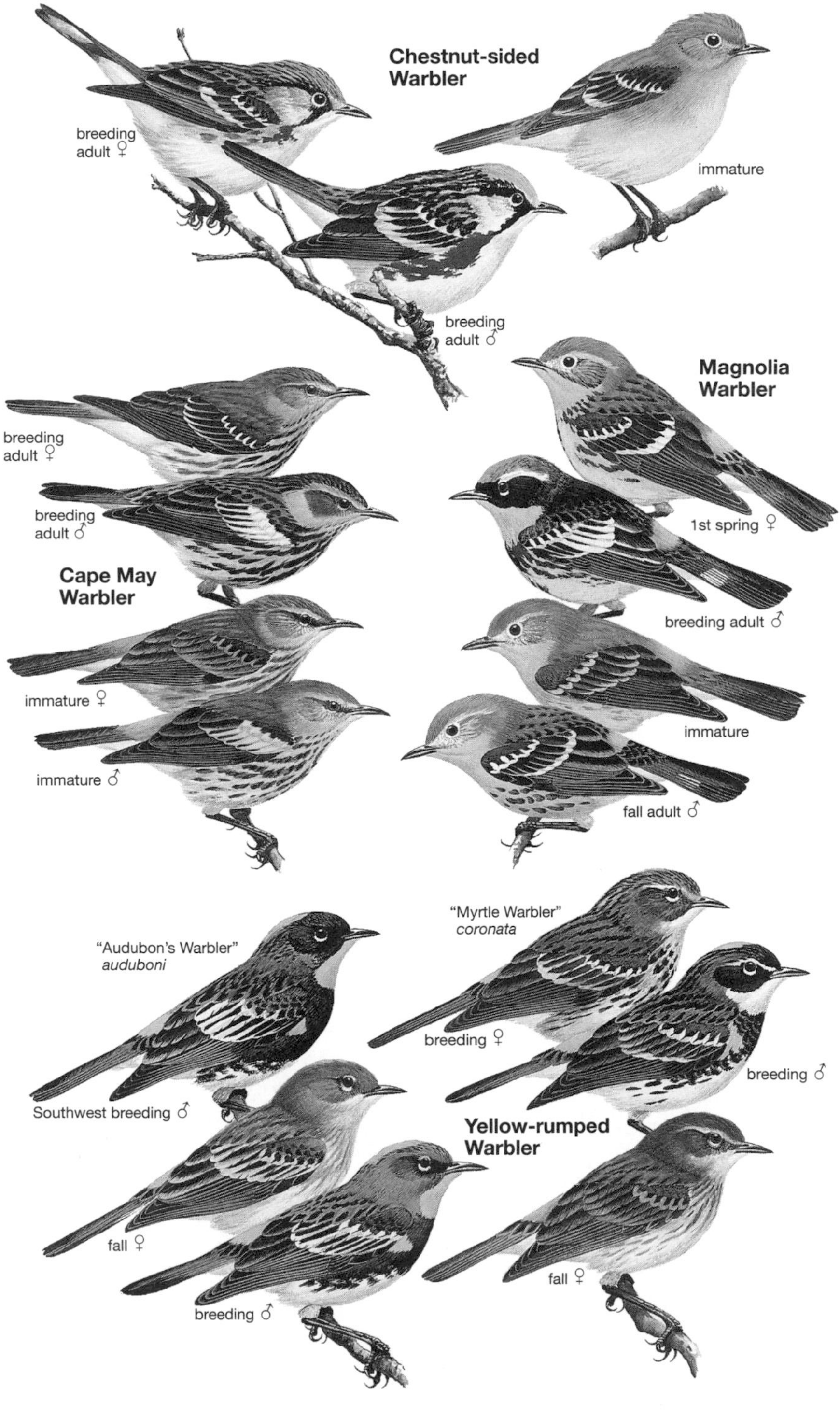
Chestnut-sided Warbler
breeding adult ♀
immature
breeding adult ♂
Magnolia Warbler
1st spring ♀
breeding adult ♂
immature
fall adult ♂
breeding adult ♀
breeding adult ♂
Cape May Warbler
immature ♀
immature ♂
"Audubon's Warbler"
auduboni
Southwest breeding ♂
fall ♀
breeding ♂
"Myrtle Warbler"
coronata
breeding ♀
breeding ♂
Yellow-rumped Warbler
fall ♀

Black-and-white Warbler *Mniotilta varia*

DATE LOCATION

Black-throated Blue Warbler *Dendroica caerulescens*

DATE LOCATION

Cerulean Warbler *Dendroica cerulea*

DATE LOCATION

Blackburnian Warbler *Dendroica fusca*

DATE LOCATION

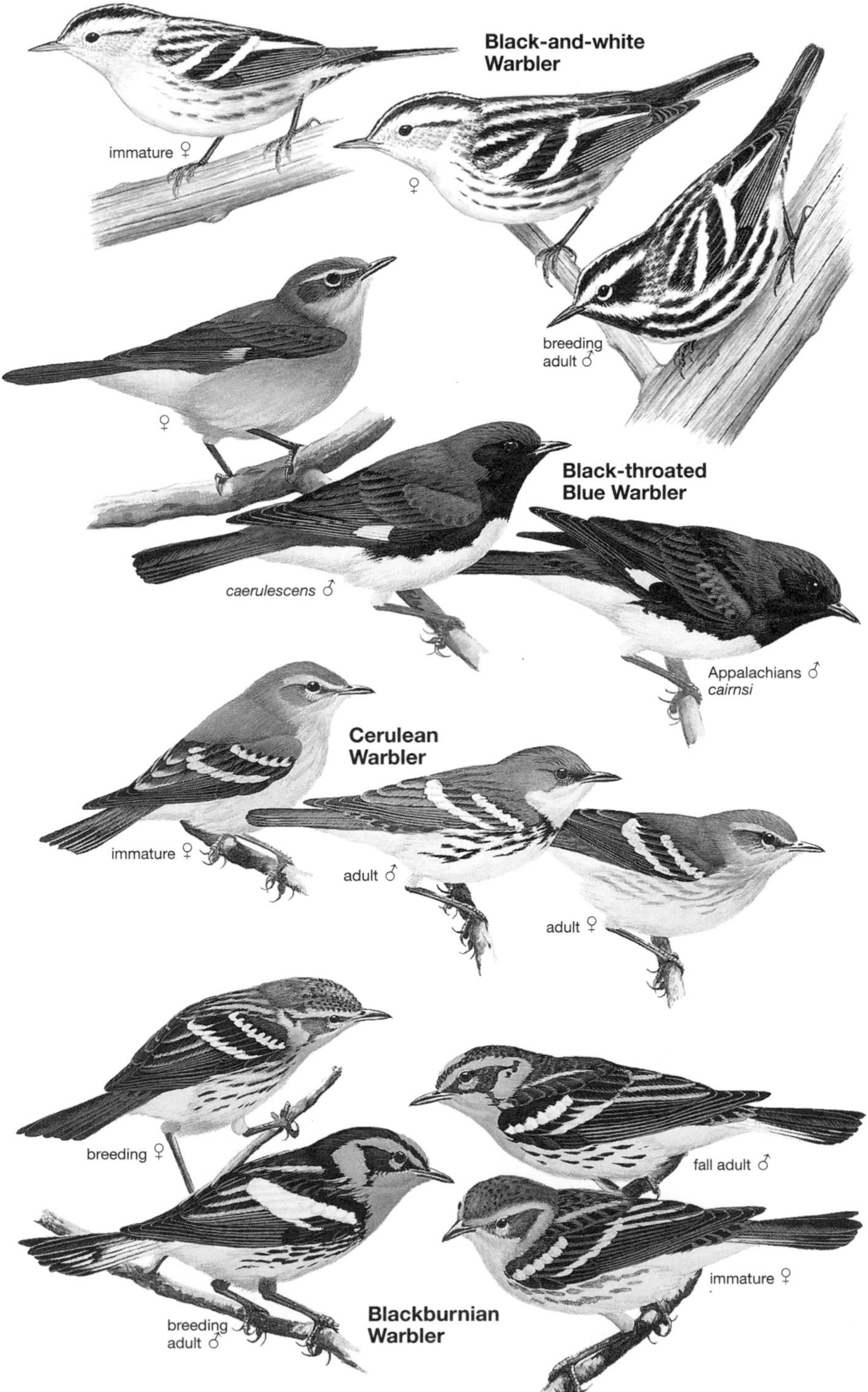

Black-and-white Warbler
immature ♀
♀
breeding adult ♂
♀
Black-throated Blue Warbler
caerulescens ♂
Appalachians ♂ cairnsi
Cerulean Warbler
immature ♀
adult ♂
adult ♀
breeding ♀
fall adult ♂
immature ♀
breeding adult ♂
Blackburnian Warbler

Black-throated Gray Warbler *Dendroica nigrescens*

DATE LOCATION

Townsend's Warbler *Dendroica townsendi*

DATE LOCATION

Hermit Warbler *Dendroica occidentalis*

DATE LOCATION

Black-throated Green Warbler *Dendroica virens*

DATE LOCATION

Golden-cheeked Warbler *Dendroica chrysoparia*

DATE LOCATION

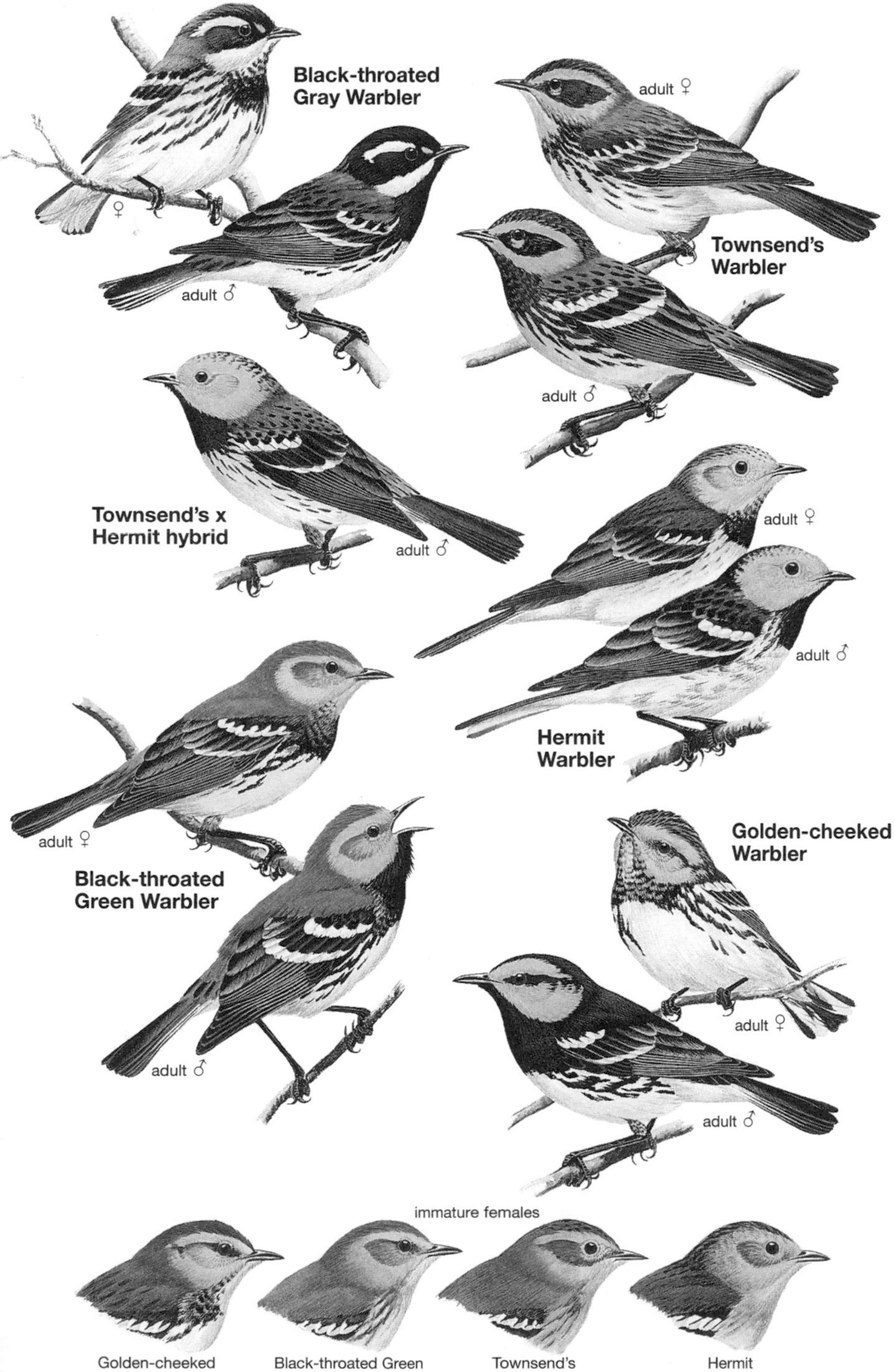
Black-throated Gray Warbler
♀
adult ♂
adult ♀
Townsend's Warbler
adult ♂
Townsend's x Hermit hybrid
adult ♂
adult ♀
adult ♂
Hermit Warbler
adult ♀
Black-throated Green Warbler
adult ♂
Golden-cheeked Warbler
adult ♀
adult ♂
immature females
Golden-cheeked
Black-throated Green
Townsend's
Hermit

Grace's Warbler *Dendroica graciae*

DATE LOCATION

Yellow-throated Warbler *Dendroica dominica*

DATE LOCATION

Kirtland's Warbler *Dendroica kirtlandii*

DATE LOCATION

Prairie Warbler *Dendroica discolor*

DATE LOCATION

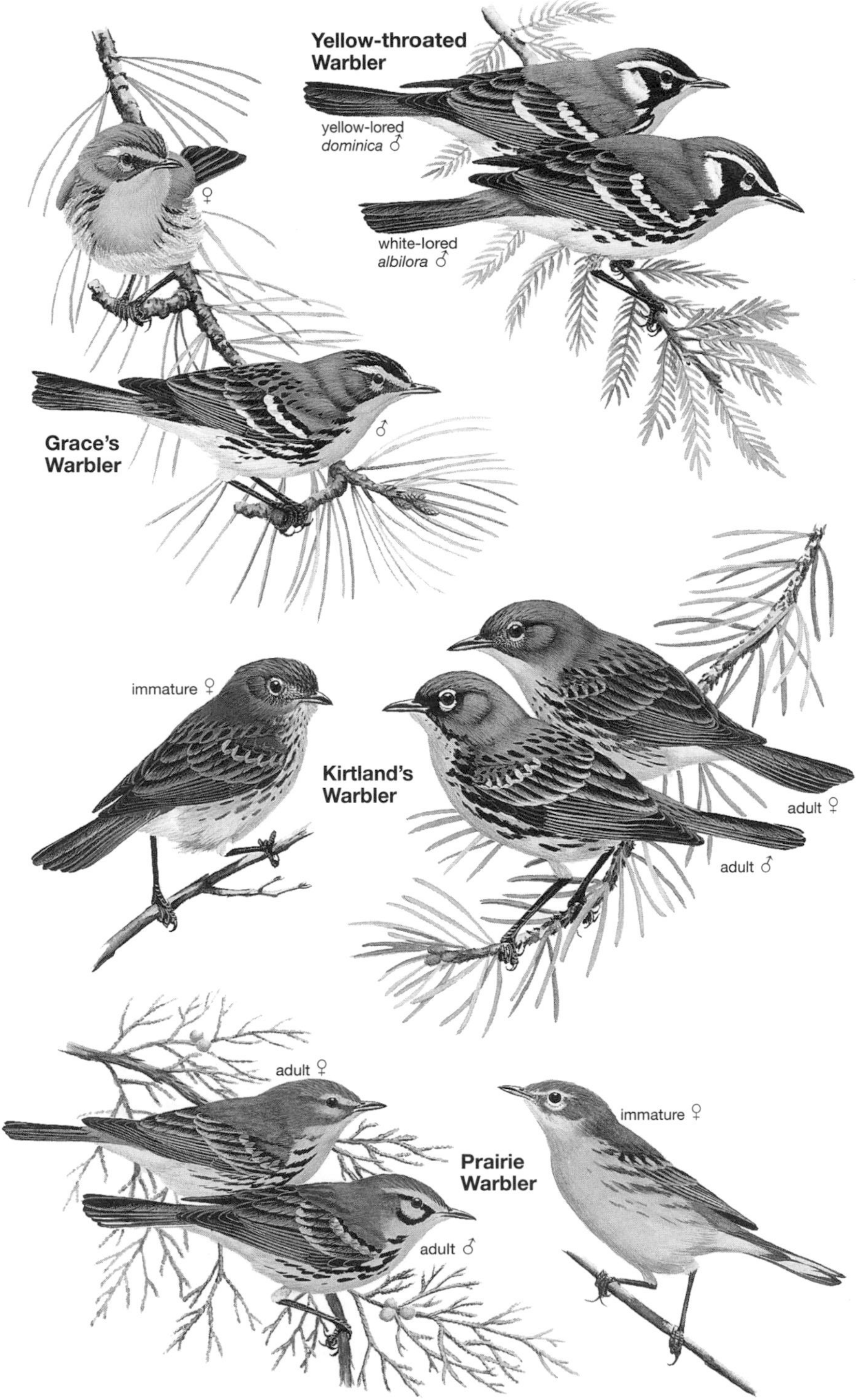
Yellow-throated Warbler
yellow-lored dominica ♂
white-lored albilora ♂
♀
♂
Grace's Warbler
immature ♀
Kirtland's Warbler
adult ♀
adult ♂
adult ♀
Prairie Warbler
immature ♀
adult ♂

Bay-breasted Warbler *Dendroica castanea*

DATE LOCATION

Blackpoll Warbler *Dendroica striata*

DATE LOCATION

Pine Warbler *Dendroica pinus*

DATE LOCATION

Palm Warbler *Dendroica palmarum*

DATE LOCATION

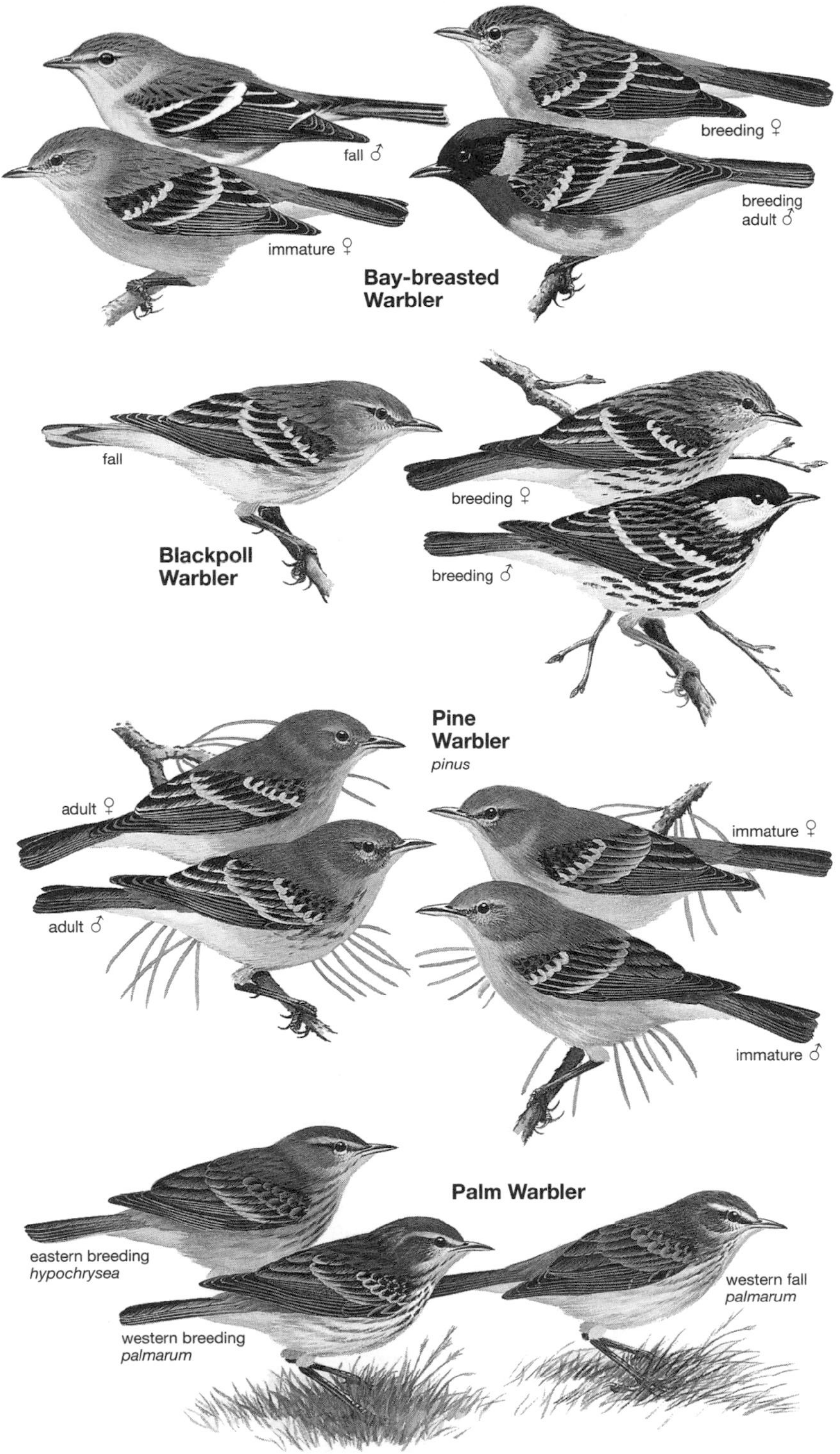

fall ♂
breeding ♀
breeding adult ♂
immature ♀
Bay-breasted Warbler
fall
breeding ♀
breeding ♂
Blackpoll Warbler
Pine Warbler
pinus
adult ♀
adult ♂
immature ♀
immature ♂
Palm Warbler
eastern breeding
hypochrysea
western breeding
palmarum
western fall
palmarum

Yellow Warbler *Dendroica petechia*

DATE LOCATION

Mourning Warbler *Oporornis philadelphia*

DATE LOCATION

MacGillivray's Warbler *Oporornis tolmiei*

DATE LOCATION

Connecticut Warbler *Oporornis agilis*

DATE LOCATION

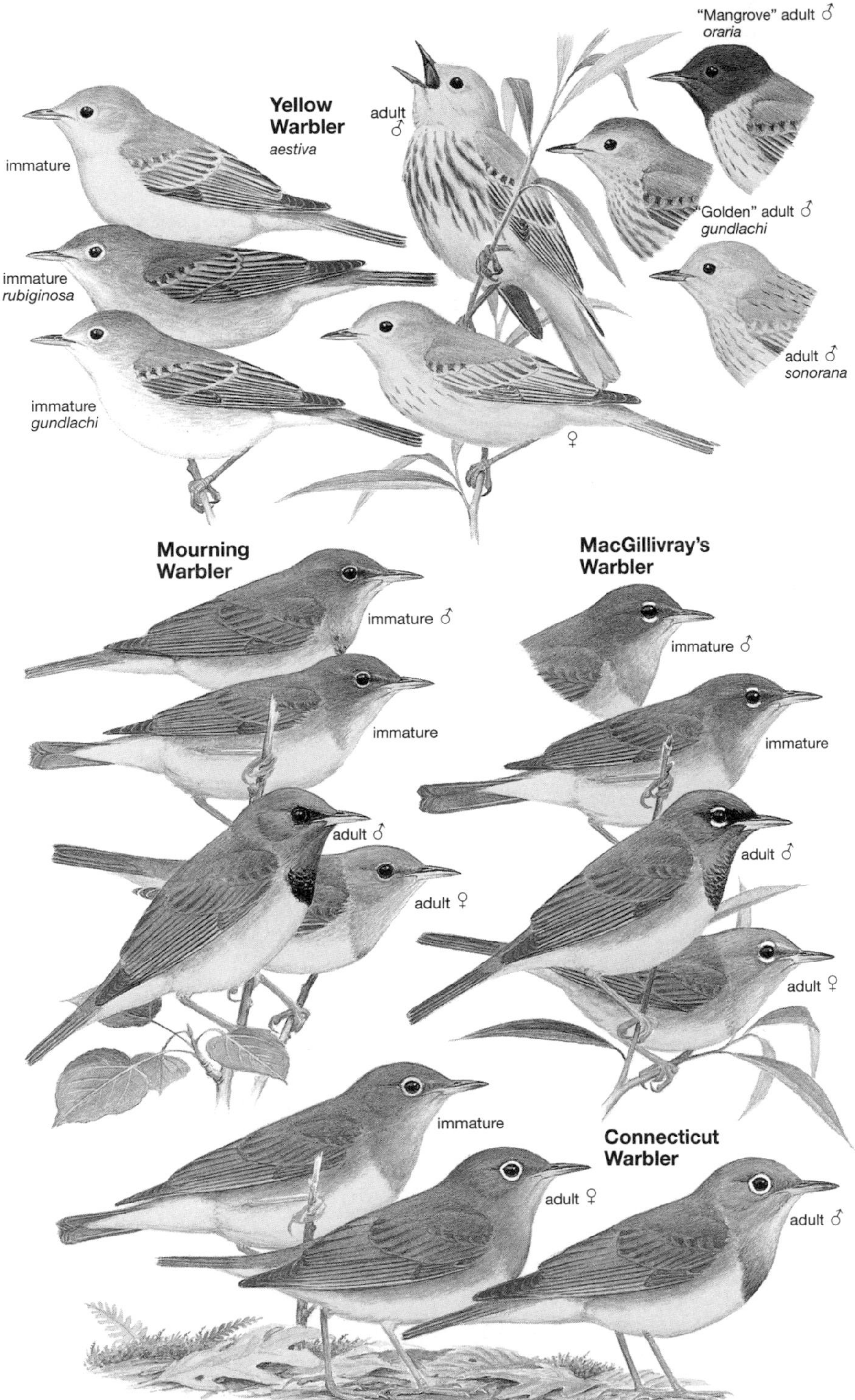
Yellow Warbler
aestiva
immature
adult ♂
"Mangrove" adult ♂
oraria
"Golden" adult ♂
gundlachi
immature
rubiginosa
immature
gundlachi
adult ♂
sonorana
♀
Mourning Warbler
immature ♂
immature
adult ♂
adult ♀
MacGillivray's Warbler
immature ♂
immature
adult ♂
adult ♀
immature
Connecticut Warbler
adult ♀
adult ♂

Kentucky Warbler *Oporornis formosus*

DATE LOCATION

Canada Warbler *Wilsonia canadensis*

DATE LOCATION

Wilson's Warbler *Wilsonia pusilla*

DATE LOCATION

Hooded Warbler *Wilsonia citrina*

DATE LOCATION

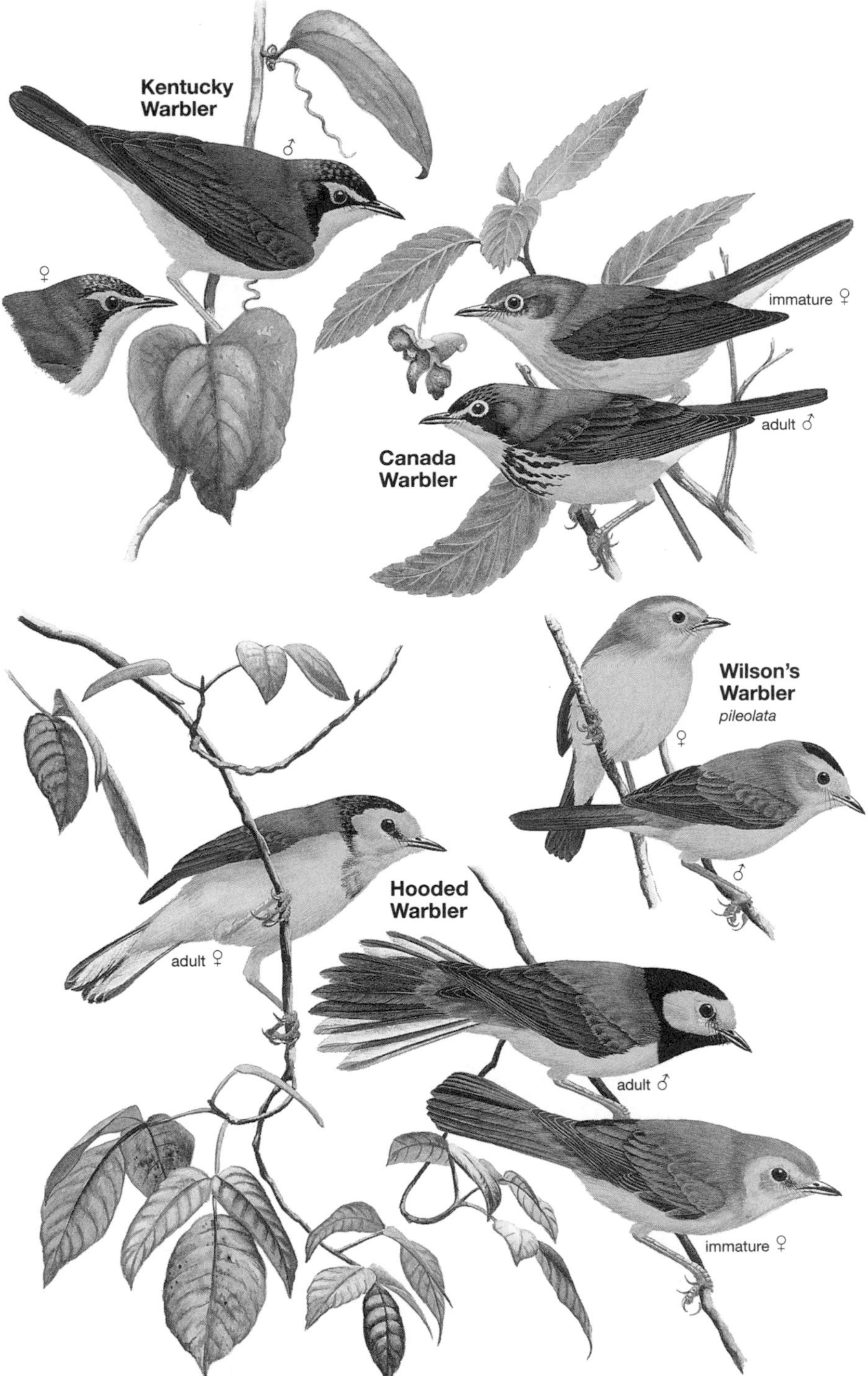
Kentucky Warbler
♂
♀
immature ♀
adult ♂
Canada Warbler
Wilson's Warbler
pileolata
♀
♂
Hooded Warbler
adult ♀
adult ♂
immature ♀

Worm-eating Warbler *Helmitheros vermivorum*

DATE LOCATION

Swainson's Warbler *Limnothlypis swainsonii*

DATE LOCATION

Ovenbird *Seiurus aurocapilla*

DATE LOCATION

Louisiana Waterthrush *Seiurus motacilla*

DATE LOCATION

Northern Waterthrush *Seiurus noveboracensis*

DATE LOCATION

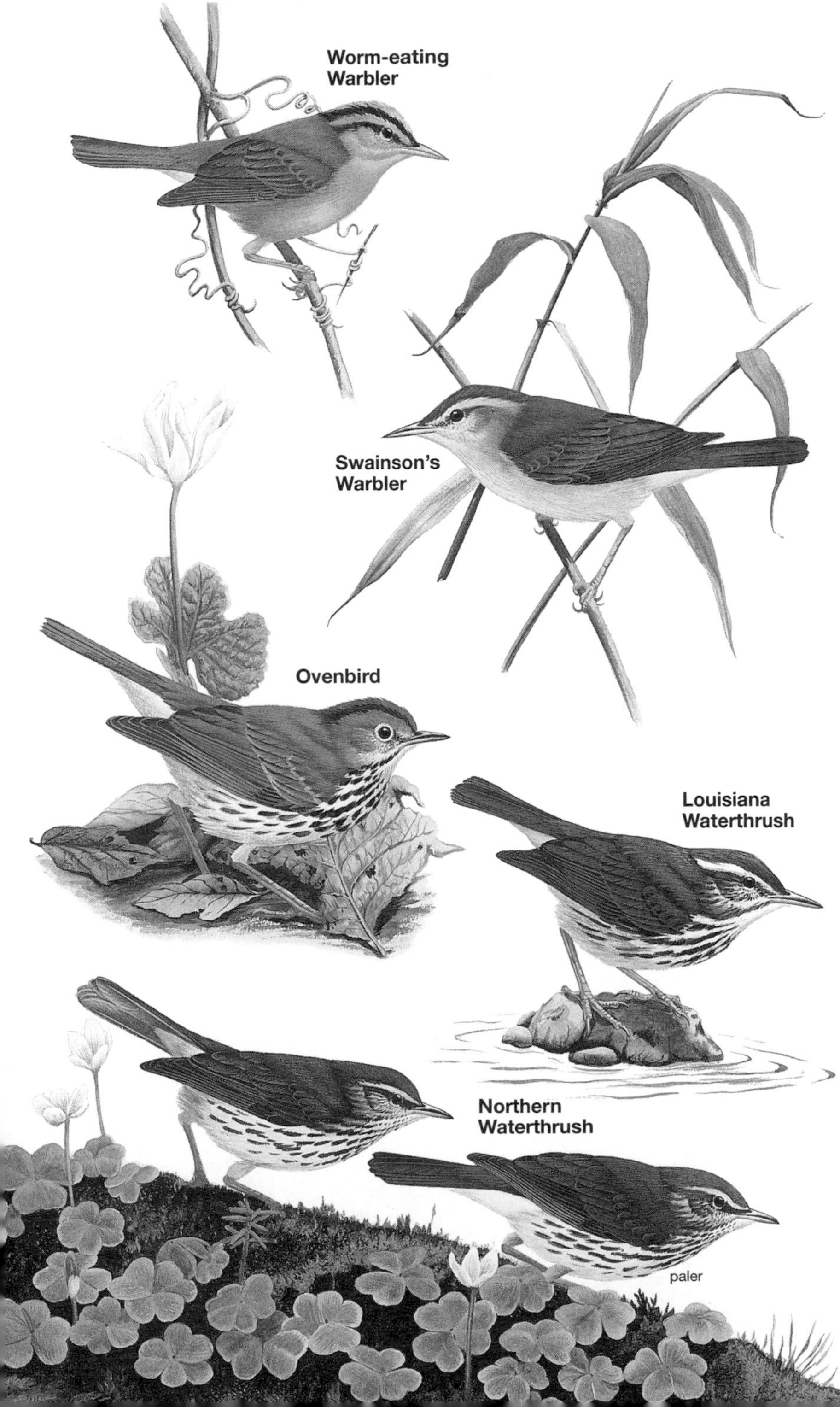
Worm-eating Warbler
Swainson's Warbler
Ovenbird
Louisiana Waterthrush
Northern Waterthrush
paler

Common Yellowthroat *Geothlypis trichas*

DATE LOCATION

Gray-crowned Yellowthroat *Geothlypis poliocephala*

DATE LOCATION

Fan-tailed Warbler *Euthlypis lachrymosa*

DATE LOCATION

Golden-crowned Warbler *Basileuterus culicivorus*

DATE LOCATION

Rufous-capped Warbler *Basileuterus rufifrons*

DATE LOCATION

Yellow-breasted Chat *Icteria virens*

DATE LOCATION

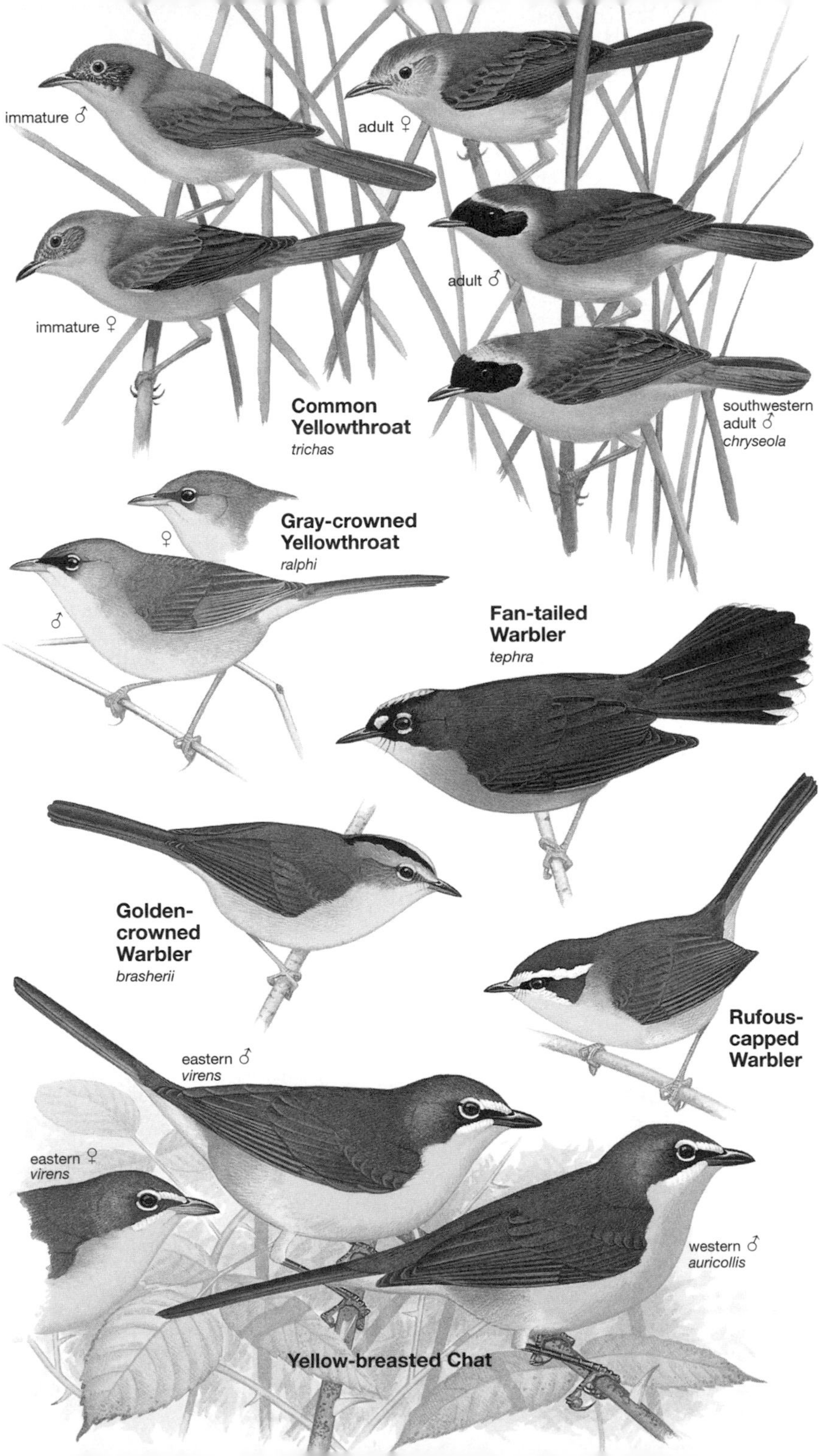

immature ♂
adult ♀
immature ♀
adult ♂
Common Yellowthroat
trichas
southwestern adult ♂ chryseola
♀
Gray-crowned Yellowthroat
ralphi
♂
Fan-tailed Warbler
tephra
Golden-crowned Warbler
brasherii
Rufous-capped Warbler
eastern ♂
virens
eastern ♀
virens
western ♂
auricollis
Yellow-breasted Chat

American Redstart *Setophaga ruticilla*

DATE LOCATION

Slate-throated Redstart *Myioborus miniatus*

DATE LOCATION

Painted Redstart *Myioborus pictus*

DATE LOCATION

Red-faced Warbler *Cardellina rubrifrons*

DATE LOCATION

Olive Warbler (Family Peucedramidae)

Olive Warbler *Peucedramus taeniatus*

DATE LOCATION

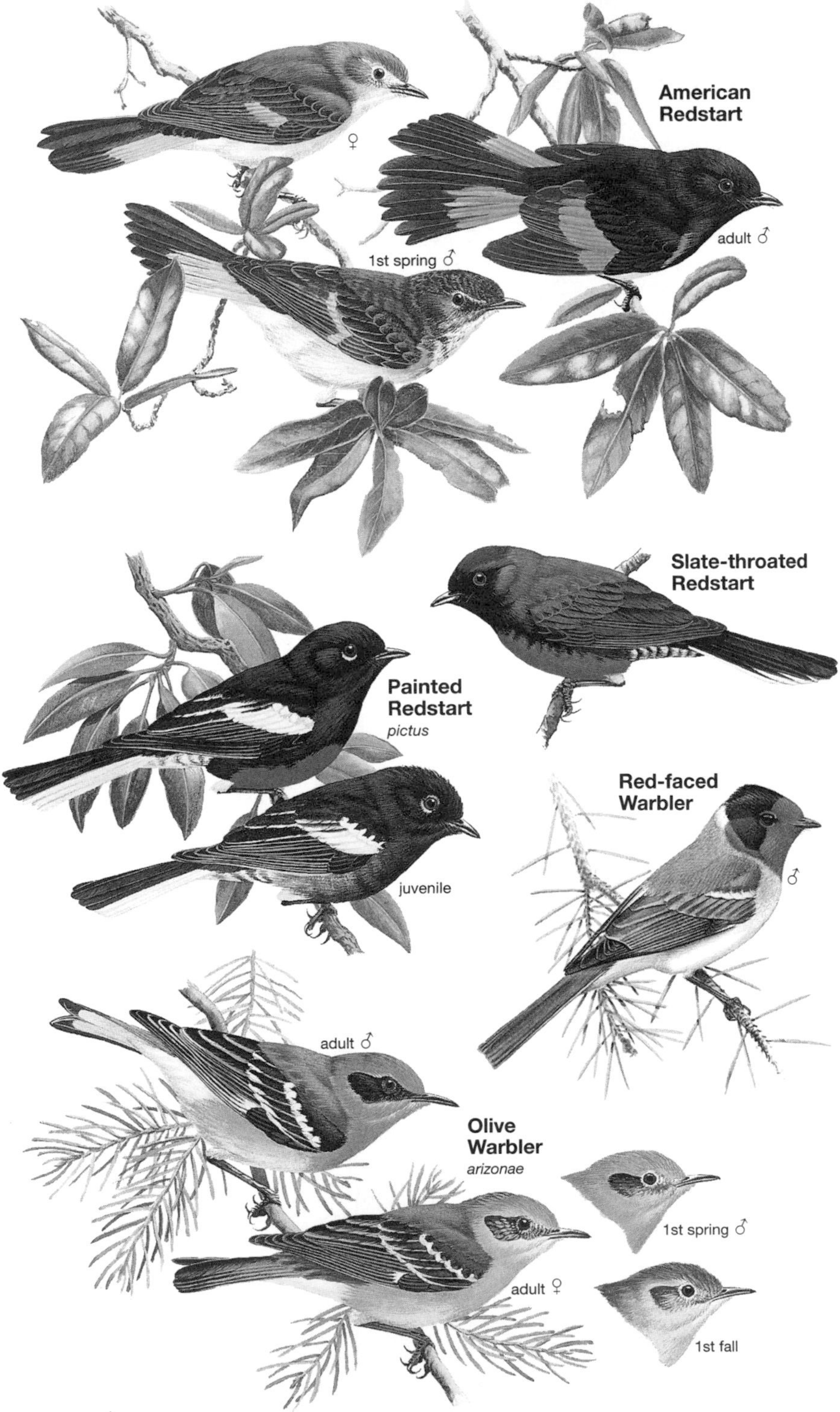

American Redstart
♀
adult ♂
1st spring ♂
Slate-throated Redstart
Painted Redstart
pictus
juvenile
Red-faced Warbler
♂
adult ♂
Olive Warbler
arizonae
1st spring ♂
adult ♀
1st fall

Tanagers (Family Thraupidae)

Summer Tanager *Piranga rubra*

DATE LOCATION

Hepatic Tanager *Piranga flava*

DATE LOCATION

Scarlet Tanager *Piranga olivacea*

DATE LOCATION

Western Tanager *Piranga ludoviciana*

DATE LOCATION

Flame-colored Tanager *Piranga bidentata*

DATE LOCATION

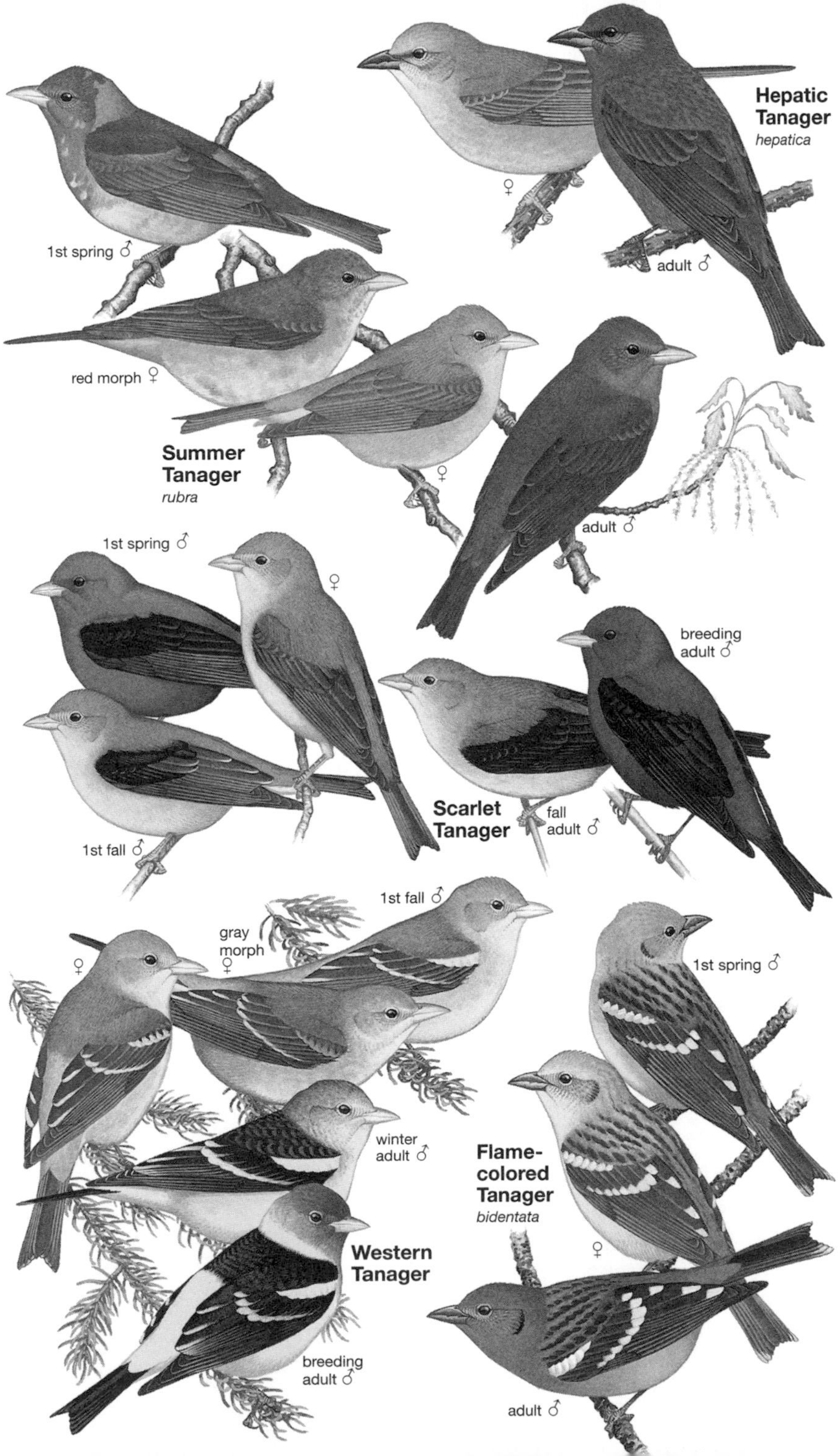
Hepatic Tanager
hepatica
♀
adult ♂
1st spring ♂
red morph ♀
Summer Tanager
rubra
♀
adult ♂
1st spring ♂
♀
breeding adult ♂
1st fall ♂
Scarlet Tanager
fall adult ♂
1st fall ♂
gray morph ♀
♀
1st spring ♂
winter adult ♂
Flame-colored Tanager
bidentata
Western Tanager
♀
breeding adult ♂
adult ♂

Western Spindalis *Spindalis zena*

DATE LOCATION

Bananaquit (*Incertae Sedis*)

Bananaquit *Coereba flaveola*

DATE LOCATION

Emberizids (Family Emberizidae)

White-collared Seedeater *Sporophila torqueola*

DATE LOCATION

Black-faced Grassquit *Tiaris bicolor*

DATE LOCATION

Yellow-faced Grassquit *Tiaris olivaceus*

DATE LOCATION

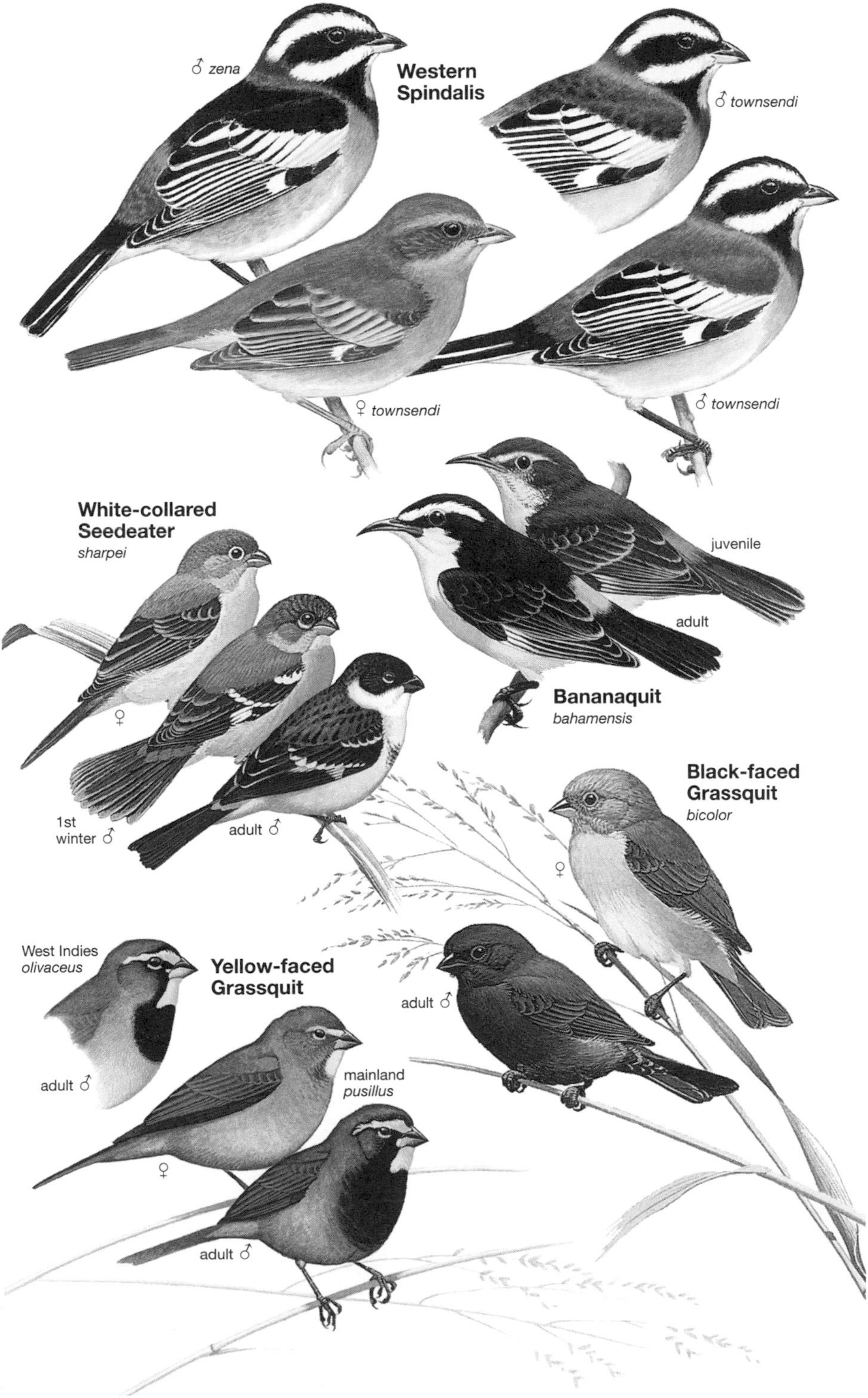

♂ zena
Western Spindalis
♂ townsendi
♀ townsendi
♂ townsendi
White-collared Seedeater
sharpei
♀
1st winter ♂
adult ♂
juvenile
adult
Bananaquit
bahamensis
Black-faced Grassquit
bicolor
♀
adult ♂
West Indies
olivaceus
Yellow-faced Grassquit
adult ♂
mainland
pusillus
♀
adult ♂

Olive Sparrow *Arremonops rufivirgatus*

DATE LOCATION

Green-tailed Towhee *Pipilo chlorurus*

DATE LOCATION

California Towhee *Pipilo crissalis*

DATE LOCATION

Canyon Towhee *Pipilo fuscus*

DATE LOCATION

Abert's Towhee *Pipilo aberti*

DATE LOCATION

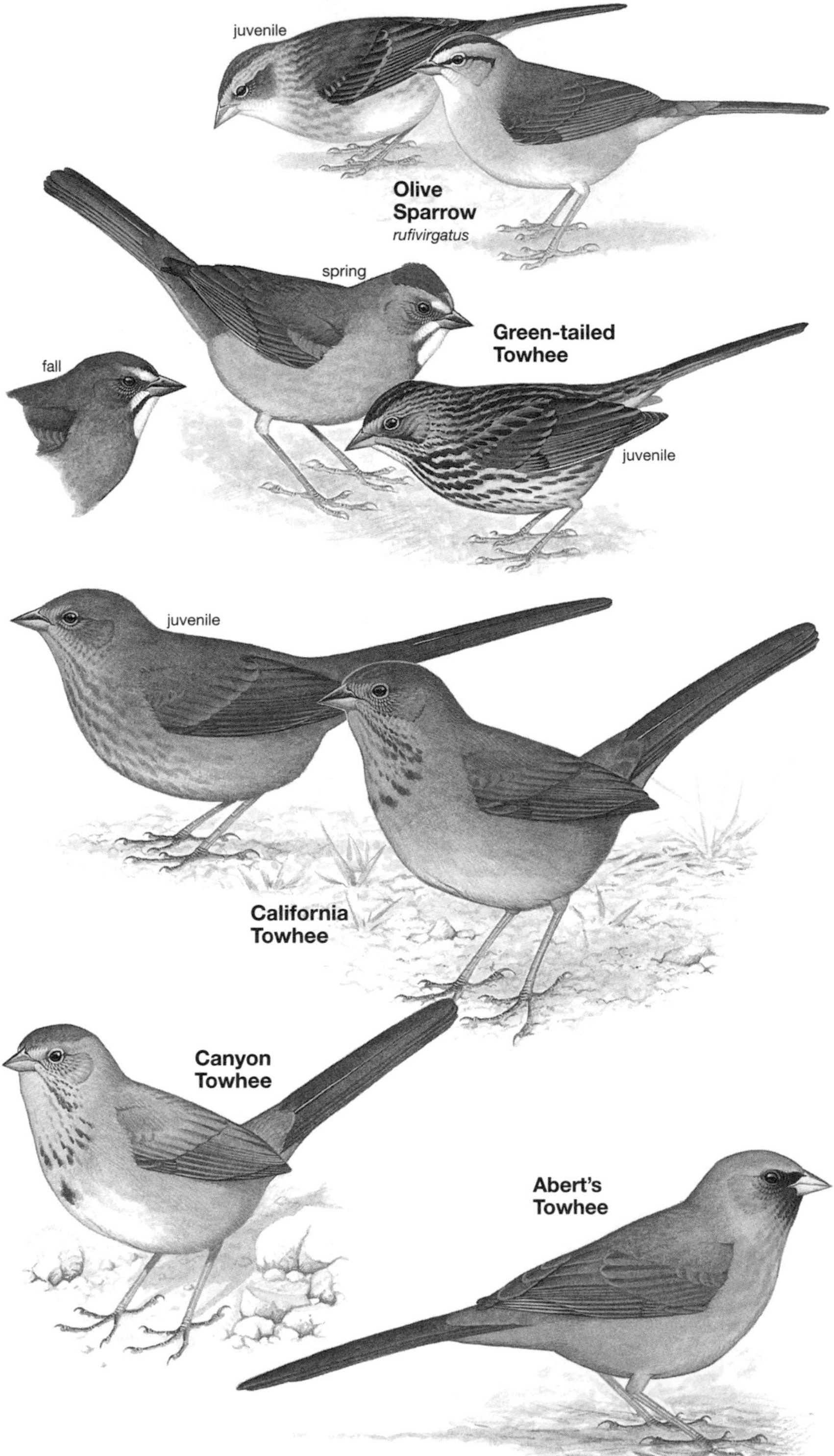
juvenile
Olive
Sparrow
rufivirgatus
spring
Green-tailed
Towhee
fall
juvenile
juvenile
California
Towhee
Canyon
Towhee
Abert's
Towhee

Eastern Towhee *Pipilo erythrophthalmus*

DATE LOCATION

Spotted Towhee *Pipilo maculatus*

DATE LOCATION

Eastern Towhee
erythrophthalmus
juvenile
♀
Florida
♂ alleni
♂
♀ arcticus
Spotted Towhee
♂ montanus
♂ arcticus
♀ oregonus
♀ montanus
♂ oregonus
♀ megalonyx
juvenile oregonus
♂ megalonyx
Eastern
erythrophthalmus
alleni
Spotted
arcticus
montanus
megalonyx
oregonus

Bachman's Sparrow *Aimophila aestivalis*

DATE LOCATION

Botteri's Sparrow *Aimophila botterii*

DATE LOCATION

Cassin's Sparrow *Aimophila cassinii*

DATE LOCATION

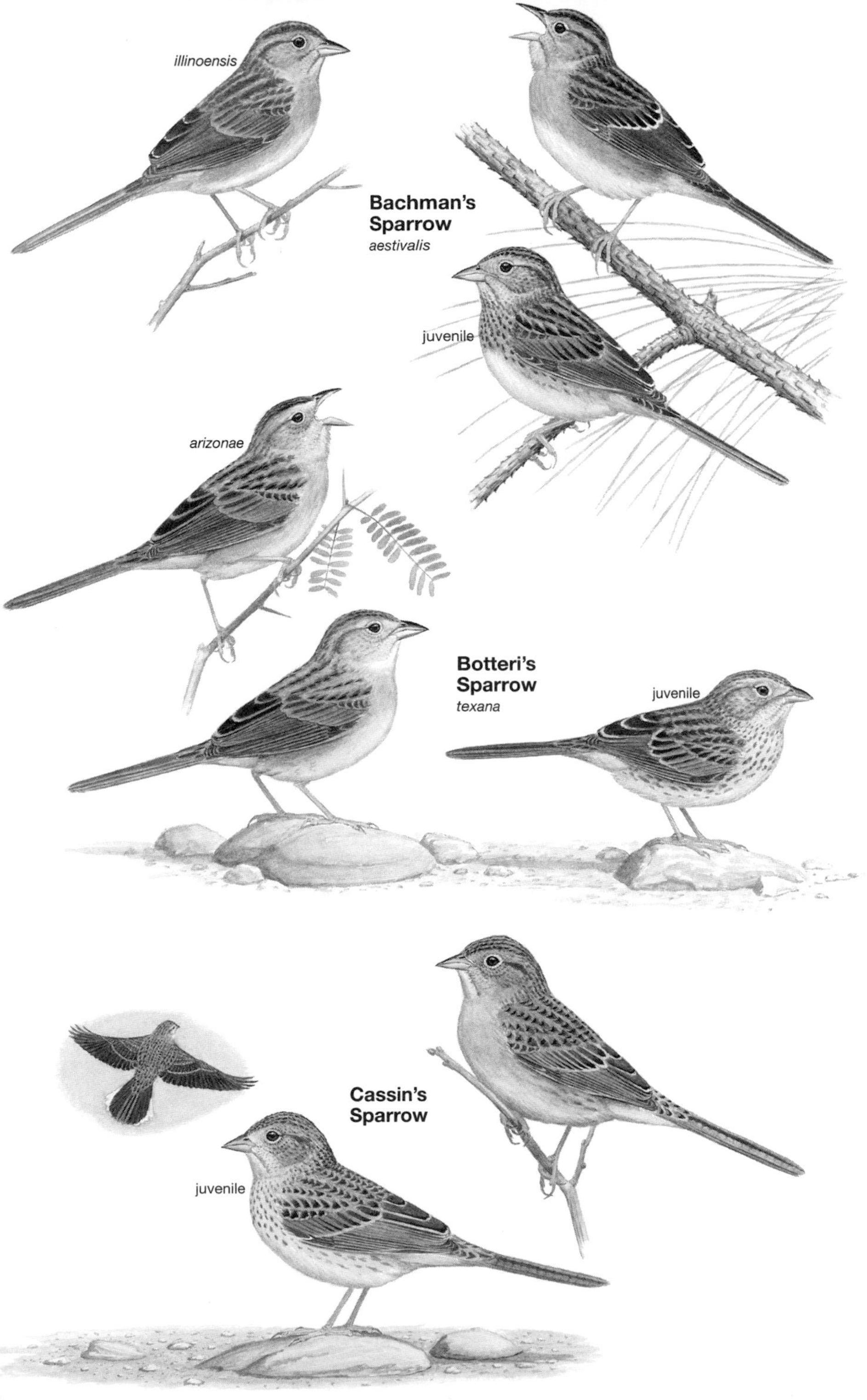
illinoensis
Bachman's Sparrow
aestivalis
juvenile
arizonae
Botteri's Sparrow
texana
juvenile
Cassin's Sparrow
juvenile

Rufous-winged Sparrow *Aimophila carpalis*

DATE LOCATION

Rufous-crowned Sparrow *Aimophila ruficeps*

DATE LOCATION

American Tree Sparrow *Spizella arborea*

DATE LOCATION

Field Sparrow *Spizella pusilla*

DATE LOCATION

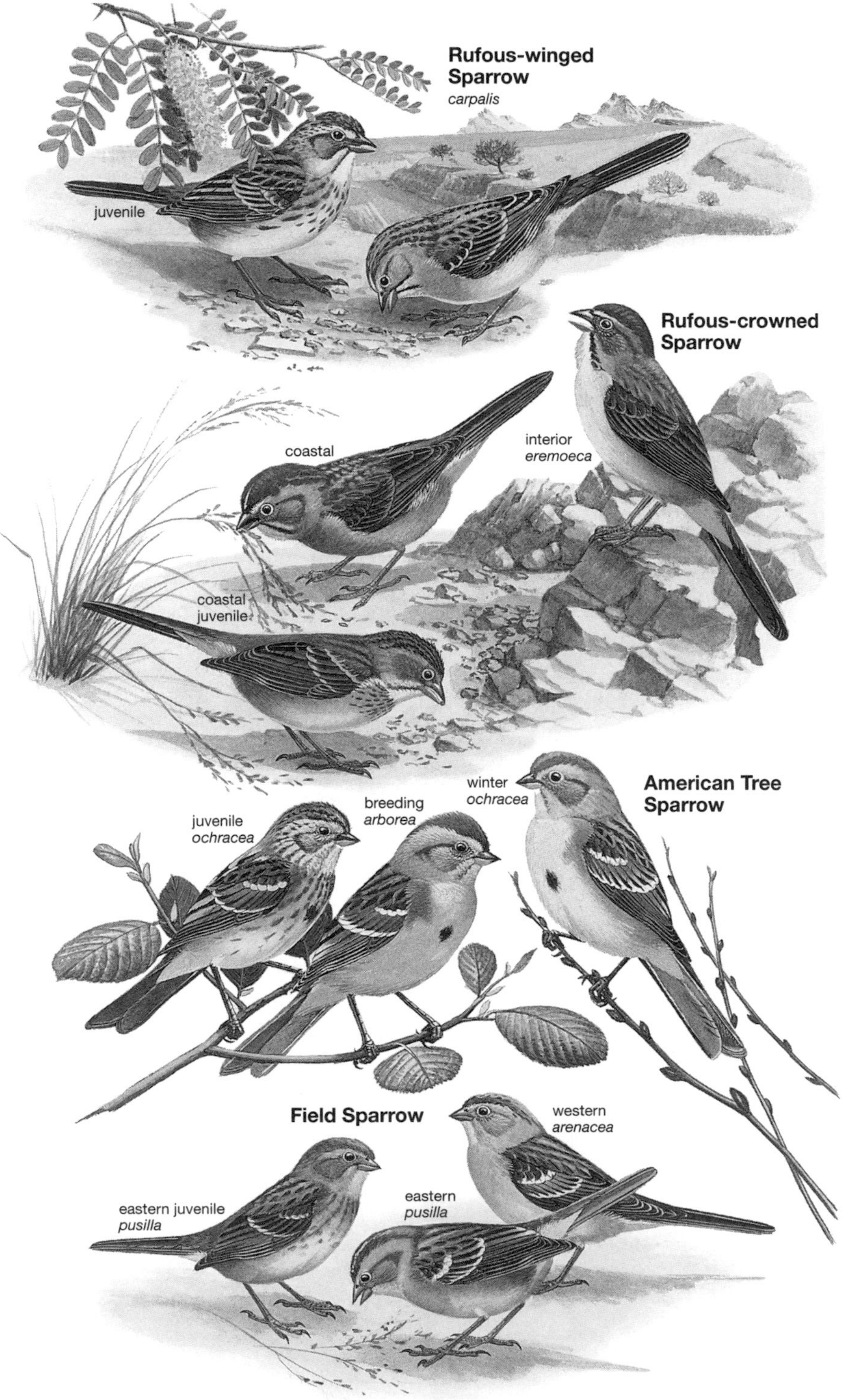
Rufous-winged Sparrow
carpalis
juvenile
Rufous-crowned Sparrow
coastal
interior
eremoeca
coastal juvenile
American Tree Sparrow
winter
ochracea
breeding
arborea
juvenile
ochracea
Field Sparrow
western
arenacea
eastern juvenile
pusilla
eastern
pusilla

Chipping Sparrow *Spizella passerina*

DATE LOCATION

Clay-colored Sparrow *Spizella pallida*

DATE LOCATION

Brewer's Sparrow *Spizella breweri*

DATE LOCATION

breeding
Chipping Sparrow
passerina
winter adult
juvenile
1st winter
immature
juvenile
breeding
Clay-colored Sparrow
juvenile
Brewer's Sparrow
breweri

Lark Sparrow *Chondestes grammacus*

DATE LOCATION

Black-chinned Sparrow *Spizella atrogularis*

DATE LOCATION

Black-throated Sparrow *Amphispiza bilineata*

DATE LOCATION

Five-striped Sparrow *Aimophila quinquestriata*

DATE LOCATION

Sage Sparrow *Amphispiza belli*

DATE LOCATION

Lark Sparrow
grammacus
juvenile
Black-chinned Sparrow
breeding ♀
breeding ♂
juvenile
Black-throated Sparrow
deserticola
juvenile
Five-striped Sparrow
septentrionalis
coastal
belli
Sage Sparrow
interior
nevadensis
interior juvenile
nevadensis
canescens

Grasshopper Sparrow *Ammodramus savannarum*

DATE LOCATION

Baird's Sparrow *Ammodramus bairdii*

DATE LOCATION

Henslow's Sparrow *Ammodramus henslowii*

DATE LOCATION

summer
perpallidus
Grasshopper Sparrow
floridanus
juvenile *pratensis*
fall *pratensis*
fall *ammolegus*
Orange Bishop ♀
for comparison
Baird's Sparrow
Henslow's Sparrow
juvenile
juvenile

Saltmarsh Sharp-tailed Sparrow *Ammodramus caudacutus*

DATE LOCATION

Le Conte's Sparrow *Ammodramus leconteii*

DATE LOCATION

Nelson's Sharp-tailed Sparrow *Ammodramus nelsoni*

DATE LOCATION

Seaside Sparrow *Ammodramus maritimus*

DATE LOCATION

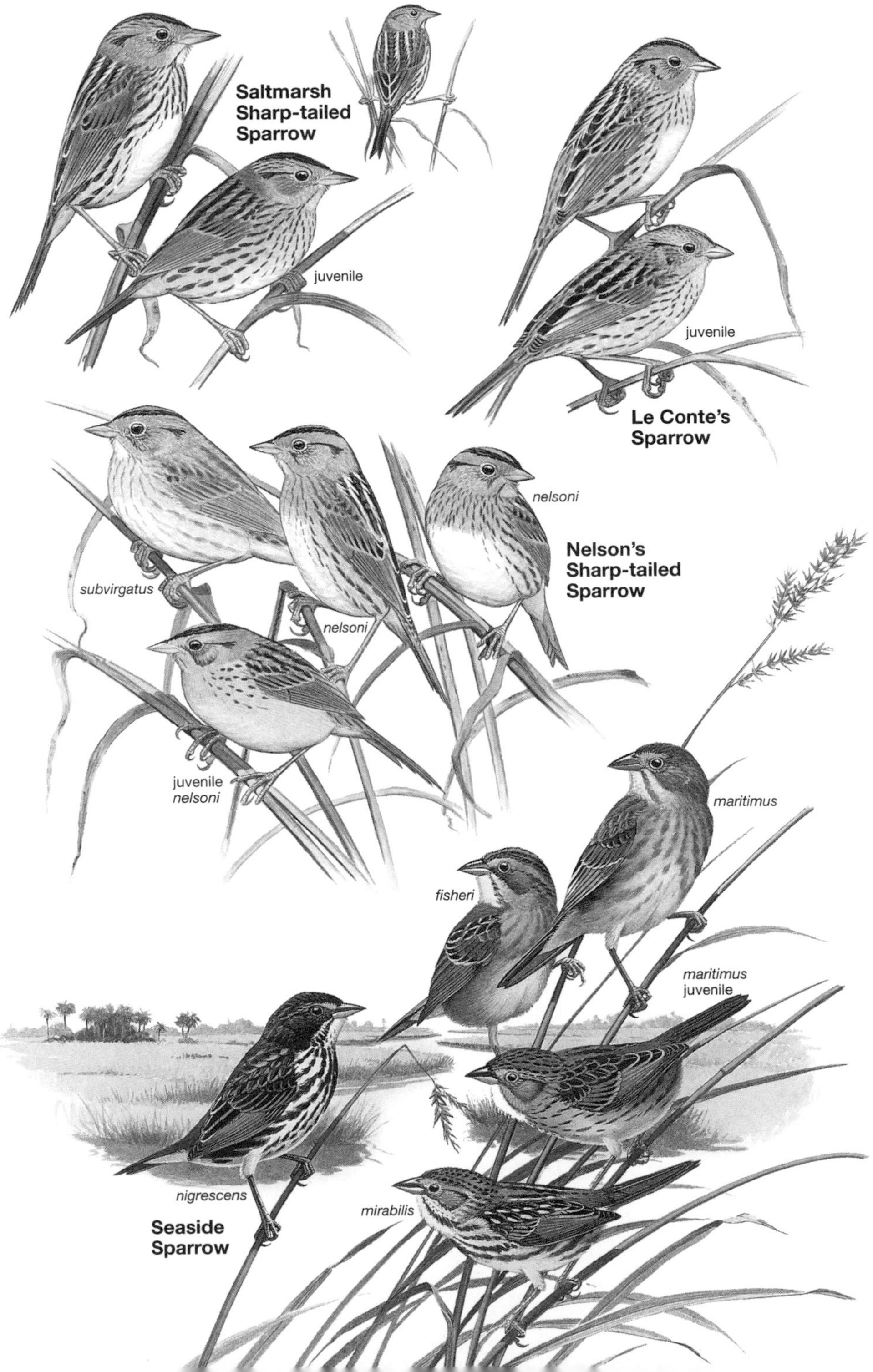

Saltmarsh Sharp-tailed Sparrow
juvenile
Le Conte's Sparrow
juvenile
Nelson's Sharp-tailed Sparrow
nelsoni
subvirgatus
nelsoni
juvenile nelsoni
maritimus
fisheri
maritimus juvenile
nigrescens
mirabilis
Seaside Sparrow

Fox Sparrow *Passerella iliaca*

DATE LOCATION

Lark Bunting *Calamospiza melanocorys*

DATE LOCATION

Savannah Sparrow *Passerculus sandwichensis*

DATE LOCATION

Fox Sparrow
"Red"
iliaca
"Slate-colored"
schistacea
"Thick-billed"
stephensi
"Sooty"
unalaschcensis
"Sooty"
fuliginosa
Lark Bunting
breeding ♂
early spring ♂
winter ♂
♀
Savannah Sparrow
nevadensis
"Ipswich Sparrow"
princeps
beldingi
"Large-billed Sparrow"
rostratus

Lincoln's Sparrow *Melospiza lincolnii*

DATE LOCATION

Song Sparrow *Melospiza melodia*

DATE LOCATION

Vesper Sparrow *Pooecetes gramineus*

DATE LOCATION

Swamp Sparrow *Melospiza georgiana*

DATE LOCATION

Lincoln's Sparrow
juvenile
melodia
juvenile melodia
heermanni
Song Sparrow
morphna
maxima
saltonis
eastern gramineus
Vesper Sparrow
western confinus
breeding
winter adult
juvenile
Swamp Sparrow
immature

Harris's Sparrow *Zonotrichia querula*

DATE LOCATION

White-throated Sparrow *Zonotrichia albicollis*

DATE LOCATION

White-crowned Sparrow *Zonotrichia leucophrys*

DATE LOCATION

Golden-crowned Sparrow *Zonotrichia atricapilla*

DATE LOCATION

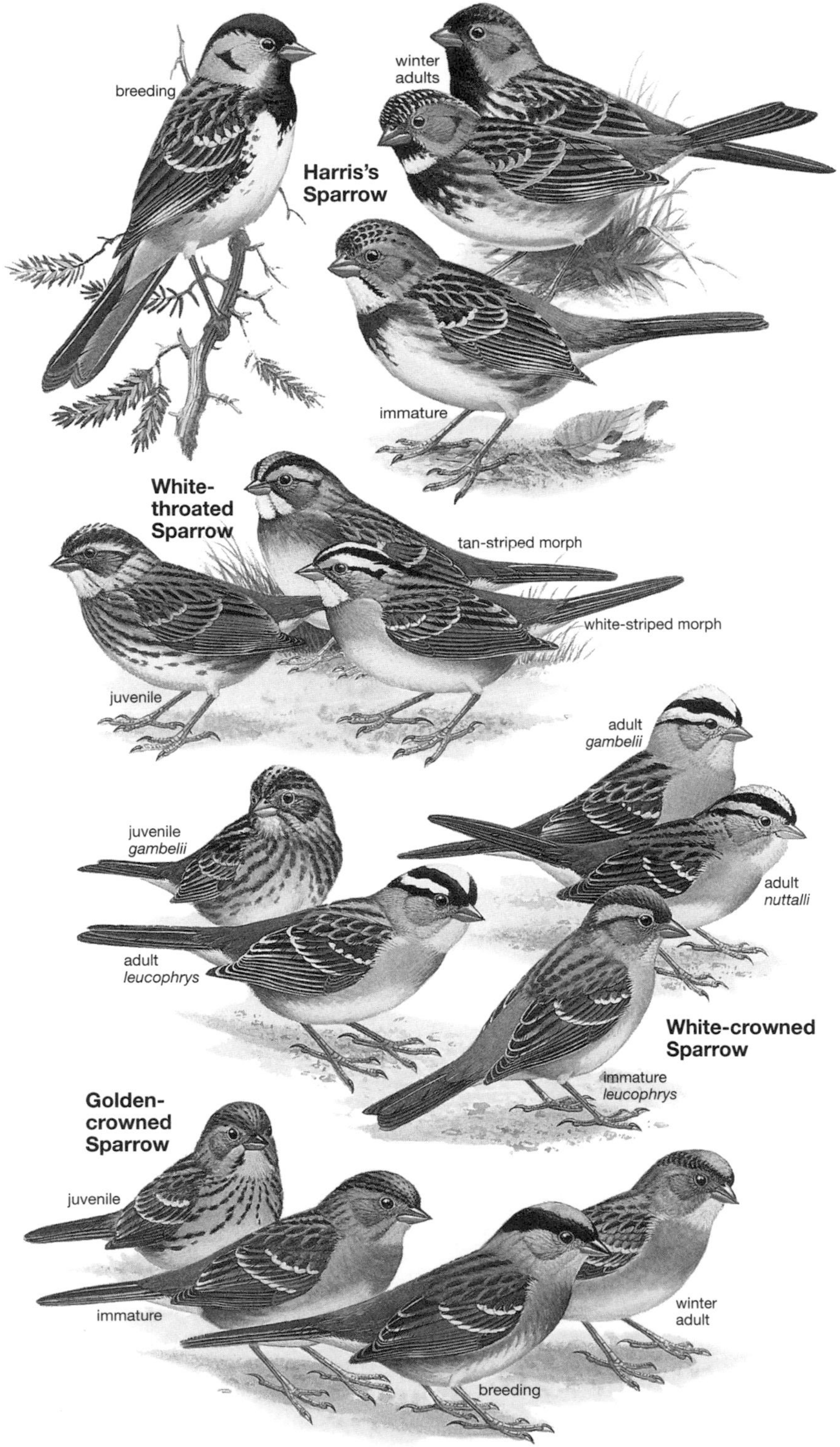

Harris's Sparrow
breeding
winter adults
immature
White-throated Sparrow
tan-striped morph
white-striped morph
juvenile
adult gambelii
juvenile gambelii
adult nuttalli
adult leucophrys
White-crowned Sparrow
immature leucophrys
Golden-crowned Sparrow
juvenile
immature
winter adult
breeding

Dark-eyed Junco *Junco hyemalis*

DATE LOCATION

Yellow-eyed Junco *Junco phaeonotus*

DATE LOCATION

"Oregon"
thurberi
♀
♂
"Slate-colored"
hyemalis
♀
♂
juvenile
"White-winged"
aikeni
♂
♂
Dark-eyed
Junco
"Slate-colored" ♂
"Gray-headed"
races
"Pink-sided"
mearnsi
caniceps
dorsalis
Yellow-eyed
Junco
palliatus
juvenile

Chestnut-collared Longspur *Calcarius ornatus*

DATE LOCATION

McCown's Longspur *Calcarius mccownii*

DATE LOCATION

breeding males
Chestnut-collared Longspur
winter ♂
winter ♀

McCown's Longspur
breeding ♂
breeding ♀
winter ♀
winter ♂
juvenile

Smith's Longspur *Calcarius pictus*

DATE LOCATION

Lapland Longspur *Calcarius lapponicus*

DATE LOCATION

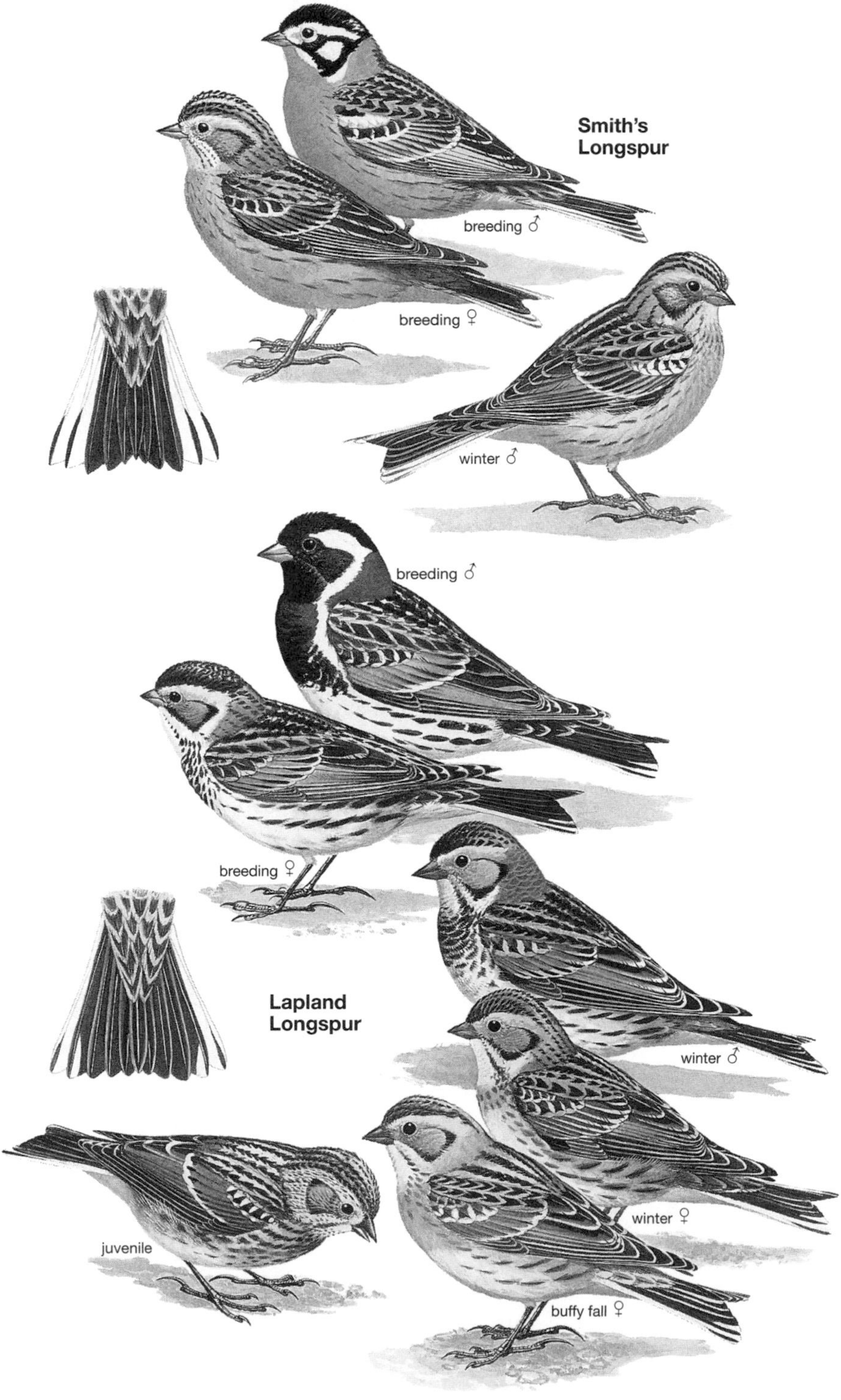
Smith's Longspur
breeding ♂
breeding ♀
winter ♂
breeding ♂
breeding ♀
Lapland Longspur
winter ♂
juvenile
winter ♀
buffy fall ♀

Snow Bunting *Plectrophenax nivalis*

DATE LOCATION

McKay's Bunting *Plectrophenax hyperboreus*

DATE LOCATION

Yellow-breasted Bunting *Emberiza aureola*

DATE LOCATION

Gray Bunting *Emberiza variabilis*

DATE LOCATION

breeding ♂
breeding ♂
1st winter ♂
breeding ♀
Snow Bunting
nivalis
winter ♂
juvenile
1st winter ♂
winter ♂
McKay's Bunting
breeding ♀
breeding ♂
breeding ♂
winter ♂
Yellow-breasted Bunting
ornata
♀
♀
breeding ♂
Gray Bunting
breeding ♂
immature ♂

Reed Bunting *Emberiza schoeniclus*

DATE LOCATION

Pallas's Bunting *Emberiza pallasi*

DATE LOCATION

Little Bunting *Emberiza pusilla*

DATE LOCATION

Rustic Bunting *Emberiza rustica*

DATE LOCATION

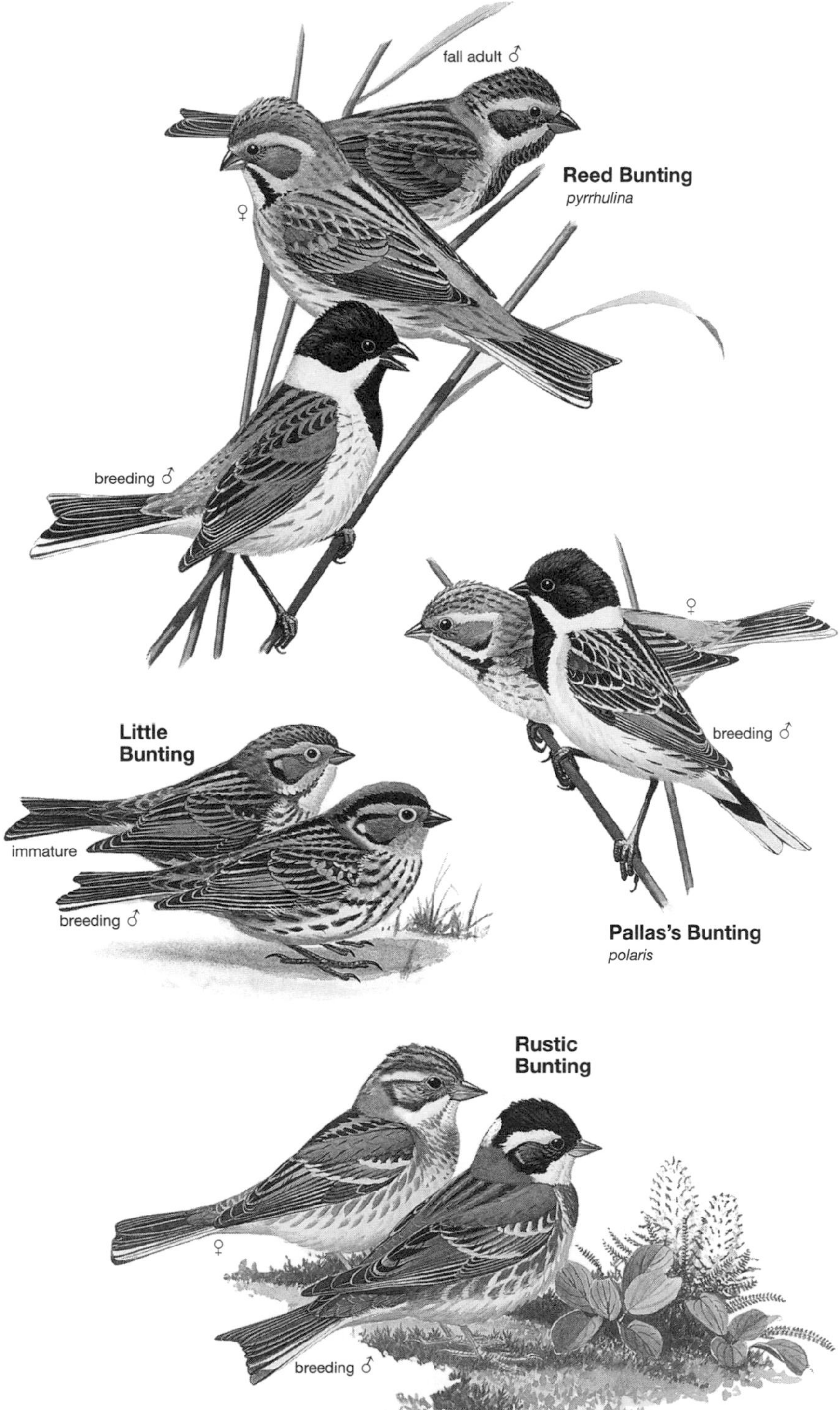
fall adult ♂
Reed Bunting
pyrrhulina
♀
breeding ♂
♀
breeding ♂
Pallas's Bunting
polaris
Little
Bunting
immature
breeding ♂
Rustic
Bunting
♀
breeding ♂

Cardinals, Saltators, Allies (Family Cardinalidae)

Rose-breasted Grosbeak *Pheucticus ludovicianus*

DATE LOCATION

Black-headed Grosbeak *Pheucticus melanocephalus*

DATE LOCATION

Crimson-collared Grosbeak *Rhodothraupis celaeno*

DATE LOCATION

Yellow Grosbeak *Pheucticus chrysopeplus*

DATE LOCATION

Rose-breasted Grosbeak
breeding adult ♂
breeding adult ♂
winter adult ♂
1st fall ♂
♀
1st spring ♂
Black-headed Grosbeak
♀
breeding adult ♂
1st fall ♂
adult ♀
adult ♂
Crimson-collared Grosbeak
adult ♂
adult ♀
Yellow Grosbeak

Northern Cardinal *Cardinalis cardinalis*

DATE LOCATION

Pyrrhuloxia *Cardinalis sinuatus*

DATE LOCATION

Dickcissel *Spiza americana*

DATE LOCATION

Blue Grosbeak *Passerina caerulea*

DATE LOCATION

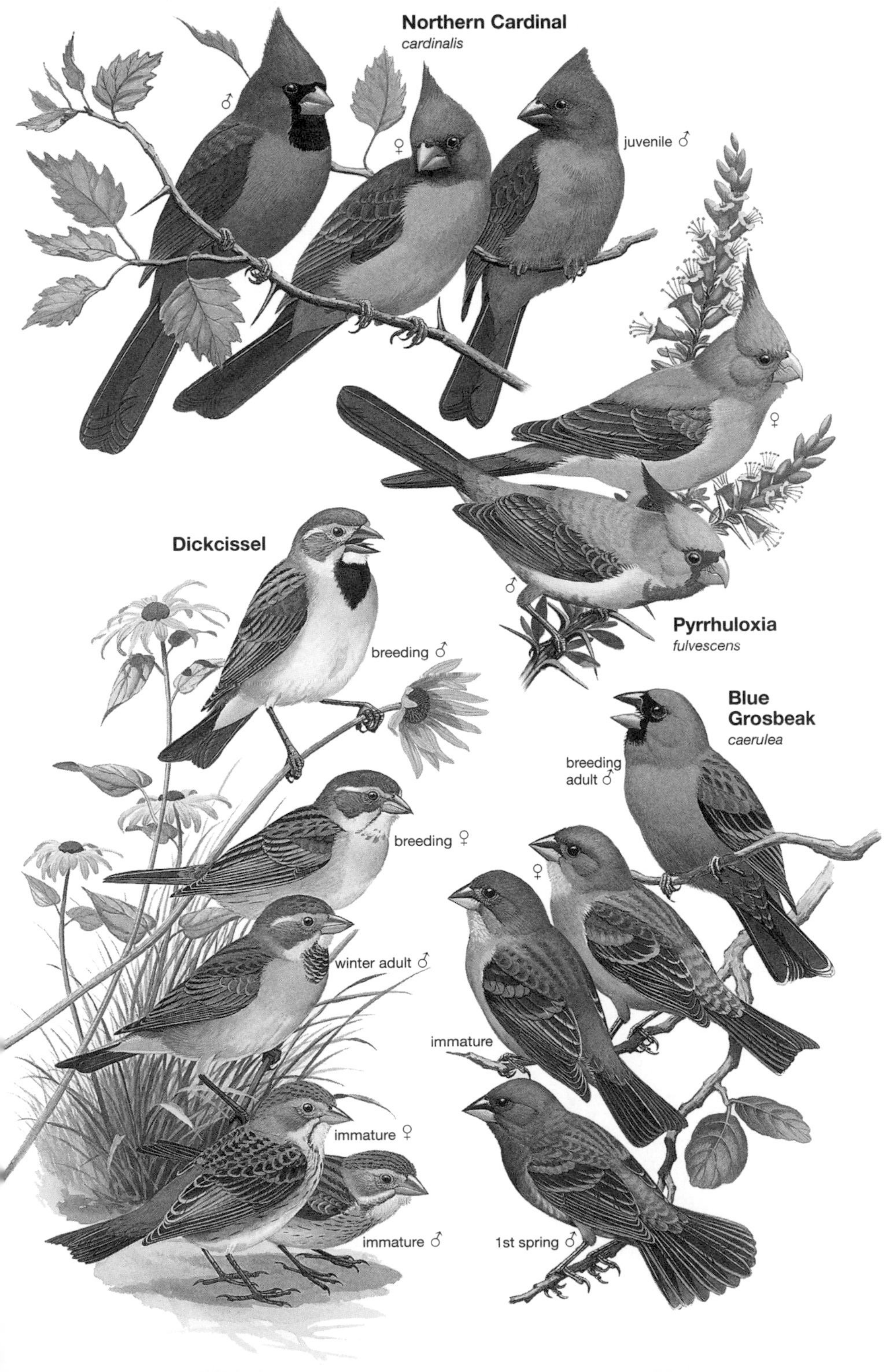
Northern Cardinal
cardinalis
♂
♀
juvenile ♂
♀
♂
Pyrrhuloxia
fulvescens
Dickcissel
breeding ♂
breeding ♀
winter adult ♂
immature ♀
immature ♂
Blue Grosbeak
caerulea
breeding adult ♂
♀
immature
1st spring ♂

Indigo Bunting *Passerina cyanea*

DATE LOCATION

Lazuli Bunting *Passerina amoena*

DATE LOCATION

Painted Bunting *Passerina ciris*

DATE LOCATION

Varied Bunting *Passerina versicolor*

DATE LOCATION

Blue Bunting *Cyanocompsa parellina*

DATE LOCATION

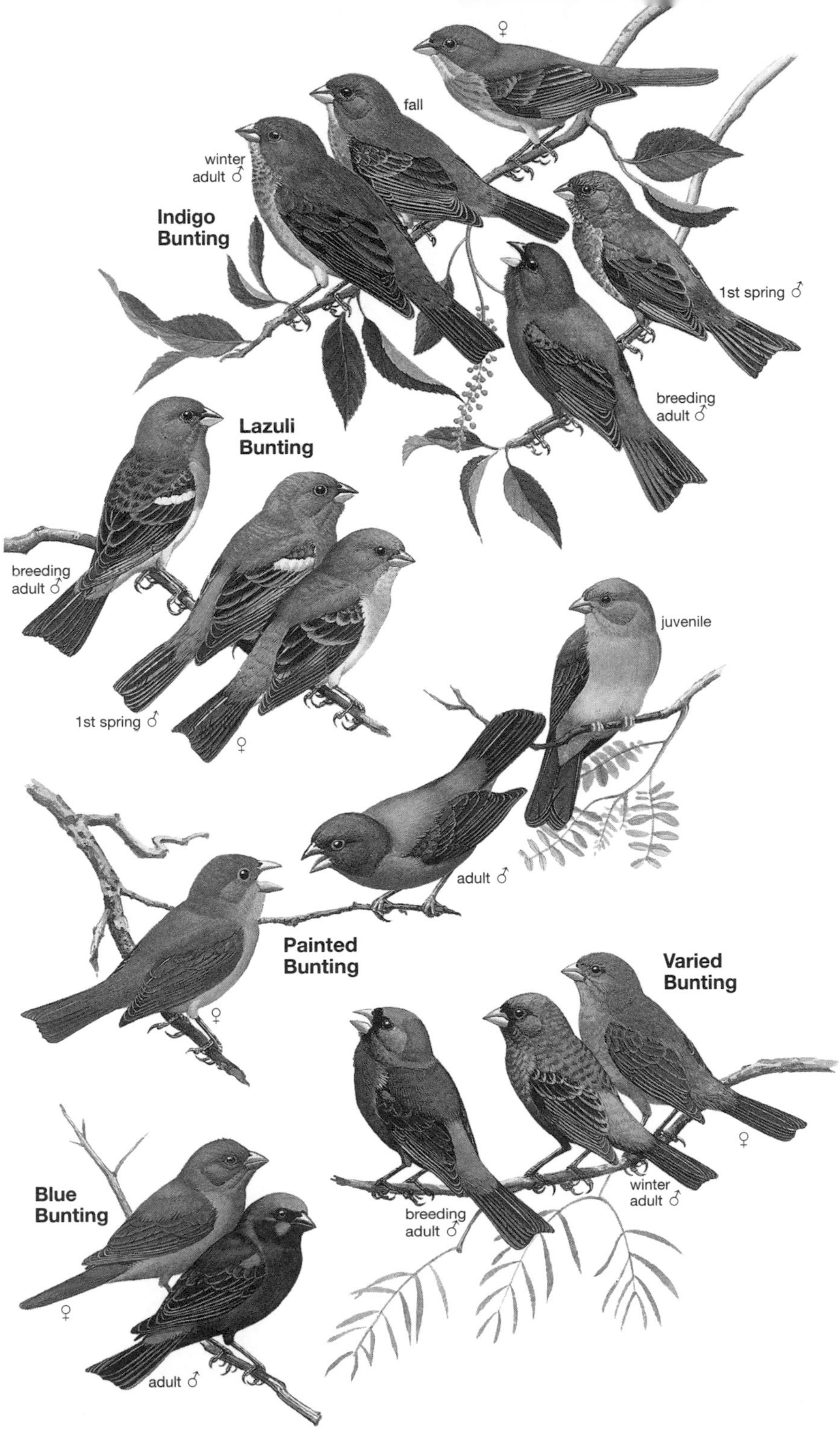

Indigo Bunting
♀
fall
winter adult ♂
1st spring ♂
breeding adult ♂
Lazuli Bunting
breeding adult ♂
1st spring ♂
♀
juvenile
adult ♂
Painted Bunting
♀
Varied Bunting
♀
winter adult ♂
breeding adult ♂
Blue Bunting
♀
adult ♂

Blackbirds (Family Icteridae)

Bobolink *Dolichonyx oryzivorus*

DATE LOCATION

Eastern Meadowlark *Sturnella magna*

DATE LOCATION

Western Meadowlark *Sturnella neglecta*

DATE LOCATION

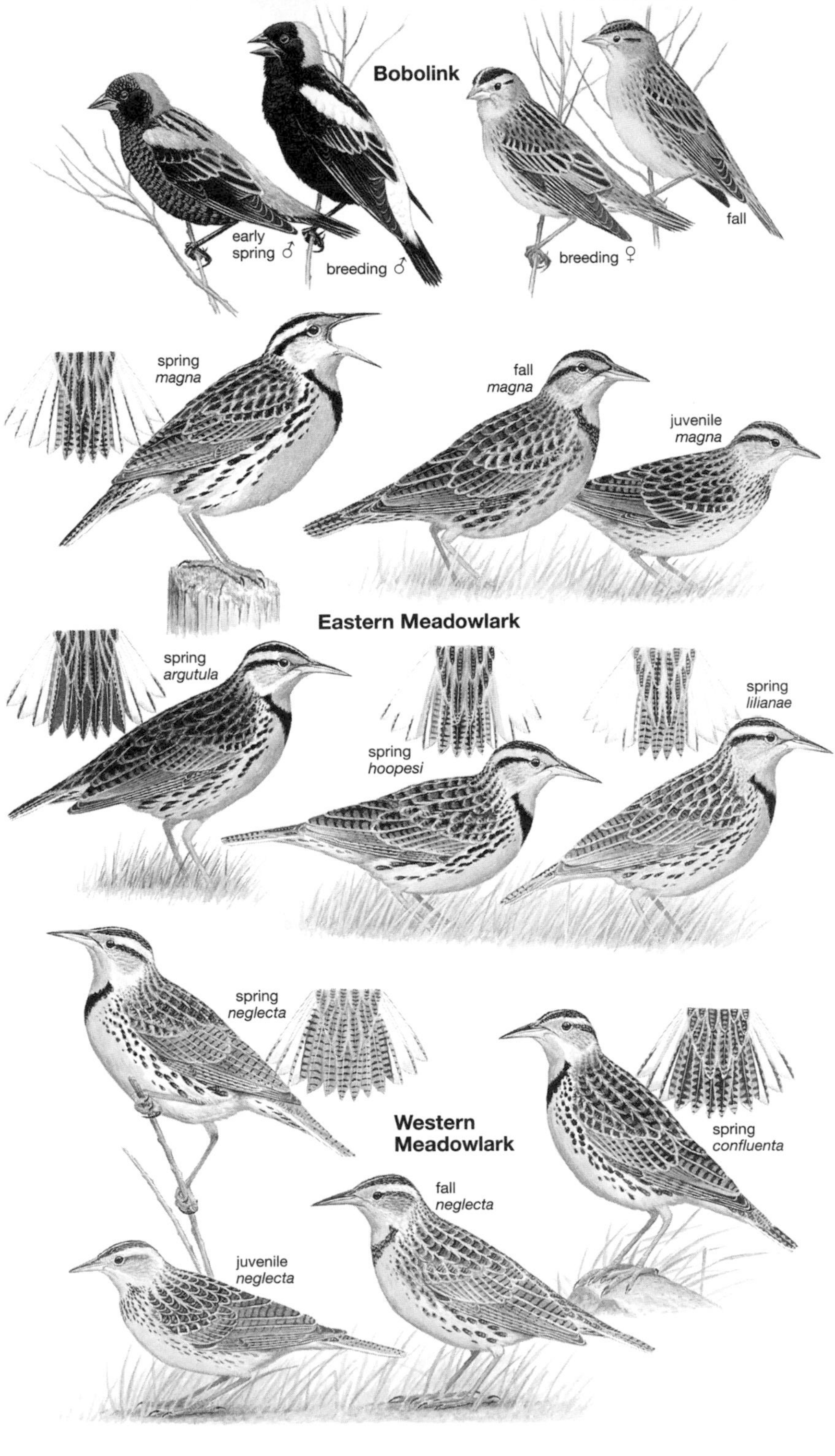
Bobolink
early spring ♂
breeding ♂
breeding ♀
fall
spring magna
fall magna
juvenile magna
Eastern Meadowlark
spring argutula
spring hoopesi
spring lilianae
spring neglecta
Western Meadowlark
spring confluenta
fall neglecta
juvenile neglecta

Yellow-headed Blackbird *Xanthocephalus xanthocephalus*

DATE LOCATION

Red-winged Blackbird *Agelaius phoeniceus*

DATE LOCATION

Tricolored Blackbird *Agelaius tricolor*

DATE LOCATION

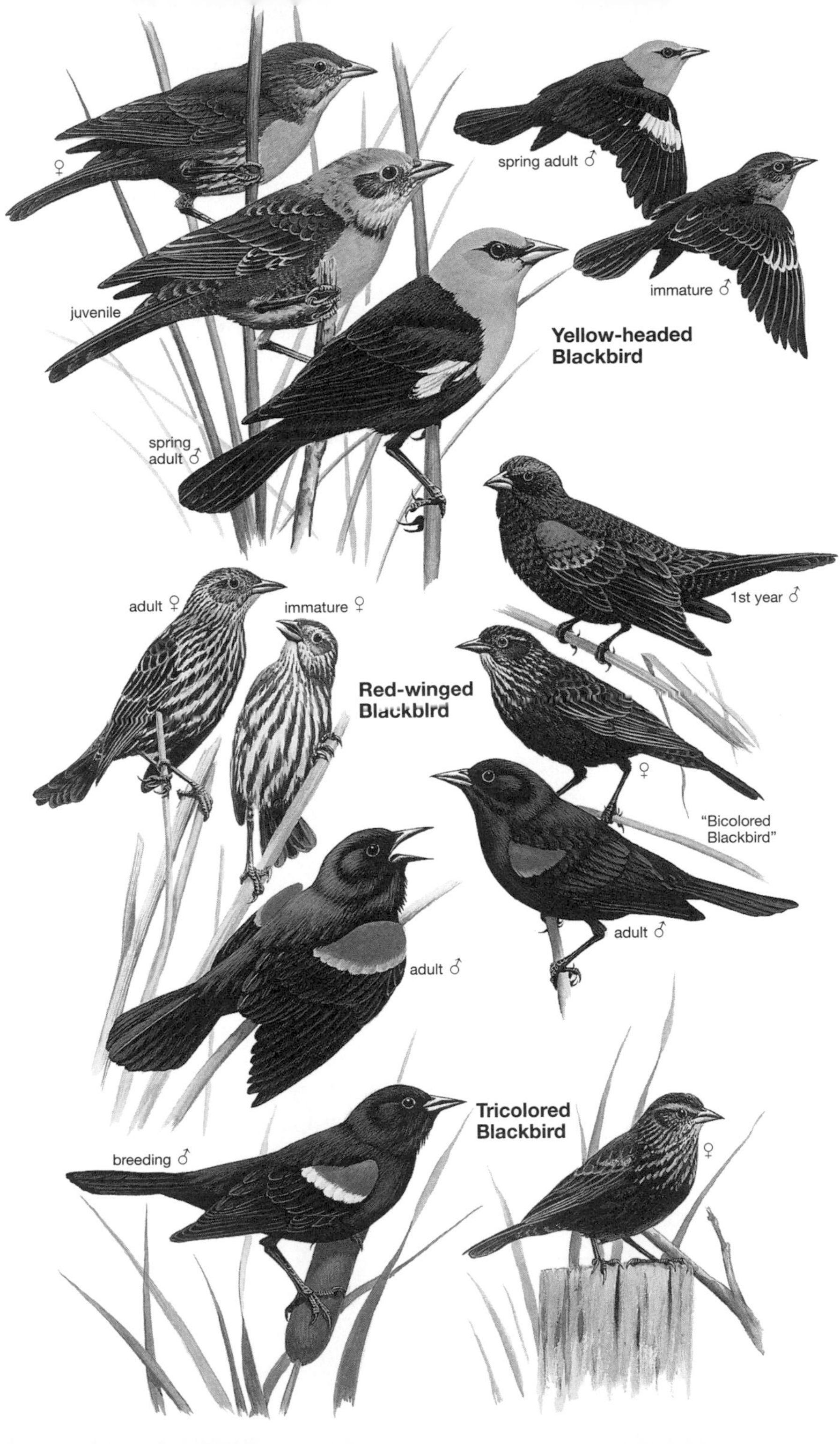

♀
spring adult ♂
immature ♂
juvenile
Yellow-headed
Blackbird
spring
adult ♂
1st year ♂
adult ♀
immature ♀
Red-winged
Blackbird
♀
"Bicolored
Blackbird"
adult ♂
adult ♂
Tricolored
Blackbird
breeding ♂
♀

Common Grackle *Quiscalus quiscula*

DATE LOCATION

Boat-tailed Grackle *Quiscalus major*

DATE LOCATION

Great-tailed Grackle *Quiscalus mexicanus*

DATE LOCATION

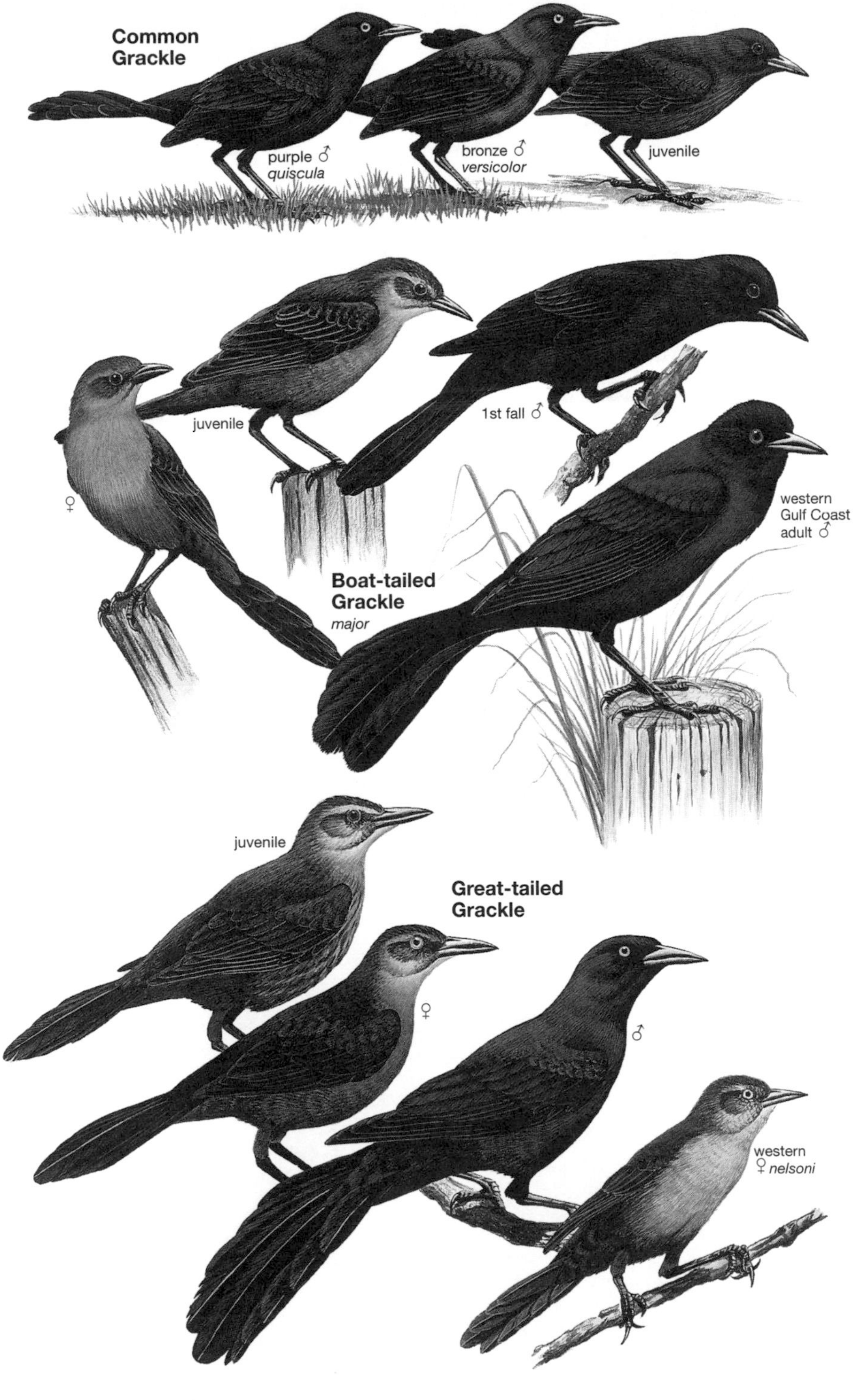
Common Grackle
purple ♂ quiscula
bronze ♂ versicolor
juvenile
juvenile
1st fall ♂
♀
western Gulf Coast adult ♂
Boat-tailed Grackle major
juvenile
Great-tailed Grackle
♀
♂
western ♀ nelsoni

Rusty Blackbird *Euphagus carolinus*

DATE LOCATION

Brewer's Blackbird *Euphagus cyanocephalus*

DATE LOCATION

Shiny Cowbird *Molothrus bonariensis*

DATE LOCATION

Brown-headed Cowbird *Molothrus ater*

DATE LOCATION

Bronzed Cowbird *Molothrus aeneus*

DATE LOCATION

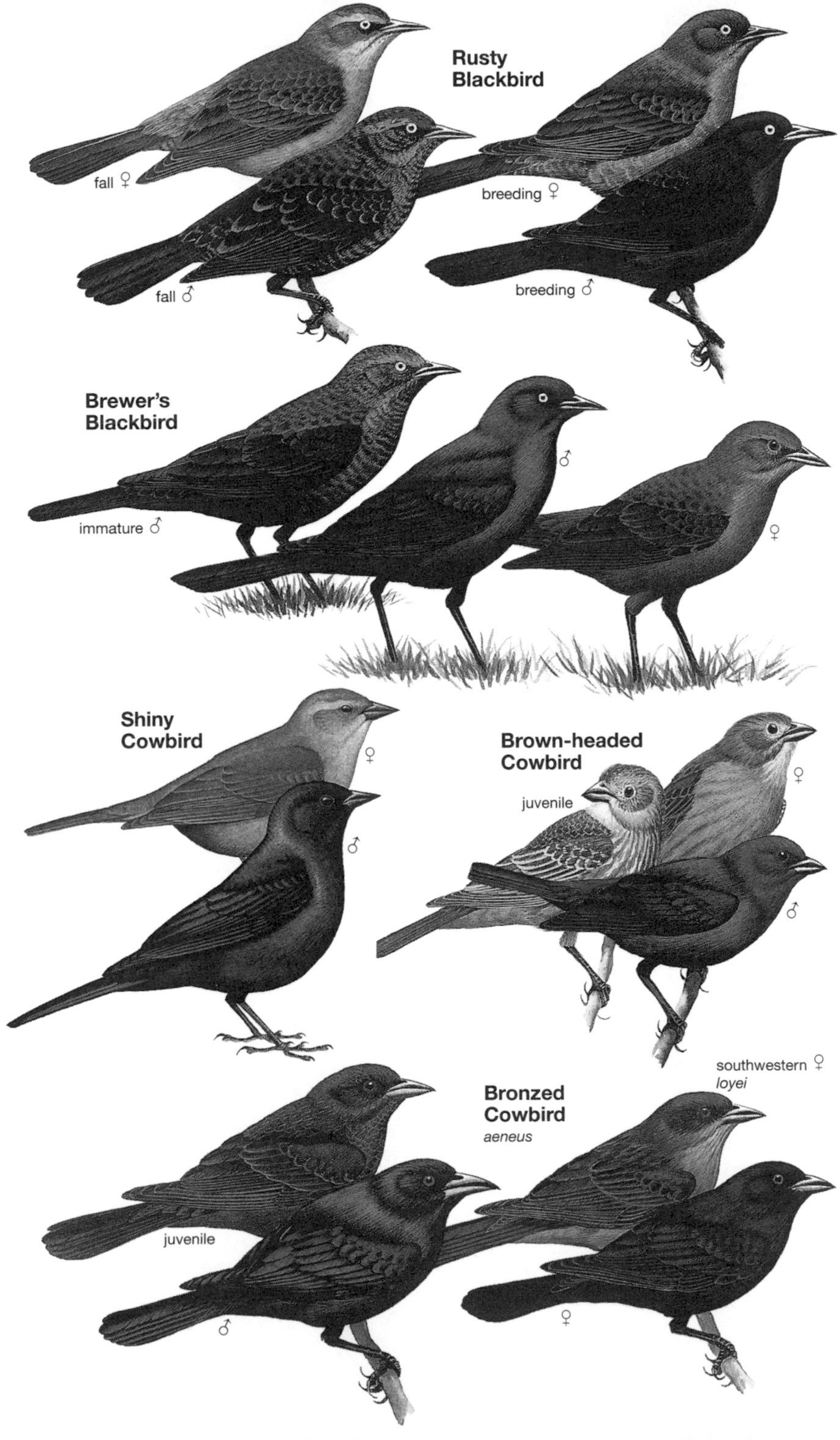
Rusty Blackbird
fall ♀
breeding ♀
fall ♂
breeding ♂
Brewer's Blackbird
♂
immature ♂
♀
Shiny Cowbird
♀
♂
Brown-headed Cowbird
juvenile
♀
♂
southwestern ♀
loyei
Bronzed Cowbird
aeneus
juvenile
♂
♀

Orchard Oriole *Icterus spurius*

DATE LOCATION

Hooded Oriole *Icterus cucullatus*

DATE LOCATION

Baltimore Oriole *Icterus galbula*

DATE LOCATION

Bullock's Oriole *Icterus bullockii*

DATE LOCATION

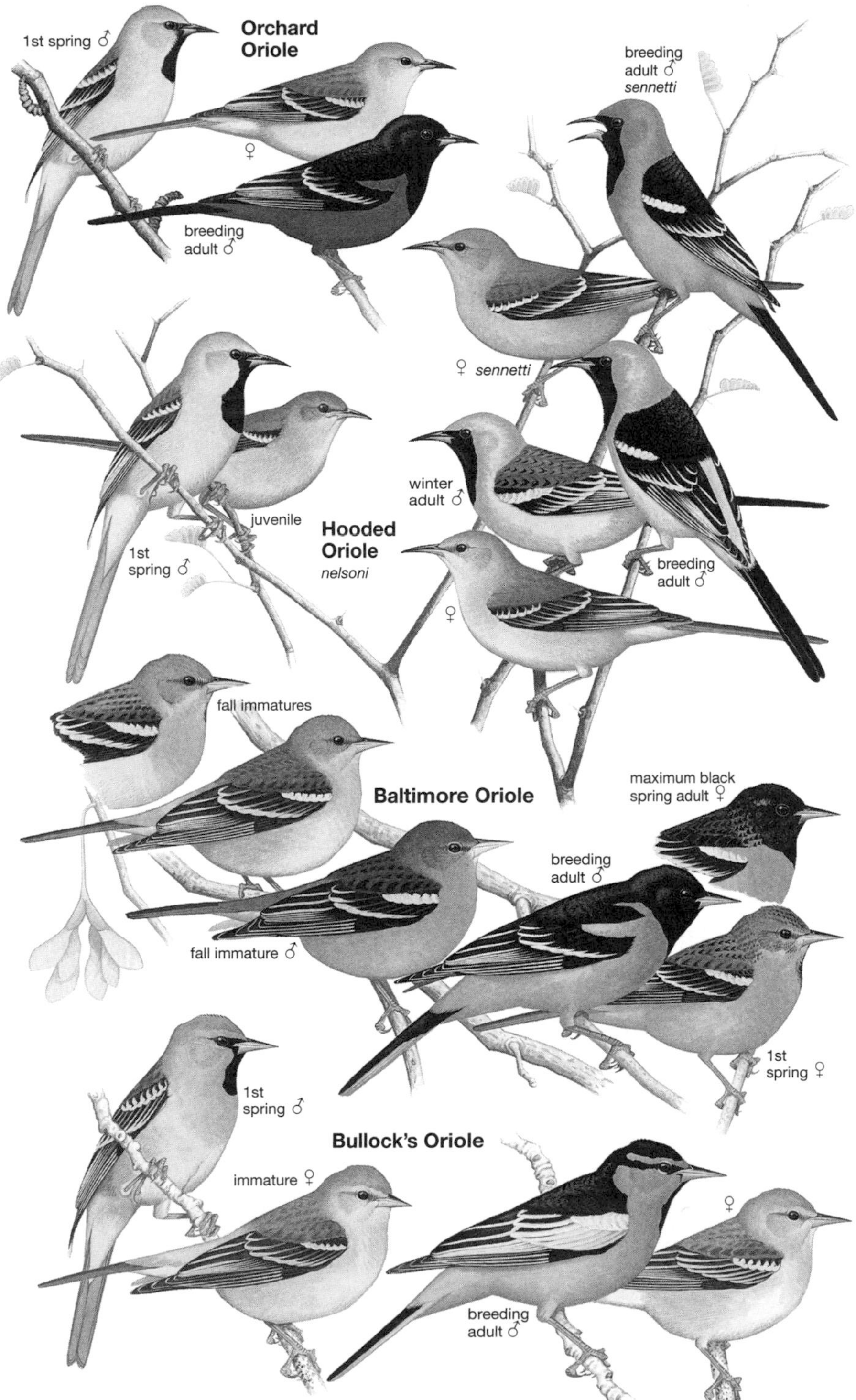
Orchard Oriole
1st spring ♂
♀
breeding adult ♂
breeding adult ♂ sennetti
♀ sennetti
1st spring ♂
juvenile
Hooded Oriole nelsoni
winter adult ♂
breeding adult ♂
♀
fall immatures
Baltimore Oriole
maximum black spring adult ♀
breeding adult ♂
fall immature ♂
1st spring ♀
1st spring ♂
Bullock's Oriole
immature ♀
♀
breeding adult ♂

Black-vented Oriole *Icterus wagleri*

DATE LOCATION

Streak-backed Oriole *Icterus pustulatus*

DATE LOCATION

Altamira Oriole *Icterus gularis*

DATE LOCATION

Audubon's Oriole *Icterus graduacauda*

DATE LOCATION

Spot-breasted Oriole *Icterus pectoralis*

DATE LOCATION

Scott's Oriole *Icterus parisorum*

DATE LOCATION

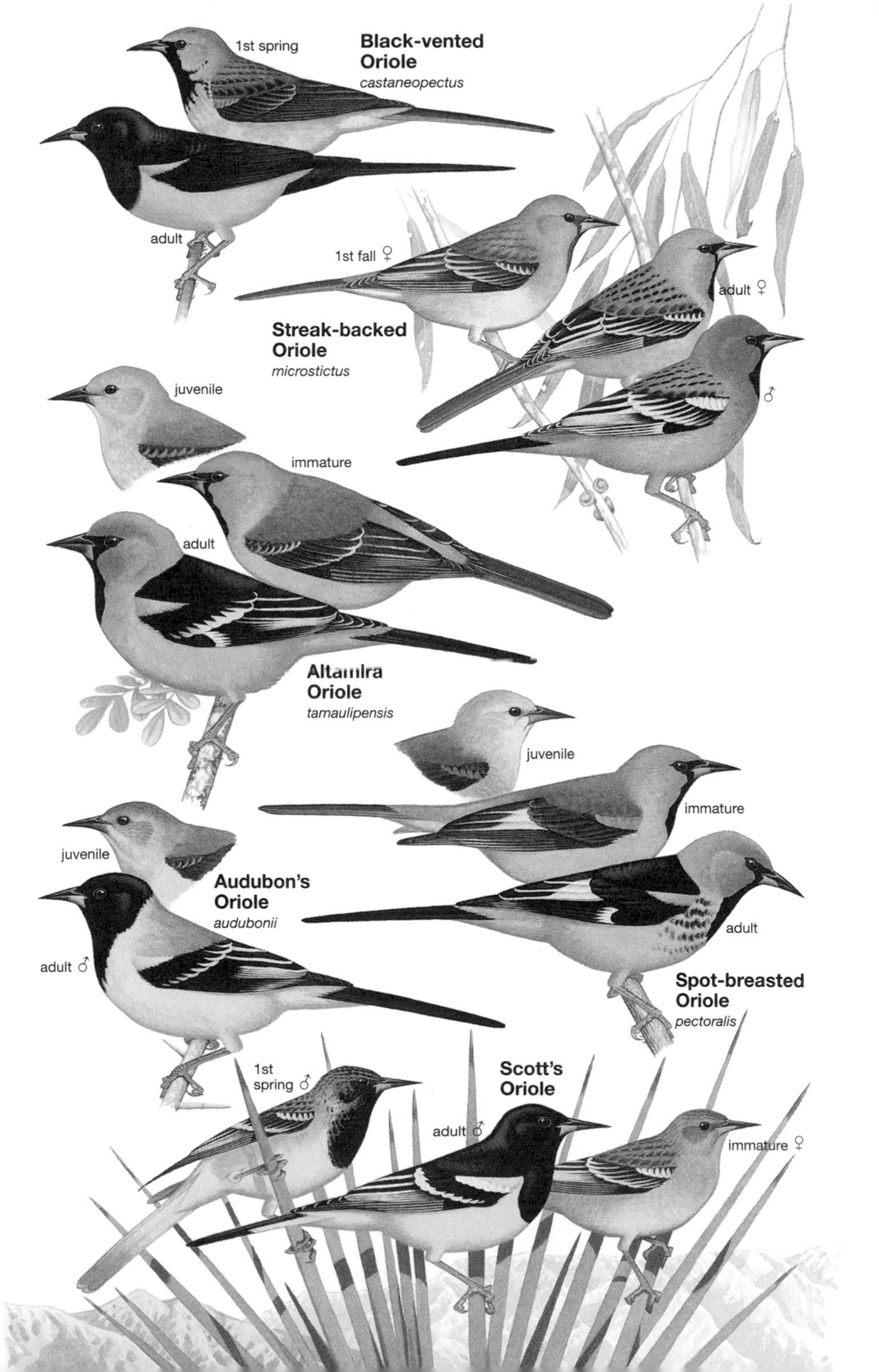
1st spring
Black-vented Oriole
castaneopectus
adult
1st fall ♀
adult ♀
Streak-backed Oriole
microstictus
♂
juvenile
immature
adult
Altamira Oriole
tamaulipensis
juvenile
immature
juvenile
Audubon's Oriole
audubonii
adult
adult ♂
Spot-breasted Oriole
pectoralis
1st spring ♂
Scott's Oriole
adult ♂
immature ♀

Fringilline and Cardueline Finches, Allies (Family Fringillidae)

Oriental Greenfinch *Carduelis sinica*

DATE LOCATION

Brambling *Fringilla montifringilla*

DATE LOCATION

Common Chaffinch *Fringilla coelebs*

DATE LOCATION

Gray-crowned Rosy-Finch *Leucosticte tephrocotis*

DATE LOCATION

Brown-capped Rosy-Finch *Leucosticte australis*

DATE LOCATION

Black Rosy-Finch *Leucosticte atrata*

DATE LOCATION

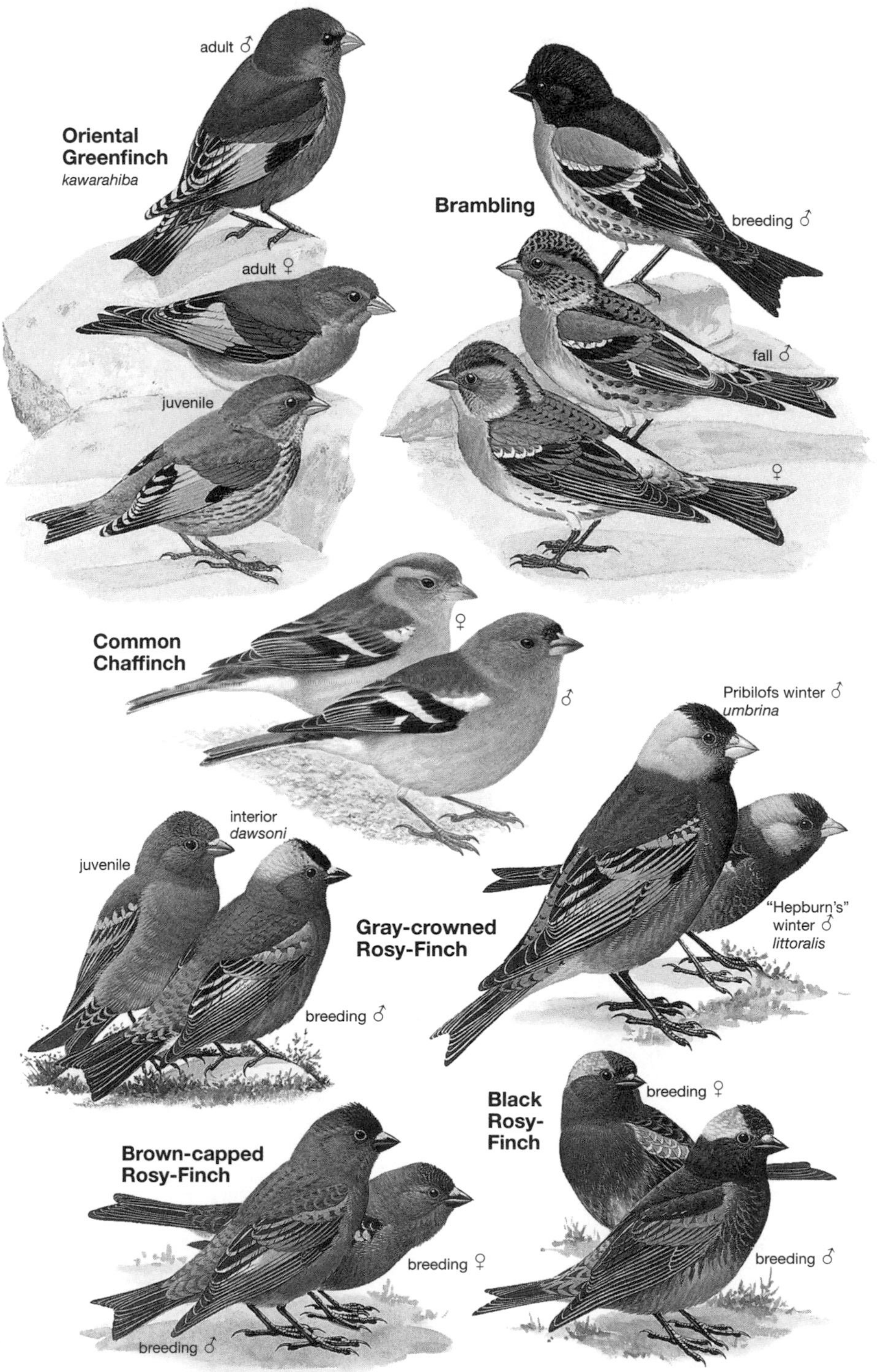

adult ♂
Oriental
Greenfinch
kawarahiba
adult ♀
juvenile
Brambling
breeding ♂
fall ♂
♀
Common
Chaffinch
♀
♂
Pribilofs winter ♂
umbrina
interior
dawsoni
juvenile
Gray-crowned
Rosy-Finch
"Hepburn's"
winter ♂
littoralis
breeding ♂
Black
Rosy-
Finch
breeding ♀
Brown-capped
Rosy-Finch
breeding ♀
breeding ♂
breeding ♂

Purple Finch *Carpodacus purpureus*

DATE LOCATION

Cassin's Finch *Carpodacus cassinii*

DATE LOCATION

House Finch *Carpodacus mexicanus*

DATE LOCATION

Common Rosefinch *Carpodacus erythrinus*

DATE LOCATION

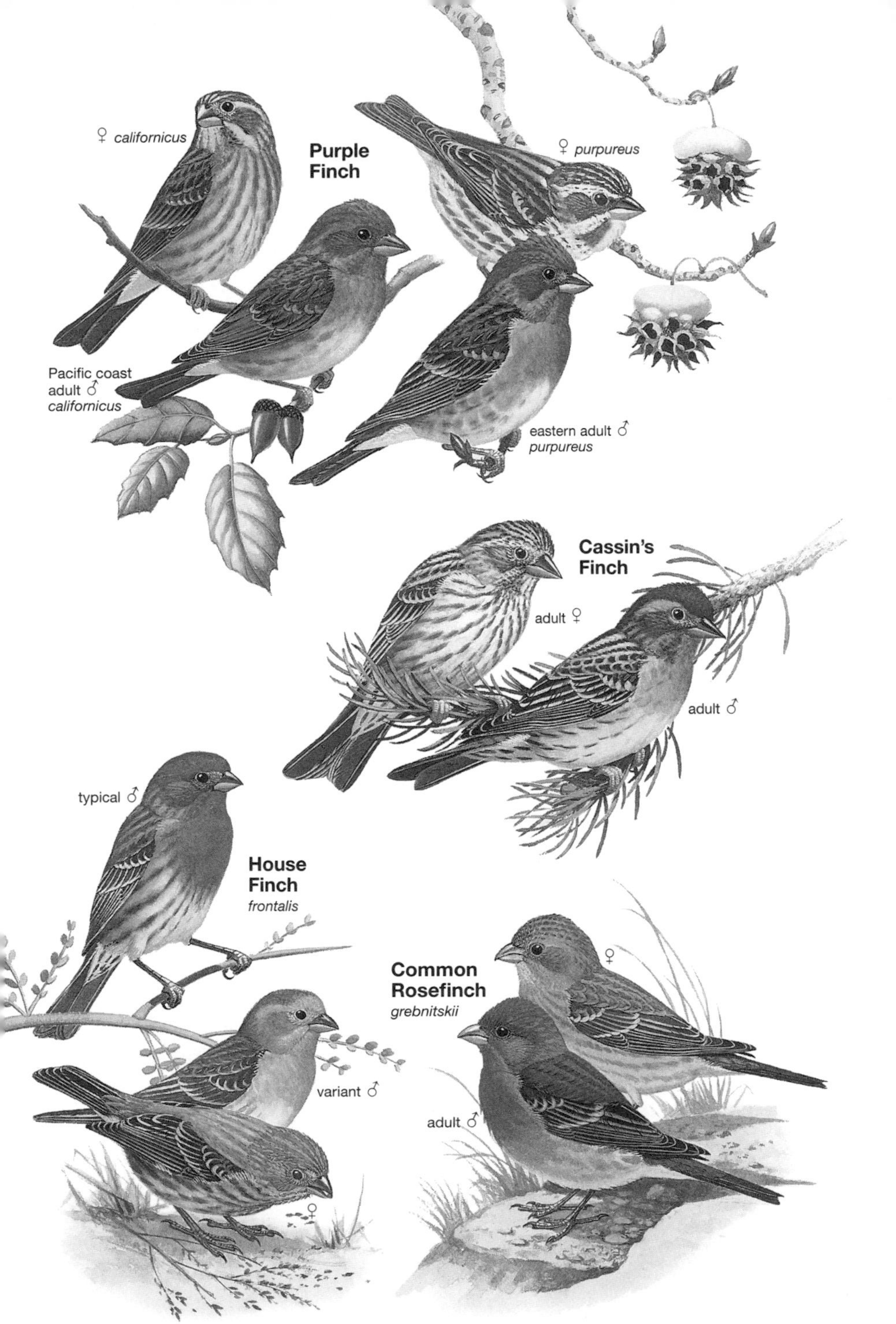
♀ californicus
Purple Finch
♀ purpureus
Pacific coast adult ♂ californicus
eastern adult ♂ purpureus
Cassin's Finch
adult ♀
adult ♂
typical ♂
House Finch frontalis
Common Rosefinch grebnitskii
♀
variant ♂
adult ♂
♀

Red Crossbill *Loxia curvirostra*

DATE LOCATION

White-winged Crossbill *Loxia leucoptera*

DATE LOCATION

Pine Grosbeak *Pinicola enucleator*

DATE LOCATION

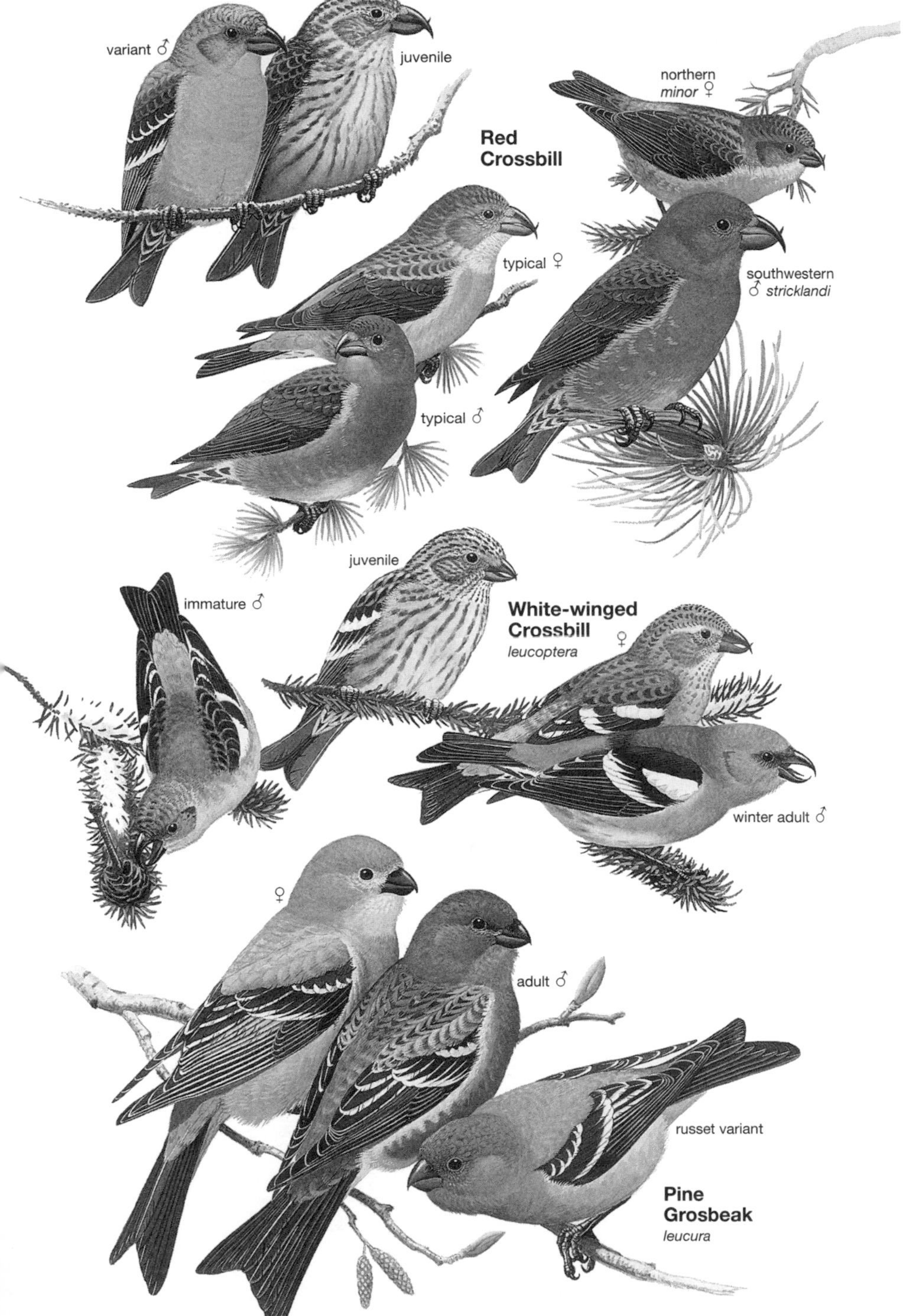

Red
Crossbill
variant ♂
juvenile
northern
minor ♀
typical ♀
southwestern
♂ stricklandi
typical ♂
White-winged
Crossbill
leucoptera
juvenile
immature ♂
♀
winter adult ♂
Pine
Grosbeak
leucura
♀
adult ♂
russet variant

Pine Siskin *Carduelis pinus*

DATE LOCATION

American Goldfinch *Carduelis tristis*

DATE LOCATION

Lesser Goldfinch *Carduelis psaltria*

DATE LOCATION

Lawrence's Goldfinch *Carduelis lawrencei*

DATE LOCATION

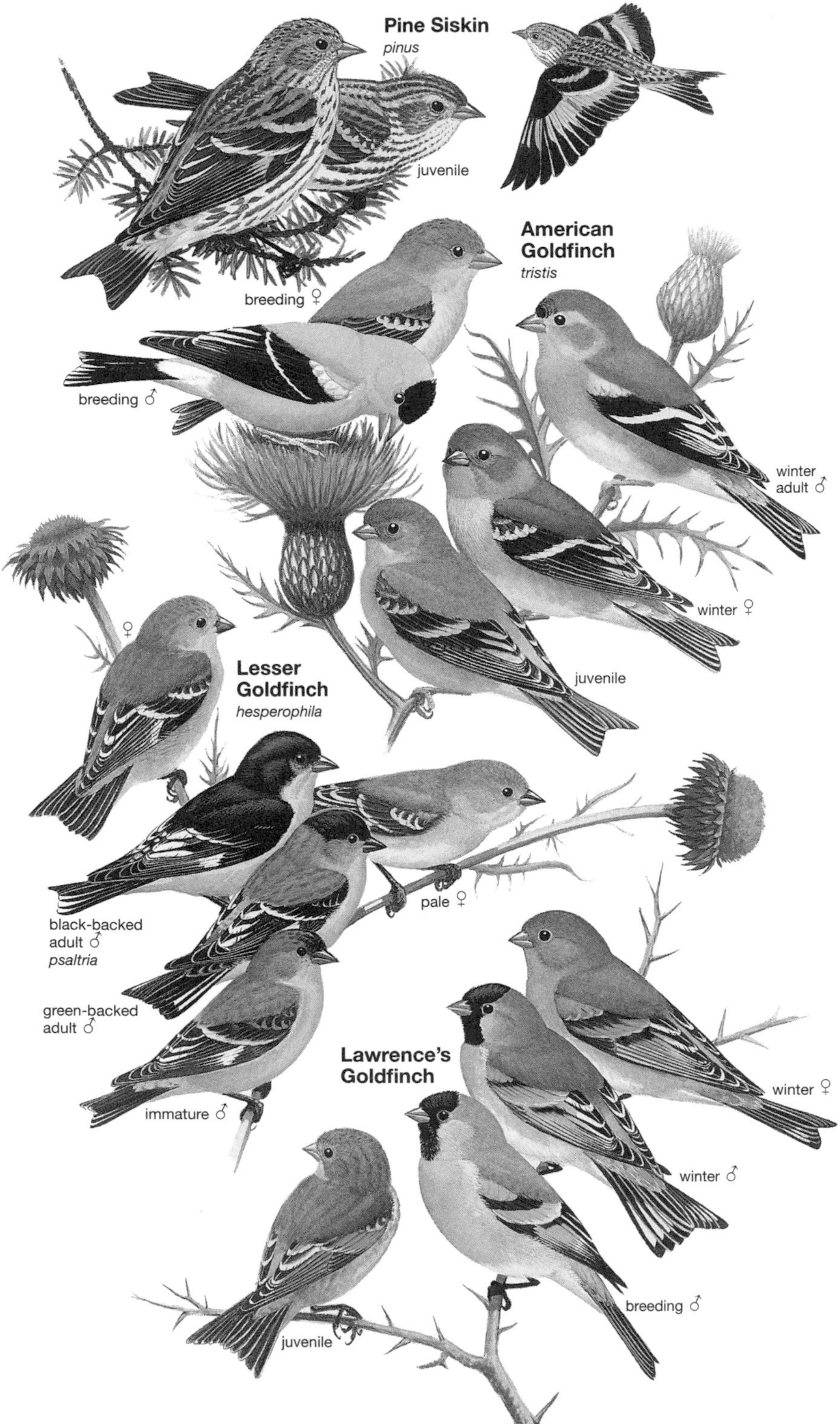

Pine Siskin
pinus
juvenile
American Goldfinch
tristis
breeding ♀
breeding ♂
winter adult ♂
winter ♀
juvenile
♀
Lesser Goldfinch
hesperophila
black-backed adult ♂
psaltria
pale ♀
green-backed adult ♂
immature ♂
Lawrence's Goldfinch
winter ♀
winter ♂
breeding ♂
juvenile

Common Redpoll *Carduelis flammea*

DATE LOCATION

Hoary Redpoll *Carduelis hornemanni*

DATE LOCATION

Evening Grosbeak *Coccothraustes vespertinus*

DATE LOCATION

Hawfinch *Coccothraustes coccothraustes*

DATE LOCATION

Eurasian Bullfinch *Pyrrhula pyrrhula*

DATE LOCATION

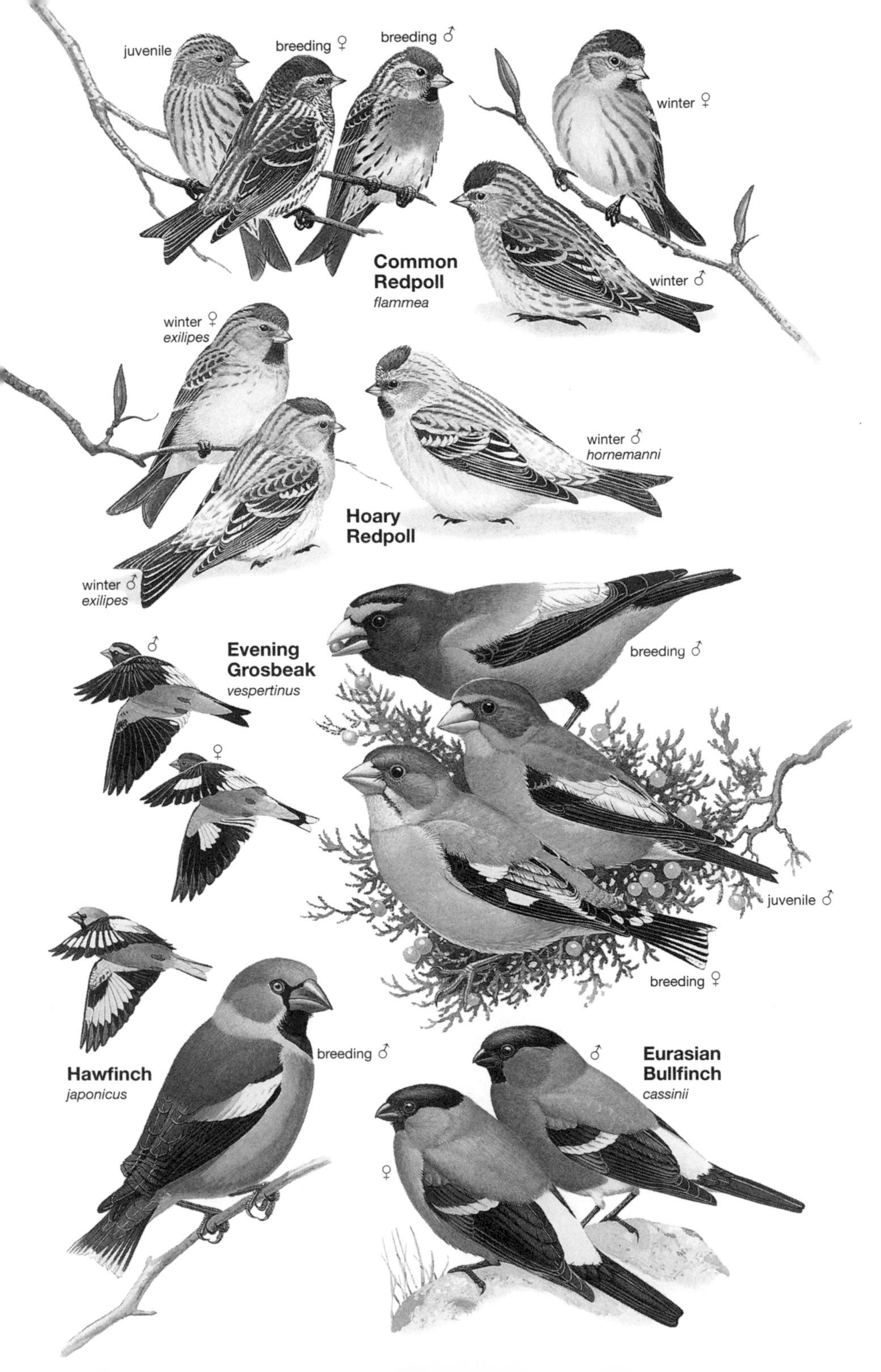

juvenile
breeding ♀
breeding ♂
winter ♀
Common
Redpoll
flammea
winter ♂
winter ♀
exilipes
winter ♂
hornemanni
Hoary
Redpoll
winter ♂
exilipes
♂
Evening
Grosbeak
vespertinus
breeding ♂
♀
juvenile ♂
breeding ♀
breeding ♂
Hawfinch
japonicus
♂
Eurasian
Bullfinch
cassinii
♀

Old World Sparrows (Family Passeridae)

House Sparrow *Passer domesticus*

DATE LOCATION

Eurasian Tree Sparrow *Passer montanus*

DATE LOCATION

Weavers (Family Ploceidae)

Orange Bishop *Euplectes franciscanus*

DATE LOCATION

Estrildid Finches (Family Estrildidae)

Nutmeg Mannikin *Lonchura punctulata*

DATE LOCATION

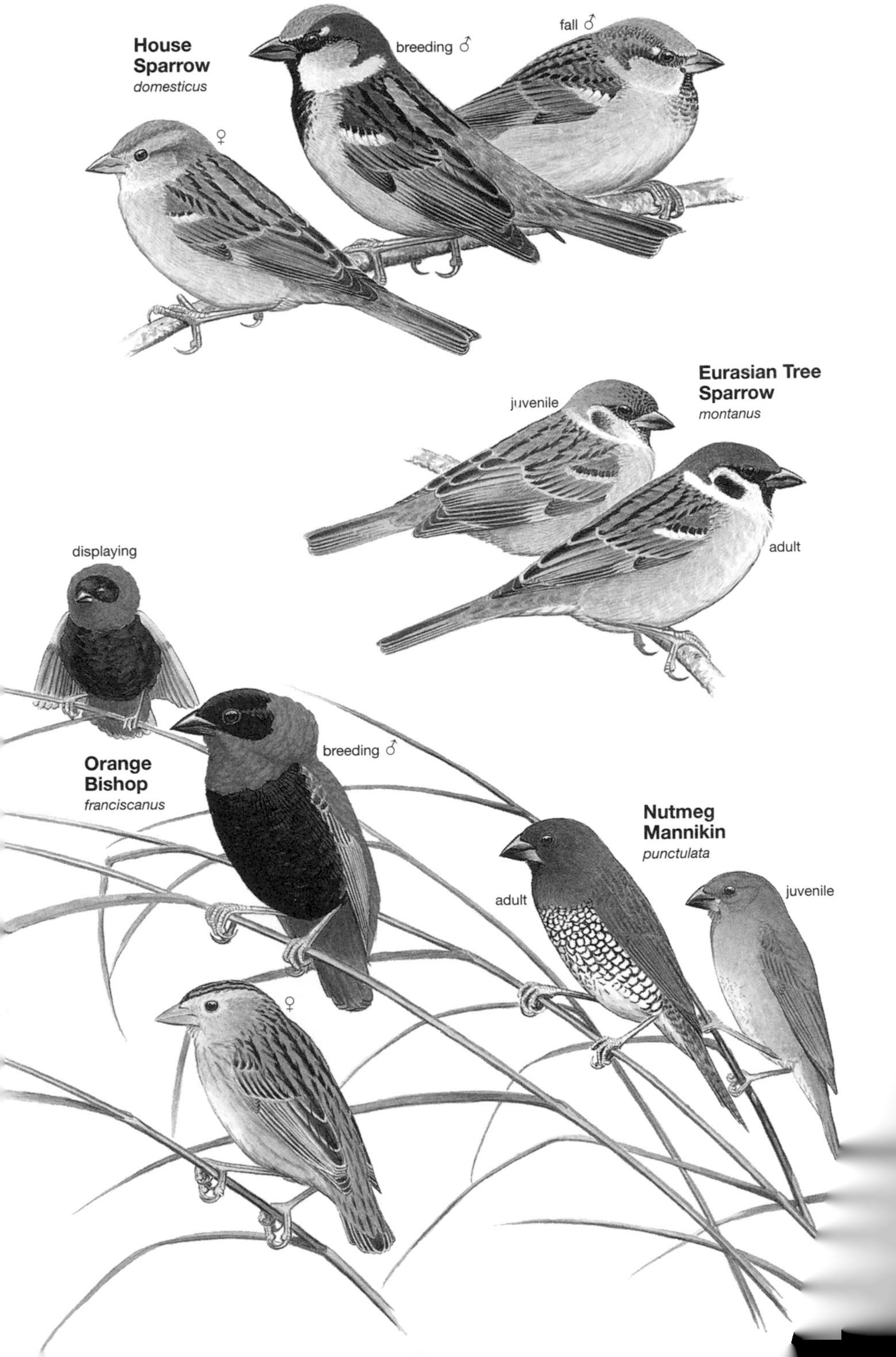
House Sparrow
domesticus
breeding ♂
fall ♂
♀
Eurasian Tree Sparrow
montanus
juvenile
adult
displaying
Orange Bishop
franciscanus
breeding ♂
♀
Nutmeg Mannikin
punctulata
adult
juvenile

Accidentals, Extinct Species

These 71 species have been recorded for North America, but for nearly all there are fewer than three records in the past two decades or five records in the last hundred years. Four species that have gone extinct in the past two centuries are also included.

Graylag Goose *Anser anser*

DATE LOCATION

Lesser White-fronted Goose *Anser erythropus*

DATE LOCATION

Labrador Duck *Camptorhynchus labradorius*

DATE LOCATION

Light-mantled Albatross *Phoebetria palpebrata*

DATE LOCATION

Wandering Albatross *Diomedea exulans*

DATE LOCATION

Black-bellied Storm-Petrel *Fregetta tropica*

DATE LOCATION

Ringed Storm-Petrel *Oceanodroma hornbyi*

DATE LOCATION

Nazca Booby *Sula granti*

DATE LOCATION

Great Frigatebird *Fregata minor*

DATE LOCATION

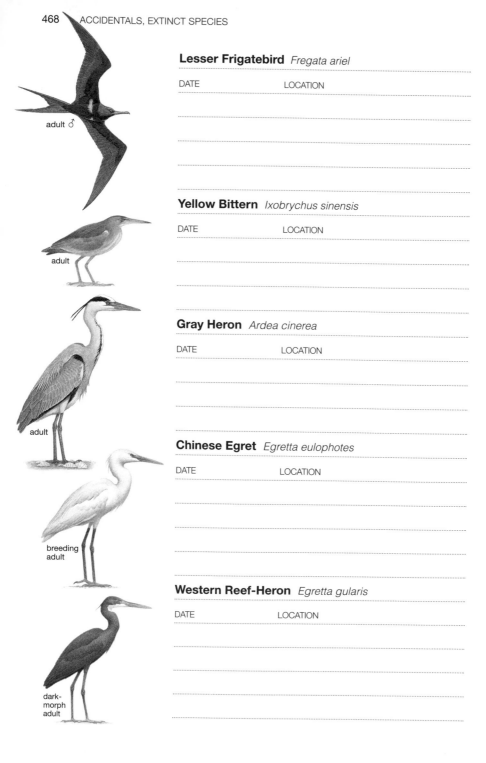

adult ♂

Lesser Frigatebird *Fregata ariel*

DATE LOCATION

adult

Yellow Bittern *Ixobrychus sinensis*

DATE LOCATION

adult

Gray Heron *Ardea cinerea*

DATE LOCATION

breeding adult

Chinese Egret *Egretta eulophotes*

DATE LOCATION

dark-morph adult

Western Reef-Heron *Egretta gularis*

DATE LOCATION

Chinese Pond-Heron *Ardeola bacchus*

DATE LOCATION

Crane Hawk *Geranospiza caerulescens*

DATE LOCATION

Collared Forest-Falcon *Micrastur semitorquatus*

DATE LOCATION

Red-footed Falcon *Falco vespertinus*

DATE LOCATION

Paint-billed Crake *Neocrex erythrops*

DATE LOCATION

Spotted Rail *Pardirallus maculatus*

DATE LOCATION

Double-striped Thick-knee *Burhinus bistriatus*

DATE LOCATION

Greater Sand-Plover *Charadrius leschenaultii*

DATE LOCATION

Collared Plover *Charadrius collaris*

DATE LOCATION

Eurasian Oystercatcher *Haematopus ostralegus*

DATE LOCATION

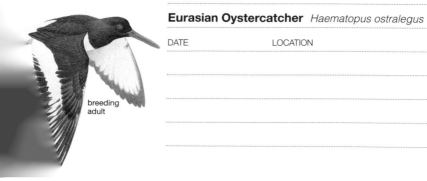

Black-winged Stilt *Himantopus himantopus*

DATE LOCATION

Slender-billed Curlew *Numenius tenurostris*

DATE LOCATION

Eurasian Woodcock *Scolopax rusticola*

DATE LOCATION

Oriental Pratincole *Glareola maldivarum*

DATE LOCATION

Gray-hooded Gull *Larus cirrocephalus*

DATE LOCATION

Whiskered Tern *Chlidonias hybrida*

DATE LOCATION

Great Auk *Pinguinus impennis*

DATE LOCATION

Scaly-naped Pigeon *Patagioenas squamosa*

DATE LOCATION

Passenger Pigeon *Ectopistes migratorius*

DATE LOCATION

Carolina Parakeet *Conuropsis carolinensis*

DATE LOCATION

Oriental Scops-Owl *Otus sunia*

DATE LOCATION

rufous morph
japonicus

Mottled Owl *Cicabba virgata*

DATE LOCATION

Stygian Owl *Asio stygius*

DATE LOCATION

Gray Nightjar *Caprilmulgus indicus*

DATE LOCATION

♂ *jotaka*

Antillean Palm-Swift *Tachornis phoenicobia*

DATE LOCATION

Cinnamon Hummingbird *Amazilia rutila*

DATE LOCATION

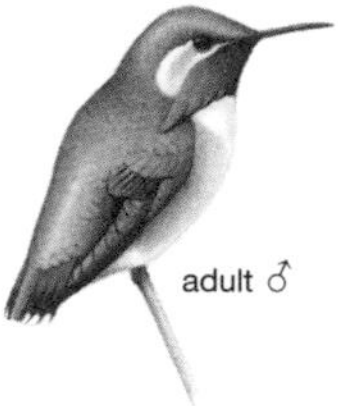

Bumblebee Hummingbird *Atthis heloisa*

DATE LOCATION

Eurasian Hoopoe *Upupa epops*

DATE LOCATION

Eurasian Wryneck *Jynx torquilla*

DATE LOCATION

Greenish Elaenia *Myiopagis viridicata*

DATE LOCATION

Caribbean Elaenia *Elaenia martinica*

DATE LOCATION

Social Flycatcher *Myiozetetes similis*

DATE LOCATION

Masked Tityra *Tityra semifasciata*

DATE LOCATION

Yucatan Vireo *Vireo magister*

DATE LOCATION

Cuban Martin *Progne crytoleuca*

DATE LOCATION

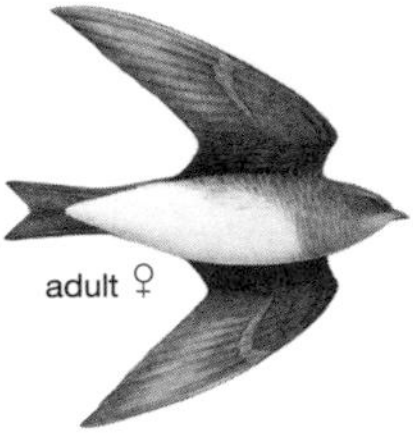

Gray-breasted Martin *Progne chalybea*

DATE LOCATION

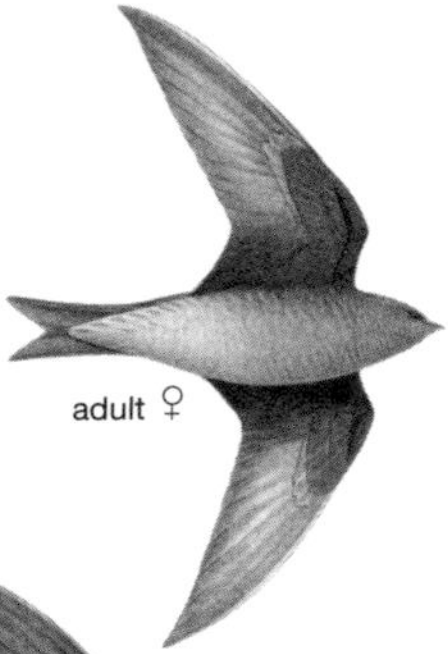

Southern Martin *Progne elegans*

DATE LOCATION

Brown-chested Martin *Progne tapera*

DATE LOCATION

Mangrove Swallow *Tachycineta albilinea*

DATE LOCATION

Willow Warbler *Phylloscopus trochilus*

DATE LOCATION

Wood Warbler *Phylloscopus sibilatri*

DATE LOCATION

Yellow-browed Warbler *Phylloscopus inornatus*

DATE LOCATION

Lesser Whitethroat *Sylvia curruca*

DATE LOCATION

Mugimaki Flycatcher *Ficedula mugimaki*

DATE LOCATION

Spotted Flycatcher *Muscicapa striata*

DATE LOCATION

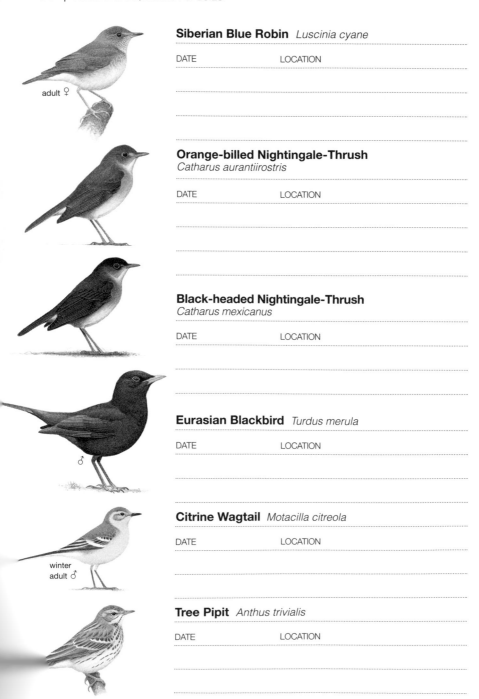

Siberian Blue Robin *Luscinia cyane*

DATE LOCATION

Orange-billed Nightingale-Thrush
Catharus aurantiirostris

DATE LOCATION

Black-headed Nightingale-Thrush
Catharus mexicanus

DATE LOCATION

Eurasian Blackbird *Turdus merula*

DATE LOCATION

Citrine Wagtail *Motacilla citreola*

DATE LOCATION

Tree Pipit *Anthus trivialis*

DATE LOCATION

Gray Silky-flycatcher *Ptilogonys cinereus*

DATE LOCATION

adult ♂

Worthen's Sparrow *Spizella wortheni*

DATE LOCATION

Pine Bunting *Emberiza leucocephalos*

DATE LOCATION

fall adult ♂

Yellow-throated Bunting *Emberiza elegans*

DATE LOCATION

adult ♂

Tawny-shouldered Blackbird *Agelaius humeralis*

DATE LOCATION

adult ♂

Eurasian Siskin *Carduelis spinus*

DATE LOCATION

fall adult ♂

Light-mantled Albatross

AOU and ABA Checklist Differences

The published checklists of the AOU and ABA differ slightly in which species they accept as being reliably recorded in North America. The differences can be summarized as follows:

Light-mantled Albatross *Phobetria palpebrata.* Origin questioned by ABA (page 466). **Azure Gallinule** *Porphyrula flavirostris.* A specimen from Suffolk County, New York, on 14 Dec. 1986 was initially accepted by both committees, but subsequent information revealed that it may have escaped from a local aviculturalist. Still accepted by AOU. **Caribbean Elaenia** *Elaenia martinica.* Not accepted by AOU (page 475). **European Turtle-Dove** *Streptopelia turtur.* One at Lower Matecumbe Key, South Florida, 9-11 Apr. 1990 (photos), was accepted by AOU; its origin was questioned by ABA.

Greenland

Redwing

White Wagtail
alba

Greenland is the largest island in the World, most of it lying north of the Arctic Circle, and forms the most northeastern part of North America. Over 230 species have been recorded there, and nearly all are substantiated by specimens. The definitive ornithological reference is *An Annotated Checklist to the Birds of Greenland* (1994) by David Boertmann (*Bioscience* 38). Boertmann divides Greenland into four regions (north, west, northeast, and southeast) and details the bird distribution for each. Greenland's avifauna is a mix of both Palearctic and Nearctic species, many of which are strays respectively from Europe (including Iceland) and mainland North America. The breeding avifauna includes Pink-footed, White-fronted (the endemic breeding subspecies *flavirostris*), and Barnacle Geese, White-tailed Eagle, Fieldfare, Redwing, White Wagtail (nominate *alba*), and Meadow Pipit. Three subspecies of Rock Ptarmigan are found in Greenland, two of which (*saturata* and *capta*) are endemic. Two subspecies of Dunlins breed in Greenland, one of which (*arctica*) is an endemic breeder in the northeast; the other (*schinzii*) breeds in southern Greenland as well as northwestern Europe. The Black Scoters recorded are of the nominate *nigra* subspecies from northwest Europe. The Merlin specimens from Greenland are of *subaesalon,* an endemic breeder on Iceland; also recorded is the more widespread *aesolon,* breeding mainly in northern Europe. The Red Crossbills collected are of nominate *curvirostra* from the Palearctic. These, along with the following list of species *not* recorded in our area of coverage, should alert observers to the potential visitors to northeast North America. For polytypic species, the trinomial subspecies name is given, if known:

Eurasian Spoonbill *Platalea leucorodia leucorodia.* One Oct. record (1909) for the West. **Ruddy Shelduck** *Tadorna ferruginea.* Four collected in the summer of 1892, an invasion year for the species in northwest Europe. (See also page 96.) **Water Rail** *Rallus aquaticus hibernans.* Four records. The subspecies *hibernans* is endemic to Iceland. **Spotted Crake** *Porzana porzana.* Eleven records, nearly all in fall, from the West! **Oriental Plover** *Charadrius veredus.* One May record (1948) from the West. A remarkable record, as it breeds on the steppes of eastern Asia and winters in Australia. **Rook** *Corvus frugilegus frugilegus.* One Mar. record (1901) for the Southeast. **Carrion Crow** *Corvus corone cornix.* Two spring records (1897, 1907) were of the "Hooded Crow." **Meadow Pipit** *Anthus pratensis pratensis.* Scarce breeder in eastern Greenland. **White's Thrush** *Zoothera aurea aurea.* One Oct. record (1954) for the Northeast. It is here treated as a separate species from the Scaly Thrush, *Z. dauma,* following other authorities. **Song Thrush** *Turdus philomelos philomelos.* One June record (1982) for the Northeast. **Blackcap** *Sylvia atricapilla atricapilla.* One Nov. record (1916) for the Southeast. **Lesser Redpoll** *Carduelis cabaret.* One Sept. record (1933) for the Southeast.

Dunlin
schinzii

Bermuda

Bermuda is a series of some 300 small islands, most of which are uninhabited. It is best known as the only breeding site of the Bermuda Petrel (also called the Cahow), which was discovered early in the 17th century and then thought to be extinct until it was rediscovered in 1951. The White-tailed Tropicbird reaches its northernmost breeding range here. The only endemic breeding land bird is a nonmigratory subspecies of the White-eyed Vireo (*bermudianus*). Established exotics not found in North America include European Goldfinch, Common Waxbill, and Orange-cheeked Waxbill. Bermuda is well known for its migrants and vagrants, which make up most of Bermuda's extensive species list—in excess of 360 species. Surprising northern species that have occurred include Northern Hawk Owl, Snowy Owl, Bohemian Waxwing, White-winged Crossbill, and Pine Grosbeak. The single Snowy Owl (1987) took to predating the endangered Bermuda Petrels and had to be collected—sometimes conservationists have to make hard choices! Most of the vagrants come from North America (including the West) or Europe, but a few (Large-billed Tern and Fork-tailed Flycatcher) are from South America. The Red-necked Stint and, even more surprisingly, the Dark-sided Flycatcher (a late Sept. specimen of nominate *sibirica*) are from Asia. The most recent birding references for Bermuda are *A Guide to the Birds of Bermuda* (1991) by Eric Amos and *A Birdwatching Guide to Bermuda* (2002) by Andrew Dobson.

The following are the species recorded from Bermuda but not from mainland North America:

West Indian Whistling-Duck *Dendrocygna arborea.* One record (1907). This species is resident on some of the Bahamian islands. (A recent record from Virginia is of uncertain origin.) **Ferruginous Duck** *Aythya nyroca.* A winter sight record (1987). **Striated Heron** *Butorides striata.* One record (1985) of a long-staying bird. **Booted Eagle** *Hieraaetus pennatus.* A Sept. sight record (1989). **White Tern** *Gygis alba.* A remarkable Dec. record (1972). Photographic evidence indicates that it was not the expected nominate race from the south Atlantic but, rather, one of the Pacific races!

Index

The main entry for each species is listed in **boldface** type and refers to the text page opposite the illustration.

Art Credits

Jonath an Alderfer: Inside front cover; 2-3; 31-Spot-billed Duck; 45-White-winged Scoter *stejnegeri;* 47-Goldeneye hybrid; 49-Goosander; 75; 77-heads; 79; 81; 83-Parkinson's Petrel and Murphy's Petrel; 85; 89-Cory's Shearwater, Cape Verde Shearwater, and small comparison figures; 91-Wedge-tailed Shearwater, Bulwer's Petrel, left Short-tailed Shearwater, and heads; 93; 101; 107; 155; 175; 177-flying Black Turnstone; 189; 191; 233-flying winter Dovekie; 235-Long-billed Murrelet; 239; 241-flying Rhinoceros Auklet; 245-with N. John Schmitt; 307; 311-Rose-throated Becard; 347-female Blue-gray Gnatcatcher tail; 363-Blue Mockingbird; 367-Common Myna; 466-except Lesser White-fronted Goose; 467-except Great Frigatebird; 468-Gray Heron; 472-except Whiskered Tern and Scaly-naped Pigeon; 475-Social Flycatcher and Masked Tityra; 476-Mangrove Swallow; 479-Gray Silky-flycatcher; 480-except Redwing. **David Beadle**: 83-Great-winged Petrel; 295; 297; 299; 301; 303-Tufted Flycatcher; 309-Gray Kingbird and Thick-billed Kingbird; 315-Thick-billed Vireo; 319-Philadelphia Vireo and Warbling Vireo; 329; 343-western Winter Wren; 379-Crescent-chested Warbler; 389-fall Bay-breasted Warbler; 399-Red-faced Warbler; 415-Sage Sparrow *canescens*; 423-Vesper Sparrow; 427-Pink-sided Dark-eyed Junco; 469-Paint-billed Crake; 470-Spotted Rail and Double-striped Thick-knee; 472-Scaly-naped Pigeon; 473-Gray Nightjar and Antillean Palm-Swift; 474-Bumblebee Hummingbird and Greenish Elaenia; 475-except Social Flycatcher and Masked Tityra; 476-except Mangrove Swallow and Willow Warbler; 478-Orange-billed Nightingale-Thrush and Black-headed Nightingale Thrush; 479-Worthen's Sparrow and Tawny-shouldered Blackbird. **Peter Burke**: 109; 117-Glossy Ibis (except flying) and White-faced Ibis; 305; 311-Piratic Flycatcher and Variegated Flycatcher; 317-Gray Vireo; 361-White-throated Robin; 397-except Common Yellowthroat; 401; 403-adult male White-collared Seedeater and Yellow-faced Grassquit; 405; 407; 437-Crimson-collared Grosbeak; 449-Shiny Cowbird; 451; 453. **Marc R. Hanson**: 83-Northern Fulmar; 89-Greater Shearwater, Manx Shearwater, Audubon's Shearwater, and Little Shearwater; 91-Flesh-footed Shearwater, Sooty Shearwater, and right Short-tailed Shearwater; 95-except European Storm-Petrel; 97; 147; 149; 151-except Purple Swamphen. **Cynthia J. House**: 21; 23; 25-except flying and Taverner's Cackling Goose and Lesser Canada Goose; 27-except juvenile Whooper Swan; 29-except flying Muscovy Duck; 31-except head of female American Black Duck and Spot-billed Duck; 33; 35; 37; 39; 41; 43; 45-except White-winged Scoter *stejnegeri*; 47-except Goldeneye hybrid; 49-except Goosander; 51-except Egyptian Goose; 52-53; 54-55. **H. Jon Janosik**: 77-except heads; 99; 103; 105; 161; 481-White-tailed Tropicbird. **Donald L. Malick:** 119; 121; 125-except Stellar's Sea-Eagle and 3rd year Bald Eagle; 127-except flying figures; 129-perched figures of juvenile Common Black-Hawk, Zone-tailed Hawk, and Short-tailed Hawk; 133; 135-except dark-morph Ferruginous Hawk and flying adult and dark juvenile White-tailed Hawks; 137-perched Aplomado Falcons and Crested Caracara; 139-all perched figures except Merlin *suckleyi* and upper flying American Kestrel; 141-except flying figures of adult male Prairie Falcon, Peregrine Falcon, and Gyrfalcon; 247; 257; 259; 261; 263; 265; 281; 283; 285; 287; 289-except Great Spotted Woodpecker; 291; 293. **Killian Mullarney**: 159; 187; 193; 196-Little Ringed Plover. **Michael O'Brien**: 87, 163-Willet; 335; 337; 339-except Verdin and Bushtit; 481-Bermuda Petrel. **John P. O'Neill**: 279-Elegant Trogan and Eared Quetzal; 339-Verdin and Bushtit. **Kent Pendleton**: 57-Gray Partridge and Chukars on ground; 59; 61; 63; 65; 67; 69; 123-except Northern Harrier; 141-flying figures of adult male Prairie Falcon, Peregrine Falcon, and Gyrfalcon; 142-except Hook-billed Kite; 143; 144; 145. **Diane Pierce**: 111; 113-except Little Egret; 115; 117-flying Glossy Ibis, White Ibis, Scarlet Ibis, and Roseate Spoonbill; 153; 409-except Bachman's Sparrow; 411; 413; 415-except Sage Sparrow *canescens*: 417-except Orange Bishop; 419-Seaside Sparrow; 421; 423-except Vesper Sparrow; 425; 427-except Pink-sided Dark-eyed Junco and Slate-colored Dark-eyed Junco; 429; 431; 433-except Yellow-breasted Bunting; 435; 437-except Crimson-collared Grosbeak; 439; 441; 455-except Common Chaffinch; 457; 459; 461; 463; 468-Yellow Bittern. **John C. Pitcher**: 157; 163-except Willet and flying Yellowlegs; 165-standing Common Grenshank and standing Spotted Redshank; 167; 169; 177-except flying Black Turnstone; 181; 183; 185. **H. Douglas Pratt**: 243; 253; 255; 273-except immature Green Violet-ear, Green-breasted Mango, and Lucifer Hummingbird; 275-except Xantus's Hummingbird; 277-except wing figures; 279-except Elegant Trogan and Eared Quetzal; 303-except Tufted Flycatcher; 309-adult Fork-tailed Flycatcher and Eastern Kingbird; 311-except Piratic Flycatcher, Variegated Flycatcher, and Rose-throated Becard; 313-except Brown Shrike; 315-except Thick-billed Vireo; 317-except Gray Vireo; 319-except Philadelphia Vireo and Warbling Vireo; 321; 323-except Island Scrub-Jay and adult Mexican Jays; 325; 327; 331-except Common House-Martin; 333; 341; 343-except western Winter Wren; 345; 347-except female Blue-gray Gnatcatcher tail; 349-except Lanceolated Warbler; 355; 359-Varied Thrush; 361-except White-throated Robin; 363-except Blue Mockingbird; 367-except Common Myna; 369-except Siberian Accentor; 373; 375; 377; 379-except Virginia's Warbler and Crescent-chested Warbler; 381; 383-except Black-and-white Warbler; 385; 387; 389-except fall Bay-breasted Warbler; 393; 395; 397-Common Yellowthroat; 399-except Red-faced Warbler; 403-female and 1st winter male White-collared Seedeater, Bananaquit, and Black-faced Grassquit; 445; 447; 449-except Shiny Cowbird. **David Quinn**: 71; 73; 95-European Storm-Petrel; 113-Little Egret; 151-Purple Swamphen; 165-Marsh Sandpiper and Common Redshank; 195-Common Redshank; 289-Great Spotted Woodpecker; 313-Brown Shrike; 331-Common House-Martin; 349-Lanceolated Warbler; 351; 353; 359-except Varied Thrush; 369-Siberian Accentor; 371; 433-Yellow-breasted Bunting; 455-Common Chaffinch; 466-Lesser White-fronted Goose; 468-Chinese Egret and Western Reef-Heron; 469-Chinese Pond-Heron; 470-except Spotted Rail and Double-striped Thick-knee; 471; 472-Whiskered Tern; 474-except Bumblebee Hummingbird and Greenish Elaenia; 476-Willow Warbler; 477; 478-except Nightingale-Thrushes; 479-Pine Bunting, Yellow-throated Bunting and Eurasian Siskin; 480-Redwing. **Chuck Ripper**: 233-except flying winter Dovekie; 235-except Long-billed Murrelet; 237; 241-except flying Rhinoceros Auklet; 267; 269-except southwestern Whip-poor-will tail. **N. John Schmitt**: 25-flying and Taverner's Cackling Goose and Lesser Canada Goose; 27-juvenile Whooper Swan; 29-flying Muscovy Duck; 31-head of female American Black Duck; 51-Egyptian Goose; 57-Plain Chachalaca and flying Chukar; 123-Northern Harrier; 125-Stellar's Sea-Eagle and 3rd year Bald Eagle; 127-flying figures; 129-except perched figures of juvenile Common Black-Hawk, Zone-tailed Hawk, and Short-tailed Hawk; 131; 135-dark-morph Ferruginous Hawk and flying adult and dark juvenile White-tailed Hawks; 137-Eurasian Hobby and flying Aplomado Falcons; 139-Merlin *suckleyi* and all flying figures except upper American Kestrel; 142-Hook-billed Kite; 171-Little Curlew; 173-standing figures of Bristle-thighed Curlew and Eurasian Curlew; 194-Little Curlew; 245-with Jonathan Alderfer; 249; 251; 271; 309-juvenile Fork-tailed Flycatcher; 323-Island Scrub-Jay and adult Mexican Jays; 365; 417-Orange Bishop; 419-except Seaside Sparrow; 427-Slate-colored Dark-eyed Junco; 465. **Thomas R. Schultz**: 179; 199; 201; 203; 205; 207; 209; 211; 213; 215; 216-217; 219; 221; 223; 225; 227; 229; 231, 357; 379-Virginia's Warbler; 383-Black-and-white Warbler; 391; 403-Western Spindalis; 409; 443; 467-Great Frigatebird; 468-Lesser Frigatebird; 469-except Chinese Pond-Heron and Paint-billed Crake; 473-except Gray Nightjar and Antillean Palm-Swift; 481-Dunlin. **Daniel S. Smith**: 163-flying Yellowlegs; 165-flying Common Grenshank and flying Spotted Redshank; 171-except Little Curlew; 173-except standing figures of Bristle-thighed Curlew and Eurasian Curlew; 194-except Little Curlew; 195-except Common Redshank; 196-except Little Ringed Plover; 197. **Patricia A. Topper**: Cover. **Sophie Webb**: 269-southwestern Whip-poor-will tail; 273-immature Green Violet-ear, Green-breasted Mango, and Lucifer Hummingbird; 275-Xantus's Hummingbird; 277-wing figures.

Acknowledgments

The editors wish to thank the following individuals and institutions for their valuable assistance in the preparation of the fifth edition:
M. Adams, Natural History Museum, Tring, UK; Jim Arterburn, Tulsa, Oklahoma; Ken Behrens, Pittsburg, Pennsylvania; Gavin Bieber, Tucson, Arizona; Chuck Carlson, Fort Peck, Montana; John Carlson, Helena, Montana; Robin Carter, Columbia, South Carolina; Allen Chartier, Inkster, Michigan; Ricky Davis, Rocky Mount, North Carolina; James Dinsmore, Iowa City, Iowa; Richard Erickson, Irvine, California; Doug Faulkner, Denver, Colorado; Dr. C. T. Fisher, World Museum Liverpool, UK; Robert Fisher, Independence, Missouri; Rick Fridell, Hurricane, Utah; Kimball L. Garrett, Los Angeles County Museum of Natural History, Los Angeles, California; Daniel D. Gibson, University of Alaska, Fairbanks, Alaska; Britt Griswold, Annapolis, Maryland; Robert Hamilton, Long Beach, California; Tom and Jo Heindel, Big Pine, California; Rich Hoyer, Tucson, Arizona; Dan Kassebaum, Belleville, Illinois; Tom Kent, Iowa City, Iowa; Rudolf Koes, Winnipeg, Manitoba; Dr M. Largen, World Museum Liverpool, UK; Tony Leukering, Brighton, Colorado; Mark Lockwood, Alpine, Texas; Derek Lovitch, Portland, Maine; Rich MacIntosh, Kodiak, Alaska; Ron Martin, Sawyer, North Dakota; Terry McEneaney, Yellowstone NP, Wyoming; Mick McHugh, Shawnee Mission, Kansas; Ian McLaren, Halifax, Nova Scotia; Steve Mlodinow, Everett, Washington; Glenn Murphy, Royal Ontario Museum, Ontario, Canada; Kenny Nichols, Pangburn, Arkansas; Jerry Oldenettel, Socorro, New Mexico; Mike Overton, Boone, Iowa; A. Parker, World Museum Liverpool, UK; John Parmeter, Albuquerque, New Mexico; Michael Patten, Bartlesville, Oklahoma; Mark Peck, Royal Ontario Museum, Ontario, Canada; Bill Pranty, Bayonet Point, Florida; David Quady, Berkeley, California; Mark Robbins, Lawrence, Kansas; Don Roberson, Pacific Grove, California; Bill Rowe, St Louis, Missouri; Larry Sansone, Hollywood, California; Larry Semo, Westminster, Colorado; John Sterling, Woodland, California; Mark Stevenson, Tucson, Arizona; Sherman Suter, Alexandria, Virginia; Peder Svingen, Duluth, Minnesota; Charles Trost, Pocatello, Idaho; David Willard, Field Museum of Natural History, Chicago, Illinois; Chris Wood, Ithaca, New York.

The editors also wish to thank the following for their contributions to previous editions of this guide:
Thomas A. Allen; David Agro; J. Phillip Angle; Stephen Bailey; Lawrence G. Balch; Dr. Richard C. Banks; John Barber; Jon Barlow; Jen and Des Bartlett; Giff Beaton; Louis Bevier; Eirik A.T. Blom; Daniel Boone; Jack Bowling; Edward S. Brinkley; the Department of Ornithology at the British Museum, Tring; Dawn Burke; Danny Bystrak; Richard Cannings; Steven W. Cardiff; Charles Carlson; Graham Chisholm; Carla Cicero; Charles T. Clark; William S. Clark; Rene Corado; Marian Cressman; Denver Museum of Natural History, Colorado; Bruce Deuel; Donna L. Dittman; Robert Dixon; Peter J. Dunn; Peter Dunne; Cameron Eckert; Victor Emanuel; Richard Erickson; Field Museum of Natural History, Chicago; Dr. Clemency Fisher; John W. Fitzpatrick; David Fix; Kimball L. Garrett; Freida Gentry; Daniel D. Gibson; Peter Grant; John A. Gregoire; Dr. James L. Gulledge; Jon S. Greenlaw; Dr. George A. Hall; J.B. Hallett, Jr.; Robert Hamilton; Jo and Tom Heindel; Matt Heindel; Steve Heinl; Paul M. Hill; Chris Hobbs; Phill Holder; Steve N.G. Howell; Rebecca Hyman; Frank Iwen; Greg Jackson; Alvaro Jaramillo; Joseph R. Jehl, Jr.; Ned K. Johnson; Roy Jones; Colin Jones; Lars Jonsson; Kenn Kaufman; Wayne Klockner; Marianne G. Koszorus; Lasse J. Laine; Los Angeles County Museum of Natural History; Daniel Lane; Dr. Malcolm Largen; Greg Lasley; Paul E. Lehman; Nick Lethaby; Tony Leukering; Rich Levad; Liverpool Museum, England; Mark Lockwood; Los Angeles County Museum of Natural History; Tim Loseby; Aileen Lotz; Rich MacIntosh; Bruce Mactavish; Laura Martin; Guy McCaskie; Terry McEneaney; Doug McRae; Dominic Mitchell; Steve Mlodinow; Joseph Morlan; Killian Mullarney; Museum of Natural History, Santa Barbara, California; Museum of Natural Science, Louisiana State University, Baton Rouge; Museum of Vertebrate Zoology, University of California, Berkeley; Glen Murphy; National Museum of Natural History, Smithsonian Institution, Washington, D.C.; Natural History Museum, San Diego, California; Harry Nehls; Michael O'Brien; Jerry Oldenettel; Gerald Oreel; Tony Parker; John Parmeter; Michael Patten; Brian Patteson; Dennis Paulson; Mark Peck; Paul Prior; Peter Pyle; Betsy Reeder; Dr. J.V. Remsen; Robert F. Ringler; Don Roberson; Mark Robins; Gary Rosenberg; Philip D. Round; John Rowlett; Rose Ann Rowlett; Royal Ontario Museum; Will Russell; San Diego Natural History Museum; Larry Sansone; Rick Saval; Robert T. Scholes; Brad Schram; Thomas Schulenberg; Scott Seltman; David Sibley; Ross Silcock; Mark Stackhouse; James Stasz; Rick Steenberg; Andrew Stepniewski; Doug Stotz; Sherman Suter; Thede Tobish; Dr. John Trochet; Charles Trost; Laurel Tucker; Nigel Tucker; Bill Tweit; Philip Unitt; U.S. Fish and Wildlife Service's Patuxent Wildlife Research Center in Laurel, Maryland; Arnoud van den Berg; T.R. Wahl; George Wallace; Western Foundation of Vertebrate Zoology; Mel White; Tony White; Hal Wierenga; Claudia P. Wilds; David W. Willard; Jeff Wilson; Alan Wormington; Louise Zemaitis; Barry Zimmer; Kevin Zimmer.

National Geographic Birder's Journal

Edited by Jon L. Dunn and Jonathan Alderfer

Published by the National Geographic Society
John M. Fahey, Jr., *President and Chief Executive Officer*
Gilbert M. Grosvenor, *Chairman of the Board*
Nina D. Hoffman, *Executive Vice President; President, Books Publishing Group*

Prepared by the Book Division
Kevin Mulroy, *Senior Vice President and Publisher*
Leah Bendavid-Val, *Director of Photography Publishing and Illustrations*
Marianne R. Koszorus, *Director of Design*

Barbara Brownell Grogan, *Executive Editor*
Elizabeth Newhouse, *Director of Travel Publishing*
Carl Mehler, *Director of Maps*

Staff for this Book
Barbara Levitt, *Editor*
Jennifer Conrad Seidel, *Text Editor*
Lyle Rosbotham, *Art Director*
Rick Wain, *Production Project Manager*
Meredith Wilcox, *Illustrations Coordinator*
Teresa Tate, Abby Leopold, *Illustrations Specialists*
Michael Greninger, *Editorial Assistant*
Cameron Zotter, *Design Assistant*

Rebecca Hinds, *Managing Editor*
Gary Colbert, *Production Director*

Manufacturing and Quality Management
Christopher A. Liedel, *Chief Financial Officer*
Phillip L. Schlosser, *Vice President*
John T. Dunn, *Technical Director*
Vincent P. Ryan, *Director*
Chris Brown, *Director*
Maryclare Tracy, *Manager*

Second Edition

Library of Congress Cataloging-in-Publication Data available upon request.
ISBN-10: 1-4262-0005-6
ISBN-13: 978-1-4262-0005-2

Printed in U.S.A.